Progress in
EXPERIMENTAL PERSONALITY RESEARCH

VOLUME 3

CONTRIBUTORS TO THIS VOLUME

IRVING I. GOTTESMAN

AUSTIN JONES

WALTER MISCHEL

JAMES SHIELDS

JACOB O. SINES

IVAN D. STEINER

PROGRESS IN

Experimental Personality Research

Edited by Brendan A. Maher

DEPARTMENT OF PSYCHOLOGY
UNIVERSITY OF WISCONSIN
MADISON, WISCONSIN

VOLUME 3

1966

ACADEMIC PRESS New York and London

ACADEMIC PRESS INC.
111 Fifth Avenue, New York, New York 10003

United Kingdom Edition published by
ACADEMIC PRESS INC. (LONDON) LTD.
Berkeley Square House, London W.1

LIBRARY OF CONGRESS CATALOG CARD NUMBER: 64-8034

PRINTED IN THE UNITED STATES OF AMERICA

CONTRIBUTORS

Numbers in parentheses indicate the pages on which the authors' contributions begin.

IRVING I. GOTTESMAN (1), *Department of Psychology, University of Minnesota, Minneapolis, Minnesota*

AUSTIN JONES (241), *Department of Psychology, University of Pittsburgh, Pittsburgh, Pennsylvania*

WALTER MISCHEL (85), *Stanford University, Stanford, California*

JAMES SHIELDS (1), *Medical Research Council, Psychiatric Genetics Research Unit, Institute of Psychiatry, Maudsley Hospital, London, England*

JACOB O. SINES (133), *Department of Psychiatry, University of Missouri Medical Center, Columbia, Missouri*

IVAN D. STEINER (195), *Department of Psychology, University of Illinois, Urbana, Illinois*

PREFACE

Contributions to this, the third volume in the serial publication, illustrate once again the diversity of concepts and techniques that are currently applied to research in personality. This is, of course, a testimony to the complexity of the variables that are found to determine individual differences; it is also evidence of the recent preference of personality psychologists for limited theories about finite realms of data, in contrast to comprehensive theories of personality in the grand manner.

Gottesman and Shields report an investigation of the genetics of schizophrenia that illustrates clearly both the growing revival of genetic approaches to problems of human personality and the increasing use of classifications based on behavioral efficiency rather than classical psychiatric nosology in research on psychopathology.

If there is one area of psychology that overlaps with personality psychology more than any other, it is the psychology of motivation. Experimental personality research continues to reflect this. Papers in this volume dealing with preference for delayed or immediate gratification, and with the effects of deprivation of information in humans provide contributions germane to problems of personality and motivation alike.

Disenchantment with global theories of personality has been accompanied by—and perhaps hastened by—a skeptical scrutiny of those methods of personality assessment that derive their conceptual structure from such theories. In the critical climate that this scrutiny generates, the actuarial approach to assessment has emerged relatively unscathed. The portents available point to the coming dominance by actuarial methods and behavioral sampling of the field of personality assessment. Sines' paper presents a systematic exposition of the actuarial method in action, and should provide the reader with an understanding of the problems and assumptions that are involved.

Previous volumes have included works dealing with the question of interpersonal perception, and we are happy to present in this issue another contribution to this complex area. The subtlety of the issues involved make it likely that many such contributions will be needed before they are resolved.

BRENDAN A. MAHER

Madison, Wisconsin
August 1966

vii

CONTENTS

Contributions of Twin Studies to Perspectives on Schizophrenia

IRVING I. GOTTESMAN AND JAMES SHIELDS

Theory and Research on the Antecedents of Self-Imposed Delay of Reward

WALTER MISCHEL

Actuarial Methods in Personality Assessment

JACOB O. SINES

Personality and the Resolution of Interpersonal Disagreements

IVAN D. STEINER

Information Deprivation in Humans

AUSTIN JONES

CONTENTS OF PREVIOUS VOLUMES

CONTRIBUTIONS OF TWIN STUDIES TO PERSPECTIVES ON SCHIZOPHRENIA[1]

Irving I. Gottesman and James Shields

DEPARTMENT OF PSYCHOLOGY, UNIVERSITY OF MINNESOTA, MINNEAPOLIS, MINNESOTA
AND MEDICAL RESEARCH COUNCIL, PSYCHIATRIC GENETICS RESEARCH UNIT, INSTITUTE
OF PSYCHIATRY, MAUDSLEY HOSPITAL, LONDON, ENGLAND

I. Introduction

A. BACKGROUND TO THE REVIEW

If schizophrenia were a clear-cut genetic disorder, simply inherited and uninfluenced in its manifestation by the environment, there would be no reason for making a special study of the condition in twins. It is

[1] We are especially indebted to Eliot Slater whose foresight made our own work possible and who has been a source of inspiration over the years. Correspondence and conversations with David Rosenthal, N. Juel-Nielsen, Einar Kringlen, Gordon Allen and E. Inouye were both valuable and stimulating. We are solely responsible for all errors of fact or interpretation. Our research was carried out at the Medical Research Council Psychiatric Genetics Research Unit, Maudsley Hospital, London to which

because the etiology of schizophrenia is complex and possibly hetero-geneous, and the meaning of its familial distribution open to conflicting interpretations, that investigators have undertaken the arduous task of collecting, analyzing, and reanalyzing samples of schizophrenic twins. Rosenthal (1963) noted that very few colleagues, if pressed, will not admit that in their opinion both genetic and environmental factors contribute to the etiology of schizophrenia. He and Meehl (1962) agree that the results of twin studies represent the most important piece of etiological information we possess about schizophrenia. In a clarification, long overdue in the field of psychopathology, Meehl goes on to point out that postulating a genetic *specific etiology* for schizophrenia means only that the genes are necessary, but not sufficient, for the disorder to occur.

Illuminating appraisal of the earlier Western twin studies of schizo-phrenia by Rosenthal (1959, 1960, 1961, 1962a, 1962b), and the appear-ance of 2 smaller studies in Scandinavia by Tienari (1963) and Kringlen (1964) that report findings markedly at variance with previous work, have led to a renewed interest in twin-based inferences about schizophrenia. What conclusions *can* be drawn from twin studies regarding the signifi-cance of genetic variability for the manifestation of behaviors disordered enough to be called schizophrenias? Were the cases of twins gathered and interpreted "with more perseverance than perspicacity," as Neel and Schull (1954) suggest for many of the applications of the method in human genetics; or, do the studies on schizophrenia in twins represent one of the more careful and successful attempts to cast light on a thorny and demanding problem?

The writers of the present chapter are concluding a further twin study, carried out in a way which allows the force of some recent criticisms to be evaluated. We believe that yet another review of this whole topic, taking our provisional findings into account, may be justified.

In the Introduction we propose to outline the principles of the twin method. More detailed discussion of problems such as sampling, diagno-sis, and concordance will be reserved until they arise in the context of particular studies.

B. Monozygotic and Dizygotic Twins

1. Biological Nature

The twin method presupposes that there are biologically two distinct kinds of twins: (1) monozygotic (MZ) pairs, arising from the splitting of the nucleus of a fertilized ovum in such a way that two genetically identi-

J. S. is seconded by the Institute of Psychiatry. It was supported in part by a USPHS Special Fellowship to I.I.G. and subsequently by PHS Grant MH 10301-01A1. I.I.G. now at the University of Minnesota.

cal individuals are produced; and (2) dizygotic (DZ) pairs, of either the same (SS) or opposite sex (OS), arising from the independent fertilization of two ova in such a way that the twins are no more alike genetically than a pair of full sibs born at different times. In contrast to twins in MZ pairs, who have 100% gene overlap, DZ pairs and sibs have only 50% on the average from the same source. Parents and children also have 50% gene overlap. This can all be deduced from the laws of genetic segregation. The possibility of a third type of twinning and the rare occurrence of MZ twins who are not genetically identical can be disregarded for practical purposes.

2. Zygosity Determination

The twin method also assumes that it is possible to distinguish MZ from SS DZ pairs with an adequate degree of confidence. The discovery, particularly over the past two decades, of an ever-increasing number of independent blood groups and serum groups, each completely determined by heredity, allows this requirement to be met (Race & Sanger, 1962). Blood-grouping has also permitted the better evaluation of the efficiency of determining zygosity by other methods, such as the difference in fingerprint ridge count (Slater, 1963), resemblance in eye color, or statements that the twins are frequently mistaken or "as alike as two peas" (Cederlöf et al., 1961). As early as 1941, Essen-Möller (1941a) estimated that an experienced observer of twins, examining a pair together, was likely to err only 2% of the time. Cederlöf et al. and Harvald and Hauge (1965) claim that postal questionnaires are sufficiently reliable for large-scale studies in the majority of cases. Gottesman (1963) found that judgment of zygosity from photographs only agreed with serological findings 78% of the time. These points are important because many twin studies were made before blood-grouping was generally available; and even when full blood-grouping is available, it is not always possible to test every twin in a complete series.

3. Frequency

The frequency of twin births varies according to country, race, year, and age of mother at the time of the birth. The expected proportion of MZ pairs among twins at birth can be calculated by means of Weinberg's (1901) differential method. This is based on the number of OS pairs born. The frequency of SS DZ pairs should be the same as that of OS pairs. Subtracting twice the number of OS pairs from total pairs will therefore give the expected number of MZ pairs. Table I, compiled from Waterhouse (1950) and Scheinfeld (1963), gives some idea of the variability in twin frequencies.

It is unique to the twin method that the proportion of MZ, SS DZ, and OS pairs, in the general population can be used as a check on the completeness of their ascertainment in a sample. Some caution is required, however, in interpreting unexpected proportions; it is hard to estimate accurately the expected number of pairs surviving unbroken

TABLE I
VARIATION IN TWINNING

Country	Twin pairs (1000 Births)	Percentage MZ
U.S. White (1918)	11.0	30.7
U.S. White (1938)	10.4	34.8
U.S. White (1956-1958)	9.9	38.4
U.S. Negro (1956-1958)	14.0	27.8
England & Wales (1938-1948)	12.1	27.8
To Mothers, 20-24	8.7	38.4
To Mothers, 35-39	16.9	21.8
Norway (1946-1954)	12.1	31.4
Japan (1956)	6.3	63.5

at a given age without extensive knowledge of the differential mortality of twins according to sex, type, and social class in different countries at different times (Allen, 1955; Gittelsohn & Milham, 1965).

4. Deductions about Etiology

Basically the comparison of MZ and DZ intrapair resemblance provides evidence for possible genetic factors, whereas the histories of pairs that differ give evidence as to environmental factors. The possibilities inherent in twin research are immense if unrealized, and they go far beyond mere nose-counting and the calculation of concordance rates. Some of the possible deductions may be mentioned; the list is far from exhaustive (cf. Allen, 1965).

a. If genetic differences are of no importance, and family environment is the major explanation for the tendency of schizophrenia to cluster in families, there should be no essential difference between the incidence of schizophrenia in the MZ and DZ co-twins of affected individuals. Such is the case with infectious illnesses, like measles.

b. If the genes are important in the manifestation of schizophrenia, MZ co-twins should be more often schizophrenic than DZ co-twins. The establishment of such a difference does not by itself prove the importance of variations in genotype; but the latter remains the most likely explanation, unless it can be shown either that MZ twins as such are predisposed to schizophrenia or that the environments of MZ twins are systematically more alike than those of DZ twins in features which can be *shown* to be of etiological significance in schizophrenia.

c. The comparison of MZ and DZ intrapair resemblance could also lead to the discovery of any subtypes of schizophrenia that may be either more under genetic influence than others or free of genetic influence.

d. Given evidence of genetic predisposition, the comparison of ill-nesses of twins who are both affected could lead to the discovery of which aspects of the illness, such as onset, symptoms, course, response to treat-ment, and outcome, may be most genetically influenced, and which aspects most susceptible to environmental influence. In appropriate cir-cumstances the co-twin control method of Gesell and Thompson (1929) can be used, for instance by treating only one of a pair of similarly affected schizophrenic twins by a given method (Benaim, 1960) or both with multiple methods.

e. The variability of psychiatric abnormality in the MZ co-twins of typical schizophrenics could lead to the identification of schizophrenic "equivalents" or an underlying "schizotypic" deviation (Meehl, 1962). Such a development could lead to an improved classification of schizo-phrenia and related disorders, as well as to the detection of "carriers."

f. The comparison of MZ twins who differ with respect to schizo-phrenia, either totally or quantitatively, allows deductions to be drawn regarding differences in the twins' previous life experiences that might relate to differences in their psychiatric states. Evidence from twins on these lines may identify interpersonal and environmental factors in schizophrenia.

Although the goal of many classical human genetic studies has been to establish the mode of inheritance of a condition, the twin method does not claim to do this. Whatever the mode of inheritance may be in schizophrenia, it is not a simple dominant or recessive without qualifica-tion. In our present state of knowledge it is difficult to distinguish be-tween sophisticated monogenic theories (Slater, 1958) and possible poly-genic models.

In a theoretical paper by Edwards (1960) on the simulation of Mendelian inheritance by polygenic inheritance, he posits that the ex-pected incidence among the first degree relatives of a proband with a polygenically determined disorder should be the square root of the general population incidence. Assuming an incidence (total life risk) of 1/100 for schizophrenia, the incidence in siblings, children, and parents would be 1/10. The latter figure fits both with the empirical data and Slater's monogenic theory of a dominant gene with a frequency of .015 and manifestation rate in a heterozygote of .26, so long as we confine ourselves to the data on siblings and children. Slater suggested that the observed frequencies of schizophrenia in the parents of probands could not be used to test his model since they had overcome various selection pressures, and therefore should have a greater resistance to developing schizophrenia.

C. SAMPLING OF TWINS

Probably more consideration has been given to the problem of un-biased sampling in schizophrenic and other psychiatric twin studies, both by the investigators themselves and by their critics, than in any other area of psychiatric or psychological research. The problem as it was originally raised by Luxenburger (see IIA) was to ensure that twins to be investigated were unselected as to resemblance. More recently the additional question has been raised (Rosenthal, 1962a) as to how representative the starting cases are of schizophrenia as a whole. In this section, we outline the problem of the sampling of twins.

The procedure by which groups of twins are obtained should be one which avoids any selective bias in favor of pairs that are alike or different. The best way to ensure this is to investigate every twin in a defined starting population, such as patients admitted to particular hospitals during a specified period of time. The problem thus becomes one of the total ascertainment of twins with twin partners who have survived to an age when they could have developed schizophrenia or any other condition under investigation. Patients discovered to be twins form the probands or index cases of the investigation. How probands are best ascertained will depend on circumstances.

Birth records providing for the indication of twinship may permit complete ascertainment. Completeness would occur provided (1) none of the starting population are immigrants, and (2) places of birth were always recorded in sufficient detail to permit tracing. Survival of the co-twin may also be established in some countries from official sources.

Ascertainment of twinship from birth records when available is a method to be recommended, especially when enquiring about twins in old material, where patients may be too deteriorated, or relatives no longer available or sufficiently motivated to answer enquiries. It is not always the method of choice. An ideal setting for complete ascertainment is one in which it can be systematically asked of every patient on admission whether he is a twin and whether his partner survived. Further relevant enquiries can be made on the spot if the investigator is notified of cases as they arise. The accuracy of this method can be checked by looking up birth registers for a sample of supposed non-twins from the starting material to see whether any cases have been missed.

D. Diagnosis of Schizophrenia and Assessment of Within-Pair Similarity

Although it is legitimate to ask whether the sample of twins is complete and representative, it cannot be asked in the same way whether a sample of schizophrenics is representative of all schizophrenia: the concept is too variable from one country to the next—or even within the same country or hospital—and at different periods of time. Progress is likely to be made, not in arguing which samples of twins have been most correctly diagnosed or are most representative of schizophrenia as a whole, but in observing how the findings vary according to sample and subsample and according to the method of analysis. The twin method as applied to schizophrenia involves, in its basic form, the diagnosis of the proband, the diagnosis of the co-twin, and an assessment in a form which can be handled numerically of the extent of resemblance. Diagnosis may be in psychiatric terms, or use may be made of tests of personality or cognition.

1. Diagnosis of the Proband

The first task facing the investigator is to decide which twins from his total starting material to count as schizophrenic. In the course of his psychiatric history a patient is likely to receive several diagnoses from different psychiatrists at different times or even simultaneously. With the advantage of hindsight and the desire to adopt a uniform standard, most investigators have decided to diagnose their own probands. This appears to be reasonable, provided what has been done is made clear. The effects of rediagnosis can be shown by the investigator's comparing the findings based on his own diagnoses with those that he would have obtained had he used official hospital diagnoses of the same patients, either at the time of their becoming probands or when last in hospital.

The findings of a twin study may well depend upon the consistency, breadth, or narrowness of the diagnosis of schizophrenia. One of the aims of a comprehensive twin or family study might be to investigate the extent to which different varieties of schizophrenic-like psychoses (as well as compensated schizotypy) occur within families. Childhood schizophrenia (Goldfarb, 1964; Rimland, 1964), pseudoneurotic schizophrenia (Hoch & Polatin, 1949), schizophreniform state (Langfeldt, 1939), psychogenic psychosis (Faergeman, 1963), atypical schizophrenia (Schulz & Leonhard, 1940; Fish, 1958), paranoia (Kolle, 1931), nonorganic paranoid psychosis of late onset (Kay & Roth, 1961), and other conditions have been added to or removed from the group of schizophrenias (E. Bleuler, 1911) in the network around the core of *dementia praecox*.

The findings may also vary according to the population sampled. A census of twins resident on a given date in hospitals catering to long-term hospitalization will contain a higher proportion of chronic schizophrenics than a sample consisting of consecutive admissions of twins to the same type of hospital. The latter will include a higher proportion of acute recoverable, relapsing (cyclic), and fatal cases, and of mild chronic cases requiring only occasional hospitalization. Samples from short-stay hospitals and from outpatient clinics will contain a higher proportion of cases with a good prognosis.

2. Diagnosis of the Co-Twin

This presents different problems.

a. The requirement that a total sample of twins be studied means that the investigator may have to make a diagnosis on insufficient information. The co-twin may have died or otherwise be unavailable for personal interview. He may have had an illness for which no medical record is available or which was diagnosed on different principles from that of the proband.

b. Criteria for diagnosis may have to be wider than those used for the proband. For instance, probands may by definition have been hospitalized, whereas the co-twin may have had an unhospitalized schizophrenia. There is no objection to having more than one level at which the concept of schizophrenia is applied. The investigator should make his standards public and preferably report his findings at different levels, indicating, for instance, how many schizophrenic co-twins have been hospitalized. Ultimately one may hope for a reliable scale measuring schizophrenic psychopathology on a continuum.

c. There is a risk that an investigator who has information about the proband will allow this fact to influence his diagnosis of the co-twin. The biases to which he may be most liable are those of calling a probably normal co-twin abnormal if he knows the pair to be MZ, and of giving a sick co-twin the same diagnosis as the proband. Various measures have been suggested for making diagnosis of proband and co-twin independent, such as arranging for them to be seen by different investigators (Rosenthal, 1962a), by having judges diagnose from case histories which do not indicate zygosity or psychiatric state of the other twin (Shields & Slater, 1966), or by using hospital diagnosis or the objective results of psychological tests. Each of these procedures has its own source of unreliability. They should be used in addition to having both twins interviewed by the same person, otherwise subtler points of similarity and difference may be missed.

3. Within-Pair Resemblance

a. Concordance. We have deliberately tried to avoid, until now, mention of the term concordant, which is used to mean that both members of a pair are, or have been, affected with the defined condition. It will be clear from what has been said on the topics of sampling and diagnosis that no single reported concordance rate can be taken to apply to schizophrenia as a whole. The term remains a useful one for handling within-pair resemblance for conditions of an all-or-none character or for variable conditions which cannot be adequately dealt with quantitatively. Whenever the term concordant is used it must be remembered what it stands for in the context of the particular investigation. Otherwise it can be misleading.

Not only does the term concordant cover the case in which one twin is more severely affected than the other, it also covers illnesses occurring at different times. Concordance has to be judged on the life history of the twins. At a given point of time both, neither, or only one of a concordant pair may be showing schizophrenic symptoms. So long as both twins are considered at some time to have been schizophrenic, the pair is termed concordant.

The concordance rate for schizophrenia depends not only on the method of diagnosis of the proband and co-twin but also on the method of calculation. In particular it depends on whether the investigator deals in terms of persons or pairs and whether he makes a correction for age.

b. Index Cases and Index Pairs. In communicating about twins it is customary to take the pair as the unit. This can cause problems in research as well as in the psychopathology of twins. In calculating the proportion of twins in a hospital population, it is evident that one should count patients: if both members of a pair have been admitted, each as a patient in his own right, and each meeting the diagnostic requirement of the series, then both twins are probands or index cases. As Allen (1955), among others, has pointed out, it is correct to count probands when calculating the distribution of the sexes and twin-types in the series. The same applies to diagnostic subtypes. Members of a pair may differ in subtype, and when both are probands they should both be included in any generalization about the sample.

On the same principle, concordance can be regarded in terms of how many co-twins of probands are affected. If both members of a pair are probands, both must also be co-twins, and the pair is therefore counted twice. To many this gives the appearance of raising the concordance rate in a misleading way. It also makes it difficult to compare investigations which happen to have a different proportion of double probands. Some studies do not indicate probands but only pairs. For the sake of simplicity we shall compare studies in terms of index pairs rather than index cases throughout the chapter.

   c. Correction for Age. Some concordance rates for schizophrenia have been corrected for age, while others have not, except for pairs excluded when the co-twin died before the age of 15. A few words about the reason for and methods of age correction are in order. Clearly, if the co-twins in a particular study tended to be around the age of 20 when information was last available about them, a crude, uncorrected concordance rate would underestimate the eventual number who might become schizophrenic, since the onset of schizophrenia is generally after the age of 20. Weinberg's Abridged Method is the one most frequently used to correct for age. It was intended originally for use in estimating the incidence of a condition in a sample of the general population. The aim was to correct the denominator, or the size of the total population, to allow for age distribution. To apply the method an empirically derived risk period must be chosen. Since the onset of nearly all cases of schizophrenia is found to occur between 15 and 39 (or 44), persons within this age group were generally considered at risk. All persons under 15 are omitted from the denominator. All those aged 40 (or 45) and over remain. The group within the risk period, provided their age distribution is not skewed, will on the average have passed half the risk; accordingly, half their number is deducted from the denominator. The numerator is the number of schizophrenics observed in the sample. The method works well enough for the relatives of schizophrenics, provided there is no correlation between age of onset in proband and relative.

   Strömgren (1935) has published tables for estimating the period of risk lived through by sibs on the assumption of a correlation of .19. He takes into account age of onset in the schizophrenic and the age of the sib. The correlation in age of onset in concordant MZ pairs is probably much higher than .19, with the result that both the Weinberg and the Strömgren methods will tend to overcorrect. If applied strictly to twins, the Weinberg method will on occasion give expectations of over 100% (e.g., Kallmann, 1950, MZ manic-depressive twins). No entirely acceptable method has been devised which is applicable to all twin samples. The best procedure would appear to be to report the age of the subjects, the length of follow-up since time of onset or hospitalization of the proband, and the crude concordance rate, with or without age correction by whatever method the investigator favors.

   Again, for simplicity, we shall report uncorrected concordance rates. This will enable one study to be compared with another, and avoid giving the impression of artificially raising concordance.

II. Critical Review of Studies, 1928–1961

A. LUXENBURGER (GERMANY, 1928)

Hans Luxenburger, of the Munich school of hereditary psychiatry (*Erbpsychiatrie*), published papers on schizophrenic twins in 1928, 1930, 1934, and 1936. The first, described as a provisional report on a psychiatric series, is the one in which he gives the fullest account of his material and the only one which divides it according to sex. The other papers, devoted primarily to a review of the literature up to 1930 or to theoretical discussions of the manifestation rate of schizophrenia in genetically predisposed persons, make use of parts of his now enlarged material in applying a formula or testing an hypothesis. There is no definitive report on the completed psychiatric series.

1. Sampling

Luxenburger was the first to draw attention to the importance of studying a complete representative series of twins, rather than combining the single cases reported in the literature or asking hospitals to send in

TABLE II

LUXENBURGER SURVEY OF CONCORDANCE FOR SCHIZOPHRENIA IN TWINS (1930)

Source	MZ	DZ	Uncertain zygosity
Single case reports in literature	31/34	3/8	9/11
Recalled by hospital doctors	7/8	0/5	5/11
Representative series	14/21	0/37	2/23

the names of patients recalled as being twins; and he was the first to attempt to put his ideas into practice. What happened when one relied on single case reports or on casually recorded twins, rather than on the results of an unselected series, is shown in Table II. Although the data relate to schizophrenia, the same applied to all the neuropsychiatric conditions analyzed. There is a gross excess of MZ pairs and of pairs in which both twins are concordant, such cases being more likely to be considered "interesting."

To obtain a representative series of twins Luxenburger pointed out that twinship should be systematically ascertained among all persons with the character under investigation in a defined place at a defined time. In his own study he started with patients on the files of the genealogical department of the Kaiser Wilhelm Institute for Psychiatric Research in Munich and the genealogical laboratory of the Basle Clinic.

This was mostly old material, already much investigated, some of it by Kraepelin himself. How many cases were from these sources, and how such cases came on to the genealogical registers in the first instance, is not specifically stated. It is possible that the cases comprised practically all patients admitted to the Psychiatric Clinics in Munich and Basle. He then obtained the names of all patients in twelve of the larger Bavarian mental hospitals on a given day. The combined sources gave him a starting material of 16,382 at the time of his first report. Luxenburger was interested initially in the "hereditary psychoses" of schizophrenia, manic-depressive psychosis, and epilepsy. The intention was to enlarge the starting material by bringing in other hospitals and diagnoses and fresh admissions. Cases of twins were ascertained by enquiring at the local registration offices for each of the starting cases whether the patient

TABLE III
COMPOSITION OF LUXENBURGER'S STARTING MATERIAL (1928)

| | Starting material | Twins ascertained | | | | |
		One member of a pair	Both members of a pair	Total twins	With adult partner	Frequency of twins
Dementia praecox	6,443	100	3	106	65	1:60.8
Manic-depressive	2,030	36	1	38	21	1:53.4
Epilepsy	1,058	19	0	19	10	1:55.7
Others (excluded)	6,851			48		
Totals	16,382			211		1:77.6

had been born one of twins. Table III shows how even a large psychiatric population of this size produces a small number of schizophrenics with a twin surviving to an age when he might develop schizophrenia; of 65 such pairs only 17 were certainly monozygotic.

Ideally, as Luxenburger realized, the birth registers could be used to ascertain all twins in the general population with a view to investigating them psychiatrically; but he pointed out the technical and financial difficulties of covering a population of several millions in this way.

By reason of the thoroughness of his sampling, Luxenburger was able to show that twins were represented in his sample of psychotics in a frequency of 1:58.5, a rate very close to the frequency of 1:55.6 which would be expected at that time in a Munich population of the same age distribution. Furthermore, the proportion of MZ pairs was close to expectation. Twinship, as such, did not affect the risk for psychosis, one way or the other. Subsequent studies have confirmed this, but none more convincingly.

While Luxenburger's ascertainment of twins could hardly be more complete and unselected, the same may not be true of his cases of schizophrenia, since he deliberately restricted himself to the classic type of dementia praecox. The group of 6851 patients which he excluded contained all uncertain cases and is larger than the group of schizophrenics. Excluded were all suspected cases of borderline, mixed and symptomatic psychosis, and psychosis with schizophrenic coloring but good outcome in persons of abnormal personality. It would have been interesting to see how the twins of such cases compared with those of the typical schizophrenics.

The complete ascertainment of twins loses some of its point if a large proportion of the material has to be omitted on account of uncertainties in the diagnosis of the index case, the zygosity of the pair, or the information about the partner. In actual practice some doubt on all

TABLE IV
DISTRIBUTION OF LUXENBURGER'S SCHIZOPHRENIC INDEX CASES (1928)
BY ZYGOSITY, SEX, AND AGE

Pairs	Male	Female	Total	Partner under 40
MZ	9	8	17	7
SS DZ	6	7	13	5
OS DZ	12	8	20	10
?Z	5	10	15	6
Totals	32	33	65	28

three scores is inevitable in any representative sample. There is a danger, however, that to reduce the possible source of error in one variable may be to increase it in another. For example, it could be that to include as MZ only such pairs as can be thoroughly investigated is to introduce a bias in favor of pairs that are both hospitalized. On the other hand, no conscientious investigator will wish to include as MZ (or as DZ) a pair about which he has serious doubts about the zygosity.

The distribution of index cases by sex and zygosity is shown in Table IV. In the series of 65 certain schizophrenic twins with partners surviving into adult life, 20 partners were of opposite sex to the index twin, 13 partners were sufficiently different in appearance for them to be classified as DZ, and 17 sufficiently alike in appearance to be classified as MZ. Unfortunately there were as many as 15 about whom, in his preliminary report, Luxenburger could not be certain; 5 of the 15, however, were probably MZ. The reasons for the uncertainty were partly that one of the twins was dead or not available for personal investigation and that information from other sources, such as accounts from relatives or old photographs, was lacking, unreliable, or inconsistent. Neither sex is overrepresented. Note also that 28 of the partners were under the age of 40 and so, conventionally, still "at risk" for schizophrenia.

2. Results, 1928 Study

Table V shows the extent of psychiatric abnormality in the co-twin. The "other abnormalities" were as follows:

A hospitalized manic-depressive among the same-sexed female DZ partners; 2 psychopaths; 1 hysteric; and 6 schizoid *Sonderlinge,* including the 2 otherwise abnormal among the MZ partners. Of the 14 schizophrenic or probably schizophrenic partners, 7 were male and 7 female. The unhospitalized schizophrenic among the partners of uncertain zygosity was thought to be probably MZ (sex not stated).

TABLE V

PSYCHIATRIC STATUS OF LUXENBURGER'S CO-TWINS (1928)

Partner	Schizophrenic (hospitalized)	Probably schizophrenic (not hospitalized)	Otherwise abnormal	Normal
MZ	10[a]	3	2	2
SS DZ			4	9
OS DZ			3	17
?Z		1[b]	1	13

[a] From 7 pairs.
[b] Probably MZ.

The outstanding feature of Table V is that there is not a single schizophrenic or probable schizophrenic among the 33 DZ partners. It is obvious that the concordance for the MZ pairs will vary according to the way in which one deals with cases of uncertain diagnosis or zygosity. Concordance will also be reduced if one counts separate pairs rather than partners of index cases. It will be recalled (Table III) that the 106 schizophrenic twins identified in the starting material came from 103 pairs, three pairs being represented by both members. Thus among the 17 MZ partners in the table there were 10 certain and 3 probable schizophrenics, from 59% to 76% concordance. The method has the advantage of allowing one to compare the risk of developing schizophrenia for different relatives of a defined sample and to compare the risk for a relative with that of the general population. It is less technical to think of concordance in terms of twin pairs rather than partners of index cases. Looked at in this way, there would be 7 MZ pairs with both twins hospitalized for schizophrenia and 3 in which the second twin was not hospitalized but was judged schizophrenic. Out of a total of 14 index pairs this yields 50% to 71% concordance. On the unlikely assumption that all the "uncertain" pairs are MZ, the minimum MZ concordance for hospitalized schizophrenia would be 7/29 pairs (24%). Maximum concordance would be 9 partners certainly or probably schizophrenic out of 10 certainly MZ pairs in which the partner has reached the age of 40. Luxenburger, in his 1928 paper, decides, probably wisely, to include the 5 "probably MZ" pairs of the "uncertain" group as MZ, counting one as concordant, four as discordant, in this way obtaining an estimated concordance rate of 14/22 (64%). In our preferred notation of index pairs versus cases, the concordance becomes 11/19 or 58%.

3. Later Papers

At the time of his 1930 paper, Luxenburger's starting material had increased to about 25,000 patients with about 200 twins of whom 81 were schizophrenics with partners who survived childhood. From the findings reported in Table V he had, since 1928, evidently had doubts about one of the discordant "probably MZ" partners, and increased his series by 4 discordant DZs and 7 pairs of uncertain zygosity, two of them concordant.

In 1934 he entered 134 in his formula for the manifestation rate in the place corresponding to 106 in his application of the formula to his 1928 material. He, therefore, presumably had 134 twins including those where the twin had died, an increase of 28. However, he stated that he had re-investigated the starting material and "carefully excluded every case which appeared in any way suspicious or doubtful." He also described the series as being very secure as to zygosity. According to the figures entered in his formula he then had only 9 MZ schizophrenic partners out of 27 "MZ partners found" (33%). The figure of 9 concordant pairs is 5 less than the 14 previously reported and even one less than the previous number of certain schizophrenics; possibly one index twin from a concordant pair had been rejected as diagnostically insecure. On the other hand, the total of MZ pairs is 6 or 7 more than the 21 or 22 previously estimated and 10 more than the 17 originally said to be clearly MZ. The figures in the formula show that there are 2 schizophrenic same-sexed partners not counted as MZ (possibly the two in the uncertain zygosity group of 1930). There is no further explanation. The figures have puzzled Schulz, Essen-Möller, Rosenthal and Kringlen; and the present reviewers are no clearer as to their explanation. It is just possible that Luxenburger's 27 MZ is not the total actually observed but the calculated number expected according to the Weinberg differential method. In the 1928 material (surviving partners) this would have been $65 - 40 = 25$. It might have been 27 in the 1934 material.

Luxenburger reported still a different concordance rate in 1936.

In this paper he was dealing principally with the sibs of 118 of the 134 twin index cases of which the family had been adequately investigated. He reports in passing a concordance for MZ twins of 52%, but it is not clear whether this related to the 118 or the 134 families. With age correction the rate rises only to 54%. From this it can be reasonably deduced that Luxenburger had followed up most of his cases. Few of the twin partners could have then been under 40 or the age-corrected figure would have been higher.

In his 1936 paper, Luxenburger was interested in whether the other sibs of the discordant MZ pairs differed from those of the concordant MZ pairs in the frequency with which they were schizophrenic. If they turned out to have a lower incidence, they might represent a different type of illness biologically, in which case the reality of the manifestation rate which Luxenburger had tried to estimate by means of his twins would be suspect. The sibs of the discordant MZ twins had a slightly higher incidence of schizophrenia, accounted for by two heavily loaded sibships, and he concluded that there was no difference genetically between the schizophrenia of the discordant and concordant pairs. The point is of some relevance. While Slater's (see Section II,E) discordant MZ schizophrenics had almost no cases of schizophrenia in their families unlike his concordant pairs, the studies of Kringlen and Tienari (Section III, B and C) are more like that of Luxenburger in that discordant MZ pairs frequently had a family history of schizophrenia.

4. Clinical and Environmental Findings

Luxenburger presented no case histories. He did, however, state that he did not often find the startling "photographic" similarity in the

TABLE VI

DIFFERENCES IN AGE AT ONSET OF SCHIZOPHRENIA IN TWIN AND
SIB PAIRS (LUXENBURGER, 1936)

Pairs	Difference in age (years)					Number of pairs
	Same age	1–1.9	2–5.9	6–10.9	$\geqslant 11$	
MZ	9 (24%)	7 (18%)	16 (42%)	4 (11%)	2 (5%)	38 (100%)
DZ and Sibs	3 (6%)	6 (11%)	14 (26%)	18 (34%)	12 (23%)	53 (100%)

illnesses of his concordant pairs that some of the early writers had claimed. Age of onset differed between the members of concordant pairs as shown in Table VI.

For the analysis of age of onset, the material was enlarged by additional cases from outside the starting material. Cases of early onset, particularly hebephrenics and catatonics, tended to be most alike.

Though there might be resemblance in prepsychotic symptoms, remissions varied in duration and quality. Paranoid schizophrenia showed the greatest variability within pairs. Some of these clinical impressions have found subsequent support.

Luxenburger said little about specific environmental causes of differences within pairs. He quotes Lange as having found in 15 pairs that the apparently more intelligent MZ twin had the earlier onset and more severe illness, while the converse was true in only 3 pairs. The attempt to function at a higher level is thought of as a possible explanation. The tendency has not been noted in later studies.

5. Conclusions

The points to be noted from Luxenburger's pioneering study are the following: (1) the need for complete, representative series of twins. Luxenburger set high standards in this respect—standards which have been rarely met in any psychiatric work. The Munich school laid the foundations of a scientific approach to psychiatric epidemiology. (2) Classical-type schizophrenia does not occur to excess in twins *per se*. (3) If one twin is affected, a genetically identical partner is much more likely to be schizophrenic than a genetically dissimilar twin. Their phenotypic illnesses, however, are not identical. (4) The concept of a single true concordance rate for a sample of schizophrenic twins is misleading. Such an estimate will vary according to the criteria and methods used, and such variation can be quite large in a numerically small and constantly expanding series.

Of later twin investigators, three studied at the Munich Institute before going on to make their own individual contributions in their own country or the country of their adoption.

Slater's London study was the first of the three to be started early in 1936, although the last to be published on account of the war. Essen-Möller began to collect his South Swedish series in 1937. He carried out a special study of zygosity determination in twins before publishing his findings in 1941. Kallmann also planned his large New York twin study in 1937, shortly after arriving in the United States. Meanwhile Rosanoff, known for his work on word association and as a textbook author, was managing to pursue his own interests in the hereditary aspects of abnormal behavior while engaging in the private practice of psychiatry.

B. Rosanoff (United States, 1934)

In April of 1931, Aaron J. Rosanoff read a paper (Rosanoff, 1932) before the neuropsychiatry section of the California Medical Association describing the beginning of an effort to locate a large sample of twins affected with conditions of interest to the section. Over a period of time from 1934 to 1941, the Rosanoff group published a series of papers, using the results of their twin survey, on the etiologies of criminality, delinquency, epilepsy, "so-called schizophrenic psychoses," mongolism, manic-depressive syndromes, mental deficiency, and child behavior difficulties. The 1934 paper by Rosanoff, Handy, Plesset, and Brush, with 142 pairs of twins in which the proband was a schizophrenic will be our major concern in this chapter.

1. Sampling

Inasmuch as the twin method is recommended for the accuracy with which the representativeness of the patients can be assured (Rosenthal, 1962b), it is crucial for the investigator to give sufficient information for the evaluation of sampling adequacy. Nowhere in the Rosanoff papers is sufficient information provided for direct evaluation of the twin sample. The 1934 paper makes reference to the Luxenburger studies of 1928 and 1930. There can be no doubt that the authors were aware of the ideal methodology to be followed in obtaining a twin sample. They state: "The obvious need is for a larger amount of material gathered by the method of uninterrupted series as developed by Lange and Luxenburger" (p. 250). *Larger* refers to the Luxenburger sample of 21 MZ pairs and 37 DZ pairs of schizophrenic twins reported in 1930.

Although the authors make no mention of the size of their total starting sample of patients or their starting sample of schizophrenics, certain estimates can be made against which to evaluate the sampling adequacy. Later, internal analyses of the schizophrenic twin sample will also be made. The Rosanoff group gathered their twins from "every part of the United States and Canada" (1932). They looked in the following settings: state hospitals, institutions for the feeble-minded, prisons, public school classes for the "subnormal," "behavior cases in the schools," and in child guidance clinics.

The survey took place between the Spring of 1930 and the Fall of 1933. It yielded 1014 pairs of twins with one or both members affected. Rosanoff stated that he expected to find no more than 1 patient in 250 with a twin who was living and accessible to investigation. He then went on to estimate that 2500 pairs of twins, roughly, should result from the survey. If he estimated correctly, the starting material contained no less than 625,000 patients. From Luxenburger's experience, in his sample of adult psychotics and epileptics, one patient in 100 had a twin who survived to adulthood. This figure would be conservative to use on the Rosanoff material since he sampled both children and adults. Nonetheless, a ratio of 1:100 applied to the 625,000 patients would yield a minimum expectation of 6250 pairs of twins contrasted to the anticipated sample of 2500 and the located sample of 1014. Rosanoff, not unreasonably, attributed the difference between his expected and located sample of twins to lack of institutional cooperation. Thus, only some 16% of the potential population of twin pairs may have been located. These data suggest remarkable and unknown types of selection bias, and we must conclude that the sample is certainly not an "uninterrupted" one.

Among the 1014 pairs of psychiatrically affected twins 142 were found with dementia praecox or schizophrenia in one or both members. It is probably safe to assume that these were diagnoses on the hospital records and that none was changed by the authors. It is possible that few of the schizophrenics were personally examined by the Rosanoff group since they say that "the material which forms the basis of this communication consists of the *clinical records* of 142 pairs of twins with schizophrenia in one or both of each pair" (p. 251) (italics added). From the 23 illustrative brief case histories it is obvious that the investigators place no restrictions on race, national origin, or whether age of onset of psychosis fit with traditional conceptions of the risk period for schizophrenia. Thus an unknown number of Negro Americans and an unknown number of foreign born and/or reared subjects are all mixed together in their schizophrenic sample.[2] Among the birthplaces of the index cases were Russia, Denmark, Canada, Australia, and "abroad." Since the starting sample of 1014 twin pairs was already so selected, it is impossible to tell whether the 142 schizophrenic index pairs is too few or too many. Rosenthal (1962a) noted that the ratio of index cases diagnosed as schizophrenic to those diagnosed manic-depressive was lower (1.6:1) in the Rosanoff material than in any of the other studies that examined both illnesses in twins. The other studies ranged in their ratios from 2.8:1 in Luxenburger to 12.7:1 in Kallmann. Only Luxenburger and Essen-Möller came close to agreement on this particular ratio even though their sampling procedures differed. There is a complex interaction between sampling procedures such as excluding broken pairs and standing population versus consecutive admissions, on the one hand, and diagnostic criteria for schizophrenia, on the other, which invalidate the ratio of schizophrenics to manic-depressives as an accurate index to sample representativeness.

It is a fairly simple matter to make an internal analysis of the 142 pairs for correspondence to expected twin types. The investigators found,

---

[2] Recent data suggest that the rates and kinds of mental illness are different in Negroes and that the rates are lower in immigrants to the United States (Locke & Duvall, 1964; Pettigrew, 1964).

using their criteria for zygosity diagnosis, 41 pairs of MZ twins, 53 pairs of SS DZ, and 48 pairs of OS DZ. The percentage breakdown, 28.9: 37.3: 33.8, is quite close to expectation. Data available for the incidence of twin births in the United States white population for 1918 (Scheinfeld & Schachter, 1963) show that 34.6% of twin births were OS DZ; thus, on the Weinberg hypothesis, the expectation by twin type was 30.7: 34.6: 34.6. However, within each of the categories, the male to female percentage split should be 50:50. For the Rosanoff sample we find the male to female percentages of 46.3: 53.7 in the MZ twins but one of 20.8: 79.2 in the DZ same-sex sample. Of course the split will be 50:50 in the opposite sex DZ group but a check on its adequacy comes from the fact that roughly equal numbers of males and females are schizophrenic probands (21 males, 22 females, and 5 unspecified). Thus, while the over-all trichotomy of twin types appears representative, a closer inspection reveals a deficiency of same-sex male DZ twins (chi square 18.3, p less than .001). For unknown reasons, the number of DZ female pairs is almost four times the number of DZ male pairs. However, even this imperfection in the sampling does not materially affect the net results reported for concordance for schizophrenia in the DZ same-sex sample (9% in males, 17% in females, 13% combined). Rosenthal (1962b) in his analysis of concordance by sex in schizophrenia errs in concluding that the Rosanoff male DZ pairs are more concordant than the female DZ pairs and thus the only instance in the literature where male pairs for any genetic relationship exceed the female rate.[3] The difference arises from the loose use of the concordance idea by Rosanoff *et al.* to mean both twins affected even though the co-twin may have been affected with alcoholism, mongolism, epilepsy, etc. This point will become clearer from Tables VII and VIII.

What happens when twinship is not systematically ascertained among all persons was pointed out by Luxenburger and shown in Table II. Neither of the major errors, over-reporting of MZ twins and of both twins affected, is pronounced in the Rosanoff sample of schizophrenic probands despite their patently incomplete ascertainment. The paradox cannot be resolved with the available information, unless we assume a fortunate balancing out of errors.

2. Zygosity Diagnosis

Perhaps the statement of the authors that "there is generally little difficulty in distinguishing between monozygotic and dizygotic twins . . ." should be held against them in the light of our current

---

[3] Tables I and II in this article by Rosenthal contain some errors stemming from Rosanoff's loose use of the concordance idea.

knowledge (Gottesman, 1963). If we could be assured that the authors had personally seen both members of a pair or that satisfactory physical descriptions were available for twins who may have been dead or abroad, we might readily accept the sense of their statement. The general similarity method was used. Blood-typing and quantitative dermatoglyphic analyses were not available at that time. One of the requirements for an uncontaminated twin study is that the diagnoses of zygosity and mental illness be done independently of each other; the Rosanoff study is among those twin studies which do not meet this criterion. Again it is difficult to judge whether appreciable damage has been done to the final results or not. Conrad (1935) suggested that some MZ pairs had been misclassified as DZ.

3. Results

The findings for Rosanoff's schizophrenic probands and co-twins are given in Tables VII and VIII. In Table VII the dependent vari-

TABLE VII

CONCORDANCE FOR PSYCHIATRIC DISORDER IN 142 SCHIZOPHRENIC TWIN PAIRS[a]

	Probably MZ		Probably DZ			
	Males	Females	Males	Females	OS DZ	Total
Both affected	10	18	3	7	5	43
One affected	9	4	8	35	M 21	99
					F 22	
Totals	19	22	11	42	48	142

[a] From Rosanoff et al. (1934).

TABLE VIII

DIFFERENT DEGREES OF CONCORDANCE AND DISCORDANCE IN MZ AND DZ TWINS[a]

Degree of concordance	Monozygotic			Dizygotic			
	M	F	%	M	F	OS	%
Similar affections	6	12	44	1	4	—	5
Quantitative dissimilarity	2	5	17	—	2	3	5
Qualitative dissimilarity	2	1	7	2	1	2	5
One affected, complete discordance	9	4	32	8	35	43	85
Totals	19	22	100	11	42	48	100

[a] From Rosanoff et al. (1934).

able, mental status, is dichotomized into both and one affected. It is a misleading manner in which to convey information about concordance for schizophrenia because the word *affected* need not mean a form of schizophrenia. Dissatisfaction with the term concordance led the authors to a clearer presentation of the actual data as set out in Table VIII. Even here however, Rosanoff *et al.* equate *qualitative dissimilarity* with *partial concordance* thus implying that the genotype for schizophrenia may sometimes manifest itself as mental deficiency, or criminality, or manic-depressive psychosis, etc. Although the pursuit of the etiology of schizophrenia has occupied many researchers since Morel and Kraepelin characterized the illness, we are not yet agreed on what constitute schizophrenic equivalents. Most investigators agree that the category schizoid personality may reflect the schizotype. The data presented in Tables VII and VIII do not allow the separating out of those co-twins who may legitimately be construed to be on the continuum of schizophrenia. A quantitative dissimilarity was defined as a diagnosis of schizophrenia in the co-twin but with marked differences in age of onset, symptoms, course, or outcome. Minimum concordances, uncorrected for age, for the Rosanoff twins can be obtained by adding the first 2 lines of the tables. This gives us rates of 42% (8/19) and 77% (17/22) for the male and female MZ samples, respectively, a total MZ concordance rate for schizophrenia of 61%. In the undersized sample of male DZ twins the rate is 9% (1/11) and for the female DZ pairs, 14% (6/42); the over-all rate for same sex DZ twins is thus 13%. The opposite sex DZ concordance rate for schizophrenia is no higher than 6% (3/48).

4. Interpretations

In a section of their paper headed "Theory of So-Called Schizophrenic Psychoses," Rosanoff *et al.* advanced the idea that schizophrenia is a heterogeneous group of psychoses, bearing little or no etiologic relationship to one another. In the same vein, it was noted that "a strong line of demarcation cannot be drawn between this group (schizophrenia) . . . cyclothymic psychoses, mental deficiency, and epilepsy" (p. 269). With these kinds of reservations in mind, it was reasonable for them to avoid any specific suggestions about the kinds of genetic mechanisms involved in schizophrenia. The words *genes, recessive, dominance, penetrance,* or *polygenic* do not appear in any of their formulations. The authors are content to conclude that "hereditary factors seem to play an important part" (p. 270), and, furthermore, that such factors are not highly specific. Granting their reservations above, the conclusions as to specificity are unwarranted and premature.

Aside from the heuristic value to research into schizophrenia, the sole advances of the Rosanoff study over that of Luxenburger, come from the diligence with which the possible causes for discordance are pursued and the broaching of the problem of sex differences in concordance. Rosanoff *et al.* endorse most strongly the proposition that a large proportion of so-called schizophrenia is caused by "partial decerebration, mainly of traumatic or infectious origin." By far the largest part of their discussion is taken up with an explication of this proposition. Some investigators might be inclined to suggest that the construct of partial decerebration tends to assume the proportion of an *idée fixe* in the writings of Rosanoff on epilepsy, mental deficiency, criminality, and schizophrenia (it is expressly ruled out for the manic-depressive syndromes). However, the observational base for the invocation of the construct in schizophrenia among discordant twins is, on the face of it, reasonable. Among 39 [sic] male probands (note that 21 are from opposite sex pairs) from completely discordant pairs, clinical histories suggested that 16 or 41% had traumatic or infectious etiologies. For the discordant females 10% (6/60) had such etiologies. More thorough histories might have raised both figures. As Rosenthal (1962b) pointed out, if physical trauma were *generally* of etiological significance with respect to schizophrenia, the incidence should be higher in twins than singletons and higher in males than females. Neither of these expectations are borne out by the literature. This is not to deny the possible importance of physical trauma in some pairs of discordant twins. Wherever potentially etiological exogenous factors differ for a pair of twins, the pair does not belong in the genetical analysis of data. It is contrary to the logic of the classical twin method to use twins where there are appreciable differences in within pair environment.

Psychic factors, "especially in the sphere of sex or love life," were implicated in the etiology of the so-called schizophrenic psychoses by the observation in discordant female twins that 35% (21/60) had such histories. Only 4 of the 60 were from discordant MZ pairs, the rest being DZ probands. Of the total sample of 39 males from discordant pairs, 6 (15%) had discernible psychic traumas. While the trend is apparent, it falls short of statistical significance (Rosenthal, 1962b). The sex difference noted earlier however, that between the concordance rates for male and female MZ twin pairs, is substantial, 42% versus 77%. The latter difference is among the provocative heritages from the Rosanoff study. The point has been taken up by Rosenthal (1959, 1962a,b) and we shall return to it.

It would appear then, that for Rosanoff, the hereditary factors in schizophrenia serve merely to determine cerebral vulnerability to a decerebration syndrome resulting from birth trauma. The data from the twins were interpreted as supporting this proposition.

The emphasis on specific neuropathology makes this particular twin study of schizophrenia different from the main line of research which has focused on biological-genetic rather than biological-anatomic factors. In what is still a unique move, Rosanoff did not use the words schizophrenia or dementia praecox in the last edition of his textbook; instead, the syndromes were discussed under "conditions of confused sexuality."

5. Conclusions

The frustrations the reviewers feel as a result of the incomplete reporting of essential details by the original authors are augmented by the paradoxical conformity of the Rosanoff results to the twin literature on schizophrenia. If our calculations about the size of the starting population are correct—625,000—only 16% of the potential sample of unbroken twin pairs were located. We have no direct way of evaluating the extent of lack of representativeness of the schizophrenic sample.

Although the absolute size of the twin sample used by Rosanoff surpassed that of Luxenburger, the former appears not to have taken the lessons of the latter to heart. The first American twin study of schizophrenia of any magnitude did support the finding that in a standing hospital population the concordance rate for MZ twins is high and greatly exceeds that of DZ twins. The qualification is repeated that the phenotypic illnesses are far from identical. Heterogeneity of both subtypes and etiologies was endorsed. Minor attention was paid to genetics *per se* with major emphasis falling on neuropathology. Sex differences were broached with the suggestion that physical trauma was more important for etiology in males, psychological factors more important for females. The discrepancy between male and female MZ concordance rates was interpreted to mean that hereditary factors were more important for female schizophrenia. The suggestion that age of onset be used as a taxonomic principle may have anticipated the process-reactive dimension now current in the literature.

All in all, the hindsight of the historian leads us to say that as of the end of 1934 the twin method in the study of schizophrenia continued to look promising, but it was in need of refinement. The Rosanoff results may have served to stave off the demise of biologically oriented thinking in the United States with respect to the so-called functional psychoses.

Seven years later the needed refinements appeared in the careful work of Essen-Möller in Sweden.

C. ESSEN-MÖLLER (SWEDEN, 1941)

The Swedish twin study of Erik Essen-Möller (1941b) resembles Luxenburger's in that the twinship of psychiatric patients was checked by reference to the local parish birth registrations. In other respects the methods differ.

1. Essen-Möller's material consisted entirely of consecutive admis-

sions. Theoretically, such material should be more representative than one based partly on the resident population of hospitals containing a high proportion of chronic cases.

2. He investigated all twins, irrespective of diagnosis and not just typical cases of specific disorders. Once again this method should secure material more representative of mental illness as it is seen in the psychiatric hospital than one restricted to clear-cut textbook examples of specific diagnoses. It could then be seen whether the findings differ between the typical and the less typical case.

3. No cases were excluded on grounds of uncertain zygosity. It will be recalled that Luxenburger's series included a high proportion of doubtful cases making interpretation difficult. The extent of personal investigation and the use of ABO and MN blood groups gave an added confidence to the classification in Essen-Möller's study.

4. The presentation of case histories enables the reader to evaluate the clinical diagnosis, which is Essen-Möller's own and does not necessarily coincide with hospital diagnosis on registration. Case histories of MZ pairs take up 110 out of the 200 pages of the monograph.

5. The approach is more clinical than statistical. The personalities of the twins, individual features of their illnesses, and environmental factors are subjected to close scrutiny. The aim was to discover what aspects of mental illness were genetically influenced, rather than to calculate the manifestation rate of a hypothetical schizophrenic gene.

Before going on to describe Essen-Möller's findings, which also differ from those of Luxenburger and Rosanoff in some important respects, it may be of value to describe his methods in greater detail. It is important to know how much differences in findings can be attributed to differences in the way in which an investigation is carried out.

1. Sampling

Essen-Möller registered all consecutive admissions to three mental hospitals and a psychiatric clinic over a period of time, which is not specifically stated in his report but probably amounted to about 11 years. His probands entered his series between 3 and 14 years before he investigated them personally. Altogether some 10,000 patients were registered. In 8586 cases he was able to look up birth registrations in the parishes where the twins were born. Even in Sweden where conditions are exceptionally favorable by reason of accessibility of parish and medical records there was a loss of 14%. A large proportion of the patients whose birth registers could not be checked were mild, voluntary cases for whom there had been no legal requirement to state the place of birth. There may have been a slight bias in favor of severity.

Of 179 patients, 1 in 48 were found to have been born one of twins. This was not significantly higher than 1 in 42 which Essen-Möller expected as the result of his special enquiries on this matter (1941a). It is, however, unexpected that as many as 85 had twins of the opposite sex.[4] Perhaps early mortality of same sex pairs accounts for their underrepresentation on the Weinberg method. Essen-Möller restricted his study to the 94 patients with twins of the same sex, a figure which was reduced to 69 when 23 cases were excluded because the co-twin had died young and 2 cases because the pair could not be investigated. Of the 138 patients and co-twins included in the report, 27 were dead at the time of investigation, and 4 had emigrated; only 6 were not seen personally by Essen-Möller for other reasons. There were 21 MZ pairs and 48 DZ. The number of MZ pairs is on the low side but not significantly lower than the 28

TABLE IX
COMPOSITION OF ESSEN-MÖLLER'S TWIN MATERIAL BY
SEX AND EARLY MORTALITY (1941b)

	Male	Female	Total
Co-twin survived	22	49	71
Co-twin died young	16	7	23
Totals	38	56	94

which Essen-Möller calculated might have been expected on the basis of his previous study (1941a). Sex distribution and early mortality are shown in Table IX. This suggests that any excess of females in samples of this kind may in part be accounted for by the excess mortality of male twins.

2. Results

Of the 69 probands, 38 were schizophrenic or probably schizophrenic. Their distribution by sex and zygosity differed little from that of the nonschizophrenics and is shown in Table X.

No pair was represented in the series by 2 probands. However, quite apart from the small size of the material, Essen-Möller and the reviewers believe that no single concordance rate for schizophrenia as a whole is capable of expressing the variability found in the clinical history of the co-twins. Essen-Möller has been quoted by others as finding anything

---

4 In Essen-Möller's starting material 3866 patients with a hospital diagnosis of schizophrenia included 69 twins, 37 (or over half) of which belonged to OS pairs. According to the Weinberg differential method there would be a negative number of MZ pairs! This deviant finding is worth mentioning if only as a warning against relying too much on the Weinberg method for estimating the expected number of MZ pairs when observations or reports of intra-pair similarity are available.

from zero concordance (Tienari, 1963) to 71% concordance (Kallmann, 1953).

There were 7 clearly schizophrenic probands in Essen-Möller's MZ group (cases 1–7). All had been ill for several years and spent over 2 years in hospital, except for one who had died during one of her repeated schizo-affective attacks. There were also 4 cases (cases 8–11) which, though not typically schizophrenic, could best be classified as belonging to the schizophrenic group of illnesses—2 agitated depressions or excitements with schizophrenic features, a reactive querulance with ideas of reference, and a senile schizophrenia. Five of the seven co-twins of the nuclear group were classified as having had a psychosis; and a sixth, developed one after Essen-Möller's investigation (Kaij, 1960). One of the four co-twins in the peripheral group had a psychosis with later deterioration, and one com-

TABLE X

SEX AND ZYGOSITY OF SCHIZOPHRENIC PROBANDS[a]

	Male	Female	Total
MZ	5	6	11
DZ	11	16	27
Totals	16	22	38

[a] From Essen-Möller (1941b).

mitted suicide a year before the onset of senile schizophrenia in the proband. In our opinion the most reasonable summary figure for MZ concordance is 7/11 or 64%.

An outstanding feature of Essen-Möller's findings is that none of the psychotic co-twins, if one omits the case followed up by Kaij, had a clear-cut schizophrenia with typical form and course. At least four, however, had symptoms of a schizophrenic kind, and nearly all the co-twins had personalities that could be regarded as schizoid. It is worth mentioning specifically what these illnesses, symptoms, or personality traits in the co-twins were.

MZ Co-Twins of Schizophrenics

Case 1 (male): At 36, there had been a recent personality change; ordinary events were experienced as unusual; he has felt a transfer of strength from himself to other people and vice versa, and has twice heard a sentence spoken out loud. He is pre-occupied with the idea of telepathy and has visited a man with whom his twin was said to have been in telepathic communication in order to get the matter clear. Regarded as a borderline schizophrenic, socially well-preserved.

Case 2 (female): In the course of a reactive depression for which she was hospitalized at 22, she thought people looked peculiarly at her; everything seemed to change as if time were standing still, all her feeling had gone, she could do only what she was told to do; monotonous speech and poor affect were observed during the illness. She had a good recovery, but at 31 was not seen personally by Essen-Möller.

Case 3 (male): He was intellectually dull but psychiatrically normal when seen by Essen-Möller at 29. Later, there was an insidious onset of delusions of jealousy; he was hospitalized for 2 years at 37, and on follow-up by Kaij at 43 in the course of a study of drinking habits in twins, in marginal employment, regarded as a schizophrenic defect state (Kaij's Case 19). (The twins in this pair were brought up apart from the age of 7.)

Case 4 (male): He had been hospitalized in a psychiatric clinic for 2 weeks at 23 with his twin, having been found in an exhausted state after living the life of a tramp since 21. Anxious, depressed, self-accusatory, but dull, lacking initiative, paranoid. On follow-up at 26, he was a ward of the parish, tense, absent-minded, and had poor affective contact. Regarded a schizoid personality; reactive psychosis largely induced by twin brother, who later developed a typical hebephrenia.

Case 5 (female): She was said to have been hallucinated during postpartum psychosis at 37; subsequently severe recurrent anxiety attacks occurred with various admissions, lasting weeks or months, to local parish institution; unemployed. When seen at 49 very dull, otherwise normal.

Case 6 (female): Somewhat obstinate, quarrelsome, suspicious under stress; no psychiatric illness, normal when seen at 63.

Case 7 (female): Postpartum depression for 6 months at 25 and later depressions at 35, 46, 49 and 57, with ideas of reference, feels watched or overheard, ordinary events take on a special meaning, liable to believe, for instance, that harm will come to her children. At 60, reported as well, but family stand in way of personal investigation by Essen-Möller.

Case 8 (female): Normal, died 36, effects of cardiac lesion. (Note: proband not hospitalized till 51, though she had an earlier psychotic attack at 24.)

Case 9 (female): Unhospitalized psychosis at 32, nature uncertain (excited, suicidal, believed her family were dead). Thereafter personality change suggestive of schizophrenia—"peculiar," lives alone and will leave the house only at 5 a.m., curses neighbors, speech disconnected; at 51 refuses to be seen by Essen-Möller.

Case 10 (male): No psychiatric illness. At 45 somewhat pedantic and withdrawn.

Case 11 (male): Unusually sensitive, irritable, violent (e.g., towards wife), heavy drinker, but could be elegant, well-spoken. At 66, after a fight, took the other man to court for accusing him of interfering with a young girl and striking him on the head. Four days before the court hearing was due, he hanged himself. Had a schizophrenic son. (Proband not hospitalized till one year later.)

Among the 24 DZ co-twins of schizophrenics (27 if questionable schizophrenic probands are included), two females had certain schizophrenias and one female and one male probable or borderline schizophrenias. Abnormalities of other kinds were not outstanding.

In assessing schizoid abnormalities Essen-Möller attached great importance to facial tonicity and emotional accessibility. Including abnormalities of this kind along with psychoses with schizophrenic symptoms, he considered that all 7 MZ co-twins were to some extent abnormal, compared with between 12 and 15 out of 24 DZ co-twins. On the genetic side he concluded that "individual symptoms within the psychosis appear to be a more constant expression of the abnormal genotypical constitution than the total psychotic picture. Similarly the characterological abnormalities that may be present at the outset in twins with endogenous psychoses appear to be a more constant expression of the abnormal genotypical constitution than the psychoses themselves." If one accepts this view, it becomes a task of future research to identify more securely those features that may be most closely related to the genotype.

On the environmental side Essen-Möller noted in general "a slight difference in the characterological abnormalities in the two twins." The one who had a psychosis, or the more severe psychosis, tended to be the one who had been the more abnormal in character. It may be noted that, contrary to the findings of some later workers, it was not particularly the weaker or more submissive who was the more severely affected. Little in the way of convincing, consistent, specific environmental causes could be found to account for the differences. Some examples may be given.

In case 1, the proband, idealistic, conscientious and energetic in personality, overworked at his studies to the extent that studying became an overvalued idea. He neglected to feed himself properly and lost weight: an attack of flu at the onset of his psychosis may have been the beginning of a later diagnosed TB. The co-twin, more withdrawn in personality, did not drive himself or neglect himself in this way.

In case 5, one of the twins was overprotected and spoiled in consequence of a leg injury at the age of 1: she later showed some degree of behavior disorder (obstinate, quarrelsome, sexually promiscuous). It was her twin who became schizophrenic.

In case 6, perhaps the most "discordant" of all, the proband, second-born, had a forceps delivery and required resuscitation: she was a weakly child and, unlike her co-twin who was normally bright, she had to repeat two grades at school. It seems probable that her later schizophrenia was related to the birth injury.

In case 10, the proband's illness, largely a reactive paranoid state, followed an unhappy marriage. The co-twin was more fortunate in his choice of wife.

Essen-Möller noted that the characterological differences between twins appear to antedate most of the environmental differences that could be established. When he conjectures that "the operative environmental difference often lies at an earlier stage of development than is generally supposed," he is probably thinking of organic rather than psychodynamic factors. Whatever the environmental factors may be, they are difficult to isolate. However, the importance of investigating them is underlined by the wide differences in psychiatric morbidity found by Essen-Möller in several of the MZ schizophrenic pairs in his study.

While Essen-Möller was conducting his twin study in Sweden, Kallmann in the United States was gathering material for the largest psychiatric twin study carried out to date.

D. KALLMANN (UNITED STATES, 1946)

1. Adult Schizophrenia

Franz J. Kallmann (1897–1965) will go down in the history of psychiatry for the strength of his commitment to the idea that genetic factors are of crucial importance in the etiology of schizophrenia and for the extensive data he gathered to support his idea. It is inevitable, when dealing with a topic and a personality which has become controversial, that uncalculating critics will dichotomize Kallmann's contributions as premature on the one hand or precocious on the other as a function of their own strongly held beliefs. They would thus be guilty of throwing out the baby with the bathwater or of keeping the baby *and* the bathwater. We are keenly aware of the pervasiveness of experimenter bias (R. Rosenthal, 1964) and have *consciously* girded ourselves against it.

The Genetics of Schizophrenia was Kallmann's magnum opus. It was published in 1938 shortly after he had arrived in the United States as a German-Jewish refugee. The book is a meticulously detailed account of work begun in 1929 as an investigation of 1087 schizophrenic probands, a total sample, who had been admitted to the Herzberge Hospital in Berlin during the first 10 years of its existence (1893–1902). Comparing the morbidity rates for representative samples of consanguineous and unrelated groups, Kallmann gathered information not only about his probands but also about their spouses, parents, siblings, children, halfsibs, grandparents and grandchildren, nieces and nephews, and even more remote antecedents and descendants. The total number of persons embraced in the study was 13,851. It is obvious that the author regarded the research as definitive and a conclusive proof of the inheritance of schizophrenia. He could well have perceived his future work in the area to be both anticlimactic and "frosting on the cake." If so, this, together with the fact that the vast majority of subsequent work on schizophrenia was presented as oral (rather than written) communication before his peers, could go a long way toward accounting for the lack of essential details in the papers that are our major concern in this chapter. Thus the 1938 book becomes essential reading for those who would fully understand the American studies on twins. In the book diagnostic criteria for the 4 subtypes of schizophrenia are clearly set out. If the criteria were changed for the American work, it should have changed the results (morbidity risks) in comparable categories; as we shall see, there were no appreciable differences. Procedures for correcting the raw data so that they are converted into empirical risk figures are set out only here in detail. Numerous case history examples are given in the book while none are given in the twin papers.

Since the earlier work on German schizophrenic probands did not satisfactorily answer the criticism that a pathological family milieu could be sufficiently etiological for the *group of schizoform abnormalities,* Kallmann's American research combined the twin and family methods. Three sibship groups in addition to the MZ, DZ SS, and DZ OS twins are observed. These groups, presumed to experience comparable environmental conditions, with respect to the trait under consideration, comprise full sibs, half-sibs, and step-sibs. "If the assumed genetic factor exists and the part played by the twinning factor is negligible, the statistical expectation will be that the morbidity rates for full siblings and dizygotic twin partners should be about the same, but they should clearly differ from the rates for the other sibship groups" (Kallmann, 1946, p. 311). Under a simplified family milieu hypothesis of causation, partners of probands in each of the 6 sibship groups should have the same risk of incurring schizophrenia.

Although Kallmann has presented his twin data on schizophrenia in a number of sources, our major concern will be with the 1946 paper originally read at the American Psychiatric Association that year since it is the most complete. Data presented at the International Congress of Psychiatry at Paris in 1950 based on additional cases will only be touched in passing; the results do not differ appreciably over the 4-year period. It should be noted that the heated exchange between Pastore (1949, 1952) and Hurst (1951) is centered almost exclusively on the 1938 book. Only in the writings of Rosenthal can an impartial review of Kallmann's twin findings be found.

a. Sampling. Over a period of 9 years (1937–1945), the 20 mental hospitals under the supervision of the New York State Department of Mental Hygiene notified Kallmann, working in its research section, of cases born by multiple birth that had been admitted with a diagnosis of mental disease. From the unspecified number of twins located in this imprecisely described fashion he made a diagnosis of schizophrenia and zygosity for 794 twin index cases, 362 male and 432 female. Since in 103 pairs both twin partners were index cases, the actual number of twin index pairs was 691. We have every reason to believe that an index case was defined as any admission to the 20 hospitals in the 9-year period (Rainer, 1962). Pairs were only used when information was available for the co-twin at age 15 or older. Of the index cases, 6.55% (52) were Negro. While the racial heterogeneity may be irrelevant to the genetic compo-

nent of schizophrenia, it introduced undesirable environmental heterogeneity.

The number and relationships of the persons included in the survey
are given in Table XI. Of the 1382 twins, 184 had died after the age of 15
but before the survey and so could only be evaluated second-hand.
Almost two thousand of the persons surveyed were dead at the time; the
number otherwise unavailable were not mentioned. The total number of
persons involved, 5776, is monumental, but still a fraction compared to
the total sample of the 1938 book. The amount of effort involved in both

TABLE XI

SAMPLE SIZES AND PRESENCE OF SCHIZOPHRENIA IN CO-TWINS AND
RELATIVES OF TWIN INDEX CASES (KALLMANN, 1946)

	Twins	Sibs	Half-Sibs	Step-Sibs	Parents	Spouses	Total
Living	1198	1682	84	47	618	221	3850
Dead	184	1059	50	27	573	33	1926
Totals	1382	2741	134	74	1191	254	5776
Cases of schizophrenia	167[a]	205	4	1	108	5	490[a]

[a] Does not include 691 schizophrenic probands.

studies is a tribute to Kallmann's tenacity and perseverance, the work
having been done in the days before large foundation and federal grants
were available.

It may be a useful exercise to attempt to evaluate some of the
aspects of Kallmann's sampling. He did not state the total number of
psychotic twins in his starting material from which he located and diagnosed 794 as schizophrenic. He did give the number of patients resident
in 1945 and the number of first admissions for that year but these are
inadequate to estimate the number of patients that furnished the twin
sample. Official New York State statistics permit us to see that at the
beginning of 1937, the 20 hospitals sampled had a resident population of
about 52,000. The hospitals had an average of 12,500 first admissions for
psychoses for the 9-year period during which Kallmann was collecting
his twin index cases. Thus the number of patients from which the twin
sample was drawn numbered some 164,500. It is interesting to note the
official hospital diagnostic practices at that time. Among patients other
than first admissions, about 73% were schizophrenic; 25% of first admissions were so diagnosed, and so were 36% of all readmissions. Although only 7% of first admissions were called manic-depressive, 23%
of readmissions were. In contrast, the Luxenburger and Essen-Möller
material had 39% and 46% diagnosed schizophrenic by the hospitals,

If we take as a rough estimate an expectancy of 1 twin with a partner surviving to age 15 for every 133 patients, the ratio found by Slater at the same time in England for a similar sample, Kallmann should have located approximately 1237 twin index cases. He could not have found this many twins since in 1950 he reported a total of 1232 psychotic twin index cases; by that time he should have found approximately 1613. A ratio of 1:100, that found by Luxenburger, would lead to a less favorable view of sampling adequacy than the ratio of 1:133. A factor complicating the assessment of the sampling is that from 1942 onward many young male schizophrenics would have been diverted to Veterans Hospitals and thus not in the state hospital system.

By using the census statistics we can estimate the number of schizophrenic twin index cases to be found and then see whether diagnostic changes imposed by Kallmann could have amounted to much. There should have been 285 cases among the resident population and 24 more for each of the 9 years for a total of 501 schizophrenic twin index cases. The figure of 794 reported by Kallmann must then include twins who had hospital diagnoses of manic-depressive, paranoia, and involutional psychosis. The changed diagnoses could well have been more accurate than admission diagnoses since Kallmann had the advantage of information about the course of the illness. As we noted earlier, diagnoses uncontaminated by knowledge of zygosity would have raised the level of confidence in all the early twin studies as would the comparison of results using first hospital diagnoses and then investigator diagnoses. If our calculations are roughly correct, more than 64% of all twins were called schizophrenic (794/1237), but how many more cannot be calculated.

TABLE XII

KALLMANN 1946 TWIN SAMPLE BY PAIRS

MZ		DZ		DZ
Males	Females	Males	Females	Opposite Sex
75	99	132	164	
174		296		221

An internal analysis of the Kallmann twin sample reveals other points worth noting. He thought that he had a "random sample" of twins. The sample, broken down by sex and zygosity is given in Table XII.

The assumption of randomness was based on finding that 25.2% of his sample were MZ and a further assumption that 25.6% of an unselected American sample of twins were MZ. As we noted before in the analysis of the Rosanoff study, the best data available for the incidence of twin births by zygosity for the United States white population shows that in 1918, 30.7% of all twins were MZ rather than 25.6%. By the Weinberg Differential Method, Kallmann should have found 249 (470 SS — 221 OS) MZ pairs rather than his 174, and 221 SS DZ pairs instead of 296. One possibility is that hospitals failed to notice some OS pairs, thus tending to weaken our estimates of expected MZ and SS DZ pairs from the Weinberg method.

Another possible explanation of departure from zygosity expectancies is that some MZ pairs are incorrectly called DZ (Essen-Möller, 1941a; Gottesman, 1963). From the birth ratios, the New York study should have had 208 MZ pairs (30.7% $\times$ 691). If roughly 34 of Kallmann's DZ pairs were really MZ (208 — 174), the proportions of MZ:DZ:DZ opposite sex would have been 208:262:221. By percentage this yields 30.7:37.3:32.0 contrasted with the census based expectation of 30.7:34.6:34.6 and his observed percentages of 25.2:42.8:32.0. The effect of this possible error in zygosity diagnosis on the final concordance results will be discussed shortly.

The male to female ratios are 43.1:56.9 for the MZ twins and 44.6:55.4 for the DZ pairs. It now appears unlikely that these departures are indicative of error but rather a reflection of sampling from a largely state hospital population of schizophrenics before the advent of chemotherapy. The Kallmann sex ratios accord almost perfectly with the data compiled by Rosenthal (1961) for Delaware with respect to all readmissions (1900–1950) who remained in hospital; 44% were male and 56%, female.

b. Zygosity Diagnosis. To the extent that the problems of zygosity diagnosis can be separately considered from the broader problems of sampling, a few additional words are in order. Kallmann personally diagnosed the zygosity of the twins on the "basis of personal investigation." He used the similarity method but apparently did not have any reservations about calling a pair MZ or DZ since he did not have a "doubtful" category. Blood-typing was not used although its use had been pioneered earlier by Essen-Möller. Like the other twin studies reviewed so far, the diagnoses of mental status in proband and co-twin were not made independently of the zygosity diagnoses. The proportion of the 691 pairs personally seen is not specified but it is known that Kallmann and his wife spent a large amount of time doing field work with the twins and their families.

c. Diagnosis of Schizophrenia. Psychiatric diagnosis in general is a thorny issue (Zigler & Phillips, 1961). It has been frequently maligned and seldom defended. Kallmann's criteria for a diagnosis of schizophrenia in his twin work have been considered to be too broad and abstract. He did not list the criteria for a diagnosis in the 1946 paper but did in 1950. The latter definition bore a marked similarity in language and intent to the one given by Kallmann's peers, Hoch and Polatin (1949), in their discussion of pseudoneurotic schizophrenia. Pseudoneurotic schizophrenia is also known variously as borderline, ambulatory, outpatient, or college-student schizophrenia. We would like to advance the speculation that the admittedly broad but clinically rich definition could only be applied to some of the co-twins and to none of the 691 index probands all of whom had to have had a psychiatric hospitalization for mental illness. It would then follow that the impact on the 1946 data is less than implied by critics and has an impact difficult to disentangle on the pairs added from consecutive admissions 1946–1950. It has already been noted that fairly complete, textbook-like criteria for the 4 subtypes of schizophrenia were given in the 1938 book. Kallmann called hebephrenic and catatonic schizophrenics *nuclear* (N) schizophrenics and paranoid and simple cases, *peripheral* (P) schizophrenics. Some 72% of the 1047 definite schizophrenics in the 1938 study were N, the remaining 28% being P. Among the 794 twin index cases in the 1946 study, we are told that 68% were N and 32% P. Thus it would seem that although separated in time and geography, the diagnostic criteria for schizophrenia for twin index cases did not differ appreciably from those Kallmann used in Germany.

TABLE XIII

KALLMANN (1946) TWIN AND SIB CONCORDANCES FOR SCHIZOPHRENIA

Relation to proband:	MZ	SS DZ	OS DZ	Sibs
Cases of schizophrenia	120	34	13	205
Crude concordance[a] (%)	69	11	6	10
Corrected morbidity rates (%)	86	18	10	14

[a] Among all persons surviving beyond age 15.

The other point in favor of our speculation comes from the analysis Kallmann did of the severity of illness in twins and co-twins in terms of deterioration. A total of 167 co-twins were diagnosed as schizophrenic. Since 103 of these were index cases in their own right, according to the investigator, they must have had a psychiatric hospitalization and so were eliminated from one of the potential diagnostic errors in the broad 1950 definition. Among the 167 co-twins, a maximum of 64 never hospitalized (167 − 103) could have been "loosely diagnosed" as psychotic.

   d. Results. The crude concordance for pairs of twins and siblings as well as the age-corrected morbidity rates for schizophrenia are presented in Table XIII. Kallmann did not present his data for the MZ and DZ twins separated by sex in an uncorrected form. The three studies reviewed earlier and the Slater study, when combined and analyzed by sex of the MZ pairs and concordance (Rosenthal, 1962b) showed that the female

MZ rate was significantly higher than that of the males, 78% versus 55%. We might therefore have expected that the MZ females in the Kallmann sample should have shown a higher concordance than the males. He stated, however, that the morbidity rates remained constant regardless of whether the co-twins were male or female; his corrected rates for DZ same sex twins support this statement—males, 17%; females, 18%.

We can now examine the possible consequences on concordance rates if the hypothesized misdiagnosis of 34 MZ pairs as DZ occurred. Kallmann reported 34/296 concordant same sex pairs of DZ twins. If we reduce the denominator by the number of "false" DZ pairs (confusingly also 34) but leave the numerator intact to maximize the DZ concordance, the new crude rate becomes 13% (34/262). If we apply this latter rate as the best estimate of concordance among the 34 pairs removed from the denominator we obtain an additional 4 concordant pairs for our now augmented sample of MZ pairs. Thus the new MZ crude concordance rate becomes $120 + 4/174 + 34$ or 60%. Our sole motive in engaging in the questionable correction of another investigator's data is to discover what effect the possible biases attributed to the study would have on the findings as well as to inquire whether some of the heterogeneity of results among twin studies may be more apparent than real in the light of "hindsight." If it were possible to analyze the sample in terms of index cases rather than pairs (Allen, 1955), it might reveal no excess of SS DZ over MZ cases. Such a finding would give less reason for supposing a bias to have occurred in the diagnosis of MZ pairs as DZ.

Many readers will be surprised to learn that Kallmann devoted about half of the 1946 paper to examining factors other than genetic that might account for the difference between MZ and DZ morbidity. Among the factors noted were prematurity, instrumental delivery, reversal of handedness, familial concordance by sex, environmental similarity, length of separation before onset of schizophrenia, and variations in the severity or outcome of the illness. In later work (1953) Kallmann stressed the importance of debilitating physical factors which does not need to be rejected along with the hypothesis linking schizophrenia to tuberculosis. None of the findings on MZ discordance preclude the importance of psychological stress. The first three factors above were found to have no bearing on the incidence of schizophrenia in twins; 82% of discordant index pairs were alike in handedness. All simple theories about schizophrenia are challenged by Kallmann's findings on the relationship between environmental similarity within a pair and the concordance rates. The method of rating environment was not mentioned. For the subset of MZ twins (114) with similar environments, 29% remained discordant thus supporting the insufficiency of a purely genetic theory. But of all the DZ pairs with similar environments (276) only 8% were concordant for schizophrenia thus supporting the insufficiency of a life experience theory of the illness. For the subset of MZ twin pairs with dissimilar environments (60), 65% were nonetheless concordant for schizophrenia.

He did not single out discordant MZ pairs for special analysis and so left that fertile area open for later investigators. Some, but not striking, support is offered to those who would like to attribute part of the high rates of MZ concordance to *folie à deux*. In twins living apart from each other for 5 or more years (59) the age-corrected risk was 77.6%, while in those not separated the risk was 91.5%.

From the similarities in severity or outcome among the twin pairs, Kallmann concluded that "heredity determines the individual capacity for development and control of a schizophrenic psychosis . . . (and) that *constitutional resistance* to the main genotype of schizophrenia is determined by a genetic mechanism which is probably non-specific and

TABLE XIV
EFFECT ON CRUDE CONCORDANCE OF SEVERITY OF SCHIZOPHRENIA
IN MZ AND DZ INDEX PAIRS

Deterioration in index case	MZ Concordance	N	DZ Concordance	N
Little or none	26%	19	2%	2
Medium	100%	53	7%	14
Extreme	100%	48	17%	31
Totals	69%	120	9%	47

certainly multifactorial" (pp. 317–320). The ramifications of this position have yet to be fully appreciated. Rosenthal (1959, 1961, 1963), for one, has gone one step further with Kallmann's data on severity and concordance. We present that step and the logical one it suggested to us in Table XIV. It is immediately obvious, if this tendency can be generalized, that the weight one gives to genetic factors will be large in a sample selected to include a majority of severely ill schizophrenics but minimal in a sample with mildly ill and recovered probands.

Implications for future research strategies will be sketched later in the chapter. Of the varieties of genetic modes of inheritance that might best account for these data on schizophrenia and severity, a polygenic theory would appear to us to hold the most promise.

It was Kallmann's final opinion that the ability to respond to certain stimuli with a schizophrenic reaction depended on being homozygous for a recessive gene. For him this did not preclude prevention and cure. A recessive hypothesis for schizophrenia as a whole has been rejected by most geneticists. At any rate to throw out recessivity is quite a different proposition from throwing out a genetic etiology for a significant proportion of schizophrenic phenotypes.

e. Discussion. It would take us far beyond the scope of the present overview to discuss adequately even a few of the important issues raised by the Kallmann twin study. One may regret the absence of sampling details and case histories. It is a fascinating armchair experience to contemplate what the effects on the data would have been had it been gathered and analyzed differently. Other important advances would have come if the author had chosen to continue the taxonomy of Nuclear and Peripheral schizophrenia and made provision for detailed symptom analyses in the twin work since no one else is likely to gather such a large sample of twins. Paranoid schizophrenics differ enough from the other subtypes to deserve separate analysis. Another issue concerns the variable of sex. Even if Kallmann found no qualitative differences between the concordance rates for male and female MZ and DZ pairs, what might the quantitative differences have been? However important these questions are, we have no firm bases for further speculations. One methodological point on which some comment can be made that seems of general importance is the kind and use of age correction for partners still in the period of risk.

Kallmann did not provide the data that would permit reconstruction of the original information on age of co-twins. However, he did provide other relevant information on age and time since onset that allows an evaluation of the appropriateness of the correction procedure. The discordant index pairs had reached the average age of 33. The discordant MZ pairs had been followed for an average of 8.5 years, the discordant same sex DZ for an average of 12.5 years since the onset of the schizophrenia in the proband. Kallmann plotted the percentages of his 120 concordant MZ pairs who became so at different intervals after the onset and first admission of the proband. These data tell us that within 8 years all but 11% of the co-twins had had their onset of schizophrenia and all but 14% had had their first admission. Thus the discordant MZ partners cannot be considered to have 50% of the risk (the routine age-correction factor) remaining for becoming schizophrenic; a more reasonable estimate would be about 10% for those co-twins within the risk period.

f. Conclusions. Kallmann's twin-family study of schizophrenia was of heroic proportions. No one has come near to finding the 953 schizophrenic index pairs he had assembled by 1950. The size of his material permitted him to go beyond fairly simple but basic nose counting. At the same time the size of the material prevented the kind of intensive analysis of lives that Essen-Möller's case histories permitted. The seeming disavowal of psychodynamic concepts has probably contributed to the resistance against wider acceptance of the data as well as the interpretations. Even if Kallmann did not write the *final chapter,* the heuristic value of his ideas on schizophrenia as evidenced by the frequency of citation is phenomenal. It is not crucial that schizophrenia may not be due to a recessive gene; it *is* crucial that researchers not abandon genetically oriented research designs. Our evaluations of possible errors in zygosity diagnosis do not change the order of magnitude of the crude concordance rates. Errors in the diagnosis of mental status were not likely of consequence to a clinician with Kallmann's experience with schizophrenia. The method of age correction chosen exaggerated the corrected risk figures, but even the raw concordances stand impressive and belong to the same domain as preceding twin work.

There then existed a need for a rapprochement among the virtues of psychiatric epidemiology, intensive description of case material, refinements of zygosity diagnosis, and flexible age corrections in a twin-family study of schizophrenia. Such a synthesis was provided in 1953 by the work of Eliot Slater. After a brief digression to describe a relatively unknown twin study by Kallmann and Roth on preadolescent schizophrenia, we will review the Slater findings.

2. *Kallmann and Roth on Childhood Schizophrenia*

The relationships among genotype, age, and phenotype are among the important unsolved problems in developmental biology that diffuse into research on psychopathology. A cogent example is provided by the work of Metrakos and Metrakos (1962) on centrencephalic epilepsy in a sample of children probands and their sibs and parents. The prevalence of 3 per second spike EEG records was 8% in parents but 37% in sibs. Only 13% of the sibs had actually had overt seizures. From the age-specific distribution of abnormal EEGs the authors postulated that the pattern was the expression of a dominant gene with a low penetrance at birth, rising to complete penetrance between ages $4\frac{1}{2}$–$16\frac{1}{2}$, declining gradually to no penetrance after age 40. The example is cited as an instance that parsimony may not always be our best master when the materials and processes are inherently complex.

Childhood schizophrenia is rare compared to the adult form; only 6 per 1000 of all first admissions to the New York State Hospitals were so diagnosed, 19 per 1000 of all schizophrenics admitted for the period 1948–1952 (Kallmann & Roth, 1956). It may or may not be the same as infantile autism (Rimland, 1964). Adding to the difficulties of psychiatric diagnosis, with children especially, is the probability of etiological heterogeneity. In our opinion inadequate data exist to say whether most forms deserve taxonomic rank with adult schizophrenia.

From a state-wide survey over an unspecified time the authors located 52 index pairs of preadolescent schizophrenics and 50 singleton index cases. On the basis of the similarity method which included some blood-typing and fingerprint data, 17 pairs were found to be MZ, 35 were DZ. The sample by sex and zygosity is given in Table XV. The number of concordant pairs is given but was not presented by sex or separately for the two DZ groups.

TABLE XV
KALLMANN AND ROTH TWIN STUDY OF CHILDHOOD SCHIZOPHRENIA

	MZ	SS DZ	OS DZ	Total	Sibs	Singletons
Male	12	16	9	37	96	37
Female	5	8	2	15	103	13
Total	17	24	11	52	199	50
Schizophrenic partners	15	8		23	18	

Apparently 17% (9) of the twin index pairs were Negro but were not analyzed separately. The disproportionate number of male probands both in the twin and the singleton material is equivalent to an excess of more than 40% over expected. The male to female ratio in the 3 twin sub-samples ranges from 2:1 to 4.5:1. Based on the birth ratios, the number of MZ pairs is very close to the expected, but there is an excess of about 7 SS DZ and a shortage of about 6 OS DZ pairs. Again the possibility must be raised that some DZ pairs were incorrectly diagnosed as such. Since they were largely discordant for schizophrenia, the addition of discordant MZ pairs to the sample would lower the MZ rate and raise the DZ. On the other hand DZ OS pairs may have been missed, making sample evaluation indeterminate.

When only co-twin onset of schizophrenia before age 15 was considered, the crude concordance rates were 71% and 17% for the MZ and combined DZ samples. After adding the 5 co-twins with onsets after age 15, the MZ and DZ rates became 88% and 23%. In the total sample of twin plus singleton parents, 18 or 9% were found to be schizophrenic. Among all sibs of index cases, 18 or 9% were found to have schizophrenia before (16) or after (2) age 15. A further 46 parents and 19 sibs were thought to be schizoid personalities.

If our earlier procedures for computing a kind of lower confidence limit on MZ concordance are applied to these data, we just change the DZ denominator by the hypothetical excess of DZ pairs to obtain the maximum DZ rate and minimum MZ. The new DZ ratio becomes $8/(35 - 7)$ or 29%. The latter rate applied to 7 presumed MZ pairs adds

2 pairs to the original 15 concordant MZ pairs. The new MZ rate then becomes $17/(17 + 7)$ or 71% contrasted with the Kallmann and Roth figure of 88%. If the adjusted rates for child schizophrenic twin probands, 71% and 29% for MZ and combined DZ respectively, are compared with the previously calculated adjusted rates for adult probands, 60% and 13%, interesting but not striking differences are revealed. From a comparison of the original concordance rates in the 1946 and 1956 studies, Kallmann and Roth concluded that, ". . . preadolescent schizophrenia is determined genetically to the same extent, and apparently by the same gene-specific deficiency state, as is assumed in regard to the adult forms of the disease. The difference between the preadolescent and adult types seems to lie, at least in part, in a number of secondary factors which lower the constitutional resistance or interfere with the containability of early cases" (1956, p. 601).

If true, the conclusion that child and adult schizophrenia are the same phenomenon is an important one for a science of psychopathology. In themselves, however, similar concordance rates in the two studies are not sufficient evidence for such a conclusion. Similar reasoning had earlier been applied to schizophrenia and tuberculosis with a consequent weakening in the genetic theorizing about schizophrenia. The interpretation of twin concordances cannot be done wisely outside of a total context of already existing knowledge from epidemiological, family, and laboratory research.

With sex per se such an obviously important factor for childhood schizophrenia, the combining of male and female data may have obscured crucial issues. At the least, the MZ to DZ contrasts should have been made separately by sex. The greater liability of the male to prenatal and perinatal trauma (Goldfarb, 1964; Taft & Goldfarb, 1964) together with Kallmann's own attention to birth complications in 1946, makes the omission of data on the latter particularly glaring in the study of childhood schizophrenia. As noted in the Introduction, the twin method can be used to search for etiological heterogeneity. Future researchers in this area would do well to separate their child probands into those with and without natal complications before calculating concordances by sex. Bender's (1956) idea that cerebral trauma merely elicits rather than causes childhood schizophrenia could be examined by looking at family histories in the concordant and discordant groups already dichotomized for natal complications.

Further consideration of childhood schizophrenia is beyond the scope of this chapter. We endorse the conclusion of Kallmann and Roth to the effect that a need exists for systematic and intensified research into the genetic aspects of both childhood and adult schizophrenia. We prefer to think of their earlier conclusion on isomorphism of both forms as a challenge to a science of psychopathology rather than a *fait accompli.*

E. SLATER (UNITED KINGDOM, 1953)

If Essen-Möller's twin study was too small to allow firm conclusions to be drawn and Kallmann's so large that he was unable to present case material for evaluation, Eliot Slater's (1953) London study of psychiatric illnesses in twins avoids both these disadvantages. It is of much the same size as Rosanoff's study, but the presentation and analysis of his material is fuller and more sophisticated.

Ascertainment of twinship by consulting birth registers is not possible in Great Britain. Direct enquiries have to be made. A major practical drawback to making such enquiries in a fresh study from a series of consecutive admissions is the time it takes to accumulate a sufficient number of cases, even of a disorder which fills as many hospital beds as schizophrenia. Essen-Möller's investigation, had his twins not been ascertained retrospectively, would have taken 11 years—an average of one MZ schizophrenic twin a year. The problem is considerable, even in large areas of dense population. Slater's plan, therefore, was to combine a study of twins who were already patients in hospital with one of twins subsequently admitted.

1. Sampling

In 1936, when he started his investigation, the ten psychiatric hospitals serving the area of the London County Council housed about 20,640 patients. The 16,632 who had relatives were surveyed in the mail. Slater asked whether the patient was born one of twins. So far as could be judged, the incidence of twins in the resident hospital population corresponded well with that in the general population. To the twins obtained from this source were added those routinely ascertained from subsequent admissions to the same hospitals and to the Maudsley Hospital. The latter is a University psychiatric clinic for inpatients and outpatients. The war put a close to the collection of cases from subsequent admissions, leaving index cases from the resident population still in the majority: of the 295 twins with partners surviving childhood, who form the probands of Slater's study, 155 were from the resident population, 140 from consecutive admissions. The investigation of previously registered cases was completed and a follow-up made in the years 1947 to 1950.

For statistical analysis all index cases, whether diagnostically typical or not, were allotted by Slater to one of four groups—schizophrenic (156), affective (38), organic (49), and personality disorders or neuroses (52). Diagnostic criteria are implicit in the case histories which account for two-thirds of the report. Official hospital diagnoses could not be used since they were couched in antiquated terms that did not include dementia praecox or schizophrenia.

The schizophrenic group included two sets of triplets, each providing two co-twins for comparison with the proband.[5] Seven pairs were represented in the schizophrenic group by two index twins.[6] Omitting two pairs of unknown zygosity, there were 147 sets of multiple births. All but five of the probands were examined by Slater or one of the two psychiatric social workers who were engaged on the field work. Four of the five who were not seen had died. Of the 149 twin or triplet partners 41 were not examined, 30 having died.

Zygosity was decided on the observed and reported resemblance in appearance; and, whenever possible, anthropometric measurements were made. Fingerprints were available for both members of 59 same-sexed pairs in the schizophrenic group. The main investigation was carried out at the time when blood-grouping was not generally available. In the absence of fingerprints, pairs considered to be MZ were indicated by the addition of a "?." No formal precautions were taken to prevent knowledge of zygosity influencing psychiatric diagnosis, or vice versa. Though it may be possible to arrange for psychiatric diagnosis to be made without reference to the other member of the twin pair, it is difficult to see how, if full blood-grouping is not available, zygosity can be reliably decided in total ignorance of clinical state; for assessment can best be made by seeing the twins side by side, a procedure in which the investigator cannot be prevented from noticing, for instance, that both twins are hospital inmates, or that one is obviously psychotic and the other apparently not.

Thirty-seven index pairs were found to be MZ, 58 SS DZ, and 54 OS. This corresponds closely to the number of pairs of the three types that would be expected on the basis of population statistics—41, 54, and 54 respectively. As we shall see there was an appreciable excess of females in the sample, a point which we shall go on to discuss. However, the proportion of the three twin types is similar taking male and female separately. This speaks in favor of the series being representative and zygosity determination accurate.

---

5 The triplets were: Case 41—2 MZ sisters, both schizophrenic, and a normal brother; and Case 289—2 DZ sisters, both schizophrenic, and a brother with a personality disorder.

6 The zygosity, source (resident, R, or consecutive, C) and sex (f or m) of the "double probands" were the following: 4 MZ pairs—RRf, RRf, CCf, and CCm; 3 SS DZ pairs—RRf, RCf, and RCf. Note that in 2 pairs one twin entered the series as an R case, the other as a C.

The report does not distinguish between probands who entered the series from the resident hospital population and those from subsequent consecutive admissions. However, one of us (J.S.), who assisted in the Slater study, has been able, using the original data, to divide the schizophrenic probands in this way. We are grateful to Dr. Slater for permission to report the results here. One hundred schizophrenic probands came from the resident population, 56 from later consecutive admissions. The proportion from the resident population is higher than in the total series. This is to be expected, since schizophrenia tends to be a chronic disorder. There is an over-representation of females, particularly among the resident hospital probands as shown in the following tabulation.

	Males	Females
Resident population	30	70
Consecutive admissions	24	32

At the time there were more women than men (all diagnoses) in the London mental hospitals, but the excess, approximately 43 males to 57 females (report of Board of Control for 1935), was not so marked as in the twin sample of schizophrenics. The official reports of the time do not break down the hospital population according to length of stay or diagnosis. However, the Registrar General's Statistical Review of England and Wales for the year 1949 (Supplement on General Morbidity, Cancer and Mental Health) (1953) gives figures for patients who had been in hospital for one year or more. Such patients would include a higher proportion of schizophrenics than all patients in residence. Carstairs et al. (1955), analyzing data from the GRO Report, show that in the four Metropolitan Regions, i.e., in London and the surrounding counties, in 1949 there were 18,621 males and 28,536 females (60.5% females) who had been one year or longer continuously in a mental hospital. The excess of females over males thus approaches a little more closely the 70% found by Slater.

Another possible reason for the excess of females comes to mind. It may well be that long-term male patients are less frequently in touch with relatives than long-term female patients. This could arise from a tendency for males to move away from their home more, and from a tendency for female schizophrenics to marry more often than males. Older female patients would therefore more often have a spouse or children who were in touch with them after their parents had died. If this were so, postal inquiries to relatives, asking about twinship, would more easily secure information about females. Unfortunately, no check could be made of the sex of the 4008 patients who had no available relatives when Slater sent out his inquiries.

Whatever may be the cause of the excess of females—excess mortality of the male is a further possibility previously mentioned—it becomes important only insofar as there is a genuine sex difference in concordance rate for schizophrenia.

2. Results

a. Concordance Rates. We shall now describe how Slater calculated his concordance rates. For him it was a question of estimating the empirical risk for schizophrenia in the co-twin of a proband who had lived through the risk period. The 4 MZ and 3 DZ "double-probands" (see footnote 5) were therefore counted twice. There were 41 MZ co-twins of index cases, 28 of whom (68%) were in Slater's judgment schizophrenic. The corresponding figure for DZ co-twins was 13 out of 115, 11%. Correction for age, using the standard Weinberg method and taking 15-39 as the risk period, yielded concordance rates of 95% MZ and 14% DZ. The MZ figure was clearly overcorrected for reasons given in Section I,E,3,c. Slater, therefore, devised an alternative method, taking into account the distribution of differences in age of onset in the concordant pairs. This yielded the rate of 76%, which he regarded as the best estimate of concordance in his material. The magnitude of the MZ and DZ concordance rates suggested to him that "genetical causes provide a potentiality for schizophrenia, perhaps an essential one, though environmental factors play a substantial role which may be decisive in the individual case" (p. 88).

Like Kallmann, Slater combined the twin and family methods. Five per cent of sibs and four per cent of parents were schizophrenic (crude and age-corrected rates differed little). The difference between the DZ and sib rates was attributed largely to the more thorough investigation of the former, though clearly environmental factors could not be ruled out. Slater noted a tendency for female relatives in general to be affected more often than males. The age-corrected risks for schizophrenia in non-twin brothers was 3%, in non-twin sisters 7%, in DZ brothers 9%, in DZ sisters 19%, in MZ brothers 70%, in MZ sisters 80%.

Table XVI displays Slater's findings in terms of index pairs rather than probands, and divided by sex and source. It can be seen that concordance is appreciably higher in female pairs than in male pairs in the resident hospital sample—2/6 (33%) male MZ, as compared with 15/20 (75%) female MZ, and 0/10 male as compared with 4/25 (16%) female SS DZ. The same tendency is barely evident in the consecutive sample—3/5 (60%) male compared with 4/6 (67%) female MZ, and 2/11 (18%) male

TABLE XVI

CONCORDANCE FOR SLATER'S (1953) INDEX PAIRS BY ZYGOSITY, SEX, AND SOURCE

Source of index pairs	MZ		SS DZ		OS (sex of proband underlined)	
	mm	ff	mm	ff	mf	fm
Resident	2/6	15/20	0/10	4/25	0/14	0/22
Consecutive[a]	3/5	4/6	2/11	2/12	0/5	2/13
Total	5/11	19/26	2/21	6/37	0/19	2/35
Concordant	45%	73%	10%	16%	0%	6%
Sexes combined	65%		14%		4%	

a Two further pairs of male twins with unknown zygosity were in the consecutively admitted sample; both pairs were discordant.

and 2/12 (17%) female SS DZ. Concordance in the consecutive sample, sexes combined, was actually a trifle higher than in the resident sample (see Table XVII).

TABLE XVII

CONCORDANCE BY SOURCE OF SLATER'S INDEX PAIRS, SEXES COMBINED

Source of index pairs	MZ	Combined DZ	All twins
Resident	17/26 (65%)	4/71 (6%)	21/97 (22%)
Consecutive	7/11 (64%)	6/41 (15%)	13/52 (25%)
Totals	24/37 (65%)	10/112 (9%)	34/149 (23%)

If the above internal analysis of Slater's material fails to show the hypothesized difference (Rosenthal, 1961) between resident population and consecutive admissions, it does not necessarily imply that there is no difference between concordance rates in severe and mild schizophrenia. It could well be that the two subsamples in Slater's series were not greatly contrasted in respect of severity, since a large proportion of the consecutive admissions consisted of readmissions and patients who later became chronically hospitalized. On the other hand, if there were a selective bias against concordant males, concordance in the resident sample when corrected for this bias would be higher.

b. Schizophrenia in the Co-Twin. We have already stressed the fact that the term concordance has little meaning without qualification. Even when restricted to "concordant for schizophrenia" one needs to know what kinds of conditions the investigator has called schizophrenic in the co-twins. An advantage of Slater's case histories is that the reader can see for himself. The histories also give an insight into the practical difficulties of observational research, involving field study of a defined group.

The probands were by definition psychiatric patients and they were all hospitalized at some time. The schizophrenic co-twins were not necessarily ever hospitalized. In fact the co-twin had a mental hospital admission in 21/24 MZ and 6/10 DZ concordant pairs. This suggests that Slater did not unwittingly let his knowledge of zygosity influence him in the direction of counting mild psychiatric illnesses as concordant more often in MZ than DZ pairs. Of the three MZ schizophrenic co-twins who were not hospitalized, one committed suicide by poison (Case 87), another died while in a mental observation ward (Case 117), and the third (Case 20) was forced to give up work on account of paranoid delusions. An interesting point emerges from the DZ pairs, suggesting that female schizophrenics are more likely to be hospitalized than males. The six DZ pairs in which both twins were admitted to county mental hospitals were all female, while the four concordant but unhospitalized co-twins were all male. One of the latter was once in a mental observation ward, another was a tramp, a third died young and untreated, while the onset in the last case was recent at time of follow-up.

Unlike the psychotic co-twins in the Essen-Möller study, the majority of the co-twins regarded as concordant by Slater had unambiguous schizophrenic illnesses. However, there were doubtful features or lack of fully adequate information in 7 out of 24 MZ co-twins. Doubt was expressed about the diagnosis in 3 out of 10 DZ co-twins "But," as Slater remarks, "it would seem captious to exclude [the doubtful cases], as in every case schizophrenia is much more probable than normality or any other diagnosis" (p. 55). He was aware of the possibility of what is now termed contaminated diagnosis, but he thought it was just as likely that he had underestimated concordance in MZ pairs by including possible schizophrenics among the discordant pairs as overestimating it by calling doubtful cases concordant. We shall refer to the discordant pairs later.

c. Clinical and Environmental Analysis. A notable feature of Slater's study and one which is apt to be overlooked is the attempt he made to analyze the nature of resemblance in pairs of relatives where both were schizophrenic. Correlations in age of onset were .5, .7, and .4 for MZ, DZ, and sib pairs respectively. There were significant resemblances in type of onset (sudden or gradual), course (one or more attacks), catatonic features, passivity feelings, presence of marked depression or elation, depersonalization, organic signs (such as confusion, disorientation), and tendencies to suicide or self-injury. There were on the other hand marked differences in duration and outcome. Though half the concordant MZ pairs fell ill within three years, differences in age of onset of 20, 22, and even 31 years occurred. One proband was in hospital for 46 years until her death at 79, while her co-twin recovered from a psychosis at 26 after about 6 months in hospital. There was no significant tendency for pairs of affected relatives to be alike in outcome. In this respect the findings are more like those of Essen-Möller than those of Kallmann or Bleuler (1941). The existence of pairs differing in severity points to the importance of nongenetic factors relevant to the treatment of schizophrenia. In the light of the Slater study the history of the Genain quadruplets (Rosenthal, 1963) is not entirely unexpected—all four MZ quads had catatonic-hebephrenic schizophrenia, but the outcomes ranged from deterioration to recovery.

Besides cases of schizophrenia, there were other psychiatric abnormalities among the relatives. Affective illnesses, when they occurred, usually took the form of an involutional depression, often with schizophrenic symptoms, which Slater considered to be related genetically to schizophrenia. Most of the non-schizophrenic abnormalities were personality disorders. By listing the words or phrases used to describe the 27 DZ co-twins, 63 sibs, and 64 parents so classified, he was able to show that they were more often paranoid, eccentric, reserved, and lacking in feeling or initiative than the abnormal relatives of non-schizophrenic probands. This lends other support to the concept of schizoidia and the schizotype.

Slater also attempted to analyze the influence of environmental and personality factors on psychosis by comparing the more severely affected twin with the less severely or unaffected twin in respect to their premorbid differences. Numbers were too small to allow clear-cut tendencies to emerge in the MZ schizophrenic group. However, the more severely ill twin tended to have the more difficult birth (in the ratio 7:3), to be the more submissive twin (7:2), to have poorer physical health (8:3), and to have been, in general, the more neurotic as an adult (13:4), in particular having more paranoid traits (9:2). While the evidence on which some of these figures are based is open to question, some of the tendencies have been noted by later workers. Kringlen (1964), Tienari (1963), and Pollin et al. (1965) all found the more submissive twin to be affected in discordant pairs. Rosenthal (1959) applied the Phillips pre-morbid check list to the discordant male pairs in Slater's series and found the future schizophrenic to have had the poorer social and sexual history.

    d. *Discordant MZ Pairs.* Based on Slater's histories, Rosenthal noted in the discordant MZ pairs an excess of males, of paranoid illnesses with late onset and better outcome, and a lack of family history of schizophrenia. He considered the possibility that the discordant pairs represented a nongenetic variety of schizophrenia. Absence of family history in discordant pairs was not found by Luxenburger, Kringlen, or Tienari. Kallmann (1938) reported a lower incidence of schizophrenia among the relatives of paranoid and simple schizophrenics than in the nuclear group.

Reviewing Slater's discordant pairs again in the light of Rosenthal's observations there is a hint of an exogenous etiology in three:

> In Case 53 Slater thought the proband's illness might have been secondary to congenital syphilis for which she first received treatment later than her co-twin. Case 61 could have been an organic paranoid psychosis precipitated by alcoholic excess. Proband 231 had a severe meningitis at age 4.

It is worth noting that in five of the thirteen discordant pairs the co-twin died before the proband was admitted to hospital. The intervals between death of the co-twin and admission of the proband were 5, 6, 8, and, in two instances, 17 years. The inclusion of such cases points to the necessity of some form of age correction. While it would be incorrect simply to exclude these five pairs it may be noted that if one did so, concordance in the MZ group would be 24 out of 32 (75%), a figure very close to Slater's age-corrected rate. The other discordant pairs may be mentioned briefly:

> In Case 13 there was rather more doubt as to zygosity than in most. In Case 291 there is the possibility of genetic mosaicism: the co-twin had one brown and one grey-blue eye, whereas both eyes of the proband were grey-blue. One could argue as to whether the pair should have been excluded from the MZ group on this account. Some psychiatrists might regard the co-twin in this pair as a pseudo neurotic schizophrenic on account of her unpredictable behavior and tendency to laugh and giggle in a strange manner rather than as a chronic anxiety state, which was Slater's diagnosis. Other pairs in which one might think of a concordance in respect of incipient schizophrenia are Cases 2 and 133. In the former, the co twin unexpectedly committed suicide before the true nature of her depressive illness had disclosed itself; the proband's clearly schizophrenic illness had a strong affective coloring early on. The co-twin in Case 133 returned to Italy, where he is said to have had "nerves" and "got funny" but was not hospitalized. There are elements of uncertainty in the remaining case, 164. Here the co-twin was understandably anxious at the time of her sister's admission to hospital but the letter she wrote to the hospital doctors suggested the possibility of something more than anxiety; it was markedly repetitive, full of anxious requests and apologies and bore a strong resemblance in style to the stereotyped psychotic letters which the proband was then addressing to Royalty. The co-twin was mistrustful on interview and evasive on follow-up.

The cases of the 13 discordant MZ pairs which we have mentioned briefly indicate a variety of possible reasons for discordance, including etiological heterogeneity within schizophrenia, lack of information, death, and possible misdiagnosis of zygosity. Some co-twins may have been borderline cases, suggesting a continuum of schizophrenic psychopathology. These reasons are in addition to the environmental and personality factors in Section II, E, 2, c. The reader will gain a better appreciation of the problems of classifying pairs as either "concordant" or "discordant." He will also be able to judge how conservative Slater was in allotting pairs to the concordant category. However, it is not our intention to suggest that Slater's concordance rates should be revised upward. His study has the merit of showing what he found in an objective way.

F. Inouye (Japan, 1961)

In 1961 Eiji Inouye, of the University of Tokyo, read a paper at the World Congress of Psychiatry in Montreal on an extensive study of Japanese schizophrenic twins (Inouye, 1963). It was not an investigation of all twins in a defined sample. The twins came from psychiatric clinics and mental hospitals and were included only when both were alive and cooperative. The proportion of MZ twins (55/72) corresponded well with that expected in Japan, suggesting that the sample may be representative. Zygosity determination and extent of personal investigation were very thorough. Two points of interest stand out.

First, concordance rates for schizophrenia in Japan are in general agreement with those of most Western studies. Uncorrected for age, and in terms of index pairs, 60% of MZ and 12% of all DZ pairs were regarded as concordant with respect to schizophrenia or schizophrenic-like psychosis. Age correction raised these figures to 76% and 22%. Professor Inouye has generously furnished the reviewers with the data divided according to sex. There was a slight excess of female probands, but no marked sex difference in concordance rates: 12/21 (57%) male and 21/34 (62%) female MZ pairs, and 1/6 male and 1/5 female SS DZ pairs. None of the six OS pairs was concordant.

Second, concordance was highest in the most severe types of schizophrenia. Table XVIII draws together Inouye's principal findings based on his clinical judgment. It can be seen that concordance was 74% (17/23) when the proband had a chronic progressive illness; 86% (6/7) in the case of relapsing schizophrenia; and 39% (9/23) when the proband was classified as having either a mild chronic or transient schizophrenia. Fifty-six per cent (18/32) concordant pairs that could be classified were alike as to type. No MZ co-twin was normal or free of schizoid traits.

A later paper by Kurihara and Inouye (1963) discusses those pairs where only one of MZ twins had a severe chronic illness. Some of the co-twins—typically passive, hypersensitive and reticent in personality—went on to develop pan-neurotic, diffuse anxiety states with hypochondriasis and/or sudden flashes of delusional ideas, akin to pseudoneurotic schizophrenia (Hoch & Polatin, 1949). The Japanese authors put forward the view that a gene or genes are responsible for pre-morbid schizoid person-

TABLE XVIII
STATUS OF INOUYE MZ CO-TWINS BY PROBAND SUBTYPE

Co-twin	Concordant				Discordant		Total
	Schizophrenia		Schizophrenic-like				
Proband	Same type as proband	Different type from proband	Psychotic episode	Chronic neurosis	Transient hypomania	Schizoid or schizothymic	
Chronic progressive	11	1	2	3	0	6	23
Relapsing	4	1	1	0	1	0	7
Chronic mild or transient	3	0	4	2	0	14	23
	18	2	7	5	1	20	53
			32		21		
Observed less than 1 year		1			1		2
Totals		33 (60%)			22 (40%)		55

ality, and that further biological or psychological agencies may lead to the further development of a mild or nuclear schizophrenia, as the case might be.

III. Recent Developments

The twin studies described so far were all carried out against a background of psychiatric opinion which held that genetic factors were likely to be important, or made by workers trained in such an environment. In a psychiatric milieu in which thinking is less along biological lines there has been a growing interest in twins by psychodynamically oriented workers, together with the possibility of an uncritical rejection or misunderstanding of genetic interpretations. Faced with the task of studying a set of schizophrenic identical quadruplets, admitted to the NIMH, Bethesda, a clinical psychologist, David Rosenthal, reviewed the roles of heredity and environment in current thinking about the etiology of schizophrenia.

A. ROSENTHAL (UNITED STATES)

1. Critical Papers

In five papers published between 1959 and 1962 Rosenthal subjected the five major twin studies (Section II, A–E) to a thorough and open-minded critical evaluation. He considered these studies to provide "the best information we now have with respect to the whole broad question of heredity and environment in schizophrenia" (1962a, p. 132). He drew attention to problems of sampling and diagnosis which he believed had led to an overestimate of the contribution of heredity. Unlike some who had pointed out weaknesses in the studies, he believed "our task is to determine their source, extent and implications, not to dismiss them offhandedly because they contain errors" (1962a, p. 132).

a. *Factors Raising Concordance Rates.* Rosenthal's reasons for believing that the concordance rates in schizophrenia are misleadingly high stem from two clusters of sources. The first cluster of biases lies in the method of acertaining twins, diagnosing zygosity, diagnosing schizophrenia in proband and co-twin, and counting probands rather than pairs.[7] We have already indicated the nature of the difficulties facing

---

[7] Rosenthal was puzzled by how it was that in 103 out of Kallmann's 691 pairs both twins were index cases, while this was so in only 7 out of 149 of Slater's pairs. The reason would appear to be that Kallmann collected cases for a longer time than Slater. Kallmann's material was collected during the years 1937-1945, Slater's from 1936-1939 with the exception of 16 out of 295 index cases (all diagnoses) from hospitals who continued to record twins during the early part of the war, i.e., the end of 1941 at the latest. No fresh probands were added when the investigation was completed after

the investigator in these areas. Rosenthal rightly stressed the importance of objectivity. The second cluster of biases lies in features common to the larger studies—the over-representation of females and of severe and chronic cases, which resulted from taking cases largely from the resident population of hospitals catering for long-stay patients.

i. Sex differences. In his 1961 paper Rosenthal pointed out that there was an excess of females over males in the studies under review, a fact which he attributed in the main to the chronicity of the illness in the samples of Rosanoff *et al.*, Kallmann, and Slater. He further noted (1962b) that male MZ pairs were twice as often *dis*cordant as female MZ pairs in the four studies reporting information on the sexes separately, 22% discordance in females as against 45% in males. (Kallmann, it will be recalled, stated that he found no MZ sex difference but gave no figures.) If the sexes had been evenly represented in the samples, as they are in first admissions of schizophrenics, the total level of concordance would have been lower. Rosenthal (1962b) believed that the closer resemblance in female pairs of twins, and in same-sexed pairs of twins or sibs, is partly due to psychological factors. His review of studies by Mott (1910), Myerson (1925), Schulz (1932), Zehnder (1941), Penrose (1942, 1945), and Greenberg (1961) showed that when parent-child or sibling pairs were counted where both were known to be mentally ill, an excess of female over male and same over opposite-sexed pairs was also found. Selective migration of the sexes and other vagaries of sampling were thought insufficient to account for all the findings.[8] Nor could the findings be explained on a genetic basis, since the same tendency did not hold for uncle/aunt–nephew/niece pairs. "Factors peculiar to the structure of nuclear family life" might therefore contribute to the sex distribution of concordant pairs of twins and other close relatives: "sex role identification" was a line of thought worth pursuing. However, Rosenthal also noted that the sex difference in concordance between female and male twin pairs was not evident in all samples.

the war. This is a point on which the Slater report may be open to misunderstanding. There is a further likely reason why Kallmann had more double probands. While his intake area covered the whole of New York State, Slater's covered only the area of the London County Council (Inner London). A co-twin hospitalized in one of the counties adjoining central London would not be a proband; nor was any first hospitalized after 1939. The point is of more theoretical than practical importance since Kallmann, contrary to some opinions, did *not* count double probands twice in the calculation of concordance rates. Though Slater did so, the fact that there were relatively few made little difference to his concordance rates.

8 One possibility Rosenthal did not consider in regard to the higher incidence of brother pairs relative to brother-sister pairs is the greater ease of identifying the former who will always have the same surname.

ii. Severity. Rosenthal argued (1961) that sampling from resident hospital populations produced inflated concordance rates. He pointed out that "the twins that get into a sample define and limit the population to which generalizations can be made," while twins "who are characteristically missed as index cases define the group to whom generalizations cannot be made unless a fresh study is done" (p. 31). In analyzing Slater's published case histories (Rosenthal, 1959) he had demonstrated it was the more chronically, and, by implication, the more severely ill twin of a concordant pair who became the proband. Kallmann's series showed differences in concordance from 100% to 26% depending on whether the proband's illness took a deteriorating course or not. Sampling from consecutive admissions and ascertaining twinship from birth records, Essen-Möller found less resemblance than Kallmann with respect to severity in concordant MZ pairs. Rosenthal therefore predicted that concordance would be lower in extensive samples from strictly consecutive admissions. It is uncertain, however, whether the fact of taking consecutive admissions, desirable though it may be, is the critical point: Kallmann's series consisted of consecutive admissions of twins to State Hospitals between the years 1937–1945 in a ratio of 2:1, consecutive: resident. Our analysis of Slater's series according to whether the index case was "resident" or "consecutive" failed to support the prediction, at least when applied to include readmissions to hospitals catering for long-stay patients. On the other hand, if the investigator's source of cases were extended to include more with a favorable prognosis, lower concordance rates might well be found. As Rosenthal (1962a) put it, "a preferable procedure would be to sample extensively from consecutive admissions to both outpatient and inpatient facilities and follow all cases until they had lived through the age of risk" (p. 131).

Despite these sources of bias, Rosenthal believed that the total weight of the evidence still strongly favored the hypothesis of a genetic contribution to the etiology of schizophrenia (1962a). In his 1959 paper it will be recalled that he considered one group of schizophrenias to have little or no genetic basis, leaving a second group which seemed to have a high genetic loading.

b. Critique of Environmental Hypotheses. If Rosenthal was critical of all-embracing genetic views of schizophrenia, he was equally critical (1960) of those who try to explain the findings in twins by concepts such as "confusion of identity." If "the identity problem of the schizophrenic . . . could find no better nidus than in the intertwining of twin identities" as Jackson (1960) believed, schizophrenia should occur more frequently among twins than among non-twins and more frequently among MZ than among DZ twins. As Luxenburger and Essen-Möller have shown more clearly than anyone else, such differential rates do not occur, thus casting doubt on the theory.

An explanation of the earlier findings in schizophrenic twins along lines other than genetic usually invokes a supposed greater similarity in the upbringing of MZ twins than DZ twins and a greater tendency for MZ twins to identify with one another. Rosenthal considers that a psychological hypothesis such as identification might be used to explain differential concordance rates in MZ and DZ twins without implying a higher incidence of illness in MZ twins. This would appear to be so provided that the same proportion of potential schizophrenics are held back from overt illness by identifying with a normal twin as those who became ill by identifying with an abnormal one. Although Rosenthal expressly states (1962b, p. 417) that he does not wish to convey the impression of espousing an identification theory of schizophrenia, some discussion of the view may be in place here.

Any greater similarity of the external or "psychological" environment of MZ twins compared with DZ loses much of its force unless the environmental factors unique to MZ twinship can be shown to be related etiologically to schizophrenia. Rosenthal makes a similar point when he suggests testing the hypothesis that some aspect of identification is the etiological mechanism in all schizophrenic reactions, not just in those occurring in twins.

It could be argued that schizophrenia is related to personality development and that personality development in general is more alike in MZ twins than DZ twins because the former are treated more alike or identify more closely with one another. This view can be tested using twins brought up apart, reared by different mothers and without the usual opportunity to identify with one another. Shields (1962), comparing 44 MZ twin pairs reared apart with 44 reared together, found no evidence that the personality resemblance between MZ twins was to any significant degree to be accounted for by their close association in childhood (cf. Juel-Nielsen, 1965, on 12 MZ pairs reared apart). Further evidence against identification theories of schizophrenia comes from a comparison of the illnesses of concordant pairs of relatives. The greater the importance of identification the greater should be the resemblance in symptoms and the occurrence of shared delusions. Unselected concordant case histories (Essen-Möller, Slater) are more conspicuous for the absence than for the presence of such features. Two pairs in which there was perhaps a suggestion of *folie à deux* (Essen-Möller, cases 1 and 4) were both male pairs and discordant as to outcome. In Tsuang's (1965) series of pairs of sibs both treated in the same hospital for any mental illness there was an excess of female and same-sexed pairs, as found by Rosenthal in other studies, but the female pairs were not more alike with respect to diagnosis than the male, or the same-sexed more alike than the opposite-sexed pairs. Such findings speak against the crucial etiological importance of problems in identification for schizophrenia.

2. The Genain Quadruplets

It is a safe bet that no one will find another set of identical quadruplets concordant for schizophrenia; Rosenthal reckoned the odds as roughly once in every one and a half billion births. Fortunately, the resources and imagination at the Clinical Center of the NIMH were such that the 4 girls could be hospitalized and studied for some 3 years together with their mother and father for varying lengths of time. Thirty years or so of the quads' lives are chronicled in the book edited by Rosenthal (1963). Collaborators ranging from handwriting analysts to electroencephalographers and totaling 24, contribute to a case study which pales all others in the literature.

One would have thought that no further proof of a genetic basis for schizophrenia would be needed after finding a set of monozygotic quadruplets all affected with schizophrenia. Clearly, however, MZ quads can tell us nothing about genetic variation. Nor can it be assumed that all schizophrenic families will resemble the extraordinary Genains. As Rosenthal put it, "The case of the Genains is presented not as a test of any theory—although some issues regarding hereditary and environmental influences on various test and behavioral patterns are critically evaluated—but, in good part, as an exemplification of the relation between life experiences and schizophrenic outcomes when heredity is controlled" (p. 5).

This section is devoted to a consideration of the quads not only because they served as the stimulus for Rosenthal's lucid series of critical papers on genetic aspects of schizophrenia, but also because the Genain girls can be construed as 6 pairs of MZ twins.

There is good reason for the allegory about the blind men describing an elephant being cited frequently as an analogue to the status of research on schizophrenia. Rosenthal and his 24 colleagues demonstrate that a multidisciplinary approach is the only way to come significantly closer to a foundation for the resolution of the elephantine problems of schizophrenia research. A close reading of the book is highly recommended; the material is presented chronologically with respect to the family as a unit. The reader should come away with the impression that an ethological, or natural habitat, approach to the observation of schizophrenics and their families could lead to new insights about the illness.

The age of onset of schizophrenia in each of the quads was difficult to pinpoint; there was an accretion of symptoms that made time of onset a nonspecific concept for the Genains. A more objective but less accurate indicator of onset was age at first hospitalization: Nora was admitted first at age 22, Iris 7 months later, Hester at about 24½ years of age, and Myra only in connection with the NIMH research about age 25. Severity of schizophrenia ranged widely as did outcome. For the quads at least, hereditary factors did not appear to be important for outcome. The status of the Genains is known as of the time of this writing (Rosenthal, personal communication, 1965). Myra, who had the best pre-morbid picture, was given 600 hours of psychoanalysis, entered marriage, and had no further hospitalizations after leaving NIMH. She is working and being an adequate mother to her 2-year-old son. Hester, with the worst pre-morbid history, has never left the state hospital she entered after the finish of the NIMH years (but writes regularly to Dr. Rosenthal). Nora, after repeated breakdowns, has not been working for the past 2 or more years, but she has not had to return to the hospital. Iris has maintained her course of marked swings so that she has been able to leave the hospital on extended leave during her better periods. She reverts to many of her earlier catatonic patterns during her poorer periods.

Despite their different life experiences and the differences in their clinical state before and during the investigation, Rosenthal was able to show that all 4 girls had catatonic-hebephrenic features in the course of their illnesses. In his Theoretical Overview he suggested that catatonia and hebephrenia may represent a single genetic effect. "What seems to be heritable is the general pattern of unfolding subtype syndromes. What seems to be environmentally determined for the most part is the point at which the process is interrupted or arrested, these points distributed over an extremely wide range" (Rosenthal, 1963, p. 528).

When entertaining the idea that life experience was a sufficient cause, Rosenthal discussed the psychopathological development of schizophrenia in terms of three theories all representing failures in learning: failure of socialization, failure of cognitive integration, and failure to contain anxiety. He suggested that "It is possible to regard the three theories as different perspectives of a common, disorganizing interpersonal process which undermines social, cognitive, and affective responses at the same time" (1963, p. 569).

The theoretical analysis presented of the heredity-environment problem in schizophrenia is likely to be an enduring source of fertile ideas. Rosenthal summarized the points illuminated by the data gathered on the Genain family. He grouped the varied proposals for theories about the etiology of schizophrenia into monogenic-biochemical, life-experience, and diathesis-stress. In sum, he favored the diathesis-stress theory with

the further implication that a combining rather than releasing relationship existed between the genetic predisposition for the illness and the
exogenous stress factors. In the case of the quadruplets, inherited constriction was augmented by environmental constriction imposed by
grossly unreasonable parents.

3. Twin-Sibling Unit

Of the many events posited as causal by advocates of a life-experience
theory of schizophrenia, some may be irrelevant or fortuitous. Since the
usual study of case histories does not permit a resolution by the pinpoint-
ing of crucial events, Rosenthal initiated a study of MZ twins discordant
for schizophrenia. A section for twin and sibling studies was then set
up in the Adult Psychiatry Branch by Pollin in conjunction with Wynne
of the NIMH. The Chief of the section is William Pollin, a psychoanalyst
and psychiatric researcher.

It will be recalled from Section I that differences in outcome between
MZ twins can be attributed to the environment and, it follows logically
that all factors applying equally to the pair must be eliminated as a
cause of the schizophrenia in the proband of a discordant pair. In the
first paper from the Section (Pollin, Stabenau, & Tupin, 1965), 5 families
in which there is a pair of discordant MZ twins are described. The investigators plan to enlarge on the sample of 5, and then study matched
samples of concordant MZ pairs, DZ pairs, and twins who are normal.
A diagnostic panel of 5 psychiatrists verified the mental status of the
proband and co-twin. A narrow diagnostic view of schizophrenia was
used so that borderline, pseudoneurotic, and childhood schizophrenias
were not included. Four, or possibly all, probands showed an acute onset,
all had had 2 or more hospitalizations prior to the one at NIMH, and
all had been previously diagnosed as schizophrenic. The length of the
period of discordance ranged from 3 to 8 years.

The screening criteria were such that a canvas of the entire United
States turned up only 5 qualified families. Both twins must have been
raised by their biological parents, and the parents must both be alive
and willing to live at the Clinical Center for an average of 25 days along
with the co-twin. The gross unrepresentativeness of the proband families
requires extreme caution in generalizing to schizophrenia in general, as
the authors themselves note. The potentially important finding that all
their families were characterized by over-protection of the proband may
reflect the screening criteria selecting for high involvement rather than a
revelation of a causal factor for schizophrenia. Other differences high-
lighted by the study include lower birth weight and slower development
of the proband. The schizophrenic-to-be did less well academically and

socially in school, and was more passive and dependent. It is possible that all these differences stem from the initial difference in birth weight or are correlated with some unanalyzed factor. All five index twins showed "soft" neurological signs; Case B has the possibility of right hemisphere abnormality; Case C, the suggestion of nonspecific cerebral disorder (co-twin had a history of convulsive disorder and a borderline EEG); and, Case E had symmetrical hyperreflexia, diminished coordination, but no abnormal reflexes.

The careful, multidisciplinary work of the Twin-Sibling Unit has already provided important leads that can now be tested by other workers. We anticipate a great deal more will come from work in progress. As yet unpublished research, in and out of NIH, on the biological and foster families of foster children who grew up to be schizophrenics (Rosenthal, Kety, Wender), and longitudinal observations of the children of schizophrenic mothers (Mednick and Schulsinger in Denmark, Heston in Oregon, Rosenthal in Israel) can be expected to add important pieces to the puzzle of the heredity-environment interaction in the schizophrenias.

B. TIENARI (FINLAND)

The critical reviews of Rosenthal might lead one to expect MZ concordance rates in a representative twin study to be lower than the 86% morbidity risk reported by Kallmann. No one would have anticipated zero concordance for schizophrenia in 16 unselected pairs. Yet this is what was reported in the next study under review. Pekka Tienari (1963) restricted his investigation to male MZ pairs where both twins were available. However, he states that there were 21 male DZ pairs with schizophrenia, of which 1 was concordant and a further 2 possibly so. Zero concordance in MZ pairs and perhaps 10% in DZ pairs is difficult to account for on any current theory of schizophrenia.

1. Sampling

It has been claimed that Tienari's study is more reliable and representative than most because his twins were obtained from birth records. Such a view is based on a misunderstanding. The studies of Luxenburger and Essen-Möller started with defined groups of psychiatric patients and used birth records to establish which of them were twins. Tienari started with birth registrations of all male twins born in Finland between 1920 and 1929. He hoped to identify all who were or had been mentally ill, a much harder task. It can be argued that such a method is likely to miss the mild or recovered case. The 16 schizophrenics Tienari identified had mostly been hospitalized and were mostly chronic; he did not find a single case of affective disorder.

Besides the difficulties inherent in finding cases in the general population rather than working from a defined sample of independently diagnosed schizophrenics, there are other possible sources of error. 2288 pairs of twins were notified in the first instance to the Finnish Foundation for Alcohol Studies, who made an extensive survey of those where both twins were available for interview. Reasons for exclusion before the start of the psychiatric study were: 1084, death of one or both twins at age unspecified; 82 emigrated; 140 not traced. Only 903 (39%) of the starting material remained. Of these 201 were MZ, 613 male DZ and 89 of uncertain zygosity, i.e., 22% or at most 32% were MZ. In most North European populations around 45% of SS pairs might be expected to be MZ. The possibility therefore arises of selective elimination of concordant or potentially concordant MZ pairs.

2. Investigation

Tienari investigated 125 MZ pairs personally using a psychiatric interview supplemented by psychological testing. His report is concerned with 44 pairs in which one or both twins had a psychiatric abnormality. Monozygosity is reasonably secure; 13 out of the 16 schizophrenic pairs were blood-grouped. The age of the co-twins on last information was between 36 and 43; 11 had been followed up for over 10 years from onset of illness in the schizophrenic partner. Uncertain zygosity and the age distribution cannot explain the discrepant findings.

3. Diagnosis

The next question to be considered is whether Tienari included as schizophrenic cases those which other psychiatrists might regard as symptomatic or organic psychoses of a kind unlikely to be concordant. Or does he tend to call the co-twin normal or neurotic when others might regard him as probably schizophrenic? Since case histories are published, it is possible for the reader to evaluate the material from this point of view. It seems possible that both these considerations may apply to some extent. In particular, 4 of the schizophrenics show well-marked organic features: intellectual deterioration associated with abnormal air-encephalogram (Case 608); head injury, facial paresis and diplopia, followed by epileptic attacks and cerebral atrophy (Case 32); attacks of unconsciousness following head wound, focal EEG signs, resection of contused area considered (Case 462); congenital glaucoma, thyrotoxicosis, cardiovascular system pathology, leading to death at 35 (Case 74). If these 4 cases were to be omitted, the schizophrenic group would be reduced to

12 pairs, including a schizo-affective psychosis (? schizophrenia), and a "borderline" schizophrenia.

Although Tienari considers none of the co-twins to be schizophrenic, he regards three as displaying "borderline features" and a further nine as showing schizoid traits. Two of these might well be regarded as concordant by other investigators. These are:

Case 989. Proband (never hospitalized) is a paranoid schizophrenic, although Tienari considers that paranoid psychopathy remains a possible diagnosis. The co-twin has expressed paranoid ideas, referring to a previous twin investigator as a Communist spy; he has avoided meeting people, has been incapacitated by symptoms for 4 years, and has received tranquillizers from his doctor for "confusion and excitement"; he has no insight into his brother's illness. Diagnosed by Tienari as "character neurosis, (?) borderline schizophrenia."

Case 881. Proband is a hospitalized hebephrenic. Co-twin was solitary in adolescence, just sat about at home, "difficult"; now he is periodically depressed, avoids company, is pedantic, has tic-like mannerisms of face and shoulders. Diagnosed by Tienari as neurotic personality, schizoid.

It is difficult to know where to draw the line when including doubtful cases. One might ask if the following were possibly borderline schizophrenics: religious conversion at 18, at 35 intolerant, inhibited, blocked, "hidden behind religious texts" (Case 67); chronic hypochondriacal neurasthenic with symptoms verging on the bizarre (Case 60); "peculiar for a while when engaged," details lacking (Case 68).

Once again we have occasion to note that the variety of forms of schizophrenia and associated disorders make it impossible to speak without qualification of *the* concordance rate. It was Essen-Möller's view that it was a predisposition to react in a schizoid way which is genetically determined rather than a tendency to develop a deteriorating psychosis; and Tienari's findings are not so very different from those of Essen-Möller.

4. Heterogeneity of Populations

After allowing for the effects of methods of sampling and diagnosis, there remains the possibility of a genuine difference in concordance rates in different parts of the world. Shields (1965) has found a significant difference between concordance in male MZ twins in the Norwegian, Swedish, and Finnish studies of Kringlen (see Section III, C), Essen-Möller and Tienari on the one hand, and those made in Germany, the United States, and the United Kingdom by Luxenburger, Rosanoff, and Slater. It is interesting that the North Scandinavian studies present similar findings despite differences in method. Essen-Möller started from consecutively admitted hospital cases and established twinship by looking up birth registers. Kringlen looked through old hospital records for cases which had been recorded in the notes as being twins. Tienari started from birth registrations of all twins and identified as best he could all those who had ever been schizophrenic.

Although no certain explanation can be given for the differences between North Scandinavian and other countries with respect to MZ twin concordance rates, there is nothing inherently unlikely in the idea that populations will vary in the extent to which schizophrenia shows itself as being genetically determined. We shall return to this point in our summary. Some of the differences between the proband and co-twin noticed by Tienari were later emphasized by Pollin. Tienari thought that the development of submissive and dependent attitudes in one of male twins gives rise to difficulties in masculine identification and that his findings support a psychodynamic interpretation of schizophrenia. However, this is clearly not the whole story. Many, perhaps most, twins differ in assertiveness, but there is no evidence that male MZ twins are especially prone to schizophrenia. It should be noted that there was a positive family history for schizophrenia in eight of the sixteen families. It would be important now to find out whether concordances in female Finnish twins are as unexpected as the Tienari male results.

C. KRINGLEN (NORWAY)

At the same time as Tienari, Einar Kringlen (1964) was studying male MZ twins discordant for schizophrenia. His conclusions also challenged earlier views. In a review of old case records from 4 mental hospitals and a psychiatric ward in a general hospital in Eastern Norway, Kringlen found 107 pairs of twins where the proband had had some sort of psychosis and where twinship happened to have been recorded. He then chose to focus on the male schizophrenics in the material of which there were 8 MZ probands and 12 DZ probands. From the total number of mental patients in the hospitals, and assuming that the incidence of twins among these patients is the same as that in the general population, the author estimated that only 40 to 50% of the expected number of twin probands had been located.

At the time of the study, the schizophrenic twins ranged in age from 25 to 68 with a median of 44; only one pair was under 35. Detailed case histories are provided for the discordant MZ pairs. Diagnosis of all twins was approved by Langfeldt, and is discussed critically by the author. In terms of concordance for schizophrenia, Kringlen reported 2/8 MZ pairs and 2/12 DZ pairs.

Considering the smallness of the material, the difficulties in evaluating the loss in sampling and the trend for concordance to be lower in males than in females, the concordance rates are not so surprising as they might at first sight appear: Slater found concordance in 4 out of 11 male MZ pairs, Kringlen in 2 out of 8. The discordance in the 6 MZ pairs cannot be explained in terms of mildness of the illness in the proband or of a negative family history for psychosis. Four probands were hebephrenic or catatonic and 2, paranoid; 1 had committed suicide, 2 were highly deteriorated, and the remainder were more or less deteriorated. In 5 of the 6 pairs there is a family history of schizophrenia or a schizophrenic-like disorder.

In the light of the possibilities mentioned in the previous section (Section III, B, 3) that the etiology of the illness in discordant MZ pairs might on occasion be organic, Kringlen's Case II may be mentioned. There is a possibility of brain disease in the proband. At 35 he developed a right-sided weakness and tremor, and at 38 was seen by a neurologist to whom the picture suggested a sequela of encephalitis. An EEG at 45 revealed "a possible, but uncertain, focus in the left parietal lobe." However, personality change was reported to have occurred from age 17 with schizophrenic-like features in evidence at 26. The majority of psychiatrists would probably agree with Kringlen's decision to count the case as most likely a genuine schizophrenia.

Turning to the author's analysis of environmental factors, retrospective accounts of the childhoods of both MZ and DZ probands in the discordant pairs suggested to Kringlen that the premorbid personality was characterized by neurotic symptoms and by introversion, inhibition, sensitivity, and dependency on the co-twin. It was his opinion that the personalities of the MZ co-twins were more or less as deviant as those of the DZ co-twins among all discordant pairs. However, we may note that the MZ co-twins would appear to be more often "quasi-philosophizing," "highly schizothymic," and introverted.

In conclusion, Kringlen said "that genetic factors do not seem to play as great a role as has been assumed for the etiology of schizophrenia. However, the material being small, one cannot rule out the possibility of accidental influences" (p. 73). The major value of this study may prove to be the impetus it has provided for a large scale project that uses the birth register of twins for all Norway 1900 to 1930 and the national register for psychosis.[9]

---

[9] Kringlen (1965) in a personal communication reports that he has found 342 psychotic twin pairs (about 400 index cases) in this fashion, of which 71 are MZ. He is trying to obtain as much first-hand follow-up information as possible in extensive field work. Psychoses other than schizophrenia, manic-depressive and reactive (cf. Meyer, 1961 and Slater, 1964) are not included. Provisional pairwise concordance rates, not age-corrected, for schizophrenia so far range from 14/50 (28%) to 19/50 (38%) MZ, 6/94 (6%) to 13/94 (14%) SS DZ and 6/81 (7%) OS DZ.

D. DANISH WORK

Brief mention may be made here of work now in progress, based on the Institute for Human Genetics, Copenhagen, register of all twins born in Denmark between 1870 and 1910. Harvald and Hauge (1965) reported some of the findings for 6893 pairs with whom they have made satisfactory contact. Zygosity and medical history were based in the first instance on questionnaires sent to the twins or their relatives. Supplemental information was obtained from blood-grouping, personal inquiries, hospital records, and general practitioners. The authors note that their twin material is not very suitable for the intensive study of psychiatric disorders because of the present age or mortality of the subjects.

Their report focused on such physical diseases as cancer and cardiovascular illness but did mention psychiatric disorders. Harvald and Hauge located 71 cases diagnosed as schizophrenia. Four out of 9 MZ co-twins, 4/33 SS DZ co-twins, and 2/29 OS DZ co-twins were similarly affected. In terms of index pairs rather than index cases, concordance was 2/7 (29%) MZ, 2/31 (6%) SS DZ and 1/28 (4%) OS pairs. The method was similar to that of Tienari in that the sampling was based on all twins born, but different in that it was not restricted to MZ males.

The figures given above represent the start rather than the conclusion of an investigation. Further work on schizophrenic twins from the register is being conducted by Juel-Nielsen and Fischer (Juel-Nielsen, personal communication, 1965).

E. GOTTESMAN AND SHIELDS (UNITED KINGDOM)

1. Sampling

The reviewers' own schizophrenic twin study is based on a register of all twins treated at the Maudsley and Bethlem Royal Joint Hospital from 1948 to 1964. The Maudsley is a short-stay post-graduate psychiatric teaching hospital in London with a large outpatient department. Over 2000 new adult patients are seen each year and over 300 new children. The social class representation of patients is similar to that of London as a whole.

On admission to any department of the Hospital every patient is routinely asked whether he was born a twin. The Medical Research Council's Psychiatric Genetics Unit (director, Dr. Eliot Slater) is informed of all such twins. Although situated in the Hospital, the Unit itself has no control over the admission of patients to the Hospital. Until 1957, twinship was not known for only 2% of patients. Since then the figure has been 7%. We believe ascertainment to be virtually complete, at least for patients with twins surviving to the age of 15. Analysis of the total register up to the end of 1957 showed no significant departure in the number of twins found or in type of twin (MZ, SS DZ, or OS) from that which would be expected in the British population, and later hospital demographic summaries confirm this. The proportion of twins diagnosed in the Hospital as psychotic and non-psychotic is close to that of all Maudsley patients.

In March, 1964 when our present series was closed there were 392 adult patients on the register with twins of the same sex surviving to age 15. Of these patients, 47 (12%) had received an official hospital diagnosis of schizophrenia (coded as 300, International List of Diseases). This is close to the 11% of all Maudsley patients who were thus diagnosed. Most of the remaining twins on the register had previously been investigated in the Unit. These twins include those from the Maudsley Children's Department and a small group of adult twins routinely ascertained between November, 1950 and June, 1953 at Belmont Hospital, a neurosis center on the outskirts of London. Some of those followed up were already known to have been rehospitalized elsewhere and diagnosed as schizophrenic. All other twins where schizophrenia had previously been suspected were followed up in 1963 1964. In all, a further 21 probands were obtained who had been diagnosed as schizophrenic subsequent to registration, making a total of 68. Three non-Caucasians were excluded. In three pairs it proved impossible to obtain information about the co-twin. The final series thus consists of 62 probands from 57 pairs, in 5 pairs both twins having been patients at the Maudsley in their own right. This series was obtained from a starting material estimated at about 45,000.

Our sample cannot claim, any more than any other, to be truly representative of all schizophrenia. Based on consecutive admissions to outpatient facilities and a short-stay, inpatient center and including probands who were first diagnosed as having neuroses, depressions, or personality disorders, it may be said to allow for a higher representation of cases with a good prognosis than previous schizophrenic twin samples. It is a total sample of Maudsley diagnosed schizophrenic twins and a reasonably complete and quite unselected representation of schizophrenics diagnosed as such elsewhere after initial registration by the Unit. Results will be presented in the first instance in terms of hospital diagnoses uninfluenced by our hindsight.

Sex and zygosity of the 57 index pairs are shown in Table XIX. The distribution supports the view that the sample is representative. It is the first twin series which has not had an excess, however small, of female pairs. In terms of probands, we have 31 males and 31 females. The twins were born between 1893 and 1945. Median age on last information was 37, range 19–65.

Zygosity was determined by a combination of blood groups,[10] fingerprints, and resemblance in appearance. So far, 20/24 (83%) of MZ pairs have been blood-grouped, and one further pair fingerprinted but not blood-grouped. Of the DZ pairs, 20/33 (61%) have been blood-grouped and a further four fingerprinted but not blood-grouped. Evidence from the appearance of the remaining pairs is sufficient to make it unlikely that zygosity has been misdiagnosed.

TABLE XIX
GOTTESMAN AND SHIELDS SAMPLE BY ZYGOSITY AND SEX

	MZ	SS DZ	Total
Female	11	16	27
Male	13	17	30
Totals	24	33	57

Of the 48 MZ probands and co-twins, 42 (88%) have been seen personally by one or both of us. Four of the others had previously been seen by other staff of the Unit or were seen by a psychologist on our behalf, and the remaining two were specifically seen by their general practitioner at the request of the Unit before they later disappeared from sight. Of the 66 DZ probands and co-twins, 49 (74%) were seen by one or both of us. Three have been seen by others in connection with the twin study; of the remaining 14, four were dead, four abroad, one untraced, and five uncooperative at the time of our follow-up, 1963–1965. All discordant pairs of twins have been followed for over 3 years from the onset of illness in the proband, one of them for as long as 16 years.

2. Interim Results in Terms of Concordance and Hospital Diagnoses

At the present stage of our research we can only offer broad outlines of the results plus the confirmation and extension of some of Rosenthal's ideas about the relationship between severity of schizophrenia and concordance. Rather than delay any communications about our initial findings until a sophisticated continuum of schizophrenic pathology can be enunciated, we have chosen to report degrees of twin resemblance in terms of old-fashioned concordance. An outline of our over-all design for the ongoing project will be given in Section III, E, 4. Results are

---

10 Over the years, all blood specimens from the Unit series of twins have been blood-typed by Drs. R. R. Race and Ruth Sanger of the MRC Blood Group Research Unit. We are grateful for their contribution to the accuracy of our work.

given in terms of a psychiatrist's diagnosis appended to those twins who ever became psychiatric patients, uninfluenced by our hindsight. We believe, for example, that some of our twins carrying a diagnosis of schizophrenia might not have been so diagnosed if the psychiatrist had had access to such information as was later available. Such information includes such things as more detailed histories of the course of the illness and the implication of toxic or central nervous system factors.

We have 4 reasonably objective and reliable grades of similarity. Grade 1 consists of pairs where the co-twin has also been hospitalized and called schizophrenic. Grade 2 co-twins have had a psychiatric hospitalization but have been diagnosed other than schizophrenic. Grade 3 co-twins are otherwise psychiatrically abnormal as determined by such

TABLE XX

CONCORDANCE FOR SCHIZOPHRENIA AND RATES OF PSYCHIATRIC HOSPITALIZATION AND
MARKED ABNORMALITY IN THE TWINS OF SCHIZOPHRENICS[a]

Grade	MZ		DZ	
	N	%	N	%
1[b]	10	42	3	9
1 + 2	13	54	6	18
1 + 2 + 3	19	79	15	45
Normal	5	21	18	55
Total	24	100	33	100

[a] All figures uncorrected for age.
[b] Chi square = 6.63, $p < .01$, one-tailed.

criteria as outpatient psychiatric care only, in the care of a general practitioner for a clearly emotional problem, a neurotic or psychotic type of MMPI profile, or, in 3 cases, being manifestly abnormal on interview. Grade 4 co-twins were within normal limits at last information.

Grade 1 pairs give the minimum concordance rates for schizophrenia in this initial analysis.[11] Table XX shows the results for the entire sample of MZ and DZ pairs without age corrections. The concordance rates for hospitalized and diagnosed schizophrenia of 42% in MZ pairs and 9% in DZ are raised to 65% and 17%, respectively when the conventional Weinberg age correction is applied for a risk period of 15 to 40. Without necessarily implying a continuum, concordance rates are also given for psychiatric hospitalization of any kind (Grades 1 + 2) and for any noteworthy degree of personality disruption (Grades 1 + 2 + 3). For exam-

---

11 By using the formula recommended by Allen (1965) that halves the number of index cases from concordant pairs, our Grade 1 MZ rate becomes 33% and the DZ, 6%. No twin researchers have yet followed Allen's recommendation.

ple, 79% of the co-twins of MZ schizophrenics are abnormal, with abnormality ranging from psychiatric hospitalization to having once been treated by a general practitioner for a transient anxiety state. The comparable DZ rate is 45%. A frame of reference for the interpretation of these data may have been furnished by Srole *et al.* (1962) in their epidemiological survey in midtown Manhattan. They reported a morbidity rate (ages 20–59) for noteworthy mental impairment of about 26%; about one-fourth of the impaired group were thought to be psychotic, two-thirds, neurotic or personality disordered.

The data of Table XX analyzed by sex are given in Table XXI. As the sample sizes are now smaller, it is difficult to prove statistical significance for the differences between sexes or types of twins. The difference between Grade 1 females, 45%, and males, 38%, is not significant but corresponds to the trends noted by Rosenthal in his analysis of

TABLE XXI

CONCORDANCE (%) FOR SCHIZOPHRENIA AND OTHER PSYCHOPATHOLOGY BY SEX

	Grade	1	1 + 2	1 + 2 + 3	Normal	N
Female	MZ	45	64	91	9	11
	DZ	12	31	62	38	16
Male	MZ	38	46	69	31	13
	DZ	6	6	29	71	17

familial concordances by sex. Given 13 male and 11 female MZ pairs, the 10 concordant Grade 1 pairs could not have been more evenly divided than 5/13 and 5/11. The uniformly higher female rates in Table XXI are most likely due to a combination of causes such as susceptibility to post-partum depressions, higher female prevalence of neuroses, and facilitated processes of identification with either co-twin or other females.

Next we analyzed the relationship between severity of schizophrenia in the proband and the degree of concordance for schizophrenia among the co-twins. Calculations are in terms of probands rather than pairs at this point since double probands need not have equally severe schizophrenias. Two variables were used as indicators of severity: total length of hospitalization in weeks in the career of the patient and then outcome at the time of follow-up with respect to remission and work status. All patients had been exposed to the prevailing therapies for schizophrenia at the time they were hospitalized, including insulin coma, electroconvulsive therapy, and, since 1954, phenothiazines. When *severe* was defined as 52 weeks or longer in hospital, MZ concordance for the co-twins of severe probands was 67% contrasted with only 20% for the MZ co-twins of mild schizophrenics. As a more stringent criterion of severity, over and under 2 years in hospital was selected. Table XXII shows that 77% of the MZ co-twins of severe schizophrenics were themselves schizophrenic, contrasted wtih 27% of the MZ co-twins of mild schizophrenics. Corresponding figures for the very small sample of DZ probands were 15% and 10%.

TABLE XXII

EFFECTS OF SEVERITY (WEEKS HOSPITALIZED) ON CONCORDANCE

Co-Twin Status	MZ Proband[a]			DZ Proband		
	< 2 Years	> 2 Years	Total	< 2 Years	> 2 Years	Total
Schizophrenic	4	10	14	2	2	4
Nonschizophrenic	11	3	14	19	11	30
Concordance (%)	27	77	50	10	15	12

[a] Chi square = 5.17, $p < .02$, one-tailed.

When outcome was used as a criterion of severity, a severe degree of schizophrenia in a proband was defined as the inability, on last information, to stay out of a hospital for at least 6 months and to be gainfully employed or, for women, to run a home adequately. Table XXIII shows the data for concordances that lend additional support to those

TABLE XXIII

EFFECTS OF SEVERITY (GAINFULLY EMPLOYED AND OUT OF HOSPITAL FOR AT LEAST 6 MONTHS) ON CONCORDANCE

Co-Twin Status	MZ Proband[a]			DZ Proband		
	Mild	Severe	Total	Mild	Severe	Total
Schizophrenic	2	12	14	0	4	4
Nonschizophrenic	10	4	11	16	14	30
Concordance (%)	17	75	50	0	22	12

[a] Chi square = 7.15, $p < .01$, one-tailed.

already presented in Table XXII. Concordances for the severe and mild MZ pairs were 75% and 17%, respectively. Corresponding figures for the DZ probands were 22% and 0%. The patent paradox of DZ higher than MZ concordance becomes transparent as soon as provision is made for the importance to be attached to the dimension of severity of schizophrenia in a twin proband.

3. Discussion

Our findings on the association between severity of schizophrenia and concordance confirm one of Rosenthal's hypotheses. The reader will recall from the Kallmann section that MZ concordance was 100%

when the proband took a deteriorating course, but only 26% when the MZ proband had a schizophrenia with little or no deterioration. The same phenomenon is paralleled by Inouye's data presented in Table XVIII; concordance for identical twins where the proband had a "progressive chronic schizophrenia" was 74%, but only 39% for identicals with a "transient mild schizophrenia." Our findings for MZ concordance for severe schizophrenia, 67% to 77%, agree quite well with over-all, age-uncorrected concordance rates in both the Kallmann and Slater studies, both of whom sampled state or county hospital schizophrenics who might be expected to have severe illnesses with poor prognoses.

What are the most likely explanations for our preliminary data analyses? Much of the data fit with a diathesis-stress model for schizophrenia mentioned in Section III, A, 2. If the diathesis takes the form of a polygenic system, having a large proportion of the genes predisposes a person to developing schizophrenia by lowering his threshold for coping with stress, and, at the same time, tends to make for a poor prognosis. In this instance we could infer that a proband with a good outcome had had few of the genes in the system, and we would expect his co-twin to have a much lower probability of decompensating than the co-twin of a severe schizophrenic. This explanation would hold whether or not one assumed with Slater (1958) and others that a further single gene was essential for the development of most schizophrenias, or whether one espoused a broader polygenic model for both etiology and course or outcome. Most instances of schizophrenia, from the most mild to the most severe, could then be conceptualized as biologically related. We have already alluded to the present difficulty in distinguishing between monogenic and polygenic modes of inheritance in a disorder as common as schizophrenia. Tienari's results, as they stand, contradict our polygenic explanation since his probands were not mild cases. Our discussion in Section II, E, 2, d of the reasons for discordance in Slater's MZ subsample of 13 pairs revealed many possible explanations.

By way of review, we can set out the kinds of questions that may be asked about MZ twin pairs discordant for schizophrenia. The answers could cast light on both the etiological heterogeneity of schizophrenia and on the environmental contributors to its exacerbation and amelioration.

(1) Has the proband been misdiagnosed, or is his illness mild, schizophreniform (Langfeldt, 1939), psychogenic or reactive (Faergeman, 1963), or symptomatic of organic disease (e.g., Slater, Beard, & Glithero, 1963)? We should not expect phenocopies of schizophrenia to be genetically related to the predominant varieties of the disorder.

(2) Should the co-twin be considered, since he is not overtly schizo-phrenic, as a compensated schizotype (Meehl, 1962; Rado, 1962)? Where information about the co-twin is vague or unreliable, this possibility may have been overlooked.

(3) Is the co-twin still within the period of risk for developing the disorder, and for how long since the onset of schizophrenia in the proband has the pair been followed?

(4) What unique factors in the life, including prenatal, of the proband might have elicited the illness, or what unique factors in the life of the co-twin might have insulated him against it?

A few examples from our unselected series of 14 discordant MZ pairs may illustrate some of these points.

In a Grade 4 pair, A, the proband, probably has an organic psychosis with schizophrenic-like features and a deteriorating course. His illness was called paranoid state at the Maudsley. The etiology of his psychosis is probably nutritional brain damage sustained as a Japanese prisoner of war. He is completely deaf, and has an EEG showing slow delta waves in the left frontal area and otherwise suggestive of a space occupying lesion. B, the co-twin, is married, has a stable job history, and an MMPI within normal limits. Projected refinement of our own data calls for the elimination of all probands where information subsequent to the initial diagnosis leads our judges to question "true" schizophrenia.

In another Grade 4 pair, A was diagnosed as an acute schizophrenic reaction after her thyroidectomy at age 43. Shortly before this surgery she had had a hysterectomy and was involved in divorce proceedings from an abusive, bullying husband. On her most recent admission she was called a depressive (Code 301). B, however, had neither surgical procedure although she also had a thyrotoxicosis. B's husband was an unusually kind and understanding man. B at age 46 is one of the pillars of her community.

A Grade 3 proband has had only one hospitalization and that for 6 weeks. He was an unusual boy with long-standing interests in oriental religion. At 20 he joined a messianic cult and 2 years later left his second wife to obtain special training at the cult's London headquarters. There he underwent "psychic realignment" and was given training in telepathy. Within a month he found he was radiating his thoughts and felt that other members knew the details of his sex life. On follow-up 4 years later, he was working, back with his wife and child, not on medication, but freely described feelings of depersonalization and aural hallucinations. He described himself as a "radiating telepath" and continued his keen interest in the occult. B, in his middle 20's, is married, has children and a

responsible position. He reported that things were "disinturbulated."
Like A he is a fanatic for the occult and on last information had left his
job to go to headquarters for special training. He told us that "Paul of
Tarsus started off in many respects a similar way to what I did." He considers himself too careful to become "insane," more self-reliant than A,
and stronger all around. Their MMPI profiles are given in Fig. 1. Both
twins have their highest scores on the clinical scales labeled *Paranoia*
(6), *Psychopathic deviate* (4), and *Schizophrenia* (8).

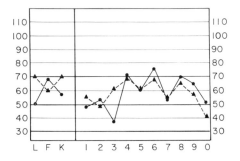

Fɪɢ. 1. MMPI profiles of a pair of MZ male twins, age 26, discordant for psychiatric hospitalization and a diagnosis of schizophrenia, concordant (Grade 3) for
psychiatric abnormality. (Proband, ●——●; co-twin, ▲---▲.)

One final example from a Grade 3 pair involves our youngest discordant proband. A has had 3 hospitalizations, the first at age 16 when he was
diagnosed as an adolescent depression. He is in the sample by virtue of a
diagnosis of schizo-affective psychosis from an area psychiatric hospital.
When treated with electroconvulsive therapy, his depression cleared but
his thinking disorder remained. When treated with phenothiazines, he
showed sufficient improvement to be discharged to outpatient status.
His brother has had no contact with the psychiatric world but has
hospitalized himself twice for physical complaints with no organic basis.
He has put himself on an ulcer diet although no physician has verified
this self-diagnosis. B has a very poor work history, never staying long
at one job. B was heavier at birth (4½ lbs. versus A's 3¼) but poorer in
school achievement; they attended different schools after the eleven plus
examination. For the past 4 years, A has lived mostly with the kindly ma-
ternal grandmother, uncle and aunt, while B has been more exposed to
the "schizophrenogenic" mother and cold, harsh step-father. At the time of
follow-up, B was clinically free of marked schizophrenic symptomatology,
but his MMPI profile was grossly abnormal and clearly of a psychotic
shape. Since B is only in his early 20's, the labeling of this pair as dis-

cordant may be premature. MMPI profiles of this pair are presented in Fig. 2.

The last 2 cases in particular illustrate some of the reasons for dissatisfaction with the concept of concordance since it imposes an artificial dichotomy upon behavior that is more fruitfully measured on a continuum.

Our 10 concordant MZ pairs tended to have rather similar illnesses with respect to subtype, age of onset, and length of hospitalization. Eight

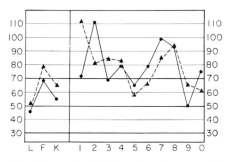

FIG. 2. MMPI profiles of a pair of MZ male twins, age 20, discordant for psychiatric hospitalization and a diagnosis of schizophrenia, concordant (Grade 3) for psychiatric abnormality. Co-twin is severely hypochondriacal. (Proband, ●——●; co-twin, ▲–––▲.)

of them were first hospitalized within 3 years of each other, 1 after a 6-year interval, the last after a 13-year interval. Using the empirical data of Slater (1953, p. 57) on ages of onset of schizophrenia in pairs of relatives rather than an arbitrary risk period, the discordant MZ and DZ twins in our series have lived through 73% of the risk. We found no striking differences between the ages at first hospitalization or ages at first diagnosis of schizophrenia when contrasting the concordant with the discordant MZ pairs; in 6/10 concordant MZ pairs, the proband was first hospitalized and diagnosed schizophrenic after age 30, while this was true for 6/14 of the discordant MZ pairs. This finding further weakens Rosenthal's conclusion (1959) that the schizophrenia observed in Slater's discordant identicals represented a nongenetic variety with a later appearance, no family history, and an over-representation of paranoid types.[12] None of the first degree relatives of our MZ pairs, concordant or discordant, has

[12] We do not wish to labor the point, but there is no reason to expect a late-appearing disorder to be either mild or nongenetic. The classical example is Huntington's chorea, caused by an autosomal, dominant gene. It has an average age of onset around 40 but onsets have been observed well into the sixth and seventh decade of life. The reasons for the delayed appearance are unknown.

been diagnosed as schizophrenic, and there does not appear to be a predominance of paranoid types in the discordant MZs.

Our discordant pairs do not fit neatly with the characteristics of the pairs described by Pollin *et al.* (1965). For example, in 7/14 pairs where birth weight is known, the future schizophrenic was the lighter in 5, the heavier in 1, and equal in the remaining pair. While it is clearly of importance to account for differences within the MZ pairs, the task is a difficult one. The environmental reasons suggested in the studies we have reviewed are not sufficient as causes of schizophrenia. Not many premature babies, or children tied to the apron-strings of constricting, inconsistent mothers, or twins who have difficulties in fending for themselves because of their close relationship, actually develop schizophrenia. Given the genetic predisposition, however, features such as those mentioned may make a crucial difference in determining which twin becomes schizophrenic. The same features, differing in degree between members of concordant pairs, may also be important determiners of within-pair differences in the severity of the illness.

4. Overall Design of the Study

Among the major pieces of information we have collected and will be analyzing are the following:

(1) Hospital notes for all psychiatric admissions for all twins, siblings, and parents.

(2) Case histories for all twins. More than half of the pairs have had a structured history form filled in by an informant (Briggs, 1959). Other information was obtained at the time of hospitalization or from follow-up interviews with twins and parents.

(3) Tape recorded 30-minute samples of verbal behavior during a semi-structured interview. The latter was intended to elicit the subtle and obvious signs of schizophrenia and the compensated schizotype (Meehl, 1962), attitudes toward self, parents, and twin, and ego strength. Interviews with 75 twins were recorded. (Three refused and 1 was missed through equipment failure). A verbatim typescript of each tape is being prepared.

(4) A Minnesota Multiphasic Personality Inventory (MMPI) from each cooperative and literate twin and parent (Dahlstrom & Welsh, 1960). The 101 profiles generated are essentially the same as those obtained in the United States. One use of the test will be to assess within-pair personality similarity on a continuum of psychopathology (Gottesman, 1962, 1963).

(5) The Goldstein-Scheerer Object Sorting Test (Lovibond, 1964; Rapaport *et al.,* 1945) completed by 90 twins and parents. It is

intended to measure concept formation and tendencies toward thought disorder. Lidz *et al.* (1962) and others have reported that half the normal-appearing parents of schizophrenics score within the schizophrenic range of thought disorder.

Our plans call for the use of various rating scales for quantifying the presence of symptoms and the severity of illness, and for locating a point on the heuristically interesting process-reactive continuum. Meehl's (1964) Radovian inspired checklist of schizotypic signs will also be tried. The most immediate advantages of adding psychometric measures to the study of schizophrenia in twins are the provisions for uncontaminated assessment of the mental status of both twins in a pair in a quantitative manner and for objective comparisons with normative data on other samples of psychiatric patients.

5. Conclusions

Our sample, to repeat, cannot be put forward, any more than any other, as being *truly* representative of the domain of schizophrenia. Based on 16 years' consecutive admissions of a population of 45,000 individuals to a short-stay psychiatric hospital with a large outpatient department, and including probands who at first appeared to be neurotic or personality disordered, it may be said to make better provision for cases with a good prognosis than the studies under review. The latter were characterized by a heavy emphasis on cases fitting the Kraepelinian description of dementia praecox. We know of no other large scale research on schizophrenic twins organized prospectively and based on the kind of population described. We thus have a study that meets many of the criticisms leveled at earlier efforts.

IV. Discussion and Conclusions

We have introduced the reader to the twin method and to the deductions that may reasonably be made from it. We have critically surveyed the 11 twin studies of schizophrenia, from Luxenburger's in 1928 to our own ongoing project, which have attempted, with varying success, to avoid the pitfalls of biased selection by ascertaining all twins in a given population. The studies came from 4 Scandinavian countries, Germany, the United Kingdom, the United States, and Japan. In none of these data was there evidence favoring the view that monozygosity or twinship per se increased the risk of schizophrenia. Some samples were quite small. Some gave admirably complete clinical details. Others were difficult to evaluate because of the absence of such details and of sampling procedures. Our survey revealed areas of heterogeneity for the concordance rates both within and between samples.

First, females tended to be concordant to a greater degree than males. Such a finding could be an artifact of sampling since only the Rosanoff and Slater female pairs showed markedly higher concordance rates. These two investigations were based on resident hospital populations with unrepresentative sex distributions for their twin pairs. Additional explanations for the sex difference that could be proposed include other selection biases, such as differential mortality, the exposure of males to greater environmental variability thereby decreasing the probability of equivalent stresses, and psychological factors facilitating identification in females. One significant and consistent difference that emerged from our analyses was a lower concordance rate for opposite-sex fraternal pairs than same-sex fraternal pairs for all studies giving information on this point.

A second source of heterogeneity was related to the severity of schizophrenia in the proband. Internal analyses of the data of Kallmann, Slater, Inouye, ourselves, and perhaps, Luxenburger showed a direct relationship between severity and concordance. Correlated with the dimension of severity are the dimensions of sampling from a standing, resident population versus sampling consecutively, and sampling from long-stay versus short-stay hospitals. Although concordances tended to be lower when sampling was done consecutively, the type of hospital was much more crucial to the magnitude of MZ concordance. Kallmann's adult twins (69% concordant) were mostly from consecutive admissions to long-stay hospitals, and Slater's series in long-stay hospitals analyzed by consecutive versus resident status showed no difference in concordance rates for schizophrenia (64% versus 65%). Our own twins from consecutive admissions to a short-stay hospital had a significantly lower MZ rate (42%).

We have compiled a master summary table of the concordance rates for schizophrenia in the 11 studies reviewed. Table XXIV shows the results by type of twin and is arranged in order of decreasing identical twin (MZ) concordance rates. All the concordances cited are without age correction and in terms of pairs rather than index cases. Kallmann corrected for age but did not count a pair twice when both members were legitimate index cases. Luxenburger counted cases rather than pairs but did not correct for age. Slater corrected for age and also counted those few pairs twice where both were index cases. Harvald and Hauge reported their data in terms of index cases. Such differences account for the departures in Table XXIV from the versions published by the investigators. Information is also provided about the status of each study with respect to the important dimensions discussed above as well as two others. Table XXIV indicates whether the author exercised the option of changing hospital diagnoses and whether fingerprints or blood were used as an aid to zygosity diagnosis. The former may or may not add to the accuracy of a study, depending on one's view;[13] the latter always add to the accuracy.

A third source of heterogeneity remains unaccounted for by the analysis above; the 4 Scandinavian studies, as they stand, have the lowest MZ concordance rates for diagnosed and hospitalized schizophrenia. The differences are not accounted for by the method of ascertainment since Essen-Möller, Tienari, and Kringlen each used different methods. For the Scandinavian studies reported in detail, the co-twins tended to be characterized by milder psychiatric problems with schizophrenic-like features, or they presented eccentricities of character termed "borderline" or "schizoid." The possibility arises that there may be real reasons, genetic and/or environmental, why "concordance" in Scandinavian twin studies does not show up at the level of a clear-cut psychosis.

There is, however, no reason to expect the degree of genetic determination (heritability) for a trait to be invariant throughout the world, even in studies using the same design. Heritability can vary according to the frequency of the genes involved and their penetrance (Huizinga & Heiden, 1957). It can vary according to the frequency and distribution in a population of the environmental influences *relevant in* schizophrenia. Since the latter are currently indeterminate, comparisons among studies done in different cultures must necessarily be somewhat elastic.

It comes as no surprise to the geneticist to find that increases in environmental variability decrease the proportion of phenotypic variance attributable to genotypic variation, and that decreased environmental variability has the opposite effect (Fuller & Thompson, 1960, p. 65). What is surprising is that the Scandinavian results are contrary to the expectation for the effects of decreasing environmental variation. Therefore, it is probably both presumptuous and incorrect to infer that Scandinavia has a less complex environment than other cultures sampled for the *schizophrenic-relevant* aspects of the environment. The possibility remains that the continuing evolution of populations (Dobzhansky, 1962; Mayr, 1963) has led to a genotype more adapted by natural selection to harbor-

---

13 Kety (1959, reprinted 1965, p. 428) reported a personal communication from Kallmann that stated 87/174 (50%) of MZ co-twins carried a *hospital* diagnosis of schizophrenia before personal investigation. Kallmann diagnosed 103 [sic], or 59%, as schizophrenic. Kallmann (1946) had earlier reported that 120 (69%) co-twins were schizophrenic. Since this chapter went to press, Dr. Kety has generously given us (personal communication, 1966) the information Kallmann freely gave him in 1958. It clarifies the apparent discrepancy in the number of affected co-twins and permits a further evaluation of certain aspects of Kallmann's 1946 study, particularly the charge of contaminated diagnoses. We hope to present an analysis of this new material elsewhere; it does not alter significantly what we have said in this chapter, but it may add to it.

TABLE XXIV
SUMMARY TABLE OF TWIN STUDIES OF SCHIZOPHRENIA

Investigator	Country	Concordance						Sampling	
		MZ		DZ SS		DZ OS		Resident vs. Consecutive admissions	Long stay vs. Short stay
		Pairs	(%)	Pairs	(%)	Pairs	(%)		
Kallmann									
Preadolescent (1956)	USA	15/17	88	8/35a	23	a		R + C	L
Adult (1946)	USA	120/174	69	34/296	11	13/221	6	R + C	L
Slater (1953)	UK								
Resident Sample		17/26	65	4/35	11	0/36	0	R	L
Consecutive Sample		7/11	64	4/23	17	2/18	11	C	L
Essen-Möller (1941)	Sweden	7/11b	64	4/27b	15	—		C	L
Rosanoff (1934)	USA	25/41	61	7/53	13	3/48	6	R	L + S?
Inouye (1961)	Japan	33/55	60	2/11	18	0/6	0	R + C	L + S
Luxenburger (1928)	Germany	11/19	58	0/13	0	0/20	0	R + C	L + S
Gottesman & Shields (1966)	UK	10/24	42	3/33	9	—		C	S
Harvald & Hauge (1965)	Denmark	2/7	29	2/31	6	1/28	4	neither	n.a.
Kringlen (1964)c	Norway	2/8	25	2/12	17	—		R + C	L
Tienari (1963)c	Finland	0/16	0	—		—		neither	n.a.

TABLE XXIV (Continued)

Investigator	Country	Is severity related to concordance	Sex with higher concordance	Sample sex surplus	Hospital vs. Author diagnosis	Blood and/or fingerprints in zygosity diagnosis
Kallmann						
Preadolescent (1956)	USA	?	?	M	A	Yes
Adult (1946)	USA	Yes	neither	F	A	No
Slater (1953)	UK					
Resident Sample		Yes	F	F	A	Yes
Consecutive Sample		Yes	neither	neither	A	Yes
Essen-Möller (1941)	Sweden	No	neither	neither	A	Yes
Rosanoff (1934)	USA	?	F	F	H	No
Inouye (1961)	Japan	Yes	neither	F	A	Yes
Luxenburger (1928)	Germany	Yes?	neither	neither	A	No
Gottesman & Shields (1966)	UK	Yes	neither	neither	H	Yes
Harvald & Hauge (1965)	Denmark	?	?	?	H	Yes
Kringlen (1964)[c]	Norway	No			H	Yes
Tienari (1963)[c]	Finland	No			A	Yes

[a] DZ pairs not broken down by type and include OS pairs.

[b] Includes psychoses with schizophrenic-like features and Kaij (1960) follow-up. On other criteria MZ concordance ranges from 0%–86% (see text).

[c] Neither Kringlen nor Tienari included female probands.

ing the genetic component of schizophrenia (Böök, 1953; Gottesman, 1965). Behavior viewed through the lenses of evolution may become more significant. There are many climates and cultures in which twin studies of schizophrenia have yet to be conducted.

It is hardly necessary to point out that the results of the 11 twin studies are time-bound. New methods of treatment can be expected to change the results of future twin studies. Concepts such as severity and chronicity which helped define aspects of schizophrenia that appeared highly heritable are also features amenable to therapeutic intervention. Perhaps in a generation or so, severe, chronic cases will be a rarity. On an analysis of variance model, schizophrenia is changing from a more to a less genetically conditioned disorder. Yet the underlying specific genes remain essentially the same in their action and at a frequency in the population not very different from recent generations.

In conclusion, the perspective afforded us by the preliminary analyses of our own data from the twins of schizophrenics, together with our reanalysis of the earlier major twin studies, lead us to suggest that we are dealing with replications of the same experiment. Heterogeneity in results among the studies is largely accounted for when provision is made for differences along key dimensions that we have tried to underscore. It seems reasonable to postulate that genetic factors are largely responsible for the specific nature of most of the schizophrenias and that these factors are necessary but not sufficient for the disorder to occur.

Biological approaches to the understanding of pathological behavior can continue to be pursued vigorously with profit. The complexities of research into the etiologies of the schizophrenias demand multidisciplinary cooperation. The reward will be a rational therapy. Our humanitarian instincts to spare the suffering of the afflicted and their families and to eliminate the dilution of human potentials demand flexible research strategies, unfettered by entrenched points of view.

References

Allen, G. Comments on the analysis of twin samples. *Acta Geneticae Medicae Gemellologiae,* 1955, **4**, 143-160.

Allen, G. Twin research: problems and prospects. In A. G. Steinberg & A. G. Bearn (Eds.), *Progress in medical genetics,* Vol. IV. New York: Grune & Stratton, 1965. Chapter 8.

Benaim, S. The specificity of Reserpine in the treatment of schizophrenia in identical twins. *J. Neurol. Neurosurg. Psychiat.,* 1960, **23**, 170-175.

Bender, Lauretta. Childhood schizophrenia. 2. Schizophrenia in childhood: its recognition, description and treatment. *Amer. J. Orthopsychiat.,* 1956, **26**, 497-506.

Bleuler, E. *Dementia Praecox oder Gruppe der Schizophrenien.* Leipzig: Deuticke, 1911. (*Dementia Praecox or the group of schizophrenias.* New York: International Universities Press, 1950. Tr. J. Zinkin.)

Bleuler, M. *Krankheitsverlauf, Persönlichkeit und Verwandtschaft Schizophrener und ihre gegenseitigen Beziehungen.* Leipzig: Thieme, 1941.

Böök, J. A. Schizophrenia as a gene mutation. *Acta Genetica Statistica Medica,* 1953, **4,** 133-139.

Briggs, P. F. Eight item clusters for use with the M-B history record. *J. clin. Psychol.,* 1959, **15,** 22-28.

Carstairs, G. M., Tonge, W. L., O'Connor, N., & Barber, L. E. D. Changing population of mental hospitals. *British J. preventive soc. Med.* 1955, **9,** 187-190.

Cederlöf, R., Friberg, L., Jonsson, E., & Kaij, L. Studies on similarity diagnosis in twins with the aid of mailed questionnaires. *Acta Genetica Statistica Medica,* 1961, **11,** 338-362.

Conrad, K., Erbanlage und Epilepsie. *Z. ges. Neurol. Psychiat.,* 1935, **153,** 271-326.

Dahlstrom, W. G., & Welsh, G. S. (Eds.) *An MMPI handbook.* Minneapolis: University of Minnesota Press, 1960.

Dobzhansky, T. *Mankind evolving.* New Haven: Yale Press, 1962.

Edwards, J. H. The simulation of Mendelism. *Acta Genetica Statistica Medica,* 1960, **10,** 63-70.

Essen-Möller, E. Empirische Ähnlichkeitsdiagnose bei Zwillingen. *Hereditas,* 1941, **27,** 1-50. (a)

Essen-Möller, E. Psychiatrische Untersuchungen an einer Serie von Zwillingen. *Acta Psychiat. Scandinavica,* 1941, Supplement 23. (b)

Faergeman, P. M. *Psychogenic psychoses: A description and follow-up of psychoses following psychological stress.* London: Butterworth, 1963.

Fish, F. Leonhard's classification of schizophrenia. *J. ment. Sci.,* 1958, **104,** 943-971.

Fuller, J. L., & Thompson, W. R. *Behavior genetics.* New York: Wiley, 1960.

Gesell, A., and Thompson, H. Learning and growth in identical infant twins, an experimental study by the method of co-twin control. *Genet. Psychol. Monogr.,* 1929, **6,** 1-124.

Gittelsohn, A. M., & Milham, S., Observations on twinning in New York State. *British J. preventive soc. Med.,* 1965, **19,** 8-17.

Goldfarb, W. An investigation of childhood schizophrenia: a retrospective view. *Arch. gen. Psychiat.,* 1964, **11,** 620-634.

Gottesman, I. I. Differential inheritance of the psychoneuroses. *Eugenics Quart.* 1962, **9,** 223-227.

Gottesman, I. I. Heritability of personality: a demonstration. *Psychol. Monogr.,* 1963, **77,** No. 9 (Whole No. 572).

Gottesman, I. I. Personality and natural selection. In S. G. Vandenberg (Ed.), *Methods and goals in human behavior genetics.* New York: Academic Press, 1965. Pp. 63-80.

Greenberg, H. P. Folie à deux: an historical and clinical study. Unpublished doctoral dissertation, Univer. of Sydney, Australia, 1961.

Harvald, B., & Hauge, M. Hereditary factors elucidated by twin studies. In J. V. Neel, M. W. Shaw, & W. J. Schull (Eds.), *Genetics and the epidemiology of chronic diseases.* Washington, D. C., U. S. Department of Health, Education and Welfare, 1965. Pp. 61-76.

Hoch, P., & Polatin, P. Pseudoneurotic forms of schizophrenia. *Psychiatric Quart.,* 1949, **23,** 248-276.

Huizinga, J., & Heiden, J. A. v.d., The percentages of concordance in twins and mode of inheritance. *Acta Geneticae Medicae Gemellologiae,* 1957, **6,** 437-450.

Hurst, L. A. Genetics of schizophrenia: reply to Pastore. *Psychol. Bull.,* 1951, **48,** 402-412.

Inouye, E. Similarity and dissimilarity of schizophrenia in twins. *Proceedings, Third*

World Congress of Psychiatry (1961), Vol I. Montreal: University of Toronto Press, 1963. Pp. 524-530.

Jackson, D. D. A critique of the literature on the genetics of schizophrenia. In D. D. Jackson (Ed.), *The etiology of schizophrenia*. New York: Basic Books, 1960. Pp. 37-87.

Juel-Nielsen, N. Individual and environment, a psychiatric-psychological investigation of monozygotic twins reared apart. *Acta Psychiatrica Scandinavica*, 1965, Suppl. 183.

Kaij, L. *Alcoholism in twins*. Stockholm: Almqvist and Wiksell, 1960.

Kallmann, F. J. *The genetics of schizophrenia*. New York: Augustin, 1938.

Kallmann, F. J. The genetic theory of schizophrenia: an analysis of 691 schizophrenic twin index families. *Amer. J. Psychiat.*, 1946, **103**, 309-322.

Kallmann, F. J. The genetics of psychoses: an analysis of 1232 twin index families. *Congrés International de Psychiatrie, Rapports VI: Psychiatrie Sociale*. Paris: Hermann, 1950. Pp. 1-27.

Kallmann, F. J. *Heredity in health and mental disorder*. New York: Norton, 1953.

Kallmann, F. J., & Roth, B. Genetic aspects of preadolescent schizophrenia. *Amer. J. Psychiat.*, 1956, **112**, 599-606.

Kay, D. W., & Roth, M. Environmental and hereditary factors in the schizophrenias of old age ("late paraphrenia") and their bearing on the general problem of causation in schizophrenia. *J. ment. Sci.*, 1961, **107**, 649-686.

Kety, S. S. Biochemical theories of schizophrenia. *Int. J. Psychiat.*, 1965, **I**, 409-430.

Kolle, K. *Die primäre Verrücktheit*. Leipzig: Thieme, 1931.

Kringlen, E. Schizophrenia in male monozygotic twins. *Acta Psychiatrica Scandinavica*. 1964, Suppl. 178.

Kurihara, M., & Inouye, E. Dissimilarity of schizophrenia in monozygotic twins. *Proceedings, Joint Meeting Japanese Society of Psychiatry and Neurology & American Psychiatric Society, Tokyo, May, 1963*. Tokyo: Kasai, 1963. Pp. 271-273.

Langfeldt, G. *The schizophreniform states*. London: Oxford University Press, 1939.

Lidz, T., Wild, Cynthia, Schafer, Sarah, Rosman, Bernice, & Fleck, S. Thought disorders in the parents of schizophrenic patients: a study utilizing the Object Sorting Test. *J. Psychiatric Res.*, 1962, **1**, 193-200.

Locke, B. Z., & Duvall, Henrietta J. Migration and mental illness. *Eugenics Quart.*, 1964, **11**, 216-221.

Lovibond, S. H. Personality and conditioning. In B. A. Maher (Ed.) *Progress in experimental personality research*. Vol. I. New York: Academic Press, 1964. Pp. 115-169.

Luxenburger, H. Vorläufiger Bericht über psychiatrische Serienuntersuchungen an Zwillingen. *Z. ges. Neurol. Psychiat.*, 1928, **116**, 297-326.

Luxenburger, H. Psychiatrisch-neurologische Zwillingspathologie. *Zbl. ges. Neurol. Psychiat.*, 1930, **56**, 145-180.

Luxenburger, H. Über einige praktisch wichtige Probleme aus der Erbpathologie des zyklothymen Kreises. *Z. ges. Neurol. Psychiat.*, 1933, **146**, 87-125.

Luxenburger, H. Die Manifestationswahrscheinlichkeit der Schizophrenie im Lichte der Zwillingsforschung. *Z. psych. Hyg.*, 1934, **7**, 174-184.

Luxenburger, H. Untersuchungen an schizophrenen Zwillingen und ihren Geschwistern zur Prüfung der Realität von Manifestationsschwankungen. *Z. ges. Neurol. Psychiat.*, 1936, **154**, 351-394.

Mayr, E. *Animal species and evolution*. Cambridge: Harvard University Press, 1963.

Meehl, P. E. Schizotaxia, schizotypy, schizophrenia. *Amer. Psychologist*, 1962, **17**, 827-838.

Meehl, P. E. Manual for use with checklist of schizotypic signs. Unpublished manuscript. Univer. of Minnesota Medical School, Minneapolis, 1964.

Metrakos, J. D., & Metrakos, K. Genetics of convulsive disorders. II. Genetics and EEG studies in centrencephalic epilepsy. *Neurology*, 1962, **12**, 474-483.

Meyer, J. E. An internationally acceptable diagnostic scheme suitable for comparative psychiatric studies. In P. H. Hoch & J. Zubin (Eds.), *Comparative epidemiology of the mental disorders*. New York: Grune & Stratton, 1961. Pp. 101-109.

Mott, F. W. The Huxley Lecture on hereditary aspects of nervous and mental disease. *British med. J.*, 1910, **2**, 1013-1020.

Myerson, A. *The inheritance of mental disease*. Baltimore: Williams & Wilkins, 1925.

Neel, J. V., & Schull, W. J. *Human heredity*. Chicago: Univer. Chicago Press, 1954.

Pastore, N. *The nature-nurture controversy*. New York: Kings Crown Press, 1949.

Pastore, N. Genetics of schizophrenia: a rejoinder. *Psychol. Bull.*, 1952, **49**, 542-544.

Penrose, L. S. Auxiliary genes for determining sex as contributory causes of mental illness. *J. ment. Sci.*, 1942, **88**, 308-316.

Penrose, L. S. Survey of cases of familial mental illness. *Dig. Neurology Psychiat.*, 1945, **13**, 644.

Pettigrew, T. *A profile of the Negro American*. Princeton: Van Nostrand, 1964.

Pollin, W., Stabenau, J. R., & Tupin, J. Family studies with identical twins discordant for schizophrenia. *Psychiat.*, 1965, **28**, 60-78.

Race, R. R., & Sanger, R. *Blood groups in man*. (4th ed.) Oxford: Blackwell, 1962.

Rado, S. Theory and therapy: the theory of schizotypal organization and its application to the treatment of decompensated schizotypal behavior. In S. Rado, (Ed.), *Psychoanalysis of behavior*. Vol. II. New York: Grune & Stratton, 1962. Pp. 127-140.

Rainer, J. D. Studies in the genetics of disordered behavior: methods and objectives. In F. J. Kallmann (Ed.), *Expanding goals of genetics in psychiatry*. New York: Grune & Stratton, 1962. Pp. 3-9.

Rapaport, D., Schafer, R., & Gill, M. *Diagnostic psychological testing*. Chicago: Yearbook Publication, 1945.

Registrar-General for England & Wales. *Statistical review of England & Wales for the year 1949: Supplement on general morbidity, cancer & mental health*. London: Her Majesty's Stationery Office, 1953.

Rimland, B. *Infantile autism*. New York: Appleton-Century, 1964.

Rosanoff, A. J. Twins—a study of certain mental disorders: preliminary report. *California & west. Med.*, 1932, **37**, 101-105.

Rosanoff, A. J., Handy, L. M., Plesset, I. R., & Brush, S. The etiology of so-called schizophrenic psychoses with special reference to their occurrence in twins. *Amer. J. Psychiat.*, 1934, **91**, 247-286.

Rosenthal, D. Some factors associated with concordance and discordance with respect to schizophrenia in monozygotic twins. *J. nerv. ment. Dis.*, 1959, **129**, 1-10.

Rosenthal, D. Confusion of identity and the frequency of schizophrenia in twins. *Arch. gen. Psychiat.*, 1960, **3**, 297-304.

Rosenthal, D. Sex distribution and the severity of illness among samples of schizophrenic twins. *J. Psychiatric Res.*, 1961, **1**, 26-36.

Rosenthal, D. Problems of sampling and diagnosis in the major twin studies of schizophrenia. *J. Psychiatric Res.*, 1962, **1**, 116-134. (a)

Rosenthal, D. Familial concordance by sex with respect to schizophrenia. *Psychol. Bull.*, 1962, **59**, 401-421. (b)

Rosenthal, D. (Ed.) & Colleagues, *The Genain Quadruplets*. New York: Basic Books, 1963.

Rosenthal, R. The effect of the experimenter on the results of psychological research. In B. A. Maher (Ed.), *Progress in experimental personality research*. Vol. I. New York: Academic Press, 1964. Pp. 80-114.

Scheinfeld, A. Bio-social effects on twinning incidence (II): the world situation with respect to twinning incidences and ratios and observations regarding genetic influences. *Proceedings, Second International Congress of Human Genetics, Rome, Sept. 1961.* Rome: Istituto Mendel, 1963. Pp. 303-305.

Scheinfeld, A., & Schachter, J. Bio-social effects on twinning incidence (I): intergroup and generation differences in the United States in twinning incidences and ratios. *Proceedings, Second International Congress of Human Genetics, Rome, Sept. 1961.* Rome: Istituto Mendel, 1963. Pp. 300-302.

Schulz, B. Zur Erbpathologie der Schizophrenie. *Z. ges. Neurol. Psychiat.*, 1932, **143**, 175-293.

Schulz, B. Übersicht über auslesefreie Untersuchungen in der Verwandtschaft Schizophrener und über die entsprechenden Vergleichsuntersuchungen. *Z. psych. Hyg.*, 1936, **9**, 130-156.

Schulz, B., & Leonhard, K. Erbbiologisch-klinische Untersuchungen an insgesamt 99 im Sinne Leonhards typischen beziehungsweise atypischen Schizophrenien. *Z. ges. Neurol. Psychiat.*, 1940, **168**, 587-613.

Shields, J. *Monozygotic twins brought up apart and brought up together.* London: Oxford University Press, 1962.

Shields, J. Review of "Psychiatric Illnesses in Identical Twins by Pekka Tienari." *British J. of Psychiat.*, 1965, **111**, 777-781.

Shields, J., & Slater, E. Diagnostic similarity in twins and the significance of biological specificity within the neuroses and personality disorders. *L'Evolution Psychiatrique*, 1966 (in press).

Slater, E. (with the assistance of Shields, J.). Psychotic and neurotic illnesses in twins. *Medical Research Council special report series, No. 278.* London: Her Majesty's Stationery Office, 1953.

Slater, E. The monogenic theory of schizophrenia. *Acta Genetica Statistica Medica.* 1958, **8**, 50-56.

Slater, E. Diagnosis of zygosity by finger prints. *Acta Psychiatrica Scandinavica*, 1963, **39**, 78-84.

Slater, E. Review of Faergeman and Labhardt. *British J. of Psychiat.*, 1964, **110**, 114-118.

Slater, E., Beard, A. W., & Glithero, E. The schizophrenia-like psychoses of epilepsy. *British J. of Psychiat.*, 1963, **109**, 95-150.

Srole, L., Langner, T. S., Michael, S. T., Opler, M. K., & Rennie, T. A. *Mental health in the metropolis.* Vol. I. New York: McGraw-Hill, 1962.

Strömgren, E. Zum Ersatz des Weinbergschen "abgekürzten Verfahrens," zugleich ein Beitrag zur Frage von der Erblichkeit der Erkrankungsalters bei der Schizophrenie. *Z. ges. Neurol. Psychiat.*, 1935, **153**, 784-797.

Taft, L. T., & Goldfarb, W. Prenatal and perinatal factors in childhood schizophrenia. *Developmental Med. Child Neurology*, 1964, **6**, 32-43.

Tienari, P. Psychiatric illnesses in identical twins. *Acta Psychiatrica Scandinavica*, 1963, Suppl. 171.

Tsuang, M. A study of pairs of sibs both hospitalized for mental disorder. Unpublished doctoral dissertation, Univer. of London, 1965.

Waterhouse, J. A. H. Twinning in twin pedigrees. *British J. soc. Med.*, 1950, **4**, 197-216.

Weinberg, W. Beiträge zur Physiologie und Pathologie der Mehrlingsgeburten beim Menschen. *Arch. ges. Physiol.*, 1901, **88**, 346-430.

Zehnder, M. Über Krankheitsbild und Krankheitsverlauf bei schizophrenen Geschwistern. *Mschr. Psychiat. Neurol.*, 1941, **103**, 230-277.

Zigler, E., & Phillips, L. Psychiatric diagnosis: A critique. *J. Abnorm. Soc. Psych.*, 1961, **63**, 607-618.

THEORY AND RESEARCH ON THE ANTECEDENTS OF SELF-IMPOSED DELAY OF REWARD

Walter Mischel

STANFORD UNIVERSITY, STANFORD, CALIFORNIA

I. Introduction

Theory and research on the process of internalization and the development of self-control have been largely confined to resistance to deviation and the occurrence of self-punitive or restitutive responses following transgression (Aronfreed, 1964). Equally important, and perhaps even more prevalent behavorial manifestations of self-control, are the willingness to defer immediate rewards in favor of delayed but more valued gratifications, and the manner in which persons regulate the self-administration of highly rewarding resources over which they have control.

The ability to delay immediate gratification for the sake of later, larger outcomes has long been recognized as a crucial prerequisite for many complex human activities, and figures importantly in a variety of theoretical formulations (e.g., Freud, 1922; Rapaport, 1951; Singer, 1955). In spite of this recognition in the abstract, there has been relatively little relevant experimental and empirical research. Recently a number of investigations (e.g., Singer, Wilensky, & McCraven, 1956; Levine, Glass, and Meltzoff, 1957; Levine, Spivack, & Wright, 1959) have inquired into the correlates of "delaying capacity," primarily as inferred from the frequency of human movement (M) Rorschach responses or other indirect indices.

In contrast to the above, the present research program investigates delay of gratification by studying direct manifestations of delay behavior. Similar direct attempts to measure voluntary delay of reward have been made in a few earlier studies (e.g., Block & Martin, 1955; Mahrer, 1956). Our studies typically employed a research paradigm in which subjects are confronted with real choices between immediately available but less valued rewards, as opposed to delayed but more valuable outcomes (e.g., Mischel, 1958, 1961a). For example, children choose between a little candy bar now or a larger one which requires waiting a week, and make a series of such choices. Choice procedures of this type were administered to samples of West Indian and U.S. elementary school children who were also tested with a variety of other measures. The results provided evidence that delay responses are relatively consistent, tend to increase with age, and are systematically related to other theoretically relevant variables usually subsumed under "ego strength" constructs.

For example, in one study (Mischel & Gilligan, 1964), yielding to temptation, in a situation in which attainment of achievement rewards is contingent upon deviant (cheating) behavior, was conceptualized to be a function of the strength of the motivation to attain the prohibited gratification, and the unwillingness to delay immediate gratification. Sixth-grade boys participated in an experimentally controlled "shooting gallery" game of skill in which attainment of achievement rewards (prizes) was contingent upon the child's falsifying his own scores. Motivation for the prohibited gratification was inferred from achievement motivation scores; preference for immediate, smaller, or delayed larger rewards in choice situations was the index of the ability to delay gratification. Achievement motivation was related to the subject's producing sufficiently deviant scores to obtain an achievement reward, and preference for delayed rewards was related negatively to the amount of cheating and positively to the latency of cheating, i.e., the number of trials before the occurrence of the first deviation.

Similar studies have been reported, demonstrating positive relationships between preference for delayed, more valued rewards and measures of social responsibility, achievement motivation, and certain rearing conditions such as the presence of the father in the home (e.g., Mischel, 1958, 1961a,b,c).

In an unpublished study (Mischel, 1962) relationships between delay behavior and a number of cognitive and personality measures were explored, using sixth-grade children as subjects. The data further supported the relational fertility of the delay measures, and also revealed sex differences in the correlational patterns obtained for boys and girls. For example, preference for delayed rewards was positively and significantly related to excellence on the Witkin Embedded Figures Test for girls but not for boys, and was negatively related to Mandler-Sarason Test Anxiety scores for boys but not for girls. Likewise, willingness to wait for larger rewards was negatively related to the subjective temporal duration of short time periods (e.g., 45 sec) for girls, whereas for boys subjective temporal experience and delay behavior appear unrelated. For both sexes preference for delayed rewards was modestly but significantly related to Performance IQ on the Wechsler Intelligence Scale for Children, but not to Verbal IQ, and significant correlations with numerous other cognitive measures (e.g., category breadth) were found.

One might view the obtained correlational patterns as indicative of a complex personality variable and pursue the associated individual differences in detail. However, our prime interest in the correlational findings is that they demonstrate that the simple, direct choice behaviors employed can be used as meaningful measures of willingness to defer gratification. We do not seek to add another trait or typology to the array already so abundant in the literature. Rather, the experiments to be reported here investigate the effects of social learning variables that might be expected to play a particularly influential role in the establishment of delay-of-reward behavior, using delay measures as the dependent variables.

It is generally assumed that the acquisition and maintenance of the various forms of self-controlling responses are primarily achieved either through direct aversive stimulation (Aronfreed, 1964), or by means of complex intrapsychic mediational processes when immediate gratification is unavailable (Freud, 1911). In contrast, our conceptualization of delay behavior is based on a social learning theory in which the probability for the occurrence of a behavior is a function of the subjective expectancy that it will lead to particular consequences in a given situation and the reinforcement value of those consequences (Rotter, 1954). Thus, whether an individual chooses an immediate, smaller reward or a delayed, larger reward in a given situation is a function of the relative strengths of the expectancies and reward values associated with each choice. Support for this comes from studies by Mahrer (1956) and by H. Mischel (1963), in which increases in preferences for delayed rewards were demonstrated by experimentally increasing the individual's expectancy that the promise maker would supply the delayed reward, or by decreasing the length of the delay interval (Mischel & Metzner, 1962).

In the present view, expectancies about response consequences are based both on direct experience with outcomes obtained by the individual for similar behaviors in earlier related situations, and on observational learning through which he observes or infers the consequences obtained by live or symbolic models for particular behavior patterns (e.g., Bandura & Walters, 1963). This formulation attempts to predict which behavior among an array of available alternative behaviors is most likely to occur in a given situation. It is clear that it does not deal with responses which have not yet been acquired or learned by the individual and which are therefore not in his repertoire of possible responses. Most of our investigations of delay behavior confront the subject with choices between alternatives, providing him with the possibility of choosing either immediate or delayed rewards. Thus they focus primarily on the antecedents of the willingness to delay gratification, rather than on the acquisition of novel delay responses. This paper describes in detail some of our recent experimental efforts with various facets of this problem.

II. The Effects of Expectancy on Working and Waiting for Larger Rewards

In previous studies subjects were exposed to choice conflicts between smaller, immediately available rewards as opposed to larger rewards which could not be attained without a waiting period. However, in most life situations the attainment of larger rewards involves contingencies other than, or in addition to, simple waiting. A recent study (Mischel & Staub, 1965) extends the investigation of the choice behavior described to contingent choices, where the smaller reward is immediately available but the larger, more valued reward is contingent on instrumental activity, both with and without additional waiting. It was reasoned that when attainment of the larger reward is contingent upon successful performance on a task, the individual's expectancy that his performance will be successful, and thus lead to positive consequences, will be a main determinant of his choice. Moreover, when attainment of the larger reward is contingent upon both successful performance and an additional delay period, then the individual's expectancy for success, as well as his expectancy that the reward will be obtained in spite of the delay period, both enter as determinants of his choice.

This experiment investigated the effects of (a) specific contingencies, (b) experimentally manipulated success and failure, and (c) pre-experimental generalized expectancies, on choices between more valued or larger rewards obtainable under various contingencies as opposed to noncontingent, immediate but less valued or smaller rewards. Eighth-grade boys were dichotomized into those with high and low generalized expectancies in ability areas on the basis of their statements about expectancies for success. Three weeks later, these children worked on a series of problems. In one treatment they obtained Success, in a second Failure, and in a third No Information. Following this, the children chose between less valuable, noncontingent immediate rewards and more valuable but contingent rewards. There were five variations in the contingencies for the more valuable rewards and each S chose under all variations, namely:

(a) successful performance on a task similar to one of the treatment tasks;
(b) same as (a) but with an additional delay period;
(c) successful performance on a task dissimilar to one of the treatment tasks;
(d) same as (c) but with an additional delay period;
(e) only a delay period.

In four conditions attainment of the larger reward was contingent upon successful performance on a task. In two of these the task was described with the same general label as one of the tasks ("Verbal Reasoning") on which success, failure, or no information had been obtained earlier. These are the *"contingent similar"* conditions (1 and 2 in Table I), and in one of them (2) attainment of the larger reward was also dependent upon a waiting period ("contingent similar delay" condition). In the next two conditions the larger reward was contingent upon successful performance on a task described with a new label ("General Information") that had not been included in the series on which Ss had performed earlier. These are the *"contingent dissimilar"* conditions (3 and 4 in Table I). Again, in one of these (4) the larger reward was also dependent upon a waiting period. Thus in conditions 1 to 4 attainment of larger rewards was contingent upon successful performance on tasks similar and dissimilar to the initial tasks, with and without an additional delay period. In the 5th condition, the more valuable reward was not contingent upon any task performance and depended only on willingness to wait ("noncontingent delay"). The same set of five choice pairs was used in each of these five conditions, resulting in a total of 25 choices.

In each of the five conditions, Ss were presented with the following five objects as smaller, immediate rewards: $1.00; two *Mad* magazines; small bag of peanuts; one hit tune record; plastic checker set. These were paired respectively against the following five corresponding larger rewards: $1.50; three *Mad* magazines; large can of mixed nuts; three hit tune records; wooden checker set. The delay conditions always involved a delay of 3 weeks before the larger reward could be obtained. For example, the "contingent similar delay" condition refers to solving a problem requiring verbal reasoning plus waiting 3 weeks in order to obtain the larger reward, whereas the "noncontingent delay" condition merely required 3 weeks of waiting before the larger reward could be obtained.

The 25 choices were presented in the same random sequence, and in group administration. Children were provided individual booklets containing on each page a brief description of a given set of paired objects and the associated contingency. After *E* had displayed both rewards and explained the contingency, the children were instructed to record their choice, and to turn the page in preparation for the next set of items. The *S*s were also advised to choose carefully and realistically because in *one* of the choices they would actually receive the item they selected, either on the same day or after the prescribed contingency, depending upon their recorded preference.

TABLE I

EXPERIMENTAL DESIGN AND MEAN CHOICES OF LARGE REWARDS BY ALL GROUPS IN ALL CHOICE CONDITIONS[a]

Groups		Choice conditions (contingencies)				
		Large rewards contingent on task				Large rewards noncontingent on task, delay only
		Similar to A		Dissimilar to A		
Treatment	Gen. expect.	Without delay 1	Plus delay 2	Without delay 3	Plus delay 4	5
Success on A	High	3.39	2.69	2.92	2.92	4.08
	Low	3.27	3.00	3.69	2.92	3.38
Failure on A	High	2.31	1.54	3.00	3.08	4.08
	Low	2.08	1.38	2.77	2.23	2.46
No information on A	High	3.77	2.85	3.54	2.85	3.54
	Low	2.08	1.54	2.15	2.15	3.23

[a] Note: "A" refers to treatment tasks.

Table I summarizes the design, and shows the mean delayed reward choices made in each condition.

First, it was anticipated that *S*s would discriminate between choice conditions as a function of the particular contingencies on which reward attainment depends. Contingent rewards should be chosen most when the probability for attaining them is greatest. Therefore, when the contingency for attaining more valuable rewards includes successful performance (work) as well as a delay period, they should be chosen less than when there is only one contingency (either working or waiting).

The data clearly supported this hypothesis and demonstrated the importance of the specific contingencies for attainment of larger rewards as determinants of the choice to wait and work for them. Larger rewards whose attainment required only a period of waiting were chosen more frequently than those that required successful work. Moreover, contingencies requiring an additional waiting period as well as successful work resulted in fewer large reward choices than contingencies requiring only successful work. A highly significant effect of choice conditions was obtained and illustrates the importance of specific contingencies as determinants of choice preference with respect to less valued but immediate, as opposed to more valued but contingent, rewards. Consequently, accurate predictions about this aspect of self-control require detailed analysis of the specific relevant contingencies for attainment of the larger or more valued outcome. This finding points to the importance of specific situational contingencies as determinants of behaviors frequently used as indices of "ego strength" and treated as if they were referents for relatively stable, general, and situation-free "traits."

Second, as anticipated, when the larger reward was contingent upon successful work on a task similar to one on which the S previously succeeded, it was chosen more frequently than when it was contingent upon success on a task similar to one on which the S previously failed. Irrespective of generalized expectancies, the effects of success and failure on similar tasks were highly significant. The extent to which individuals discriminate between specific contingencies was again illustrated by the fact that, when attainment of larger rewards was contingent on performance *dissimilar* to those on which subjects had previously succeeded or failed, these success and failure experiences did not significantly affect their choices.

The specific situational expectancies produced by the experimentally manipulated success and failure experiences minimized the effects of generalized expectancies in the Success and Failure treatments. In these two treatments choices were not significantly affected by pre-experimental generalized expectancies. However, in the absence of success or failure directly relevant to the contingencies upon which larger rewards depend, generalized expectancies affected choices. In the No Information group, children with low generalized expectancies behaved as if they had failed, whereas those with high expectancies behaved as if they had succeeded. The differences between Ss with high and low generalized expectancies were strongly significant, the former choosing more contingent rewards in the No Information treatment.

There was an unpredicted significant effect of generalized expectancy in the noncontingent (delay only) choice condition. In this condition children with high generalized expectancies for success waited for larger rewards more frequently than those with low expectancies. This difference was significant after the Failure treatment but not after either

Success or No Information. It seems plausible that generalized expectancy as measured in this study was also correlated with expectancies that the promised delayed reward will indeed be forthcoming, even when this was objectively independent of the S's own performance and contingent primarily upon the promise maker. However, since there were no significant differences between Ss with high and low generalized expectancies on nontask-contingent choices in the No Information and Success groups, and since the difference was significant only in the Failure group, it appears more reasonable that "confirmed failure" for Ss with low generalized expectancies for success decreased their discriminations about specific contingencies and caused them to generalize to choice situations in which reward attainment was independent of their own performance.

Extrapolating to life situations, in the absence of new information about outcomes relevant to the contingencies upon which reward attainment depends, individuals with highly generalized low expectancies for success behave as if they are unable to fulfill the contingency; that is, they behave like individuals who have already failed on tasks highly similar to those upon which the larger reward is contingent. Following actual failure on tasks similar to those upon which larger rewards are contingent, they are less willing to wait for them than subjects with high generalized expectancies for success, even when the larger reward is not contingent upon their own work and requires only waiting. However, when they are given information indicating that they can probably fulfill the relevant contingencies (Success treatment) their task-contingent large reward choices increase and are not significantly different from those made by subjects with high generalized expectancies for success. The implications for obtaining increased willingness to work and wait for larger rewards are clear: increase the probability that the person can fulfill the necessary specific contingencies. While this is hardly a startling conclusion it is one that needs to be taken seriously in therapeutic programs concerned with increasing "ego strength."

In sum, the first study demonstrated some of the determinants of working and waiting for larger, more valued outcomes and revealed some of the interactions between generalized expectancies, situational expectancies, and specific contingencies that affect this behavior.

III. The Effects of Expectancy on Reward Value

Having demonstrated that expectancy may be an important determinant of delay behavior, we come to the question of the relationship between the expectancy for attaining a delayed reward and the value attributed to that reward. The next experiment (Mischel & Masters, 1966) was designed to investigate this.

In this experiment children were subjected to a frustration, in the form of an externally produced delay of reward. The experimental treatments involved variations in the probability that the frustration would be terminated and the blocked reward attained. More specifically, elementary school children viewed an exciting motion-picture film which was interrupted near the climax on the pretext of a damaged electrical fuse. The experimentally presented probability that the fuse could be repaired and the film resumed was either 1., .5, or 0. A control group viewed the film without interruption. Response measures of the perceived value of the film, and the children's delay of reward behavior with other goal objects, were administered before and after the imposed delay period. Thereafter the fuse was "fixed" and the remainder of the movie was shown to all subjects, with another rating of its value and attractiveness obtained at the end.

There is some suggestive indirect evidence that the nonavailability of a reward increases its attractiveness or value (e.g., Aronson and Carlsmith, 1963). Likewise, Metzner (1962) found that preschool children who were required to wait for a reward (marble) tended to overvaluate it more than those who could obtain it by completing a puzzle game. However, the relationship between expectancy or subjective probability and reward value or utility remains unclear. For example, Lewin *et al.* (1944) and Atkinson (1957) assume an inverse relationship between subjective probability and reward value, whereas Rotter (1954), Edwards (1954), and others argue for the independence of these constructs.

In a cogent discussion of this issue, Feather (1959) has reasoned that, at least in our culture, persons learn to place greater value on the attainment of goal objects which are difficult to get because of the relatively consistent occurrence of sizable rewards for the successful achievement of difficult goals and deprecation or punishment for failure to attain easy goals. Moreover, achievement of the difficult is probably more typically and highly rewarded when it is due to the person's own efforts or skill, rather than to chance factors beyond his control, and likewise failure to achieve the easy is chastised more when it is due to the person's lack of skill than when it is a chance occurrence. In view of this, Feather hypothesized that an inverse relationship between attainment attractiveness (goal value) and success probability would be more apparent in "ego-related" than in chance-related situations, and in achievement-oriented as opposed to relaxed conditions. Feather's empirical results supported an inverse relationship between attainment attractiveness and success probability and indeed suggested that the independence assumption may be an oversimplification even for chance-related situations under achievement-oriented conditions. Similarly, Atkinson (1957) suggests that "the incentive value of winning *qua* winning, and losing *qua* losing, presumably developed in achievement activities early in life, generalize to the gambling situation in which winning is really not contingent upon one's skill and competence" (pp. 370-371).

In the present experiment, it was reasoned that the learned inverse association between reward value and attainment probability in achievement-related situations generalizes to nonachievement-related frustration conditions in which goal attainment is not in the S's control and is not contingent on his behavior. If in our culture persons acquire the generalized expectation that unlikely or unavailable positive outcomes are more valuable than likely or assured positive outcomes, then the value ascribed to an unattainable reward should be greater than that attributed to a reward that either may be attainable or whose attainment is assured. Accordingly, it was predicted that the perceived value of the delayed reward (film) would be greater when it is ultimately unattainable ($P = 0$) than when its attainment is assured ($P = 1$). Moreover, it was anticipated that certainty of reward attainment minimizes the effects of the imposed delay or frustration and therefore no differences were expected between the $P = 1$ treatment and the control group. Likewise, it was anticipated that the perceived value of the reward would be greater in the $P = 0$ condition than in the $P = .5$ group and that subjects in the latter would value the reward more than those in the $P = 1$ treatment or the control group. A posttest was included to determine whether differences between treatments in the perceived value of the delayed reward are maintained even after the frustration is terminated and the delayed reward is obtained.

It also seemed plausible that when the perceived frustration is greater subjects will more frequently self-administer other available immediate rewards. Therefore, when the delayed reward is permanently unattainable, immediate self-reward (in the form of increased preference for immediate smaller as opposed to delayed larger rewards) should be greater than when it is ultimately attainable ($P = 0 > P = 1$). This was not hypothesized on the basis of any "compensatory mechanisms" but on the assumption that immediate self-reward is more acceptable following strong frustration than following minimal frustration.

METHOD

Subjects

The Ss were 56 boys and 24 girls, all sixth-grade students at two public schools in Mountain View, California.

Design and Procedure

Pre-experimental Assessment of Delay-of-Reward Responses. In a pre-experimental session the children were administered in their classroom groups a series of 14 paired rewards (Form A), in each of which they were asked to select either a small reward that could be obtained immediately, or a more valued item contingent on a delay period ranging from 1 to 4 weeks. The administration proceeded in the following manner. Children were provided individual booklets containing on each page a brief description of a given set of paired objects and the associated time interval. After the E had displayed both rewards and explained the temporal contingency, the children were instructed to record their choice, and to turn the page in preparation for the next set of items. The Ss were also advised to choose carefully and realistically because in one of the choices they would actually receive the item they selected, either on the same day or after the prescribed delay period, depending upon their recorded preference.

Half of the sets of paired rewards involved small amounts of money (e.g., 25¢ today, or 35¢ in one week), while the remaining items included edibles (e.g., small bag of salted peanuts today, or a can of mixed nuts in 2 weeks), children's magazines, and various play materials (e.g., small rubber ball today, or a large rubber ball in 2 weeks).

Assignment to Treatments. The total pool of Ss was divided into quartiles on the basis of the distribution of delay-of-reward responses. An equal number of children from each quartile was randomly assigned to each of the three experimental groups and the control group, thus producing groups similar in their initial willingness to defer immediate rewards for the sake of delayed, larger gratifications. The same proportion of boys and girls was assigned to each group.

At each of the two schools each of the four experimental conditions was administered once, with an approximately equal number of children from each school in each condition. Two new Es, unconnected with the pre-experimental session, were used and each administered half the treatments in one school and the other in the second school. The temporal sequence of treatments at the two schools was balanced, the sequence in the second school being the reverse of the one used in the first school.

Experimental Treatments. Approximately 4 weeks after the assessment of delay preferences, the experimental sessions were conducted in a research trailer stationed at the school. The E was introduced as coming to prescreen an "exciting space movie" and to obtain the children's opinions about it. The film was a 20-minute documentary on space exploration. The children were told that they would fill out "audience estimate and opinion sheets" several times to determine their "feelings at different points." These contained the value ratings described below. The E explained that he was also interested in children's expectations about how attractive the film would be and therefore they would be asked to rate it before it actually commenced. This rationale was used to obtain a base level of attractiveness ratings in all groups to serve as a comparison point for any subsequent changes in the rated value of the film.

In the experimental groups the movie began as soon as the first value ratings were completed and collected. After 5 minutes, at a predetermined climactic point in the film (just as the space ship was being launched) the projector failed. A confederate, posing as the "district electrician," entered and explained that the power failure was due to his overloading the circuits with electrical tools. This rationale was used to avoid connecting the cause of frustration with either the E and his procedures or with the Ss' own behavior. The experimental treatments consisted of the following variations in the probability of resuming the interrupted film, announced by the confederate:

$P = 1$ I'm positive I can fix it—I've had things like this happen in the past, and I've always managed to fix them.

$P = .5$ I've had things like this happen before—sometimes I was able to fix them, sometimes I wasn't. I never know for sure . . . there's probably about a 50-50 chance.

$P = 0$ It takes a special fuse for this circuit, and there are none around here . . . I can't possibly fix it . . . there's no chance.

To increase credibility, E asked if the confederate was sure of his evaluation and the confederate reiterated his initial statement confidently in paraphrased form and left. The E expressed his regret at the interruption but reminded the Ss that repeated "audience estimate" sheets were needed and circulated the second set of value ratings.

In the *control group* the movie was not interrupted and both sets of ratings were obtained before the movie began. The second set of ratings was administered approximately 5 minutes after the first set, and during the intervening period the E prepared the film and projector. The rationale given to the children for readministering the ratings was in terms of the need for repeated measurements of their feelings at different times.

Following these second value ratings the Ss in all groups were administered a measure of immediate or delayed self-reward (described below).

Approximately 10 minutes after his first entry, and after the second ratings of the film and the delay-of-reward measures were completed, the "electrician" returned to all experimental groups, announcing that he had been able to fix the fuse and the movie would continue. The remainder of the film was shown and, when it ended, ratings of the movie were obtained for the third and final time.

Assessment of Reward Value. A four-item measure of reward or goal value was administered in printed booklets, the S checking his response to each item on a seven-point intensity scale. For example:

"Let's pretend that you are the manager of a movie theater. Instead of charging a set price for letting people see the movies you have, you do things different—when you have a movie that you think is very good, you charge a lot for them to get in; when you think a movie is bad, you don't charge very much at all. Now let's pretend that the movie I have today is at your theater—check about how much you would charge for tickets (0 to $1.00)."

These measures were given in the same random sequence to all Ss, with a different sequence used in each of the three administrations.

Assessment of Changes in Delay Behavior. Immediately following the second set of ratings the Ss were administered a new series of 14 independently pretested paired choices between immediately available smaller rewards and delayed larger rewards (Form B).[1] The rewarding objects differed from those employed in the pre-experimental sessions, but the money items were the same since pretesting revealed that Ss were unable to recall the exact amounts and temporal intervals involved. The E indicated at the outset that these choices were unconnected with his own project and were being administered for a Stanford researcher during the available period in order to save time.

RESULTS AND DISCUSSION

Prior to the experimental manipulations the groups did not differ appreciably in their initial evaluation of the film. Figure 1 shows the mean value rating of the film at each of the experimental phases for each group.

To assess the effect of the independent variable, change scores were computed for the difference between each pair of value ratings in each group. Analysis of variance of the mean change in value ratings immediately after interruption of the film (difference between phase 2 and phase 1 ratings) revealed a highly significant treatment effect. Subjects who were told they would definitely not see the remainder of the film ($P = 0$) increased their evaluation of it significantly more than those in all other conditions. None of the other groups ($P = 1$, $P = .5$, control) differed from each other.

---

[1] The delay scales were developed through extensive earlier pretesting. Responses to the 14 items in Form A and those comprising Form B were found to be reasonably intercorrelated ($r = .77$) in pilot work with 34 sixth-grade children from the same area.

Moreover, as Fig. 1 indicates, the increased evaluation of the film in the $P = 0$ condition was maintained even after the interruption was terminated and the movie completed. Subjects in the $P = 0$ condition tended to maintain their overevaluation of the movie even after they viewed the entire film, although the difference between the over-all increment in the $P = 0$ group and the $P = 1$ condition fell short of acceptable significance.

The data clearly showed an increase in the evaluation of an unattainable goal but there was no evidence for a linear inverse relationship between the probability of attaining a goal and the value attributed to it.

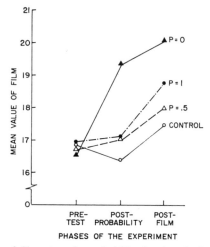

Fɪɢ. 1.   Mean value of film at each probability level and phase of the experiment.

Value changes in the $P = .5$ condition were not significantly different from those in the $P = 1$ or control groups. Indeed, the mean terminal value rating was slightly (not significantly) higher in the $P = 1$ treatment than in the $P = .5$ condition.

The effects of treatments on changes in delay of reward behavior were examined by comparing the number of pre-experimental and post-experimental immediate reward choices made in each condition. The control, $P = 1$, and $P = 0$ groups all showed slight mean increases in immediate reward choices, whereas in the $P = .5$ condition there was a fractional decrease, but these differences were not significant.

Summarizing, the results show that the value of a blocked or delayed reward can be affected by the expctancy for its ultimate attainment. When the probability for seeing the interrupted film was stated as zero, its rated value increased significantly more than when P was 1 or .5. When resumption of the film was presented as a certainty, children evaluated the film no differently than those who saw it without interruption. Although the value of the film increased most when its completion seemed nonattainable, and this change was maintained even after the film was completed, significant increases did not occur when an intermediate probability $(P = .5)$ was given. Subjects given an intermediate probability did not differ from those in the $P = 1$ and control conditions. An extension of the present study, using a large number of probability levels, would clarify whether the obtained effect of probability on value is restricted to unattainable outcomes $(P = 0)$ or holds for highly unlikely outcomes (e.g., $P = .10$).

Since subjective probability does not necessarily match experimentally presented probability statements, it would also be interesting to assess the S's expectancies for attaining the delayed reward and to examine the relationship between subjective probability and reward value in the present situation. For example, in the $P = .5$ treatment, most children may have had subjective expectancies for seeing the film which exceeded .5 considerably. Such effects may account for the lack of difference obtained from the $P = 1$ and $P = .5$ manipulations.

The results indicate that in our culture unattainable positive outcomes may be more valued than those which are attainable and that the unavailability of a positive outcome enhances its perceived desirability. Moreover, the findings support the view that the higher value attributed to unlikely outcomes in achievement-related situations generalizes very broadly even to nonachievement-related situations in which the probability for goal attainment is clearly independent of difficulty level and in which goal attainment is entirely outside the S's own control. These results have clear implications for understanding responses to imposed delay of reward. If the nonattainability of a reward increases its desirability, persons who, on the basis of their previous histories, expect that delayed or blocked rewards are lost irrevocably will respond quite differently from those who anticipate their ultimate attainment. The individual who has learned that blocked goals tend to be unattainable remains on the unhappy treadmill, expecting that what he wants cannot be obtained and overevaluating and wanting what he cannot have. Certainly this is not an unfamiliar clinical phenomenon. In contrast, the person who has learned that frustrated goals ultimately tend to become available may respond to delay of reward with equanimity.

The obtained results point to the importance of clearly distinguishing between voluntary and imposed delay-of-reward situations. The former offers the S a choice of immediate or delayed reward, whereas the latter forces him to wait. There is strong evidence that in voluntary delay situations there is a linear positive relationship between the probability of attaining the delayed reward and the willingness to wait for it. Suggestive evidence for this was found by Mahrer (1956), Mischel and Metzner (1962), Mischel and Staub (1965), and, most directly, by Mischel and Grusec (1965), who found linear increments in voluntary delay of reward as a function of the probability for attaining the delayed reward. Thus, although the expectancy for attaining delayed rewards increases the likelihood of choosing to wait for them, the nonattainability of a reward in an imposed delay-of-reward situation increases the value attributed to it.

The treatments did not significantly affect self-reward behavior in the form of changes in willingness to defer immediate rewards for the sake of larger but delayed outcomes. Unexpectedly, there was a slight, nonsignificant trend toward increased *delay* behavior in the $P = .5$ condition, whereas in all other treatments Ss tended to increasingly choose immediate rewards. It may be speculated that when the ultimate attainment of the blocked reward is uncertain, children try to be especially "good," deferring immediate gratification in the irrational hope that their "good" behavior will increase the probability of obtaining the blocked goal. This is sheer speculation but may be interesting to pursue.

The present experiment was designed to minimize the occurrence of cognitive dissonance at the onset of frustration and therefore the frustration was deliberately unconnected with the S's own behavior and not contingent on his own decisions. In contrast, when a temporary or permanent delay of reward is a consequence of the S's own behavior, dissonance theory (Festinger, 1957) might generate predictions opposite to those of the present study. In a recent study by Carlsmith (1962), Ss were exposed to the possibility of electric shock with variations in the probability that they would actually receive the shock. The probability was ostensibly determined by the S's performance on a fictitious personality test. Carlsmith's prediction of an increase in the rated "pleasantness" of the shock as a function of the probability of receiving it was supported and is consistent with dissonance theory. Comparisons between the present study and the Carlsmith experiment are precarious because they differ in several critical ways, e.g., the latter was not a frustration paradigm, involved aversive rather than positive outcomes, and presented probabilities ostensibly determined by the S's own performance. Perhaps most important, in the Carlsmith study the postmanipulation ratings were obtained after brief temporal delays (15 minutes), whereas in the present experiment the re-evaluation occurred almost immediately after the announced probabilities. It may be that such temporal effects are critical determinants of the relationship between expectancy and value. The initial response to an unattainable positive goal may be to overevaluate it (as in this study), but after the individual has been faced with its unattainability for some time justification processes commence and the value of the reward becomes minimized. To test for a positive relationship between probability of goal attainment and reward value under dissonance-producing conditions (in which the frustration is the consequence of the S's own behavior), an extension of the present experimental design is planned. This extension will include a temporal variation with respect to the amount of time elapsing between the onset of frustration and the measurement of reward value.

IV. Modification of Delay Behavior by Exposure to Live and Symbolic Models

The third study (Bandura and Mischel, 1965) investigated the vicarious transmission of delay behavior without the mediation of direct reinforcement. In accord with recent evidence (e.g., Bandura and Walters, 1963) on the potency of vicarious learning, it is plausible to hypothesize that self-imposed delay of reward is likewise determined by the delay patterns displayed by social models. Moreover, there have been no systematic comparative studies of the relative magnitude and stability of changes in social behavior as a function of exposure to real life and symbolic modeling cues. Consequently, the present investigation studied the relative efficacy of both live and verbally presented symbolic models in modifying children's delay-of-reward behavior.

In this experiment children who exhibited predominantly either delayed-reward or immediate-reward patterns of behavior were assigned randomly to one of three treatment conditions. One group of children observed live adult models who exhibited delay-of reward responses counter to the group's self-gratification pattern; a second group was similarly exposed to a model displaying the opposite delay-of-reward behavior with the exception that the modeling cues were presented in written form, while a third group had no exposure to any models. Immediately following the experimental procedure the children's delay-of-reward responses were measured in the absence of the model. In order to test the generality and stability of changes in delay behavior, the Ss were reassessed by a different E in a different social setting approximately 1 month after completion of the experimental phase of the study.

It was predicted that the modeling procedures would alter the children's delay-of-reward behavior in the direction of their model's response dispositions. Observation of a prestigeful and presumably successful model's behavior should increase the observer's expectancies that such behaviors lead to positive consequences and thus increase the likelihood of his performing them. Since an actual performance is apt to provide substantially more relevant cues with greater clarity than can be conveyed by a verbal description, it was also expected that live models would prove more effective than symbolic models in modifying children's self-imposed delay tendencies.

The maintenance of response patterns established through vicarious experiences is highly dependent upon reinforcement-related variables (Baer & Sherman, 1964). In view of the absence of any information concerning the naturalistic reinforcement contingencies that were operative during the relatively long period of time elapsing between the postexposure and the generalization test phases of the experiment, no predictions were advanced regarding group differences based on the terminal assessment.

Method

Subjects

The S's were 60 boys and 60 girls selected from the fourth and fifth grades of three elementary schools in the Stanford vicinity.

Design and Procedure

Pre-experimental Assessment of Delay-of-Reward Responses. In the initial phase of the experiment approximately 250 children were administered in their classroom groups the series of 14 paired rewards described earlier (Form A) in each of which they were asked to select either a small reward that could be obtained immediately, or a more valued item contingent on a delay period ranging from 1 to 4 weeks. From the total pool of Ss those falling in the extreme top and bottom 25% of the delay-score distribution, computed separately for boys and girls, were selected for the succeeding phases of the experiment.

Experimental Treatments. Approximately 4 weeks elapsed between the initial assessment of the children's delay behavior and the experimental phase of the study. The Ss were brought individually from their classrooms to the experimental room where a new experimenter explained that the adults had been invited to appear at the school, since it was difficult on week days to see them in their various places of employment. To insure that the model was endowed with adequate prestige the adults were described as recent college graduates. All children who were assigned to the experimental treatments observed same-sex models.

For children subject to the *live-model* condition, the adult entered shortly after the child was seated and introduced himself to the E and the S. In order to further increase credibility, the E described the choice procedure to the model in considerable detail as though he were a naïve S. The instructions stated the objects would be presented in pairs and in each case the Ss were to select either a less valued item that could be obtained immediately, or a more valued item conditional on a specified delay period. The participants were also informed that they would in fact receive one of their 14 choices.

On the pretext of the model's "busy schedule," the E first administered the items to the model while the child waited for his turn. The model's paired rewards included such adult-appropriate items as chess sets, paperback books, *Hi-fi* magazines, gourmet candy bars, jars of instant coffee, and monetary choices.[2] Although the items differed from those subsequently administered to the children, the delay intervals necessary for attaining the more valuable rewards were similar in both sets of items. During the modeling phase the E displayed each pair of items to the model who then indicated his choices verbally.

With *high-delay* children, the model consistently selected the immediately available rewards and in several instances commented briefly, according to a prearranged script, on the benefits of immediate self-reward (e.g., "Chess figures are chess figures. I can get much use out of the plastic ones right away.") In addition, after the fourth item, the model casually summarized his immediate-gratification philosophy of life as follows: "You probably have noticed that I am a person who likes things now. One can spend so much time in life waiting that one never gets around to really living. I find that it is better to make the most of each moment or life will pass you by." While the model periodically extolled the virtues of immediate self-gratification he carefully refrained from depreciating delay behavior; otherwise, it would be impossible to determine whether any changes in the children's behavior were a function of positive modeling of immediacy, or the modeling of negative attitudes toward postponement of gratification.

With *low-delay* children the procedure was identical to that described above except the model consistently selected the more valued delayed rewards. The model likewise commented periodically on the virtues of self-imposed delay (e.g., "The wooden chess figures are of much better quality, more attractive, and will last longer. I'll wait two weeks for

---

2 In the adult choices, just as in the children's, in each pair the more valuable or larger item required delay. Thus, for example, the choice was between a set of plastic chess figures obtainable now or a more expensive wooden set requiring a waiting period of 2 weeks; two issues of *Hi-Fi* magazine now or three issues in 1 week, etc.

the better one."), and expounded his postponement-of-gratification philosophy of life in the following manner: "You have probably noticed that I am a person who is willing to forego having fewer or less valuable things now, for the sake of more and bigger benefits later. I usually find that life is more gratifying when I take that carefully into account."

In both of the above experimental treatments, the models departed immediately upon completion of the choice task so as to remove situational pressures on the children to adopt the model's self-rewarding disposition.

In the *symbolic-model* condition, the E explained to the child that the adult who was scheduled for the same time had to leave early and, consequently, he had already made his selections. In addition, the S was told that children and adults are typically seen simultaneously to expedite matters; therefore, in order to keep the conditions as similar as possible for all participants, he would first be shown the paired items that were administered to the adult together with his recorded preferences and comments. The child was then handed the answer booklet in which were written both the model's choices and accompanying philosophy-of-life commentaries. The E then exhibited each choice pair sequentially while the S read the corresponding verbal accounts of the model's behavior.

In the *no-model-present* condition the children were informed that, because of scheduling difficulties, no adult would be present, but in order to ensure intersubject comparability the items between which adults ordinarily make choices would be shown. The E then simply displayed the series of paired objects. This procedure was adopted in order to control for any effects that mere exposure to a set of reinforcers might have on children's subsequent delay behavior.

Postexposure Assessment of Delay Behavior. Immediately following the above procedures each child was individually administered his own new set of 14 paired items (Form B).

Test for Generalization and Stability of Altered Delay Patterns. About 4 weeks after the experimental treatments all Ss were readministered the initial set of 14 items within their classroom settings utilizing the same group procedure described earlier. The same E who had conducted the pre-experimental measurement of delay responses presided over the follow-up assessment. Considering the relatively long temporal intervals separating the various phases of the study, the variation in Es, and the fact that in the terminal assessment children recorded their preferences privately in the context of their natural classroom situation, it was assumed that the follow-up data would provide a particularly stringent test of both the generality and the stability of modeling effects.

Dependent Measures. Change in the *S*'s behavior was measured in terms of the relative number of delayed responses produced by the low-delay groups and conversely, the number of immediate responses displayed by children in the high-delay groups, at each of the three phases of the experiment.

RESULTS AND DISCUSSION

Figure 2 shows the mean percentage of immediate-reward responses produced by the high-delay children on each of the test periods as a function of treatment conditions.

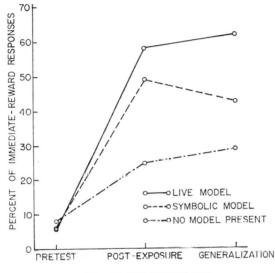

FIG. 2. Mean percentage of immediate-reward responses by high delay children on each of three test periods for each of three experimental conditions.

Analysis of variance of these data revealed that the main effects of modeling and experimental phases were highly significant sources of variance. In addition, the two modeling procedures proved to be differentially effective at the immediate postexposure and the later generalization phases of the experiment. Further comparisons by the *t* test of pairs of means across experimental phases showed that high-delay children in all three conditions not only altered significantly their delay-of-reward behavior in favor of immediate gratification, but also maintained the response changes long after the experimental interventions.

Moreover, comparisons between groups at each of the test phases revealed that children who had been presented either live or symbolic models differed substantially in their postexposure delay behavior from the no-model controls, with the live-model condition yielding the greatest differences. It should be noted that while the live and symbolic models were equally effective within the immediate social-influence setting, the changes in delay responses induced by the live model were significantly more stable over time. This is shown in the finding that high-delay children who had observed the live model continued to display in the generalization test a significantly higher level of immediate-reward responses than children in either the symbolic model or the control groups, which did not differ significantly from each other.

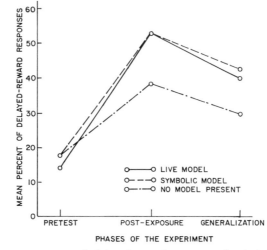

Fig. 3. Mean percentage of delayed-reward responses by low-delay children on each of three test periods for each of three experimental conditions.

The corresponding set of data for low-delay children exposed to models exhibiting a preference for more valued delayed reinforcers is presented graphically in Fig. 3. Analysis of variance of these scores revealed that the children's willingness to delay gratification increased substantially across the phases of the experiment.

Although the over-all differences among the three experimental groups were not of statistically significant magnitude, it was evident from supplementary analyses that the two conditions employing modeling procedures were chief contributors to the obtained increases in delay behavior. Within-treatment comparisons disclosed that both forms of modeling produced highly significant temporary and long-term increases in self-imposed delay of reward. On the other hand, although the no-model control Ss exhibited a temporary change, their subsequently assessed delay behavior did not differ significantly from their pre-experimental level. In contrast to the findings based on the high-delay children, however, the low-delay Ss were not differentially affected by the live as compared with the symbolic model. Another noteworthy difference between the two sets of data is the finding that experimentally induced immediate-reward responses generally remained more stable over time than did self-imposed delay behavior.

The results of this investigation provide further support for the influential role of modeling variables in the social transmission of self-controlling responses. Children who had shown a predominantly delayed-reward pattern displayed an increased preference for immediate and less valued rewards as a function of observing models who favored immediate gratification; conversely, Ss who had exhibited a marked disposition toward immediate rewards increased and maintained their willingness to wait for more highly valued delayed reinforcers following exposure to models displaying high-delay behavior.

Both forms of modeling procedures were essentially equally efficacious within the immediate social-influence setting. With high-delay children, however, the symbolic model yielded relatively weaker long-term effects. There are several possible explanations for the fact that similar long-term differences between modeling conditions were not obtained in the findings for low-delay Ss. This discrepancy may partly reflect the effects of differential reinforcement contingencies characteristically associated with high- and low-delay behavior. In social training in our culture self-imposed delay-of-reward behavior is actively modeled, encouraged, and generously rewarded by socialization agents, whereas immediate self-gratification is negatively reinforced on many occasions. To the extent that adoption by high-delay children of immediate self-gratification responses requires some reduction of previously established inhibition, it would be expected that actual observation of a moderately prestigeful adult exhibiting low-delay behavior would have stronger disinhibitory cue value than a verbal description of his responses. This factor, if operative, would suggest that predictions about the relative efficacy of live and symbolic models should consider not only the number and clarity of modeling cues associated with different modes of presentation, but also the possibly greater inhibitory or disinhibitory influence of performances by live models.

An alternative explanation, and one that accounts for other obtained differences, is in terms of the temporal variations in reinforcement invariably associated with immediate and delayed reward responses. There is considerable empirical evidence that behavior can be more effectively maintained by immediate reinforcement than by delayed re-

wards (Renner, 1964). Consequently, self-imposed delay behavior, which
is accompanied by less favorable reinforcement conditions, would be
harder to establish and even more difficult to maintain in the absence
of intervening positive reinforcements. This interpretation would help
to explain both the greater stability of changes in immediate compared
with delayed-reward behavior among Ss in the no-model conditions and
the larger decrement in delay responses on the generalization test among
Ss whose behavior was being altered in the direction of delayed gratification. Although Ss who were exposed to high-delay models continued to
exhibit a higher level of delay behavior than they displayed in the pre-
experimental phase, their difficulty in maintaining the newly acquired
behavior in the prolonged absence of the model may have reduced the
possibility of obtaining significant long-term differences between modeling
conditions. These over-all findings point to the necessity for supporting
newly established self-control behavior, particularly when it is associated
with less optimal reinforcement conditions, as in the case of self-imposed
denial of readily available rewarding resources.

The results of this study also provide an interesting contrast between
traditional psychoanalytically based theories of personality and those
derived from principles of social learning. According to the psychoanalytic theory of delay behavior (Singer, 1955; Freud, 1911), aroused im-
pulses press for immediate discharge of tension through overt motoric
activity. As a function of repeated association of tension reduction with
goal objects, and development of greater ego organization, absence or
imposed delay of satisfying objects results in the substitution of hallucinatory satisfactions, and other thought processes that convert free
cathexes into "bound cathexes." The capacity to delay or inhibit motor
discharge by substituting cathected ideational respresentations presumably reflects the gradual shift from primary-process activity to reality-
oriented secondary-process thinking.

The psychoanalytic approach thus leads one to seek determinants of
delay behavior in terms of hypothetical internal events in the form of
ego organizations and energy-binding ideations. In contrast, social-learn-
ing theory, as illustrated in the present experiments, views manipulable
social-stimulus events as the critical determinants of self-controlling behavior.

V. Effects of Discrepancies between Observed and Imposed Reward Criteria on Their Acquisition and Transmission

Thus far the focus has been on only one aspect of delay of reward.
Another related critical aspect of self-control is the individual's own
self-administration and regulation of the rewards and punishments which

are available to him without external constraints. Human beings evaluate their own performance and frequently set standards which determine, in part, the conditions under which they self-administer or withhold numerous readily available gratifications and a multitude of self-punishments. Failure to meet widely varying self-imposed performance standards often results in self-denial or even harsher self-punishment whereas attainment of difficult criteria more typically leads to liberal self-reward and a variety of self-congratulatory responses. Although research concentrating on infrahuman beings may find it easy to neglect this phenomenon, it is apparent that for man self-administered rewards constitute powerful incentives for learning and potent reinforcers for the maintenance of behavior patterns. In spite of the importance of self-reward as a human process there have been relatively few experimental investigations of its antecedents.

Kanfer and Marston (1963a) provide some support for the direct conditioning of "self-reinforcing responses"; they found that adults who were encouraged for judging their responses as accurate on an ambiguous noncontingent task increased their rate of self-reinforcement and rewarded themselves more frequently on a new learning task than those who were discouraged from judging their responses as accurate. The same authors also found that the frequency of self-reinforcement is partly dependent on such variables as the correctness of the individual's responses and the degree of similarity between the training and generalization tasks (Kanfer, Bradley & Marston, 1962; Kanfer & Marston, 1963b).

An effective means of influencing children to adopt particular self-reward criteria consists of exposing them to the criteria exhibited by models. It has been demonstrated that mere observation of a model's self-reward patterns, without direct reinforcement to the observer, can result in their adoption by the O even in the model's absence (Bandura & Kupers, 1964).

In life situations reward standards usually are transmitted by individuals who exhibit their own self-reward criteria and also reinforce the observer's adherence to particular criteria. The modeled and directly reinforced behaviors may not be congruent and the criteria used by social agents for administering rewards to themselves often are discrepant with the standards which they directly impose on others. Consider, for example, the father who tries to influence his child toward delay, self-denial, and work while he simultaneously and persistently indulges himself. Although frequent reference is made to the importance of "consistency" in child-rearing practices, usually this refers to consistency in the use of direct training techniques across different situations and the effects of consistency or discrepancy between direct training and modeling procedures remain unexplored. This study (Mischel & Liebert, 1966) therefore investigated the effects of discrepancies in the stringency of the self-reward criteria used by an adult and the standards imposed on a child.

Children participated with a female adult model in a task which seemingly required skill but on which scores were experimentally controlled. A plentiful supply of tokens which could be exchanged for rewards was available to both the model and the S. In one experimental group the model rewarded herself only for high performances but guided the S to reward himself for lower achievements; in a second condition the model rewarded herself for low performances but led the S to reward himself only for higher achievements; in the third group the model rewarded herself only for high performances and guided the child to reward himself only for equally high achievements. After the children had been exposed to these experimental procedures, measures were obtained of the self-reward patterns they displayed in the model's absence.

It was reasoned that the reward criteria adopted by Ss would be a function of both the criteria they observed a model use for herself and those she imposed on them directly. When the observed and imposed criteria were consistent, expectancies about the appropriate behavior would be clear and the criteria should be adopted readily. Therefore, greatest stringency would be shown by children who were held to a stringent standard and also observed a model who was stringent with herself. These children would be more likely to use higher standards for reward than either children who had received the same stringent direct training but observed a lenient model, or those who were permitted leniency themselves. Moreover, when the observed and imposed criteria were discrepant, the less stringent alternative would be adopted. When the criterion leading to more reward is the one that Ss have been directly trained to adopt, they should have little conflict about rewarding themselves generously in the model's absence and should maintain the lenient criterion to which they were trained. In contrast, those who had been trained to be stringent but had observed a more lenient model should be tempted to reward themselves more liberally when there were no external constraints. In the model's absence their behavior should reflect conflict about adopting the lower criteria yielding more frequent reward used by their own model and the more stringent standards which had been imposed on them. Therefore it was anticipated that Ss would adopt lenient criteria more frequently when they had been permitted greater leniency themselves than when they observed it in another.

The design also investigated the effects of the children's role on their self-administered reward schedules and on the criteria they imposed upon others, although a detailed presentation of this aspect is not given here. Briefly, after the child's interaction with the adult model, half the children became "demonstrators" of the game for another younger child, alternating with him for a series of trials, and thereafter performed alone on additional trials (Demonstrator-Performer or D-P sequence). Half the Ss participated in the reverse sequence, first performing alone and then alternating trials with a younger child to whom they demonstrated the game (Performer-Demonstrator or P-D sequence). Both sequences took place in the absence of the E as well as the model.

It is apparent from the above that the design permitted investigation of the effects of the independent variables not only on the acquisition of self-reward criteria but also on the transmission of these standards by Ss to others (the younger child) when the S controlled the available reinforcers. No differences in the criteria used by the S for himself and those he imposed on the other child were anticipated. That is, the same between-treatment differences predicted for self-reward criteria were expected for the transmission of these standards to another person. On the whole, this was indeed found. In this presentation only the main treatment effects will be discussed.

METHOD

Summary of Design

Each S was randomly assigned to one of three model-subject interactions. One third of the children observed stringent reward criteria modeled but were led to use lenient criteria; one third observed lenient reward criteria modeled but were led to use stringent criteria; the remainder observed a model who used stringent criteria for himself and applied the same criteria to the child. Thereafter, in the absence of the model, half the Ss in each group demonstrated the game to another younger child and then performed alone, whereas the other half went through the reverse sequence, first performing alone and then demonstrating.

Apparatus

The apparatus was a bowling game consisting of a miniature bowling alley with a 3-foot runway at the end of which there were seven signal lights. Each light was labeled with a score, the score of 5 occurring once whereas scores of 10, 15, and 20 each appeared twice. The lights and scores were displayed on an upright partition facing the bowler. A series of electronic relay switches, concealed in the machine, were preset for each S in order to control in a standardized manner the entire sequence of scores for all trials. This apparatus permitted all trials to occur in the absence of the *E* and the latter recorded all data from behind a one-way observation window. The target area was screened from the *S*'s view by shields which covered the terminal area of the runway and encircled the ostensible targets so that the *S* had no knowledge of whether or not the bowling balls were striking the target area and was dependent on the electric score signals for feedback. Pretesting indicated that the procedure appealed to the *S*s and no doubts were raised about its credibility.

Discrepancies between Modeled and Imposed Reward Criteria

The model-subject discrepancy treatments involved the following variations in the discrepancy of the scores for which the model rewarded herself and those for which she guided the *S* to reward himself. The reward consisted of small tokens (chips) which were abundantly available and which were described to the children as exchangeable for "valuable prizes" at the end of the experiment. These prizes actually consisted of small gifts (e.g., notebooks) given to all subjects upon completion of the study.

In the *stringent criterion modeled, lenient criterion imposed* treatment the model rewarded herself only for scores of 20 but led the *S* to reward himself for scores of 15 or 20 (*M* 20, *S* 15/20). Whenever the model's score was 20 she took a token and made approving comments such as, "That's a good score. That deserves a chip," or "I can be proud of that score. I should treat myself for that." In contrast, whenever her score was below the criterion of 20 she refrained from taking a token and commented with obvious self-disapproval, "That's not a very good score. That doesn't deserve a chip" or "Well, I can't be very proud of that. I can't treat myself for that low score." Using a fixed memorized script she addressed similar approving comments to the *S* whenever his score was either 15 or 20 and made parallel critical comments whenever his score was below 15.

In the *lenient criterion modeled, stringent criterion imposed* condition (*M* 15/20, *S* 20) the reward and disapproval pattern of the previous condition was reversed, the model rewarding herself for scores of 15 or 20 but rewarding the *S* for scores of 20 only.

In the *stringent criterion modeled, stringent criterion imposed* condition (*M* 20, *S* 20) the model displayed her self-reward pattern only for scores of 20 and likewise commented positively on the child's performance only when he obtained scores of 20, indicating for all other performances that they did not deserve a chip and showing dissatisfaction.

After both model and *S* completed 10 trials the model said she had to leave and did so, collecting her own chips with enthusiasm and noting that they would be exchanged now for valuable prizes.

Measures of Reward Patterns

The measures collected from Ss in both sequences were the scores for which self-reward occurred when performing alone (Self-reward when Performer); when demonstrating the game to another younger child (Self-reward when Demonstrator); as well as the scores for which the S rewarded the other child (Rewards Other). These were collected immediately after the child's interaction with the model but in the absence of both the model and E and were recorded by the latter through an observation window.

Results and Discussion

Figure 4 shows the percentage of Ss who administered rewards for scores below 20 in each treatment group in all model-absent phases of the experiment. Note that whether the child was a Performer first or a Demonstrator first did not appear to affect appreciably his reward criteria within each model-subject discrepancy treatment. Comparisons of Ss who rewarded for scores below 20 as opposed to scores of 20 only in the Performer-Demonstrator as opposed to the Demonstrator-Performer sequences within each discrepancy treatment yielded no p values approaching significance. Therefore, subsequent comparisons between discrepancy treatments combined Ss from both sequences.

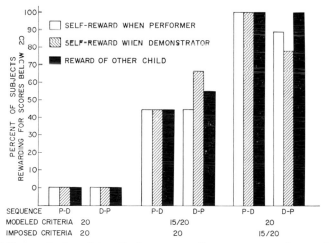

Fig. 4. Self-reward when S is a Performer or a Demonstrator, and reward of other child, as a function of the Performer-Demonstrator (P-D) or Demonstrator-Performer (D-P) sequence and the initial criteria exhibited by the model and imposed on S.

Comparisons of the discrepancy treatments for each phase of the experiment separately supported the hypotheses clearly. The greatest stringency was shown by Ss who observed a stringent model and were themselves held to the same stringent criterion (*M* 20, *S* 20). These children made reward contingent on a higher performance level more often than those who obtained identical direct training but from a model who used a more lenient criterion for her own self-reward (*M* 15/20, *S* 20).

Moreover, these differences held at each phase of the experiment: the treatments affected the *S*'s self-reward both as a performer and as a demonstrator as well as the reward criteria he imposed on the younger child when demonstrating the game to him. The effects resulted in *p* values less then .01 in all but one instance.

The results of this experiment show that patterns of self-reinforcement may be affected jointly by the criteria displayed by social models and the standards directly imposed on the *O*, with the resultant behavior determined by a predictable interaction of both factors. The hypothesized effects of discrepancies and consistency between observed and imposed reward criteria received strong support. As predicted, when modeled and imposed reinforcement criteria were of different stringency, Ss adopted the more lenient alternative for themselves and this occurred more frequently when they were permitted self-reward for a relatively low standard but observed a model rewarding herself only for higher achievements than when they were held to stringent criteria while observing a model displaying a more lenient self-reward pattern. Subjects in both these conditions adopted more lenient self-reward patterns than those who were held to a stringent self-reward criterion and observed the model using an equally stringent reward schedule for herself. Most interesting is the fact that Ss who were trained on a stringent criterion by a model who was similarly stringent with herself adopted and transmitted more stringent reward criteria than those who received the identical direct training but from a model who exhibited greater leniency in her own self-reward.

When the modeled and imposed standards were consistent they were adopted in the model's absence without a single deviation in spite of the relative stringency of the criterion and the desirability of the rewards which were freely available for self-administration without external constraints. The fact that in the present study children who witnessed a model rewarding herself for a high standard and who were led to use the same high criterion for themselves adopted it in her absence without any deviations reflects the potency of combining modeling procedures with direct behavior guidance and reinforcement. The maintenance of the predicted reward patterns in the absence of all external restraints further indicates that the variables studied in this experiment are determinants of behaviors frequently used as indices of self-control or "internalization."

The predicted effects of the model-subject discrepancy treatments were so strong, both when the modeled and imposed behaviors were identical, and when the S was permitted lenient self-reward but observed the model rewarding herself stringently, that there was virtually no variance in the S's subsequent behavior. However, when the child was held to a stringent criterion but observed a model who was lenient with herself, approximately half the children adopted and transmitted the stringent standards imposed on them and half used the more liberal criteria that they had observed. The prediction and manipulation of behavior in this kind of discrepancy condition appears intriguing for future research and an investigation is planned to isolate some of the determinants affecting whether the individual adheres to the more self-denying schedule which was imposed on him or adopts the more generous patterns which he observed exhibited by a social agent. In addition to individual differences in previous social learning histories, such factors as the attributes of the model, including his similarity to the S, and the S's role seem to be relevant variables.

In the present experiment, data on the children's willingness to delay immediate but less valued gratification for the sake of more valued but delayed rewards, elicited in simple, real choice situations, were collected in the manner described previously. No relationships approaching significance were found between this aspect of self-control and the children's behavior following the discrepancy treatments. Although certainly not definitive, this finding is in accord with numerous other recent investigations on self-control in pointing to the specificity of different aspects of self-control behavior and suggesting that such behaviors as delay of gratification and the regulation of self-reward schedules for particular performance contingencies may be relatively independent and governed by different antecedents without any underlying unitary moral agency (Aronfreed, 1964; Bandura & Walters, 1963).

The over-all findings of this experiment appear to have clear implications for socialization practices and therapy. The study demonstrated that consistency in the standards which an individual is trained to use for himself, and those he observes used by social agents, facilitates the adoption and transmission of these standards, and pointed to some of the variables that can determine the performance levels which the person adopts for his own self-reward and for rewarding others. Many cultural and individual differences reflect differences in the kinds and liberalness of criteria used for the administration of rewards and punishments. There is abundant clinical evidence that for troubled individuals the inappropriate regulation of self-administered rewards and punishments often is a central problem. A host of deviant behavior patterns, such as psychopathy, masochism, depression, sadism, etc., may be construed as reflecting the inappropriate regulation of self-administered rewards and punishments and the imposition of excessively harsh or generous standards on other people. The isolation of antecedents of this aspect of self-control therefore seems to have particular importance.

VI. Some Determinants of the Rehearsal and Transmission of Neutral and Aversive Behaviors

The next study examined the manner in which the characteristics of a social agent, manifested in his interactions with a child, affect the degree to which his behaviors are adopted by the child when the latter is both the observer and the object of the agent's behaviors. The behaviors of main interest were constraints or punishments, such as delay-of-reward periods imposed by the agent with direct aversive consequences for the child.

It has been commonly noted, anecdotally and in clinical observation, that individuals rehearse and transmit to others behaviors which had aversive consequences for them. For example, parents often claim they behave, albeit unwillingly, toward their children in ways similar to those that produced pain for them when followed by their own parents. At present the factors governing the reproduction of a model's novel behaviors which were aversive to the individual in his interactions with that model remain ambiguous. Several theories (e.g., Maccoby, 1959; Sears, 1957; Whiting & Child, 1953), including the well-known theory of "identification with the aggressor" (Bettelheim, 1943; A. Freud, 1946), have been invoked to account for this reproduction and transmission of social punishments, and the difficulties of a secondary reinforcement interpretation have been noted (e.g., Aronfreed, 1964). Relevant data, however, have been primarily clinical and informal and the very occurrence of the phenomenon itself has been rarely demonstrated in laboratory research.

There is considerable evidence that the characteristics of the model, such as his rewardingness and power or control over resources, affect the extent to which some of his displayed behaviors are imitated by an observer (e.g., Mussen & Distler, 1959; Bandura & Huston, 1961). The unresolved question is whether the characteristics of the model can affect the reproduction of social punishments, such as imposed delay of reward, which the individual not only observed but also directly received from the model.

The two characteristics of the model which were manipulated in the present study are considered determinants of imitation in several prominent theories of identification. The conceptualization of Sears (1957), Mowrer (1950), and Whiting and Child (1953) all give the rewarding characteristics of the model a central role for the development of identification. For example, in Mowrer's (1950) formulations, if the model's behavorial attributes are paired with positive reinforcement they acquire secondary reinforcing properties on the basis of classical conditioning and, through stimulus generalization also become rewarding when performed by the child. After the model's behaviors have been paired with positive reinforcement the child can self-administer secondary reinforcers by reproducing components of the behavior. In addition, Maccoby (1959) and Mussen and Distler (1959) focus on the model's control of resources as well as his rewardingness, stressing the model's social power as the characteristic which enhances identification. Maccoby, for example, suggested that the control exercised by a model over resources important for the needs of the child will determine the amount of role practice in which the child engages. He will rehearse both the rewarding *and* the punishing characteristics of the model since both are relevant to him in guiding his plans about future actions. Because these behaviors have been well rehearsed they are more likely to be performed when relevant eliciting stimuli evoke them by contiguity.

In this study (Mischel & Grusec, 1966) rewardingness was manipulated by varying the degree to which the model provided the child with both material and social noncontingent reward. Power or control over both positive and negative outcomes was manipulated cognitively by varying the model's role. For half the children the model was introduced as a visiting teacher who would never reappear while for the other half she was introduced as the child's new teacher.

Thus, we investigated the effects of the model's rewardingness or use of noncontingent reinforcement, and his control over the S's future resources, on the degree to which behaviors displayed by the model without direct consequences for the S ("neutral" behaviors) and those directed at the S with negative consequences for him ("aversive" behaviors) are rehearsed and transmitted. The main purposes of this study were to demonstrate the occurrence of both rehearsal and transmission of aversive behavior; to investigate the relative effectiveness of noncontingent reinforcement by the model and his control over future resources in producing this rehearsal and transmission; and to compare the determinants of the rehearsal and transmission of such initially aversive behaviors with those of neutral behaviors displayed by the model.

Preschool children were exposed to an adult female whose non-contingent rewardingness and future control over the child were varied. Thereafter, the children participated with the model in a "special game" which involved playing with a cash register, making change with play coins and bills, etc. The model included the following behaviors during this interaction: (1) she was aversive to the child in novel ways ("aversive" behavior) and (2) she exhibited novel behaviors with no direct reinforcement consequences for the child ("neutral" behaviors). More specifically, the aversive acts consisted of imposing delay of reward, removal of reward, and criticism. The modeling of neutral behaviors consisted of emitting distinctive verbal and motor behaviors (e.g., marching around the room while saying, "March! March! March!"). The aversive behaviors were designed to have direct negative consequences for the S whereas the neutral behaviors were merely modeled without direct reinforcement consequences for him. In the former instances the child was the object of the behavior whereas in the latter he was only the observer of the displayed behaviors. Following these treatments the S's task was to show another person who was dressed as a clown how to play the cash register game in the model's absence. Measures were taken of the rehearsal and reproduction of novel behaviors in the model's presence and of the transmission of neutral and aversive behaviors to the "clown" in her absence.

In accord with the above-mentioned theories of identification which stress both the model's rewardingness and power, it was anticipated that the reproduction of both neutral and aversive behaviors would be more frequent when the model's noncontingent reinforcement was high than when it was low. The combination of noncontingent reinforcement and future control over resources was expected to result in the most frequent reproduction of the model's behaviors. Conversely, it was expected that reproduction would be least frequent when the combination of non-contingent reinforcement and future control was lowest.[3] The other combinations of rewardingness and control were expected to fall between these extremes, with no prediction made concerning their relative strength.

---

[3] These predictions are consistent with an expectancy-reward value conceptualization to the extent that in our culture social learning experiences generate expectancies that emulating the behaviors of individuals who control and dispense valuable resources, and who have power, is likely to lead to positive consequences for the imitator. Likewise, the reward value of particular behaviors may be enhanced or decreased by the social characteristics of the agent who displays them.

METHOD

Subjects

The Ss were 56 Stanford nursery school children ranging in age from 37 months to 64 months with a mean age of 52 months. There were 31 boys and 25 girls and the same adult female E was used with all children. The children were assigned randomly to each treatment, with separate assignments for each sex to assure that similar proportions of boys and girls were included in each condition.

The Model's Rewardingness and Control

Four manipulations were used to vary the model's rewardingness and control:

High Noncontingent Reward (High Reward). Attractive toys were available (e.g., a bowling set, battery-operated cars and planes, musical tops, hand puppets) and the model and S played together with them, the model showing interest, affection, and warmth, and frequently praising the child. In addition, she dispensed attractive stickers and cookies to the child. The intent was to establish the model as noncontingently rewarding, with highly attractive resources at her disposal. These operations were similar to those usually labeled "nurturance" (e.g., Bandura & Huston, 1961).

Low Noncontingent Reward (Low Reward). There were less attractive toys available (e.g., coloring books, used crayons, broken toys) and the model informed the child that she had some work to complete saying, "I don't have too many toys here, but you can play with them for awhile. I'll be right over here working [pointing to corner of room]." The model responded minimally but pleasantly to attention bids, indicating that she had to finish her work.

High Future Control (High Control). The model structured her role as that of the child's new nursery school teacher, and she commented that they would therefore be seeing a lot of each other.

Low Future Control (Low Control). The model structured her role as that of a visiting teacher who was leaving the nursery school in an hour to take the bus back home to Milwaukee. She commented that they would therefore not be seeing each other again.

Experimental Groups

Each of the four experimental treatment groups contained 14 children and consisted of these combinations of the above-described operations: High Reward–High Control; High Reward–Low Control; Low Reward–High Control; Low Reward–Low Control. Each involved a 20-min inter-

action between the adult and child. There were six girls and eight boys
in each group except the Low Reward–High Future Control condition in
which there were seven boys and seven girls.

Procedure

The E introduced herself to the child, identifying herself either as his
new nursery school teacher or as a visiting teacher who was leaving that
same day (High or Low Control). The 20-min play session followed in
which she displayed either High or Low Reward behavior. The E again
reminded the S of her future role, and then took him to another experimental room to "play a special game with a toy cash register." On enter-
ing the room the S was shown a large container of toys and was allowed
to select the one he wanted most. This toy was placed in a bag and given
to the child and he was told that he could take it home.

Presentation of Neutral and Aversive Behavior

The E and S seated themselves in front of the toy cash register. The
game involved playing store with a cash register, making change, opening
and closing the register drawer, hitting the register keys, etc. During the
game, all Ss were exposed to the following two kinds of behaviors:
(1) Neutral behaviors. The model hit a key on the cash register and said
"Bop," marched around the table saying, "March, march, march, march,
march," and repeated this sequence two more times. (2) Aversive behaviors. (a) Imposed delay. When the S touched the cash register for the
first time, the model immediately said that if one wants to play with
anything badly enough one ought to be able to wait for it, and instructed
the S to sit still with his hands in his lap until she finished counting.
She then very slowly and methodically repeated the numbers "one, two,
three" fifteen times. (b) Criticism and removal of reward. The cash register was constructed so that, unknown to the S, the model could make the
drawer come all the way out when it was opened, giving the appearance
that it was broken. When this happened, as the S "broke" the drawer the
E exclaimed sharply, "Oh my! Do you know what this makes you? It
makes you a storewrecker, and when you're a storewrecker, you lose your
toy." She then removed the toy the child had received previously, saying
sternly "You try not to be a storewrecker again."

The model performed the neutral behaviors and the counting at two
different times in the course of playing cash register with the child
whereas the drawer was broken once. The children's reactions to the
aversive behaviors varied from tears to silent but obvious tension and
indicated that the behaviors had painful consequences for them. This

was further substantiated by the fact that seven Ss (not included in the total N) had to be eliminated because they cried and became too upset to continue participating. This occurred with similar frequency across treatment conditions. At the conclusion of the learning session the child was left alone to play with the cash register in the experimental room for 3 minutes, during which he was observed through a one-way mirror by the E and her confederate. The purpose of this interval was to reduce any immediate emotional arousal stemming from the interaction and to observe any additional practice of the model's behaviors during her absence.

Transmission

The E returned to the experimental room and led the S back to the room in which the play session had taken place. She informed him that, as a special treat, he was going to be allowed to show someone else how to play the cash register game. All the events that had occurred during the game, including the neutral and negative behaviors, were reviewed verbally by the experimenter who also reminded the child again of her future role (High or Low Control). The S was told that the person he was going to teach was a girl dressed up as a clown. The adult and child then returned to the experimental room where an adult female experimental confederate was seated in front of the cash register. The confederate was dressed as a clown to disinhibit children who might be reluctant to relate with a strange adult in novel and aversive ways. As the S and the model came into the room the clown began to play with the cash register. The model playfully tapped the clown's hand and told her not to play until she was told what to do by the S. The model then left the S and clown together, and observed them through a one-way mirror in an adjoining room.

The clown behaved in a pleasant way to the S, nodding and bowing occasionally. When asked any questions about her background she answered minimally, e.g., she was just pretending to be a clown, she lived down the road, she didn't have any age when she was a clown. If the S did not immediately show the clown how to play, the clown attempted twice to elicit this behavior by saying, "Can you show me what to do," and "I really want to learn how to play." If the S still made no response the clown began to play with the cash register and money by herself. Always, in the course of the transmission session, the clown broke the drawer and exclaimed, "Oh look what happened!" When the S stopped demonstrating the clown said, after 10 seconds had elapsed, "Is there anything else? Can you show me what else to do?"

Measures of Rehearsal and Transmission

"Behavior rehearsal" refers to reproduction of any aspects of the model's distinctive neutral or aversive behaviors, either in her presence while she participated with the children in the cash register game or during the interval in which the child was alone before his interaction with the clown. "Behavior transmission" was scored when the S enacted any aspects of the model's neutral or aversive behaviors directly toward the clown while showing him the game. Because the referents for behavior rehearsal and transmission involved the presence or absence of clear overt behaviors (e.g., marching, counting) scoring was unambiguous. Independent scoring was done by the E and the confederate who served as clown and yielded perfect agreement with only one exception. In the transmission phase the confederate recorded her independent scoring of the child's behavior at the end of her interaction with him. After the experimental procedure was completed each child obtained toys and warm approval for his performance in a brief play session.

RESULTS AND DISCUSSION

Twenty-six children, or almost 50% of the total, did not rehearse or transmit either neutral or aversive behaviors. The percentage of children in each treatment condition who reproduced none of the model's behaviors was 21 in the High Reward–High Control group, 50 in the High Reward–Low Control group, 64 in the Low Reward–High Control group, and 50 in the Low Reward–Low Control group. Because of this highly skewed distribution the data were analyzed with chi-square tests. Inspection of the data for sex differences indicated no trends and scores for males and females were therefore combined. Chi-square comparisons between treatment conditions were computed separately for neutral and aversive behaviors and for behavior rehearsal and behavior transmission. In view of the lack of appropriate eliciting stimuli during the rehearsal phase it was not expected that "storewrecker" would be repeated and indeed only one child did so, all other rehearsals of aversive behaviors consisting of slowly counting "one, two, three," aloud in the manner modeled by the E during the imposed delay periods. In contrast, during the transmission phase, children called the clown a storewrecker and imposed delay periods on him by counting repetitiously with approximately equal frequency. With the exception of the virtual absence of "storewrecker" responses during rehearsal, inspection of the data for reproduction of each separate aspect of the model's neutral behaviors on the one hand, and her aversive behaviors on the other, revealed no systematic pattern differences within these two classes of behavior. There-

fore these separate aspects were combined and the four final scores assigned to each S indicated the presence or absence of imitative neutral
behavior, and imitative aversive behaviors, respectively, computed for
the rehearsal phase and the transmission phase separately.

Figure 5 shows the number of Ss in each treatment condition who
rehearsed neutral and aversive behaviors. Chi-square tests comparing the
relevant treatment groups and treatment combinations on rehearsal of
each class of behavior showed that significantly more Ss rehearsed both
aversive and neutral behaviors when the model was both highly rewarding and had future control than when her rewardingness and control
were low (all tests one-tailed).

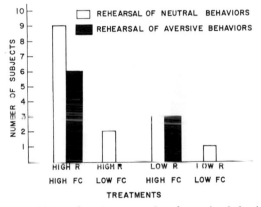

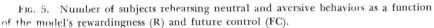

FIG. 5.   Number of subjects rehearsing neutral and aversive behaviors as a function
of the model's rewardingness (R) and future control (FC).

Comparisons of the two High Control groups showed that rewardingness significantly affected the rehearsal of neutral but not aversive
behavior, although the trend was in the same direction. That is, with
high control, high as opposed to low rewardingness produced greater
rehearsal of neutral behavior but the effect was not significant for aversive
behavior. Likewise, significantly more Ss in the two High Reward groups
combined rehearsed neutral, but not aversive, behaviors than in the two
Low Reward conditions combined.

In the High Reward–High Control group, significantly more Ss rehearsed both aversive and neutral behaviors than in the High Reward–
Low Control group; that is, with equally high rewardingness, high as
opposed to low control produced greater rehearsal of both aversive and
neutral behavior. The potency of future control, with reward constant,
is further demonstrated by the fact that, as predicted, significantly more
children in the two High Control groups combined rehearsed both

aversive and neutral behaviors than in the two Low Control conditions combined. Thus, rewardingness significantly increased the rehearsal of neutral but not aversive behaviors whereas control affected the rehearsal of both aversive and neutral behaviors. It is striking that in the two low control treatments not a single S rehearsed aversive behavior (Fig. 5).

It should also be noted that when either reward or control was low the other variable did not produce significant differences in the rehearsal of either aversive or neutral behaviors. That is, when the model's rewardingness was low, differences in her control did not affect behavior rehearsal and, conversely, when her control of the child's future was low, variations in her rewardingness did not result in significant differences

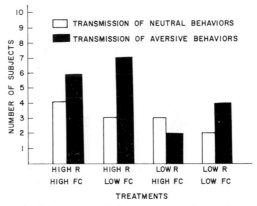

Fig. 6. Number of subjects transmitting neutral and aversive behaviors as a function of the model's rewardingness (R) and future control (FC).

in behavior rehearsal. Likewise, there were no significant differences in behavior rehearsal between treatments in which either reward or control was high when the other variable was low and the condition in which both reward and control were low. If it were possible to measure an interaction effect in these data, it would probably be sizable.

The number of Ss in each group who transmitted neutral and aversive behaviors to the clown is shown in Fig. 6. Comparison of the combined High Reward conditions with the combined Low Reward groups showed that the model's rewardingness led to greater transmission of aversive behaviors but did not affect the transmission of neutral behaviors. The model's future control did not affect the extent to which the Ss transmitted any of her behaviors. Likewise, the condition in which the model was both rewarding and had high control did not produce more behavior transmission than the treatment in which the model's rewardingness and control were both low.

Summarizing, the results demonstrate that observed behaviors could be reproduced and transmitted to others without external reinforcement for their performance, even when the observer was the object of the modeled behaviors and received aversive consequences from them. Indeed, the percentage of aversive behavior transmitted (34) exceeded the percentage of neutral behavior transmitted (21). Moreover, the extent to which the model's behaviors were reproduced was affected by her rewardingness or use of noncontingent reinforcement and her future control over the S.

These results support theoretical formulations stressing the rewardingness of the model and his power as determinants of the degree to which his behavior is adopted and indicate that both variables are useful for an adequate theory of imitation. The findings indicate, however, that these two variables have somewhat different effects as a function of the type of behavior displayed by the model and the stimulus situation in which the S reproduces it. Reward and control appear to interact in their effects on the *rehearsal* of neutral behavior. Aversive behaviors were rehearsed only when the model had high control, and even with a highly rewarding model not a single child rehearsed them if the model's control was low. Both neutral and aversive behavior rehearsal was rare in all conditions in which either reward or control was low (see Fig. 5). Indeed, when reward was low variations in control did not affect behavior rehearsal; conversely, when control was low variations in reward did not produce differences in rehearsal. The fact that the differences produced in behavior rehearsal by one variable were enhanced by the presence of the other suggests that reward from the model may be a necessary condition for the effectiveness of his control and likewise that a rewarding model who has little control over the S's future resources is no more effective than one who is not rewarding and does not have control.

However, the model's rewardingness, rather than his future control, was the only variable affecting the *transmission* of aversive behaviors. Children who had been exposed to a noncontingently rewarding model transmitted components of her aversive behavior to another person more frequently than those who had received little noncontingent reinforcement. Although not impressively strong, this result was significant, whereas there was no indication that the model's future control over the child affected the extent to which he transmitted the model's behavior. Indeed, rewardingness and future control may have opposite effects on the transmission of aversive behavior and these antagonistic effects may have tended to cancel each other. Exposure to a noncontingently rewarding model may have disinhibited the children about transmitting aversive behaviors to another person, whereas exposure to a model who had great control over the child's future may have served to inhibit the transmission of such aggressive behavior, even in the physical absence of the model. Calling an adult, albeit one dressed as a clown, a "storewrecker" and making him wait while the child repetitiously counts "one, two, three" is unlikely to incur the pleasure of a "new nursery school teacher" even if the same behavior was originally displayed by her. To be sure, the model was absent in this phase of the study but it is not unlikely that the child's behavior was influenced by expectations concerning what would please her. Subjects may also have feared that the clown would report their behavior to the teacher. Fear of negative consequences from the model for aggression to the other adult would inhibit children who believed the model was their new teacher more than those who believed she was about to leave their school forever. Although the differences were not significant, children transmitted aversive behaviors most frequently when the model had been rewarding and had low control and least frequently when she was not rewarding but had high control (see Fig. 6). These trends suggest that rewardingness disinhibited the transmission of aversive behaviors, while a powerful model (high control) inhibited them.

The results on transmission of aversive behaviors are in direct opposition to those anticipated by theories of defensive identification with the aggressor. Such formulations predict that the punitive behaviors displayed by a highly powerful, and thus potentially threatening, model would be transmitted most frequently. Instead, the data indicate that such transmission was facilitated by the model's rewardingness, irrespective of her control over the S. The effects of high control when the model himself strongly encourages and disinhibits the Ss about transmitting punitive behaviors remain unknown and merit investigation.

An attempt was made in the present study to determine whether the two variables of rewardingness and control affect only the child's performance of a model's behavior or whether they affect the acquisition or learning of those behaviors. If the obtained treatment effects were due to differences in learning these were probably mediated by differences in the amount of attention given the model as a function of her manipulated social characteristics. It is plausible that a new teacher or rewarding adult was more closely observed than a stranger or nonrewarding adult. Immediately after the transmission phase the child was asked by both the model and the clown to recall what had happened when the model had first showed him how to play store. For each item of the model's behavior which the child correctly recalled he was given an attractive sticker and warmly praised. There were no differences between the groups in the number of children recalling either aversive or neutral behaviors, although there was a slight, but not significant, trend for more children in the Low Reward–High Control group to recall neutral behavior. These data were considered unsatisfactory, however, since many of the children who reproduced behavior did not recall it. This was true of 40% of the children with respect to aversive behavior and 50% of the children with respect to neutral behavior. In spite of their obvious inadequacy as a measure of total learning it is clear from these data that the behaviors which the children learned considerably exceeded those which they performed. Thus 21% of the Ss recalled aspects of the model's aversive behavior that they did not perform while 25% recalled aspects of the model's neutral behavior that they did not perform. In addition, of the 26 Ss who performed none of the model's behaviors only 11 were unable to recall any of her behaviors. The discrepancy between performed and acquired behaviors was most striking in the Low Reward–High Control group. Whereas only five Ss performed aspects of the model's behavior, six who did not perform it recalled it. The deficiencies of the measure prevent firm conclusions but these data suggest that the obtained differences between the experimental groups may reflect differences in performance and not necessarily in acquisition.

A recent follow-up study (Grusec & Mischel, 1966) was conducted to clarify this. Nursery school children were exposed to an interaction with a model who was either high or low in both rewardingness and future control. The model then proceeded to enact both neutral and aversive behaviors, using procedures similar to those employed in the above study. Thereafter the children were immediately tested for the degree to which they had learned the model's behaviors. This acquisition test was conducted by a female confederate who offered attractive rewards to the child for reproducing the model's behaviors. The results indicated a significant difference between groups in the degree to which they had learned all aspects of the model's behavior. The behaviors of the rewarding model with high control over the child were learned to a greater degree than those of the model who was low in rewardingness and control. These findings suggest that the characteristics of the model affect the degree to which the O attends to his behaviors and influence the acquisition as well as the performance of the behaviors he displays.

VII. Summary

Our earlier investigations into the correlates of voluntary delay of reward provided the bases for reasonably meaningful direct measures of delay behavior and demonstrated systematic relationships between the willingness to defer immediate reward for the sake of delayed but more valuable consequences and a variety of other measures usually subsumed under an ego strength construct. The more recent experimental investigations presented in this paper pointed to some of the variables that control this behavior and that can be used to modify it.

The first study investigated the effects of situational and generalized expectancies for success on choices of immediate, less-valuable, noncontingent rewards as opposed to more valuable contingent rewards. Measures of generalized expectancy for success were administered to eighth-grade boys who later worked on a series of problems and obtained either Success, Failure, or No Information for performance. Thereafter, each subject chose between less valuable, noncontingent rewards and more valuable rewards whose attainment was contingent on successful solutions of problems varying in their similarity-dissimilarity to the original problems and/or an additional delay period. As predicted, contingent rewards were chosen more after success than failure and subjects discriminated between specific contingencies. The effects of situational success and failure tended to minimize the effects of generalized expectancies. However, in the absence of such situational success or failure experiences, generalized expectancies affected willingness to work and wait for larger rewards. Thus, children with low generalized expectancies for success who received no information about their performance behaved like those with similarly low generalized expectancies who had obtained failure. Following failure, generalized expectancies for success affected willingness to wait for large rewards even when their attainment was independent of performance.

The next experiment investigated the manner in which expectancies for ultimately obtaining a blocked or delayed reward in a frustration situation affect the value of the reward. Children viewed a film which was interrupted near the climax on the pretext of a damaged fuse. The probability that the film could be resumed was 1, .5, or 0. Measures of the film's value were administered before and after the interruption. Thereafter, the fuse was "fixed" and all subjects saw the remainder of the film, with final value ratings obtained at the end. The hypothesis that the nonavailability of a reward increases its value was supported. Subjects who were given a zero probability for seeing the remainder of the film increased their evaluation of it more than those in the other groups, and this increase was maintained even after the entire film was shown. Thus, in an imposed delay of reward situation, the nonattainability of a reward may increase its value. In contrast, in voluntary delay of reward situations, in which subjects are given choices between immediate or delayed rewards, willingness to delay rewards is a positive linear function of the probability for attaining the delayed reward.

The third study provided a comparative test of the relative efficacy of live and symbolic models for modifying delay-of-reward behavior. Groups of children with marked preferences for either immediate but less valued rewards, or more valuable delayed reinforcers, were assigned randomly to one of three experimental conditions. One group observed live models who exhibited delay behavior that was counter to the children's pattern; a second group was presented essentially the same modeling cues except in symbolic verbal form, while a third group had no exposure to any models. Changes in the subjects' delay-of-reward behavior were measured immediately following exposure to the modeling procedures and reassessed approximately 1 month later within a different stimulus situation. Both live and symbolic models produced substantial modification in delay-of-reward behavior within the immediate social-influence setting, but the changes induced through symbolic models were less stable over time.

The fourth experiment investigated the effects of discrepancies between the self-reward criteria modeled by an adult (model) and those he imposed upon a child (subject) on the latter's adoption of self-reward criteria and transmission of reward standards to another younger child (O). The model and subject alternated turns in a bowling game with experimentally controlled scores and abundantly available rewards. There were three discrepancy treatments: The model rewarded himself only for high performances and guided the subject to do the same; he used a high criterion for his own self-reward but permitted the subject to reward himself more leniently; the model rewarded himself for low achievements but led the subject to reward himself only for high achievements. Thereafter the children continued the game in the model's absence, with free access to rewards. To examine role-taking effects, half the subjects in each treatment performed alone first and then demonstrated the game to O, with the sequence reversed for the remainder. As anticipated, reward schedules in the model's absence were most stringent when both the model and subject had initially adhered to a high criterion for self-reward and least when the subject had been permitted to reward himself for low achievements. Children who were trained to reward themselves only on a stringent criterion and observed the model reward himself similarly maintained more stringent schedules than those who had been given the same stringent direct training for self-reward but by a model who rewarded himself leniently. The criteria subjects imposed on O tended to be identical with those they imposed on themselves and role taking had only indirect effects.

A final experiment investigated the manner in which the social characteristics of a model affect the degree to which children rehearse and transmit his behaviors. These included neutral behaviors which the model merely displayed, although the focus was on aversive behaviors which involved his imposing delay periods on the subject and criticizing him directly. Preschool children interacted with an adult female model who was either rewarding or nonrewarding and whose control over the child's future resources was either high or low. Thereafter, the children participated with the model in a game during which she behaved toward the child in ways designed to be directly *aversive* for him (e. g., imposed delay of reward) and also displayed novel *neutral* behaviors (e.g., distinctive marching). Later, in the model's absence, an experimental confederate provided eliciting stimuli that permitted the subject to re-produce the model's behaviors. Measures were taken of the child's rehearsal of the model's neutral and aversive behaviors and of his trans-mission of these behaviors to the confederate. More children rehearsed the neutral behaviors of a rewarding than of a nonrewarding model and high as opposed to low control over the child's future resources resulted in greater rehearsal of both neutral and aversive behaviors. Rewarding-ness and control interacted in their effects on behavior rehearsal, and children rehearsed both neutral and aversive behaviors most frequently when the model was high in rewardingness and control and least fre-quently when both these variables were low. The transmission of aversive behaviors was increased by the model's initial rewardingness but not by her control. It was unclear whether the model's rewardingness and control affected only the child's willingness to adopt the model's be-haviors or also the extent to which those behaviors were learned by the child. A follow-up study suggested that the model's characteristics may affect the degree to which his behaviors are learned by the observer, presumably by affecting the degree to which the observer attends to them.

Acknowledgments

The studies reported here were supported by research grant M-06830 from the National Institutes of Health, United States Public Health Service. Complete de-scriptions of the five main experiments reported here are in the *Journal of Personality and Social Psychology*. Acknowledgment is due to that journal, and to my collaborators, for permission to reproduce here major portions of the original experimental papers. Thanks are also due to the administrators, teachers, and children who generously cooperated and participated in these studies.

References

Aronfreed, J. The origin of self-criticism. *Psychol. Rev.*, 1964, **71**, 193-218.

Aronson, E., & Carlsmith, M. C. Effect of severity of threat on the devaluation of forbidden behavior. *J. abnorm. soc. Psychol.*, 1963, **66**, 584-588.

Atkinson, J. W. Motivational determinants of risk-taking behavior. *Psychol. Rev.*, 1957, **64**, 359-372.

Baer, D. M., & Sherman, J. A. Reinforcement control of generalized imitation in young children. *J. exp. Child Psychol.*, 1964, **1**, 37-49.

Bandura, A., & Huston, Aletha C. Identification as a process of incidental learning. *J. abnorm. soc. Psychol.*, 1961, **63**, 311-318.

Bandura, A., & Kupers, Carol J. The transmission of self-reinforcement through modeling. *J. abnorm. soc. Psychol.*, 1964, **69**, 1-9.

Bandura, A., & Mischel, W. Modification of self-imposed delay of reward through exposure to live and symbolic models. *J. pers. soc. Psychol.*, 1965, **2**, 698-705.

Bandura, A., & Walters, R. *Social learning and personality development.* New York: Holt, 1963.

Bettelheim, B. Individual and mass behavior in extreme situations. *J. abnorm. soc. Psychol.*, 1943, **38**, 417-452.

Block, J., & Martin, B. Prediction of behavior of children under frustration. *J. abnorm. soc. Psychol.*, 1955, **51**, 281-285.

Carlsmith, M. C. Strength of expectancy: its determinants and effects. Unpublished doctoral dissertation, Harvard Univer., Cambridge, Massachusetts, 1962.

Edwards, W. The theory of decision making. *Psychol. Bull.*, 1954, **51**, 380-417.

Feather, N. T. Subjective probability and decision under uncertainty. *Psychol. Rev.*, 1959, **66**, 150-164.

Festinger, L. *A theory of cognitive dissonance.* Stanford, California: Stanford Univer. Press, 1957.

Freud, Anna. *The ego and the mechanisms of defense.* New York: International Univer., 1946.

Freud, S. Formulations regarding the two principles of mental functioning. 1911. *Collected Papers.* Vol. IV, pp. 13-21. New York: Basic Books, 1959.

Freud, S. *Beyond the pleasure principle.* New York: Boni & Liveright, 1922.

Grusec, Joan, & Mischel, W. The model's characteristics as determinants of social learning. *J. pers. soc. Psychol.*, 1966, in press.

Kanfer, F. H., & Marston, A. R. Determinants of self-reinforcement in human learning. *J. exp. Psychol.*, 1963, **66**, 245-254. (a)

Kanfer, F. H., & Marston, A. R. Conditioning of self-reinforcing responses: an analogue to self-confidence training. *Psychol. Rep.*, 1963, **13**, 63-70. (b)

Kanfer, F. H., Bradley, Marcia A., & Marston, A. R. Self-reinforcement as a function of degree of learning. *Psychol. Rep.*, 1962, **10**, 885-886.

Levine, M., Glass, H., & Meltzoff, J. The inhibition process, Rorschach human movement responses and intelligence. *J. consult. Psychol.*, 1957, **21**, 41-45.

Levine, M., Spivack, G., & Wight, B. The inhibition process, Rorschach human movement responses and intelligence: Some further data. *J. consult. Psychol.*, 1959, **23**, 306-312.

Lewin, K., Dembo, Tamara, Festinger, L., & Sears, P. S. Level of aspiration. In J. McV. Hunt (Ed.), *Personality and the behavior disorders.* New York: Ronald Press, 1944. Pp. 333-378.

Maccoby, Eleanor E. Role-taking in childhood and its consequences for social learning. *Child Develpm.*, 1959, **30**, 239-252.

Mahrer, A. R. The role of expectancy in delayed reinforcement. *J. exp. Psychol.*, 1956, **52**, 101-105.

Metzner, R. Work and delay of gratification. Unpublished Ph.D. Thesis, Harvard Univer., Cambridge, Massachusetts, 1962.

Mischel, Harriet. Trust and delay of gratification. Unpublished doctoral dissertation. Harvard Univer., Cambridge, Massachusetts, 1963.

Mischel, W. Preference for delayed reinforcement: An experimental study of a cultural observation. *J. abnorm. soc. Psychol.*, 1958, **56**, 57-61.

Mischel, W. Preference for delayed reinforcement and social responsibility. *J. abnorm. soc. Psychol.*, 1961, **62**, 1-7. (a)

Mischel, W. Delay of gratification, need for achievement, and acquiscence in another culture. *J. abnorm. soc. Psychol.*, 1961, **62**, 543-552. (b)

Mischel, W. Father-absence and delay of gratification: cross-cultural comparisons. *J. abnorm. soc. Psychol.*, 1961, **62**, 116-124. (c)

Mischel, W. Delay of gratification in choice situations. NIMH Progress Report (mimeo), Stanford Univer., Stanford, California, 1962.

Mischel, W., & Gilligan, Carol F. Delay of gratification, motivation for the prohibited gratification, and responses to temptation. *J. abnorm. soc. Psychol.*, 1964, **69**, 411-417.

Mischel, W., & Grusec, Joan. Determinants of the rehearsal and transmission of neutral and aversive behaviors. *J. pers. soc. Psychol.*, 1966, **3**, 197-205.

Mischel, W., & Grusec, Joan. The effects of probability and time on voluntary delay behavior. Unpublished paper, Stanford Univer., Stanford, California, 1965.

Mischel, W., & Liebert, R. M. Effects of discrepancies between observed and imposed reward criteria on their acquisition and transmission. *J. pers. soc. Psychol.*, 1966, **3**, 45-53.

Mischel, W., & Masters, J. C. Effects of probability of reward attainment on responses to frustration. *J. pers. soc. Psychol.*, 1966, **3**, 390-396.

Mischel, W., & Metzner, R. Preference for delayed reward as a function of age, intelligence and length of delay interval. *J. abnorm. soc. Psychol.*, 1962, **64**, 425-431.

Mischel, W., & Staub, E. The effects of expectancy on waiting and working for larger rewards. *J. pers. soc. Psychol.*, 1965, **2**, 625-633.

Mowrer, O. H. *Learning theory and personality dynamics.* New York: Ronald Press, 1950.

Mussen, P. H., & Distler, L. Masculinity, identification, and father-son relationships. *J. abnorm. soc. Psychol.*, 1959, **59**, 350-356.

Rapaport, D. *Organization and pathology of thought.* New York: Columbia Univer. Press, 1951.

Renner, K. E. Delay of reinforcement: a historical review. *Psychol. Bull.*, 1964, **61**, 341-361.

Rotter, J. B. *Social learning and clinical psychology.* Englewood Cliffs, New Jersey: Prentice-Hall, 1954.

Sears, R. R. Identification as a form of behavioral development. In D. B. Harris (Ed.), *The concept of development.* Minneapolis, Minnesota: Univer. of Minnesota Press, 1957. Pp. 149-161.

Singer, J. L. Delayed gratification and ego-development: Implications for clinical and experimental research. *J. consult. Psychol.*, 1955, **19**, 259-266.

Singer, J. L., Wilensky, H., & McCraven, Vivian G. Delaying capacity, fantasy and planning ability: A factorial study of some basic ego functions. *J. consult. Psychol.*, 1956, **20**, 375-383.

Whiting, J. W. M., & Child, I. L. *Child training and personality.* New Haven, Connecticut: Yale Univer. Press, 1953.

ACTUARIAL METHODS IN PERSONALITY ASSESSMENT

Jacob O. Sines

DEPARTMENT OF PSYCHIATRY,
UNIVERSITY OF MISSOURI MEDICAL CENTER,
COLUMBIA, MISSOURI

I. Introduction

For quite a few years after the issue of actuarial prediction was brought into clear focus (Meehl, 1954), there were longer lists of psychological characteristics attributed to the opponents and the proponents of actuarial methods than there were actuarially derived data describing any clinical group. The interested reader is referred to Meehl (1954), Gough (1962), and Marks and Seeman (1963) for reviews and for compilations of the epithets.

Most psychologists who use psychodiagnostic tests continue to do so in the traditional clinical fashion wherein the clinician's personal preferences determine his choice of tests, the patient's test responses are viewed and interpreted subjectively and creatively, and behavior potentialities and personality characteristics are inferred from the test data and attributed to the patient on the basis of the clinician's unspecified experience and training. There is a great deal of readily expressed doubt that actuarial methods of prediction can be successful because, unlike the clinician, they fail to consider either the subtleties of the test data, the uniqueness of human personality, the exceedingly complex ways in which test data relate to personality characteristics or behavior, or all of these.

It is interesting to speculate that essentially similar expressions of shock and dismay from colleagues prompted the following comment from another well known clinician over 30 years before Meehl's book (1954) was published.

> The use of the test for diagnostic purposes may arouse occasional objections. It might be said that the test would reduce the difficult art of diagnosis to a mechanical technic and that, eventually, every laboratory diener could produce psychograms by following certain instructions just as he stains tubercle bacilli. Such an objection would be untenable. To be able to draw conclusions from the scoring of so large a number of factors requires a great deal of practice in psychological reasoning and a great deal of experience with the test. To acquire this experience demands a great deal of clinical material for comparative study, and every person wishing to use the test has to get the experience for himself. Only studies on varied types of individuals can furnish the basis for the acquisition of experience. The test lends itself to psychiatric diagnosis only in the hands of workers capable of collecting psychologically comparable material. . . . Rorschach, H. *Psychodiagnostics,* Berne: Verlag Hans Huber, 1942, p. 122. (Quoted with permission of the publisher.)

Although both Meehl (1954) and Gough (1962) have presented detailed reviews of the data clearly indicating the superiority of actuarial over clinical prediction, Meehl is quite correct in noting that the actuary is still largely unrecognized in the clinic (Meehl, 1965). Even so there are some indications that the resistance to actuarial methods in personality assessment is softening and recently published work (Gilberstadt & Duker, 1960, 1965; Marks & Seeman, 1963) as well as reports now in preparation by Marks on adolescent MMPI's will undoubtedly further stimulate a much needed re-examination of psychodiagnostic practices.

The arguments for and against actuarial prediction will not be reviewed in this chapter. Rather, the first section will present an overview of a number of the basic problems that must be dealt with in any attempt to predict from tests, and the following pages will be devoted to a discussion of several actuarial procedures that have been used. In addition, there are at least two procedural models, distinctions already made by Meehl (1956) and by Gleser (1963), within which actuarial methods have been employed. Research involving both models will be described and the several methodological problems to be dealt with in each of the two predictive strategies will be discussed. Greater emphasis will be given to the work done on prediction from a taxonomic class because at the present time this particular strategy seems to hold the greater promise.

Finally, since the work done so far on actuarial prediction has significant implications for a number of issues beyond the day-to-day activities of the clinician, some of these will be explored.

This review will be organized around some of the distinctions and methodological issues that seem most central to attempts to derive actuarial predictions. It is hoped that this initial focus on the issues involved will help remove some of the confusion and misunderstanding regarding actuarial prediction that persists even now, some 10 years after Meehl's lucid examination of the question.

Before continuing it should be made clear that by actuarial prediction is meant the empirical determination of the regularities that may exist between specified psychological test data and equally clearly specified socially, clinically, or theoretically significant non-test characteristics of the persons tested. This point is of crucial importance in that the clinician is specifically ruled out only as the source of data on the *relationships* that may obtain between test scores and real-life behavior even though the judgment of some person may be, and often is, the only possible source of information concerning the real-life characteristics in which we are ultimately interested (Gough, 1962; Lindzey, 1965). In this sense, the relationships between Minnesota Multiphasic Personality Inventory (MMPI) (Hathaway & McKinley, 1951) scale scores and personality characteristics that have been automated at the Mayo Clinic (Pearson, Swenson, Rome, Mataya, & Brannick, 1964; Rome, Swenson, Mataya, McCarthy, Pearson, & Keating, 1962; Swenson & Pearson, 1964) are not actuarial, nor will the results of Piotrowski's computer program (1964) qualify as actuarial, while the behavior and personality characteristics found, independently of the test, to be characteristic of persons who generate certain types of MMPI profiles are actuarially derived data (Gilberstadt & Duker, 1960; Marks & Seeman, 1963). For the purpose of defining "actuarial" we need not put any limit on either the source of data that are used as predictors or on the range or types of the characteristics that are predicted; we are concerned only with the way in which one determines the regularities or contingencies between these two sets of data. The test data that are the predictor variables need not be derived from traditionally objective tests although, for a variety of practical reasons to be mentioned below, the whole procedure is facilitated if they are; and the characteristics to be predicted may be judgments or numerical data about the person even though there are severe technical and methodological limits on the types of data that will serve as acceptably dependable criteria. Thus we may, in an actuarial or statistical fashion, determine the contingencies between ratings of structured interviews, Rorschach protocols, or MMPI profiles, and the patient's observable behavior or inferred personality characteristics that have been judged by his family, his therapist, or reported by nonprofessional ward personnel.

II. Basic Considerations

Even though the primary purpose of this review is to examine current work on actuarial methods for determining the regularities between persons' test behavior and their socially or clinically significant behavior or personality characteristics, we must nevertheless be concerned with the selection of these two sets of behaviors. The choice of the tests to be used as predictors, and the selection of the criteria to be predicted involve decisions that will not only determine the success or failure of the entire predictive venture but whether the clinician will even consider the possibility that clinically useful predictions and descriptions can be produced actuarially.

A. SELECTION OF THE TEST DATA

In many of the discussions of actuarial versus clinical prediction there appears to be the implicit assumption that the test data in hand, whatever they happen to be, are valid; that is, if they are combined appropriately, either by the clinician or the actuary, the criterion of interest can be predicted with greater accuracy than the raw base rate affords. An extreme statement in this regard is to be found in Berg's (1959) deviation hypothesis where he wrote ". . . any content which produces deviant response patterns will serve. . . ." While such a position regarding the choice of predictors seems to be somewhat brash, the psychologist would be seriously embarrassed if he were required to select as his predictors only those tests or test scores that have already been found to allow highly accurate prediction of the criterion of interest.

There is a large middle ground (between "everything is a predictor" and "nothing is a predictor") that, although insufficiently explored, may yield a number of tests and test scores that logically hold some promise as predictors of the events or behaviors we seek to understand in the clinic. Cronbach (1960) and Cronbach and Gleser (1965) have provided the most thorough discussion of the factors to be considered in choosing tests and test scores, and it is appropriate to review some of them briefly here. It will be seen later in this paper that each of the points raised here has particular relevance to one or more of the specific procedures involved in actuarial prediction.

1. Validity

As Cronbach (1960) has pointed out, validity is the major consideration in choosing a test, even though there are few reports in the literature that offer convincing evidence that any of the available tests are particularly valid as predictors of behavior or personality characteristics. The usual test manual and the typical published validation study most often provide data only on the degree to which test scores discriminate between various criterion groups. Examples of reports that are not atypical are those by Canter (1951), Cattell and Moroney (1962), Meier and French (1965), and Moos and Solomon (1964) in which statistically significant differences on several objective test scales were found between various criterion groups. Reports comparable to those just cited are easily to be found concerning most of the widely known psychological tests, describing the degree to which they discriminate between a variety of socially or clinically important criterion groups.

This type of information may be called partial validity data and is generally not an adequate basis on which to judge the value of a test or test pattern in predicting the criterion of interest. In a brief but very important note Dawes (1962) has clearly shown that such data do not provide the logical basis for test interpretation, and Sines (1964) has argued that studies reporting only that type of data do not appropriately test the validity of a psychodiagnostic instrument. In Dawes' notation (Rj) is a test response or test pattern and (Ci) is membership in a class or criterion group. The usual validity study and test manual present data concerning the most probable test response to be expected from members of a specified criterion group or class of persons or in Dawes' notation, $P(Rj/Ci)$. In order logically to interpret a test or test pattern or to determine the validity of a test or test pattern, we must know the probability with which persons who generate a particular test pattern are members of a specified class or criterion group; or in Dawes' notation, $P(Ci/Rj)$. As Dawes pointed out, the second value may be derived from the values $[P(Rj/Ci)]$, $P(Rj)$, and $P(Ci)$; $P(Ci/Rj) = P(Rj/Ci)/P(Ci)/P(Rj)$. Or, as Sines (1964) argued, $P(Ci/Rj)$ may be calculated directly from an examination of the behavior and personality attributes of persons who generate test pattern (Rj).

It is by no means certain that in any particular instance $P(Rj/Ci) \neq P(Ci/Rj)$ although there appear to be only two examples in the literature in which both values have been found to be essentially identical. In one case a test pattern was found that was both characteristic of persons who admit to thoughts of suicide $[P(Rj/Ci)]$ and also predictive of persons who admit to thoughts of suicide $[P(Ci/Rj)]$. The first value may be found in a report by Rosen, Hales, and Simon (1954) in which they present the average MMPI profile of a group of psychiatric patients who admitted to suicidal thoughts. Some years later Marks and Seeman (1963) noted that a very high percentage of psychiatric patients who generated MMPI

profiles that fit their 278 pattern were said to have suicidal thoughts. The
mean MMPI profile for Rosen, Hales, and Simon's suicidal thought group
fits Marks' and Seeman's 278 pattern pretty well. These two studies were
done several years apart, in quite widely separated institutions, using
different samples of patients and different investigational strategies.

A second study in which $P(Rj/Ci) = P(Ci/Rj)$ was reported by
Lindzey (1965) and concerned a set of TAT (Thematic Apperception
Test) dimensions that both (a) were characteristic of the test responses of
college students who admitted to homosexual behavior $[P(Rj/Ci)]$ and (b)
allowed the prediction of college students who admitted to homosexual
behavior $[P(Ci/Rj)]$. Although there may be other instances in which it
can be shown that $P(Rj/Ci) = P(Ci/Rj)$, such an equality must be demonstrated empirically, it cannot safely be assumed.

These comments should underscore the growing awareness that the
presumed validity data concerning most of our tests are based on only the
first step in determining the predictive or concurrent validity of such
instruments relative to real-life behavior. In most instances we may
increase the probability of successfully achieving our goal of accurate
prediction if we begin with test data that do possess some nonnegligible
$P(Rj/Ci)$ but this is not always so. Consideration of those instances in
which this stricture does not hold (Wheeler, Burke, & Reitan, 1963;
Meehl, 1950) is beyond the scope of this chapter. We should recognize,
however, that if we consider *only the available validity data* [which is
actually most often partial validity data in the form of $P(Rj/Ci)$] there
is little support for the use of most of our tests in most of the clinically
important prediction situations, much less justification for our individual
preferences for using one particular test or even one type of test to the
exclusion of others.

2. Multiple versus single variable tests

In principle and within limits, a multivariate test or test battery can
be expected to have greater value than a univariate test or one that
narrowly limits the possible variance on its dimensions (Cronbach &
Gleser, 1965). The most frequently used projective techniques are
certainly not criticized for any failure to provide the clinician with seemingly multivariate data and indeed it is the very lack of restriction on
the variability of the subject's responses that is offered as a basic advantage of such techniques. Similarly, many different profile configurations
are possible on objective instruments such as the MMPI or 16 PF (Cattell,
Saunders, & Stice, 1957). This question of multiple scores and possible
variation is basic to the problem of prediction whether it be clinical or

actuarial and is given significant treatment by Cronbach and Gleser (1965).

But in the prediction situation the sheer presence of variability on a multivariate test is not the critical issue. Whether or not the variation is detectable or specifiable is the crux of the matter. For the clinician this may be translatable as "can the psychologist note and retain enough of the several predictor variates and their possible configurations to recognize their relationship to the criterion?" For the actuary this may be translated as "are the necessary information-bearing test scores included and are the formalized rules for combining and weighting the several variables and their possible configurations sufficiently comprehensive and sensitive so that any relationship they may have to the criterion can be detected?"

It is clear that such questions do not require the clinician consciously to verbalize the cues he may use or to which he may respond. It does however require that the variates be available to him. The question becomes one of whether he is able to perceive and process the available information, and there is strong suggestion that the human animal, too, is sharply limited in this respect (Miller, 1956; Miller & Bieri, 1963). At the same time such questions do require that the test variates be consciously verbalized or specified and available to the actuary: whether the actuary's methods are sufficiently sensitive to assign appropriate weights to the cues and their possible configurations cannot be determined unless the data are available for him to process.

Proponents of the clinical approach may argue that the psychologist makes use of cues in the test data that may not have been previously specified, and Meehl (1959) has expressly cited this as a possibility that might allow the clinician to achieve predictive accuracy superior to that of the actuary. Furthermore, Lindzey (1965) has reported a study in which this has apparently occurred. It cannot be overemphasized, however, that there are no data to support the contention that the clinician will be more accurate than the actuary when both the clinician and the actuary are responding to the same test data.

When one considers this issue then, the availability of detectable variability in several dimensions, Lindzey's notion of the "psychometric intractability" of the TAT (Lindzey, 1965) takes on considerable significance relative to the selection of the test one is to use as a source of predictor data. It would certainly be unwise to reject a test because it provided too great a range of potential predictors—one can always sample the pool of predictors to identify those that have a usable degree of validity in various situations. There is, however, little justification for using psychometrically intractable instruments in the absence of reasonable data to suggest that the wealth of potential but subtle predictor variables that most projective devices provide will result in predictions that are more accurate or more comprehensive than are possible from other psychometrically quite tractable instruments. Thus, while the validity data do not provide the basis on which to decide which test to use for prediction in the clinic, the importance of having detectable or specifiable variation on several variables does argue for the use of objective test instruments. The data reported by Sarbin (1943) concerning the relative accuracy of statistical and clinical prediction of college grades and the more recent work of Hoffman (1960) indicate a strong likelihood that predictor variables that are relatively easily specified and easily subjected to statistical analysis may in fact be the most important ones to which the clinician responds. It is this last point that is at issue in the interpretation of a recent report in which clinical prediction was found to be superior to predictions based on the mechanical combination of objectified TAT signs (Lindzey, 1965). This particular study will be discussed below.

3. Cost

Another important factor, the cost of testing, must be considered in selecting the variables we wish to employ as predictors. The question of cost has not been given a great deal of attention in clinical settings although it is more seriously considered in the planning of industrial and personnel testing programs. Cronbach (1960) and Cronbach and Gleser (1965) discuss this topic in detail and Meehl (1960) has clearly shown that testing in the clinic may be a surprisingly expensive procedure unless both the test data and accurate inferences from them can be produced rather quickly—under some conditions in a matter of 2–4 hours. When we add to this embarrassing constraint the fact that there is an increasing relative shortage of trained psychological testers it becomes unavoidably clear that the cost of any test is a major consideration, when cost is determined by the ease of administration and scoring and the interpretive time required of the test user.

In view of considerations such as those just mentioned it seems reasonable, *at this time*, to expect a greater return or greater weighted utility value from objective psychometric devices. Even though there are few if any data on this matter, and it is an empirical question that can be decided only after viewing the appropriate data, this reviewer is betting heavily on objective multivariate instruments. While it is absolutely clear that objectively specified test data are essential for any study of actuarial prediction, the investigator should feel equally comfortable (or uncomfortable) whether he uses the "time-worn MMPI scales" or the "validity-shorn Rorschach protocol."

B. Selection of Criterion Information

By virtue of the procedures involved in an actuarial approach to personality assessment the criteria to be predicted, as well as the predictor variables, must be specified clearly at the outset. Actuarial methods do not allow for the identification and prediction of behavior or personality characteristics that have not previously been noted. Investigators who have published reports of actuarially derived personality descriptions have generally made use of a limited set of descriptors; Halbower (cited by Meehl, 1956) used 154 descriptive statements in his Q pool; Gilberstadt and Duker (1960) reported on only 70 characteristics; and Marks and Seeman (1963) selected from a Q pool of 108 statements plus a fairly large array of psychometric and case history material. The descriptors used were either considered to be representative of statements made about personality or were terms selected from psychiatric summary descriptions of patients. This apparent rigidity has been discussed by Meehl (1959), criticized by Holt (1958) and Taft (1959) and seems to be one of the basic reasons why many clinicians feel that actuarial methods are too limited and do not warrant serious consideration.

Let us examine this problem a bit more closely. If we are concerned with predicting a specified or fixed criterion such as success in a training program, improvement under certain treatment, or an event such as suicide, this particular criticism of actuarial methods is certainly not a legitimate one. Only when our task is to respond to a question of the sort "Describe this person's personality structure" or "What is this patient's characteristic behavior pattern" or in Gleser's words, to predict a set of "free" criteria (Gleser, 1963) does this inflexibility appear to be a handicap. In these last situations it is conceivable that the clinician's memory or past experience or mental manipulation of theoretical constructs may provide him with specific correlates of the test data that the actuary has either never experienced, failed to note, or failed to include in his experience table. These points have been cited by Meehl (1959) as some of the possible conditions under which the clinician might do better than the actuary.

It is instructive to consider in this connection what clinicians do in fact say about patients. In an unpublished study (Sines, 1960) a count was made of the descriptive words and phrases that were used in a sample of the psychological reports on 60 patients seen in a university affiliated psychiatric hospital by one or another of a group of 8 different psychologists. The psychologists included 4 staff members and 4 predoctoral interns supervised by one or more of the staff members. One of the staff psychologists had over 25 years of experience, and was a diplomate of ABEPP in clinical psychology, two of the clinicians each had 4 years of post-doctoral experience and one had 2 years of post-doctoral experience. The reports selected were all that were written during a 2-month period and there was no reason to assume that the patients described were atypical for that particular clinical setting. Finally, there were no restrictions on the source of the information on which the psychological reports were based; all patients had been interviewed by the psychologist, and most had been given a battery of objective and projective tests. It was clear from the reports that some of the descriptive statements were based on the behavior the patient showed in the interview or in the testing situation and other statements specifically referred to test data or scores. Many of the statements were not attributed to a specific source.

There were only 261 differently worded statements that could be extracted from that sample of 60 psychological reports. This list quite probably included as separate statements a number of phrases and terms that had essentially identical meanings because only obviously synonymous terms or phrases were combined. It is admitted that these data do not bear on the question of the validity of the psychological reports nor do they reflect universal practice. They do indicate, however, that in at least one clinical setting a surprisingly limited range of behavioral potentialities and personality characteristics were attributed to patients on the basis of a psychological evaluation. It seems not unreasonable to hypothesize that the characteristics attributed by clinicians to persons in other settings may be drawn from equally restricted descriptor pools.

If such is indeed the case the actuary would be well advised to study carefully the contingencies between his test data and a technically quite manageable set of behaviors or personality attributes that are known or believed to have practical or theoretical significance in his particular clinic.

But the number of descriptors to be used is of course not the only question or even the most important one here; in an attempt to devise actuarial prediction, the actuary is forced to consider, as the clinical clinician often does not explicitly do, the validity of the descriptors or free criteria he may wish to predict. It is certainly here that the actuary must rely on someone's clinical judgment concerning the presence or absence of the characteristics he wishes ultimately to predict mechanically. It is appropriate that we examine some of the major determinants of criterion validity at this point. The extent to which the relevant variables have been considered in several studies of actuarial prediction will be noted when those reports are discussed in the next two sections.

The problems inherent in determining criterion validity and the unfortunate tendency among psychologists to gloss over or ignore them have been reflected in a literature that, although it is briefer and apparently less widely read, is almost as stimulating as the controversy over clinical versus actuarial prediction (Ebel, 1961; Jenkins, 1946). Here one of the major issues involves the selection of those characteristics of persons that can be judged reliably without the mediation of the test data we wish to use in predicting them. There appear to be two fundamental considerations necessary in devising or selecting criteria that are themselves valid. First, we must determine the content or type of material that can be judged reliably. A second consideration deals with the identification of who or what type of persons are able to make reliable judgments of the criteria selected.

1. Criterion Content

Gage and Cronbach (1955) have drawn clear distinctions between four types or patterns of studies of interpersonal perception and their patterns B and D are precisely relevant here. Both patterns B and D involve a judge observing another person, with whom the judge is not well acquainted, and then describing certain characteristics of that subject or patient. Patterns B and D differ in that in pattern B the judge is required to report on observed characteristics of the subject while in pattern D the judge must not only observe the subject's phenotypic characteristics but he is required to make inferences about genotypic processes or attributes that are not directly observable. There appear not to be any studies that are directly concerned with the relative reliability with which observable, phenotypic characteristics and inferred, genotypic attributes can be judged. Most studies of clinical judgment, judgment of others, empathy, or interpersonal perception have been designed for other purposes and either do not include data relevant to this question or include such data almost incidentally to the main findings.

The reliability of complex criteria such as formal psychiatric diagnosis has been much discussed and found wanting by many investigators (Ash, 1949; Mehlman, 1952; Zigler and Philips, 1961). There are also impressively clear data to indicate that clinical judgments of many seemingly more simple personal characteristics and symptoms are almost equally unreliable (Garland, 1960; Giedt, 1955; Grigg, 1958; Grosz & Grossman, 1964; Lewinsohn, Nichols, Pulos, Lomont, Nickel, & Siskind, 1963; Weiss, 1963).

Giedt (1955) reported that in his study of clinical judgment an initial list of 33 traits and personality dimensions most frequently used in staff conferences and psychological reports was reduced first to the 11 variables considered most necessary for description of personality and then further reduced to five variables because *the criterion judges were unable to achieve an acceptable degree of reliability* ($P = .02$ or better) in their estimates of the other six variables. While the 6 variables that could not be rated reliably were not given, 4 of the 5 variables that were included in Giedt's study seem to require only a moderate degree of inference, or in the terms used by Gage and Cronbach, judging them does not appear to require a great deal of extrapolation from the patient's observable behavior.

Data somewhat more relevant to the issue are to be found in the study by Lewinsohn *et al.* (1963) in which the inter-rater reliabilities for a set of traits and personality characteristics judged from hospital charts and from psychological test data were reported. This reviewer roughly categorized the items as "relatively close to observable behavior" or more "inferential." Considering those judgments based on hospital charts, the reliability coefficients for the first group of attributes ranged from $+.11$ to $+.79$ with three below $+.25$, and the average reliability coefficient was .51 (using the z transformation). The coefficients for the more inferential judgments ranged from $-.03$ to $+.41$, with only 3 larger than $+.25$ and the average z-transformed coefficient was .17.

Lewinsohn *et al.* noted that among those ratings based on test data, reliabilities were higher if the ratings were more directly derivable from the test data whereas lower reliabilities were obtained when the ratings "required remote inferences or elaborate interpretations." In this connection, Briggs and Wirt (1960) indicated that their raters reported greater difficulty in sorting Q items that required interpretation of covert behavior whereas the easiest judgments involved items referring to observable behavior. Livson and Nichols (1956) reported similar comments from their Q-sort judges. Grosz and Grossman (1964) have gone a bit further in their interpretation of their data concerning the unreliability of psychiatric residents' judgments of observed and inferred characteristics of psychiatric patients when they stated that ". . . (highly inferential) judgments are less informative about the patients whom they are meant to describe than about the clinician who makes them."

The recommendation, made several years ago by Gage and Cronbach (1955), that (as a first step) we study the determinants of judgments that require only a small degree of extrapolation from observable behavior has not yet generated the necessary research on criterion validity. It is quite unlikely that many clinicians, either producers or consumers of psychological reports, would calmly approve of test interpretations containing statements that referred only to their patient's behavior. In view of the lack of data to support any other position, however, it does seem eminently reasonable that, as Hathaway (1956) and Marks (1961) have suggested, the criteria we select to predict from psychological tests should be descriptors that are most directly and reliably rated from, or descriptive of, observable behavior rather than characteristics requiring remote inference or much extrapolation from behavior.

2. Criterion Judges

Three major attributes of good judges emerge from the extensive literature on research designed to identify the factors responsible for accurate judgments of others (Allison, Korner, & Zwanziger, 1964; Bendig & Sprague, 1954; Borke & Fiske, 1957; Cline & Richards, 1960; Cronbach, 1955; Estes, 1938; Gage, 1953; Gage & Cronbach, 1955; Giedt, 1955; Grebstein, 1963; Grigg, 1958; Kostlan, 1954; Oskamp, 1962; Taft, 1955; Wedell & Smith, 1951). As Taft listed them they are: (1) appropriate judgmental norms, (2) a combination of general and social intelligence, and (3) the motivation to make accurate judgments. By far the greatest amount of work has been devoted to attempts to specify the details of the first attribute, "appropriate judgmental norms." As will be noted later, many investigators erroneously assume that training in clinical psychology provides adequate assurance that a judge possesses the appropriate judgmental norms. When the criteria to be judged are not phrased in peculiarly psychological jargon, psychologists are found to be no better than nonpsychologists and often less accurate in their judgments of others. This particular lack of relationship between training in psychology and ability to predict the behavior of others has been reported in 1938 by S. G. Estes, most recently by Weiss in 1963, and by several investigators in the interim.

A judge may possess appropriate judgmental norms by virtue of his sharing a variety of characteristics in common with the subject who is judged. In this case similar socioeconomic backgrounds, extended acquaintance with the subject, or the accuracy of a judge's stereotype of the class of persons of which the subject is a member, all may contribute to the observed accuracy of judgment (Cronbach, 1955). Robins and Braroe (1964) studied the information obtained when a structured interview schedule was used by trained professionals and lay interviewers to obtain psychiatrically relevant data. These investigators reported that ". . . psychiatrists, medical students, and social scientists . . . obtained essentially the same kind of information, and that the information obtained by each equally well enabled a psychiatrist to make a diagnosis."

The major difference between the information obtained by the psychia-
trist-interviewers and the lay interviewers was the failure of the latter
group to omit any data—they made no on-the-spot decisions concerning
the relevance of a questionnaire item as the sophisticated judges often did.

Oskamp's (1962) report of the ability to judge whether an MMPI
profile was generated by a patient hospitalized in a psychiatric or in a
medical unit is particularly relevant here too. By making appropriate
judgmental norms (the best numerical cues relating to the correct decision) available to a group of intelligent and motivated but initially
naive judges, Oskamp was able to train a group of undergraduate college
students to classify MMPI profiles as accurately as highly trained Ph.D.
psychologists who were experienced in the use of the MMPI.

The conclusions one may draw from the literature on criterion
validity and characteristics of good judges do not offer the clinician a
great deal of comfort. They should motivate the psychologist to consider
carefully what it is he wishes to predict and to restrict himself more
often than seems to be the case in his reports to those characteristics of
persons that are as closely as possible related to observable behavior,
realizing that as distance from "observable" increases so does the unreliability of judgment, even among expert professionals (see Garfield,
Heine, & Leventhal, 1954). The data also clearly support the notion that
when one does attempt to describe the observable behavior of others or
predict the specific behavior of others the reports of intelligent non-
professionals are at least as reliable as those of social workers, psychiatrists, and clinical psychologists. These conclusions seem to offer good
justification for carefully expanding the range of sources of criterion
data about persons while at the same time cautiously reducing the range
of characteristics we try to attribute to others.

III. Actuarial Prediction

With the preceding comments in mind we may now move on to
consider a number of examples of actuarial prediction. It will help clarify
the discussion if, at the outset, we make the distinction between predicting a fixed criterion and predicting from a taxonomic class. We will then
examine selected studies that involve actuarial prediction in each of those
two general types of prediction situations.

In one of his series of discussions of actuarial prediction Meehl
(1956) distinguished between two different types of prediction problems
that often face the clinician. The first general class of situations involves
"gross outcome-type administrative" decisions such as assigning a diagnosis, deciding whether a given patient would do well in psychotherapy, or
determining the presence or absence of some other specific event or charac-

teristic. Gleser (1963) referred to a situation of this sort as prediction of a fixed criterion. We will use Gleser's term here to denote prediction problems in which the task is to predict some specific attribute of the patient. In the second prediction situation the psychologist's task is much more open-ended and general. As Meehl (1956) characterized it this second enterprise is "describing the person" and in relation to such efforts Gleser (1963) referred to the prediction of "free criteria." We will refer to such activities as prediction from a taxonomic class. This latter term seems to describe quite accurately what the actuary does in this second prediction situation even though many clinicians, including Meehl, resist the suggestion that the clinician who attempts to predict "free criteria" functions in such a manner.

In the first instance the investigator's attention is initially focused on a specific event, bit of behavior, or characteristic of the patient, while in the second model we focus at first on test scores or patterns. This distinction between predicting a fixed criterion and predicting from a taxonomic class will be used throughout the remainder of this paper not only as a matter of convenience but also because it does seem rather effectively to indicate the very important methodological differences that result from the type of problem the investigator chooses and the way in which he phrases the question to be investigated. The strategies employed by the actuary in either of these two prediction situations can be shown not to be in any respect mutually exclusive and it can be seen as Tellegen has noted (1964) that they both faithfully reflect the same basic covariational structure. Three discussions that are particularly instructive in this regard are those by Birnbaum and Maxwell (1965), Ledley and Lusted (1962), and Turner (1965). Ledley and Lusted in particular describe the relationships between the search for predictor patterns that will be discussed in a following section of this paper as well as two other strategies involving configural rules such as those of Meehl and Dahlstrom (1960) and conditional probabilities as discussed by Meehl and Rosen (1955) and Dawes (1962).

Since applied psychologists, from Binet to Wechsler, have traditionally been occupied with attempts to predict fixed criteria, and since most of the research on the validation of psychological tests and prediction from them has involved the use of fixed criteria, some of the relevant actuarial attempts to predict a fixed criterion will be discussed first.

A. PREDICTION OF A FIXED CRITERION

In the situation frequently encountered in the clinic, the psychologist is asked to predict a specific criterion such as, "Is this particular patient a suicide risk?" or "Will this patient improve with psychotherapy?" These questions may be restated as "Does the patient belong to that class of persons who attempt to commit suicide?" or "Is the patient a member of that class of persons whose psychological disorder improves with psychotherapy?" In each of these not unusual prediction situations, one specific behavioral attribute is used to define the large initial class of persons.

There are, of course, many reasons why actuarial attempts to predict any such fixed criterion might fail. The first would appear to be the actual lack of any relationship between the test variates and the criterion of interest. Even though our partial validity data are far from satisfactory there is no reason to reject out of hand the possibility that when subjected to appropriate validation study some of our test instruments may be predictive of some real-life behavior. A second problem to be dealt with, even assuming valid tests, results from the fact that there may be and often are several differentiable subclasses in any larger class defined by the gross criteria that Meehl referred to as "administrative decisions." Assuming the actuary's formula to be capable of accommodating several, possibly quite different, configurations of test data he might still be unsuccessful unless the configurations of test data that characterize each of the N possible subclasses of the criterion class are available to him. Third, if the relationship between test data and criterion is grossly nonlinear, a linear model may not allow for the optimal combination of the test data. A fourth and final major consideration is the possibility that the criterion to be predicted is itself so unreliably judged that its prediction under any circumstances would be highly unlikely.

It is clear, when we inspect the psychological test performances of patients who are members of a gross criterion class such as "suicide risk," that there may be N number of subclasses of persons, with each subclass characterizable by different configurations of scores on the same test; and each of those possibly quite different test patterns may be validly predictive of "suicide risk." Specifically, it can be shown (for instance, Marks & Seeman, 1963) that persons who are judged to present a risk of "suicide attempt" or who are judged to possess the capacity to show "good response to psychotherapy" are found to generate any one of several MMPI profile patterns or, in other words, may be found in any one of several MMPI definable subclasses of these potential larger criterion groups. Reports by Gilberstadt (1962), Gilberstadt and Farkas (1961) and Levitt and Fellner (1965) also clearly point out the gross error involved in assuming that a group of persons, defined by the possession of some arbitrarily chosen single criterion attribute, all share a common configuration of test scores. It should be obvious that when he attempts to predict a fixed criterion the psychologist cannot safely assume that all members of that larger class of persons defined by the criterion of interest will be characterized by one, or even in most cases, by a few patterns of his test data. In the same sense, of course, it would be entirely premature for the psychologist to conclude that a test is not valid for predicting a given criterion when he finds that a particular set of scores on that test is not predictive of all instances of the criterion of interest; a specific configuration of his test scores may indeed be quite acceptably valid for the prediction of a specifiable subclass of the criterion group as Ghiselli (1956, 1960) has repeatedly shown.

Most of us who use psychological tests in the clinic, even though most of the classical literature on the validity of such tests does not justify our continued use of them, feel that the generally negative published data do not somehow accurately reflect the real worth of these instruments. This intense feeling of dissatisfaction with the necessary interpretation of the available (part) validity data may be logical as well as visceral. As the writer has pointed out in a previous note (Sines, 1964), the predictive validity of a particular configuration of test scores may be inversely related to the representativeness of the criterion samples on which it has been derived and with which it is subsequently used.

Too often there is just the above sort of implicit assumption that all (or even most) members of a class, that has been defined by some arbitrarily chosen bit of behavior, share some discernible and specific set of nonclass-defining test characteristics. To state this differently, the psychologist may operate as if he denied or discounted the possibility that the criterion behavior he wished to predict could be related to more than one configuration of test data. If, in the larger criterion class there are subclasses within each of which there is some common configuration of test data, but between which the test patterns differ, the prediction problem becomes much more complex than if all of the members of the criterion-defined class share a common (nonclass-defining) pattern of test data. The test data that might be used to predict the criterion in one particular subclass of the criterion class may be totally non-predictive of the same criterion in a different sub-class of the initial criterion class; that is, the validity of the test data may not generalize to another subclass of the same initial criterion group or class (Meehl, 1959, 1965). Therefore, in order to be able to identify all (or most) members of the initial large criterion class (potentially including N different test-definable subclasses) a first necessity for successful actuarial prediction is that the actuary have access to the test data that may characterize each of the possible subclasses. A discussion of the possible varieties of subclasses of the larger criterion class defined by "suicide" has recently been presented by Kubie (1964).

Furthermore, many psychologists maintain that the test data available to them are related to the criterion of interest in some (unspecified) complex nonlinear fashion, and therefore in order to be successful any model used for actuarial prediction of a fixed criterion must be based on statistical techniques that are sensitive to highly configured functions. This is an issue quite separate from the matter of validity generalization mentioned above and would be relevant even if there were only one (nonlinear) combination of test data that were predictive of all instances of the criterion of interest. Fisher (1959), Ghiselli (1956, 1960), and Meehl (1950, 1959) have discussed several aspects of the nonlinearity of the relationships between test predictors and various criteria, and in sum have marshalled strong evidence in support of the clinician's argument. A review of selected studies of actuarial prediction of a fixed criterion will illustrate the varying degree to which the several issues have been considered.

1. Linear versus Configural Models

Actuarial prediction of a fixed criterion by means of both configural and linear combinations of test scores is well exemplified by studies using the MMPI to discriminate between psychiatric patients diagnosed either psychotic or neurotic (Goldberg, 1965; Meehl, 1959; Meehl and Dahlstrom, 1960) and between psychiatric and medical patients (Oskamp, 1962). Meehl reported (1959) that of the six methods he studied the linear discriminant function was the least effective in classifying MMPI profiles as psychotic or neurotic. Since the other four statistical methods and the clinicians who sorted the profiles all were presumed to be responding to configural aspects of the test scores Meehl concluded that the relationship between MMPI profile pattern and psychiatric status of psychosis versus neurosis was a configurated relationship.

On the basis of his detailed reanalysis of the original Meehl–Dahlstrom data, Goldberg (1965) has reported that ". . . the simple linear nonweighted composite . . ." of $(L + Pa + Sc) - (Hy + Pt)$ achieved a cross-validated hit rate of 70% with no indeterminate class; that is, the linear index allowed 70% of the profiles to be correctly classified when a decision was required for every profile. When forced to classify every profile the configural rules devised by Meehl and Dahlstrom (1960) correctly assigned 66% of the profiles. Goldberg's linear index and the Meehl–Dahlstrom rules achieved the same degree of accuracy (74%) when both were allowed to use an "indeterminate" category, but Goldberg's indeterminate class included only 20% of the sample while the Meehl–Dahlstrom indeterminate group accounted for 31% of the original sample.

Application of the Meehl–Dahlstrom rules to several other samples have been reported by Henrichs (1964) and Oskamp (1962). Henrichs found that the Meehl–Dahlstrom rules correctly classified 66% of a group of 69 state hospital patients with 27.5% called indeterminate. When the original rules were modified to accommodate a group of character disorders added to the patient sample, Henrichs found a hit rate of 72.2% with an indeterminate group of 18.2%. These figures compare favorably with Oskamp's report that when an indeterminate category was not included the Meehl–Dahlstrom rules allowed correct assignment of 67% of 200 MMPI profiles, 100 of which were obtained from psychiatric patients and 100 from medical patients. Oskamp further reported that his seven most accurate judges averaged 73.6% correct predictions while 75% of the profiles could be correctly classified on the basis of the two best nonlinear actuarial signs.

In this context there are three major conclusions to be drawn from these data. First is the fact that the MMPI scales do appear to possess sufficient cross-validated concurrent validity $[P(Ci/Rj)]$ to warrant their continued use in the clinic (Henrichs, 1964; Goldberg, 1965; Meehl, 1959; Meehl & Dahlstrom, 1960). Second, when used to predict the fixed criterion of formal psychiatric diagnosis (psychosis versus neurosis) any of a number of relatively simple statistical decision rules will result in accuracy that is at least equal to and often greater than that attainable even by a variety of more complex configurated models or by clinicians who are experienced in the use of the MMPI (Goldberg, 1965; Meehl, 1959; Meehl & Dahlstrom, 1960; Oskamp, 1962). And third, even though Meehl (1959) has pointed out the Meehl–Dahlstrom rules certainly accommodate the presumed necessary configural relationships between test data and criterion and the way in which the rules were devised allowed highly competent clinicians to express their considerable experience with the test, the best statistical index to apply to the MMPI in order to predict this particular fixed criterion among psychiatric patients is ". . . the simple linear nonweighted composite of . . ." $(L + Pa + Sc)$ — $(Hy + Pt)$ (Goldberg, 1965). It seems abundantly clear that we have no good evidence to support the clinical psychologist who maintains that formal psychiatric diagnosis (of psychosis or neurosis at least) is predictable best from a complex configuration of MMPI scores.

2. Availability of Predictor Data

An additional study reported by Lindzey (1965) and Meehl's comments on that study (1965) point out most clearly the importance of each of several methodological problems that must be considered in actuarial prediction.

Quite briefly, Lindzey found that an experienced judge was able to correctly classify 95% of the TAT protocols of 40 male undergraduates, 20 of whom admitted to homosexual behavior and 20 of whom had no known history of homosexuality. The judge was familiar with but did not use a number of objectively scored TAT indices of homosexuality that were also formally used to classify the TAT protocols. Only 85% of the protocols could be classified correctly on the basis of an unweighted sum of scores on 20 different objectified TAT variables. A second study was an attempt to discriminate between the TAT protocols obtained from 14 homosexual and 16 nonhomosexual male prisoners. On the basis of clinical examination of the entire TAT protocols one judge achieved 80% accuracy and a second judge's classification was 60% accurate. Even the most lenient arrangement of the 20 previously used objective TAT indices of homosexuality resulted in only 57% correct classifications in the prisoner groups.

Lindzey and Meehl both pointed out that the dramatic failure of the objective TAT scores to be of any predictive value in the second study is most probably attributable to the many marked discrepancies in a number of highly relevant class-defining characteristics of the two sub-classes (college students versus prisoners in a maximum security penitentiary) of the larger criterion class of persons who had exhibited homosexual behavior. The lack of validity generalization of the objective signs, so clearly found in that second study, illustrates most effectively a point too often unrecognized; the actuary must have access to the test data that can in principle be combined somehow to predict the criterion of interest. In this sense the appropriate test of the relative efficiency of clinical versus actuarial prediction was carried out in Lindzey's first study in which the clinician's accuracy was 95% and the actuary was correct in 85% of his decisions. The second study was more legitimately a test of the degree of generalizable validity of the objectified TAT signs. We may conclude that Lindzey's signs appear to have a high degree of validity when used for predicting homosexual behavior among selected college students but no appreciable validity when used to predict the same criterion among male maximum security prisoners.

In their report of an attempt to predict a fixed criterion, Allison et al. (1964) presented disappointingly little data but concluded that "The contrast between the findings for the objective measures and the clinical judgments is strong evidence that critical information was available in the pre- and post-stress (TAT) stories which was not appearing in the objective measures." This observation seems to be equally appropriate in reference to the decline in the predictive significance of Lindzey's TAT signs in the prisoner sample.

To the considerable extent that accurate prediction of homosexual behavior among prisoners has administrative importance we may be justified in attempting to formalize the scoring of test variables that allow its prediction; but only then will we be able to determine the relative accuracy of clinical and mechanical prediction of the "prisoner subclass" of homosexual persons. On the basis of Lindzey's two studies (1965) it is clear that there are TAT variables that have not yet been identified for formal scoring that possess predictive significance for the socially significant behavior of homosexual behavior among prisoners. One of the basic issues is whether the clinician is capable of specifying those test cues and variables so that they may be objectively scored. But even assuming that the relevant cues in each of our several types of tests can be objectively specified, there remains the more fundamental question of the weighted utility of the several methods of predicting the criterion and that question is yet to be answered. The weighted utility value is determined in large part by the cost of the procedures involved in generating the predictor data as Cronbach and Gleser (1965) have pointed out. In recommending the use of psychological tests that require expensive procedures for either administration or scoring, the cost must be seriously considered and in many cases it *cannot be* assumed to be negligible (Rimm, 1963).

3. Bayesian Approach

A number of years ago Meehl and Rosen (1955) raised the issue of base rates in relation to the predictive efficiency of psychological tests, and in a later note Dawes (1962) explicitly introduced Bayesian terminology to the discussion of the problem of prediction from psychological tests. Although there has been frequent reference to the limitations that the numerical values of base rates or antecedent probabilities place on the predictive value of test data, there have been no large scale prediction studies in psychology that make explicit use of Bayes' theorem. There is, however, a rapidly growing literature on medical diagnosis based on the application of Bayes' theorem to specific signs and symptoms and selected diagnostic categories. Birnbaum and Maxwell (1965), Ledley and Lusted (1962), and Turner (1965) have discussed the logical and statistical framework within which medical diagnosis may be subjected to formal mathematical analysis. As mentioned earlier, all of those writers have developed the basic concepts so as to clearly illustrate the logical and statistical relationships between the several strategies employed in predicting a fixed criterion and predicting from a taxonomic class.

One study of predicting a fixed criterion using Bayes' theorem to be described as an example is a preliminary report of the attempt to predict the histologic diagnosis of primary bone tumors by means of roent-genograms, a situation that has a number of interesting similarities to the problem facing the clinical psychologist who attempts to predict a patient's psychiatric diagnosis from psychological tests. Lodwick, Haun, Smith, Keller, and Robertson (1963) noted that prior to subjecting their actuarially derived diagnostic decisions to cross-validation, several essential factors must be considered. The first question to which those investigators addressed themselves was the diagnostic validity of the roentgenogram itself. The accuracy with which expert radiologists are able to predict the histologic diagnoses from the X-ray films clearly indicate that there are roentgenographic characteristics that do in fact relate to differential criterion diagnoses. Since the method used for determining the relationship between the predictor characteristics of the X-ray films and the criterion diagnoses required objective data, a method was devised that allowed all of the presumedly relevant features of X-ray films to be coded in digital form. Because the diagnostically relevant characteristics that are presented in the roentgenogram are in large part qualitative, the specificity of the rules for analysis and coding of the films was recognized as an important potential source of error. For that reason a great deal of care was devoted to the detailed specification of the X-ray film cues that were to be used in objectifying those ratings.

The serious problem of criterion validity was also noted by Lodwick *et al.* and they recognized the fact that there is a sufficient degree of unreliability in the criterion judgments made by the histologist to limit somewhat the predictive accuracy that is attainable using the roentgenogram.

Having objectified a set of predictor variables derivable from a "clinically validated" technique, Lodwick *et al.* used Bayes' theorem to determine the relationship between the various configurations of the several predictor variables and a set of fallible criterion diagnoses. In order to ensure stable estimates, the several conditional probabilities were determined on the basis of observed contingencies between each of the diagnostic classifications in a large number of cases. The Bayesian formula into which the roentgenographic and the diagnostic data were inserted and for which a computer was programmed was:

$$Pd_j/(S_1, S_2, \overline{S}_3 \ldots Sn) = \frac{(Pd_j)\ (Ps_1/d_j)\ (1 - Ps_3/d_j)\ \ldots\ (Ps_n/d_j)}{Pd_k(Ps_1/d_k)\ (1 - Ps_3/d_k)\ \ldots\ (Ps_n/d_k)}$$

where Pd_j = the over-all probability of a particular diagnosis, d_j, in the sample of cases available

Ps_1 = the probability of the particular symptom or X-ray film characteristic, S_1

$\overline{S}_3 =$ the absence of the particular symptom or X-ray film characteristic, S_3

$Ps_1/d_j =$ the probability of symptom S_1 among patients with diagnosis d_j

$Pd_j/(S_1, S_2, \overline{S}_3 \ldots S_n) =$ the probability of diagnosis, d_j among patients who possess symptoms S_1, S_2, S_n and do not have symptom S_3

The results of the initial computer run indicated that 77.9% of the bone tumors were correctly diagnosed by this actuarial method. This may be compared with a "hit rate" of 80% correct diagnoses, from clinical reading of the X-ray films of similar tumors. There was a good deal of variability in the accuracy with which the several diagnoses could be predicted (37% to 100% accuracy) and the one diagnosis made least accurately clinically proved to be least accurately predicted by this particular actuarial method. In subsequent analyses of these and additional data other diagnostic groups of tumors will be added to the matrix and symptoms not found to carry diagnostic significance may be dropped. This system of actuarial prediction thus retains the high degree of flexibility necessary to allow it to be periodically and regularly updated with current clinical material.

4. Nonactuarial Automated Techniques

There is an additional group of studies, involving test data that are in objective form and making use of formalized decision rules for relating the test variables to characteristics of persons tested, that cannot be classed as actuarial methods in the context of this discussion. Prominent among those are the reports by Eber (1964), Finney (1965), Fowler (1964, 1965), Gravitz and Davis (1965), Kleinmuntz (1963a,b,c, 1964), Pearson et al. (1964), Piotrowski (1964), Rome et al. (1962), Swenson (1965), and Swenson and Pearson (1964). Most of these studies share the common feature of having the skilled clinician specify at the outset those criterion characteristics that later will be automatically attributed to the persons who generate certain test scores or patterns. Published research or the clinician's experience is the basis for estimating the relationship between test data and the criteria of interest. The results of the procedures reported by Piotrowski (1964) using the Rorschach are indeed encouraging (86% agreement between machined Rorschach psychiatric diagnosis and the purified criterion of follow-up actual diagnosis), and Kleinmuntz (1963a) has reported somewhat lower but nonetheless encouraging validity for his computerized MMPI decision rules relative to maladjustment among college students, a criterion that is far less valid and dependable than the one employed by Piotrowski. So far the only external check on the validity of the automated test interpretations in use at the Mayo clinic has been the utility of the reports as judged by the clinicians to whom they are provided. The expressed acceptance of the reports has been overwhelmingly positive (Swenson, 1965; Swenson & Pearson, 1964).

As Seeman has noted (1964), one of the continuing misconceptions about the nature of actuarial prediction is the assumption that ". . . all mechanical methods (of combining test data to derive descriptions of persons) are statistical or actuarial." The studies just mentioned involving the mechanical combination of clinician-derived test interpretations appear to hold promise relative to a number of theoretical as well as applied questions but their success or failure does not reflect on the issues basic to the question of actuarial prediction per se.

B. Prediction from a Taxonomic Class

Although prediction of a fixed criterion will undoubtedly continue to occupy a significant portion of the clinician's professional time, we ought seriously to consider the possibility that we may be taking the long way around when we focus initially on the criterion of interest instead of the test data. As Tellegen has noted (1964), general reliance on the approach described here as "predicting a fixed criterion" would require a prohibitively large amount of skill and labor to carry out the necessary analyses of even a limited number of test variables in relation to the many individual criterion variables if the prediction task were to "describe this patient's personality or behavior pattern." Tellegen goes on to suggest that a more parsimonious approach would be to classify persons in terms of the pattern or configuration of the test scores they generate and then to determine the high probability attributes of persons who have produced very similar test data. This procedure, proposed by Meehl in 1954, has led to only three published reports to date (Gilberstadt & Duker, 1960, 1965; Marks & Seeman, 1963). Some of the major problems to be dealt with in this approach to actuarial prediction will now be considered.

The strategy in this case is to classify persons in terms of the configuration or pattern of scores on the test variables we have selected as relevant to the type and range of behavior we wish to predict. The task is to generate classes that are at the same time large and homogeneous: large enough to provide us with a base for reliable estimates of the non-test characteristics that are shared by members of each class, and sufficiently homogeneous so that we may increase our chances of avoiding important individual differences in criterion characteristics between persons within each class (Tellegen, 1964). We may attempt to satisfy this latter requirement by defining the classes in terms of scores on a large number of finely differentiated and valid test variables but as we increase the number of class defining characteristics and simultaneously increase the degree of homogeneity required within classes, it is readily apparent that we increase even more rapidly the size of the sample of persons needed to yield classes of any specified size. And even after one has identified acceptably large groups of persons, groups that meet some specified degree of homogeneity in test scores or test pattern, the procedures necessary for determining the presence or absence of the criterion characteristics provide us with a variety of problems that require, among other things, some detailed examination of our clinical frame of reference.

The failure of any attempt to predict socially or clinically important characteristics from membership in somewhat arbitrary, test-defined classes of this sort may be due to any one or more than one of the following reasons: (1) the class-defining test variables may not be valid; they may in fact be unrelated to the criterion characteristics we wish to predict; (2) valid test variables are used but the index of profile similarity may fail to take into account some particular important component of the test pattern, for instance elevation, scatter, or shape of a profile pattern; (3) the test variables may indeed be valid and the index of pattern similarity may include all of the important components of the test pattern but class membership (similarity of test pattern) may be defined so broadly that persons are grouped together who are different in test pattern and therefore different in criterion characteristics as well, or (4) the criterion variables may be so highly unreliable that successful prediction of them by any method is unlikely. Possibilities 1 and 4 are problems shared in common with attempts to predict a fixed criterion.

There is an extensive literature in which a wide variety of methods for use in assessing profile similarity or grouping persons are proposed, criticized, refined, compared with one another, or tested with real or artificial data (Block, Levine & McNemar, 1951; Cattell, 1949; Cronbach & Gleser, 1953; duMas, 1946, 1949, 1950, 1953; Gaier & Lee, 1953; Gengerelli & Butler, 1955; Gilberstadt & Duker, 1960; Gleser, 1961; Guertin, 1963; Haggard, Chapman, Isaacs, & Dickman, 1959; Harris, 1955; Heerman, 1965; Helmstadter, 1957; Horst, 1954; Lubin & Osborn, 1957, 1960; Lykken, 1956; Lykken & Rose, 1963; Marks & Seeman, 1963; McHugh & Apostolakos, 1959; McQuitty, 1963, 1964; Meehl, 1959; Meehl & Dahlstrom, 1960; Melda & Linden, 1965; Mosel & Roberts, 1954; Nunnally, 1962; Overall, 1964; Overall & Hollister, 1964; Sawrey, Keller, & Conger, 1960; Sines, 1964; Sullivan & Welsh, 1952; Ward, 1963; Ward & Hook, 1963; Webster, 1952). The types of problems to which most investigators have typically addressed themselves are subsumed under one or another

of the questions originally listed by Cronbach and Gleser (1953) and later
by Sawrey *et al.* (1960) as follows:

1. How similar are the profiles generated by different individuals?
2. How similar are the mean profiles of several groups of persons?
3. How similar is an individual profile to the mean profile of one
   or more groups?
4. How homogeneous are the individuals who make up one or more
   groups?

As Sawrey, Keller, and Conger have noted most writers have not been
concerned with grouping individual profiles into arbitrary test-pattern-
defined classes that have no *a priori* dependence on an outside criterion.

With only a few exceptions there has thus been a notable reluctance
among psychologists to separate themselves from the real-life behavioral
(or theoretical) criterion attributes of their subjects, even for the brief
time needed to consider the possibility that a set of taxonomic classes
defined solely in terms of some of the available psychological test dimensions may provide effective means of predicting these criteria of interest.
It is in this connection that Cronbach and Gleser (1953) have cautioned
that since "similarity is not a general quality . . . the investigator who
finds that persons are similar in some set of scores cannot assume that
they are similar in general. He could begin to discuss general similarity
only if his original measurement covered all or a large proportion of the
significant dimensions of personality." Lykken (1956) vehemently emphasized this commitment to the criterion when he noted that ". . . . the
psychologist is not interested in geometrical configurations (of test data)
but in people." Traces of this attitude are to be found in Gilberstadt and
Duker (1960) and Marks and Seeman (1963) when, in explaining their
choice of methods for identifying clusters of MMPI profiles, they indicate
that the procedures selected allowed them to bring into play their clinical
experience with psychologically equivalent profile types.

Ebel (1961), Meehl (1954 and subsequently), Sawrey *et al.* (1960), and
Sines (1964) have explicitly argued for using psychological test dimensions
as the initial bases on which to classify persons in order then to determine
whether the criteria of interest may be predicted with a meaningful
degree of accuracy. Cattell and Morony (1962) seem to have made a
similar proposal when they wrote "It is to be hoped that the true typology
of the pathological field will soon be systematically attacked by obtaining
the profiles for, say, some 30 recognized sorts of deviants, intercorrelating
them (by r_p) in all possible ways, and grouping them in the demonstrable
clusters."

The first of several points made by Gleser (1961) in her paper on the "Logical Constructs Underlying Various Methods for Grouping Persons" is most relevant here. She commented on the erroneous notion that there exists some "true or right way to classify people that can be discovered in the data" and continued by emphasizing the fact that "any particular classification will be meaningful only to the extent that it is based on variables which are related to the broader class of behavior that we are trying to predict or control."

In these terms a taxonomy is justified, or is good, or is meaningful to the extent that it allows us to generalize accurately (Simpson, 1961). The accuracy with which one may generalize from membership in a taxonomic class is in turn dependent upon the degree to which the taxonomic class-defining variables are related to those broader characteristics to which we wish to generalize. This brings us back to the question of which test variates to choose as class-defining characteristics and, as noted above, few of our psychological test variables individually (Rjs) have demonstrably high $P(Ci/Rj)$s. But the moderate $P(Rj/Ci)$ of many of the available test dimensions appear to be high enough to warrant further use and study.

Rather than continue to put off a crucial test of the validity of our assessment techniques and rather than continue to await the development of measures of the "true" dimensions of personality we may profitably examine the utility of prediction from taxonomic classes that are defined in terms of existing psychological test dimensions; dimensions that have been found to discriminate between many socially or clinically significant groups of persons. It is to be hoped that increasing numbers of psychologists view this proposal made by Meehl in 1954 as lying somewhere between the "galloping empiricism" rejected by Allport (1965) and the psychological realism rejected by Ebel (1961). It is of much more than passing interest that similar apparently arbitrary methods are now being investigated in biochemistry (Irvine, 1961; Williams, Reed, Berry, Cain and Rogers, 1956) and biology (Sokal, 1964) in current efforts to develop or revise taxonomic systems in those disciplines.

1. Published Research on Prediction from a Taxonomic Class

There are only four published reports of actuarial prediction from arbitrary test-defined taxonomic classes (Gilberstadt & Duker, 1960, 1965; Halbower, quoted in Meehl, 1956; Marks and Seeman, 1963). Each of these investigators defined a number of classes of MMPI profiles and then, independently of the test, identified a variety of psychologically significant characteristics of persons who had generated profiles that fit into each of the profile classes. We will now examine the methods used in those studies to achieve the goal of accurate prediction from test defined classes. Many of the following comments will refer only to the work of Gilberstadt and Duker (1960) and Marks and Seeman (1963) because Halbower's unpublished dissertation is not available in the psychological literature.

As the literature on methods for grouping profiles or persons clearly indicates, and as Meehl noted (1956), the questions of how to identify clusters of profiles, and how to specify the limits of intragroup dissimilarity are ". . . very complicated matter(s) involving both theoretical and practical considerations." In all of the three investigations cited in this section classes of profile types were selected and defined using ". . . the investigator's clinical experience with the MMPI, knowledge of the reliability of the scales over time, and knowledge of frequencies of single and mutiple scale high points" (Marks & Seeman, 1963). Specifically, classes of profiles that in the investigator's experience occurred frequently and conveyed similar psychological information about the patients were collected and assigned to one of several groups. At that point the investigators undertook to formulate a set of decision rules that would specify the MMPI profile characteristics of members in each profile class. It should be pointed out that using this approach the *initial* grouping of MMPI profiles is not entirely divorced from expert clinical judgment of the psychological significance of the several profiles. This will be viewed as a strength or weakness of the method depending upon the reader's willingness to consider "geometrical configurations" of test data or his need to stay close to the criterion at all times.

It is clear from inspection of the rules, developed by Gilberstadt and Duker (1960) and Marks and Seeman (1963), to specify each of the classes of MMPI profiles that profile elevation, pattern, and shape are all included among the class-defining characteristics. If one uses the methods employed by these investigators for generating classes of profiles without primary reliance on an outside criterion, there is no readily apparent way in which one could more efficiently incorporate these three essential aspects of test profiles into the rules. It must be pointed out, therefore, that configural rules such as those that have been published for the identification of classes of MMPI profiles do take the important information-bearing components of test patterns into consideration.

The parameters used in this particular method of grouping profiles may of course be defined with whatever degree of precision the investigator chooses, but the smaller the variance desired within a class the larger the original sample of profiles must be if a group of N profiles is sought. Gilberstadt and Duker indicated that about 2300 MMPI profiles were available to them and even so, the numbers of profiles in the three classes they described were 22, 13, and 27 respectively. Marks and Seeman required 20 profiles for each class they would attempt to describe, and from a total sample of 826 profiles were able to specify 16 groups that accommodated 78% of their available tests. It should be noted that when Marks and Seeman's configural rules were applied to the 468 male and 634 female MMPI profiles available in the files at the University of Missouri Medical Center (UMMC) 18.4% of the male profiles and 16.4% of the female profiles, or 17.2% of the total sample of profiles were classifiable.

None of the available reports have so far included information on the variability within the profile groups that have been identified. Data concerning the variability within the 2-7, 2-7-4, and 2-7-8 profile classes as defined by Gilberstadt and Duker (1960) and by Marks and Seeman (1963) are presented in Figs. 1–6. The mean profile for the group of 7 UMMC patients whose profiles fit Marks and Seeman's 2-7 type is given in Fig. 1, and the mean profile for the 8 men whose MMPIs fit Gilberstadt and Duker's 2-7 type is given in Fig. 2. In each figure, and those to follow, plus and minus 1 SD are indicated by the upper and lower dashed profiles. The mean of the 8 profiles that fit Marks and Seeman's 2-7-4/2-4-7/7-4-2 type and the mean of the 10 profiles that fit Gilberstadt and Duker's 2-7-4 type are presented in Figs. 3 and 4, respectively. Finally, in Figs. 5 and 6 the mean profiles for our 5 instances of Marks and Seeman's 2-7-8 and our 14 examples of Gilberstadt and Duker's 2-7-8 type are presented. Although there is considerable reduction in the variance within these profile classes compared to a randomly selected group of MMPI profiles, it is obvious that *the specification rules as currently stated* still allow marked variability among profiles within each group.

To the extent that the variance on the MMPI scales validly relates to socially and clinically significant individual differences among patients, specification rules that allow the degree of profile variability noted above generate groups of persons who show a good deal of clinically significant heterogeneity. The resulting profile classes therefore include patients to whom an undetermined number of the group-derived descriptors do not validly apply. It must be clearly noted, however, that until data are available on patients who generate profiles that are grouped into much more narrowly defined classes than those available so far, the degree of error that results from applying the class descriptors to each member of that class cannot be specified.

Although the 2-7, 2-7-4, and 2-7-8 profile types were defined somewhat differently by each pair of investigators, the findings reported by Gilberstadt and Duker (1960) and by Marks and Seeman (1963) may be viewed as approximate cross-validational studies of the predictive significance of those 3 MMPI profile patterns. It can be seen in Figs. 1–6 that the essential pattern of each of the MMPI profile types is easily dis-

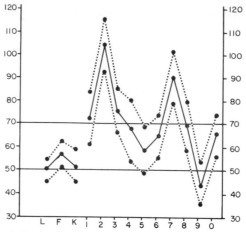

Fig. 1. Mean of the 7 UMMC MMPI profiles that fit Marks and Seeman's 2-7 type.

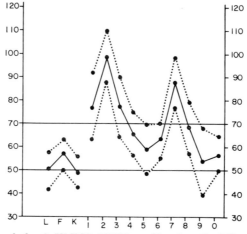

Fig. 2. Mean of the 8 UMMC MMPI profiles that fit Gilberstadt and Duker's 2-7 type.

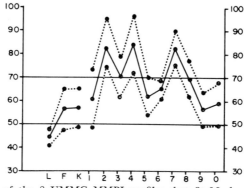

Fig. 3. Mean of the 8 UMMC MMPI profiles that fit Marks and Seeman's 2-7-4 type.

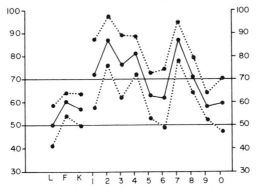

FIG. 4. Mean of the 10 UMMC MMPI profiles that fit Gilberstadt and Duker's 2-7-4 type.

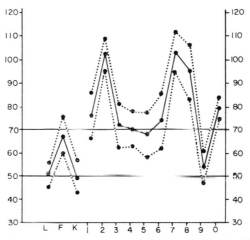

FIG. 5. Mean of the 5 UMMC males whose MMPI profiles fit Marks and Seeman's 2-7-8 type.

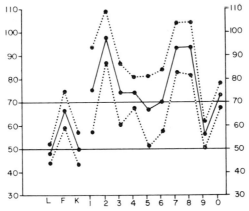

FIG. 6. Mean of the 14 UMMC MMPI profiles that fit Gilberstadt and Duker's 2-7-8 type.

cernible whichever set of rules were used to define the group. There is, moreover, a great deal of similarity in the frequency with which those descriptors obtained from the medical records were found to be associated with a particular profile pattern in both investigations. The similarity is sufficiently great so that the statement made by Gilberstadt and Duker that patients whose MMPI profiles fit their 2-7-8 type ". . . appear to fit the characterization of the group of pseudoneurotic schizophrenics . . ." seems to apply equally well to the patients in Marks and Seeman's 2-7-8 group.

If one assumes, however, as do Lykken (1956) and Meehl (1956), that the measurement error in the MMPI is so great that a coarsely defined set of classes will not result in the loss of much information, the investigator may still attempt to be more selective in the procedures used to identify the criterion descriptors that are applied to each of the patients in each test-defined class. Marks and Seeman had judges describe 9 or 10 patients in each of their groups using a 108 item Q sort. These 9 or 10 Q arrays on patients in a given group were then intercorrelated and from the resulting matrix the 5 most similar Q sorts were selected. The average Q sort placement of each descriptor item in those 5 sorts was taken as the best clinical estimate of the degree to which each of the descriptors could validly be applied to patients in a particular MMPI defined class. This procedure was similar to that used by Halbower and served further to refine the already carefully selected test-defined groups.

In each of the three investigations referred to above a number of efforts were made to insure the maximum possible reliability of the criterion variables used. Meehl (1956) indicated that the majority of the Q items used by Halbower were phenotypic or intermediate statements with only a minority being genotypic. Similarly, it can be seen that the Q pool on which Marks and Seeman's patients were sorted consisted primarily of phenotypic items, thus allowing the judges to make use of information concerning observable behavior rather than having to attempt to draw distant inferences or to extrapolate far beyond such information. In order to avoid the additional possibility that interjudge consistency might be based on "Barnum" type statements that could be sorted reliably merely because of their triviality or universal applicability, the Q items used were those that had shown an acceptable degree of interpatient variability in previous research.

The criterion descriptors that were derived from the case records were considered to be acceptably reliable by Gilberstadt and Duker and by Marks and Seeman only if 2 out of 3 judges agreed on their presence or absence. Finally, that such judgments could be made reliably was indicated by the fact that there were test-defined patient groups within which certain Q items or case history data were differentially but consistently ranked high or consistently ranked low [see particularly Marks and Seeman (1963), Table 28, p. 68 and Appendix A, p. 222].

In all three of these investigations expert clinical judges were used to determine the applicability of each criterion descriptor to the patients studied, although some of the preliminary ratings of the hospital records in Marks and Seeman's program were made by medical students. While the literature reviewed earlier does not support the notion that experts can judge the presence or absence of observable behavioral characteristics of persons more accurately than motivated intelligent laymen, the fact is that since many of the criterion statements were phrased in technical language and some of the statements required inferences to be drawn from behavior, trained judges were necessary.

Before proceeding to a discussion of the program of research on actuarial prediction being developed at the University of Missouri Medical Center it may be well to summarize briefly the procedures used in the three published reports of actuarial prediction from taxonomic classes.

In each of the studies cited above the MMPI, an inexpensive multivariate instrument with moderate partial validity $[P(Rj/Ci)]$ was employed. Classes of persons were defined solely in terms of the test scores; that is, non-test criterion attributes were not included among the parameters that determined class membership. The class-defining characteristics were specified in such a way that the important information-bearing components of the test profiles (shape, elevation, and scatter) were fully represented. The rules for determining class membership were sufficiently narrowly specified so that, although profiles in each class were not identical or strictly homogeneous, the variance in test scores within groups was markedly reduced compared to the variance encountered in a randomly chosen set of profiles. At the same time the specification rules for class membership were broad enough to include a sufficient number of individuals in each group so that an acceptable degree of stability in socially and clinically relevant attributes could be expected if the derived classes were valid.

A variable but fairly large number of clinically significant descriptors or criterion characteristics were then selected for study. Great care was exerted to select descriptors that were clinically or socially relevant, nontrivial or not universally applicable, and capable of being reliably judged. Efforts to enhance the reliability of the judgments included the use of descriptors most of which were relatively closely tied to observable behavior and the use of multiple expert judges. The presence or absence or degree of applicability of each of the criterion attributes to each of the members of each test-defined class was then determined without knowledge of the test data. Those criterion attributes that were found to be regularly associated with membership in each of the classes were considered to be characteristic of a particular class if it occurred more frequently or with greater intensity among members of that class than among psychiatric patients in general.

Although precisely appropriate cross-validation studies of the data reported by Gilberstadt and Duker or by Marks and Seeman have not yet appeared, a comparison of the specification rules and the descriptors applied to each of the three profile patterns described in those two studies reveals markedly good agreement in both the means of similarly coded profiles and in attributes found among members of the similarly coded profile classes.

2. *The Missouri Program of Research on Actuarial Prediction*

The purposes of the Missouri program were quite simple and straightforward. We wished to devise a system whereby patients referred to the Medical Psychology Section could be evaluated economically and quickly with a minimum of professional time being required for the task. We further desired to be able to return to the referring clinician a psychological report that was both comprehensively broad and yet an accurately detailed description of the clinically relevant characteristics that could be inferred from psychological testing. In view of the further fact that we found many of our medical colleagues receptive to the notion of having some indication of the level of confidence they could have in specific statements or some indication of the probability with which certain characteristics could be expected to occur in their patients, we sought a means of indicating the degree of confidence that each descriptive statement seemed to warrant.

a. The Test. The MMPI was chosen as the test around which the program was to be developed. It can be argued rather firmly that relative to other test instruments available to the clinician at this time, the MMPI possesses partial validity $[P(Rj/Ci)]$ that is at least as encouraging as any other—even though one must admit that such a recommendation leaves a great deal to be desired. And if one considers the criteria for test selection that are discussed by Cronbach (1960) and Cronbach and Gleser (1965) it is not unreasonable to expect the weighted utility value of this type test to exceed that of other psychometrically intractable devices that are truly quite expensive. An additional fairly weighty argument for using the MMPI, even in preference to several other objective tests, is the fact that data now becoming available indicate that when its validity is assessed properly [by empirically determining $P(Ci/Rj)$] the

MMPI is found to be meaningfully related to a number of clinically significant characteristics of medical and psychiatric patients.

b. Development of Test Defined Classes. Several different methods were considered for use in grouping the MMPI profiles. The two basic factors that determined our choice were, first, the index must take into account all three of the information-bearing components of the profile, shape, elevation, and scatter, and second, calculation of the index could not require a great deal of time or be excessively complex.

The reports by Helmstadter (1957) and Mosel and Roberts (1954) were particularly instructive in that they had compared a number of proposed indices of profile similarity using actual test data (Mosel & Roberts) and artificial data relating to geometric solids (Helmstadter). Helmstadter's findings particularly, indicated that the D statistic proposed by Cronbach and Gleser (1953) and Osgood and Suci (1952) was as efficient or more efficient than many other methods in assigning objects to the appropriate independently defined criterion classes. We agreed with Sawrey, Keller, and Conger's statement (1960) that of the various measures of profile similarity that have been proposed, the only one that ". . . preserves all three of the basic elements of elevation, shape, and scatter—without encountering serious objections on technical or logical grounds—is that of linear geometric distance." We therefore used D^2 to identify classes of MMPI profiles ($D^2 = \Sigma d^2$), where $d =$ the difference in T score points between corresponding scales on the MMPI.

While many writers who have been concerned with the development or evaluation of indices of profile similarity have noted that the use of the D statistic is based on the assumption that the profile components are uncorrelated (Guertin, 1963; Nunnally, 1962; Overall, 1964; Melda & Linden, 1965), this is not strictly the case. A more precisely accurate statement is that the magnitude of the D measure of profile similarity reflects the factors underlying the test scores in proportion to their representation in the test pattern. Thus, a factor that may be represented in several MMPI scales is weighted much more heavily than some other less pervasive and therefore less well-represented factor. As Cronbach and Gleser (1960) and Sawrey *et al.* (1960) point out, there is no ready answer to this criticism of the use of most profile clustering methods with non-orthogonal variates but it is conceivable that there may be instances in which it is appropriate to give relatively greater weight to the general factors that are basic to several of the scores in a test. The apparently direct approach to the solution of this problem, that is, making use of multivariate tests whose components are orthogonal, is not possible at this time and can only be approximated even with factorially derived tests. It is clear that when one groups MMPI profiles that consist of 13 intercorrelated scales the resulting D^2 values do not reflect the distance between profiles in 13 dimensional space. There is little doubt, however, that profiles that are *geometrically* highly similar can be selected by the use of this measure simply by limiting the magnitude of the D^2 or the component d^2s that will be accepted for defining similar profiles. Whether MMPI profiles that are similar geometrically are generated by persons who are similar psychologically is an empirical question. The data that have been published by Gilberstadt and Duker and Marks and Seeman suggest that geometrically similar MMPI profiles do indeed imply a statistically and clinically significant degree of psychological similarity among the persons who generated those profiles.

The procedures developed at UMMC to group MMPI profiles was programmed for computer processing and the steps will now be described. There are many similarities between the UMMC profile clustering program and the method proposed by Sawrey *et al.* (1960).

Each patient's hospital number, age, sex, date of test, and k-corrected raw scores on the 13 MMPI scales (L, F and K plus scales 1 through 0) were punched into data cards. Each MMPI profile was then compared to every other profile and the D^2 value was the sum of the squared differences in T score points between the 13 corresponding scales. If the D^2 value for any pair of profiles was equal to or less than 625 the following information could be printed out:

1. the hospital numbers of the two patients whose test profiles were being compared.
2. the D^2 value.
3. the value of the largest d^2 that resulted from the comparison of those two profiles.
4. the designation of the scale on which that largest d^2 occurred.

Next, the largest set of profiles that compared to some particular "target" profile, each with a D^2 of 625 or less, was then located. All profiles that compared to the target profile with a D^2 of 400 or less were then selected for further attention. The profiles that related to each of these last profiles with a D^2 of 625 or less were identified. Next, a matrix was formed of the D^2 values resulting from the comparison of each of the profiles in this rather large group with each other. This matrix was successively reduced by eliminating profiles until only those profiles remained that related to at least 60% of the other profiles in the group with a D^2 of 625 or less.

The profiles in this final group were then averaged and the resulting mean profile was set as "Prototype #1." The prototypic profile number and MMPI scale raw scores were then punched into a data card and re-run comparing it to every profile in the original sample. The hospital number, D^2, largest d^2, and scale on which the largest d^2 occurred were printed out if the D^2 for "Prototype" versus the individual profile was 484 or less. By following this procedure, a number of profiles not originally used to construct the prototype were usually located. All profiles that were thus defined as examples of a prototype were then removed from the sample before recycling the program to develop the second profile cluster.

It should be noted that 625 was set as the critical value for the first D^2 only after a sample of 350 profiles had been run through the program several times using other limiting values. The only justification for using this particular value is that a configuration of the test pattern is much more readily apparent when one inspects a cluster so defined than if the group is defined by an interprofile D^2 of 900, for instance, and further, requiring that degree of similarity still allows several groups of 10 or more profiles to be identified in a moderate sample of test records. These particular rather arbitrary procedures for developing profile classes and for determining membership in a profile group were our compromise with the two requirements of (1) achieving relatively homogeneous groups that (2) are large enough to yield stable estimates.

Although it has not been used so far in our program for developing clusters of MMPI profiles, the magnitude and source of the largest d^2 in any comparison is retained. We anticipate the time when our sample of profiles will be large enough to allow us to impose even more stringent limits on the parameters that define profile class membership. At that time we hope to be able to set a maximum value on the magnitude of any d^2 that will be tolerated within a specified class.

c. Criterion Descriptors. The institutional records of the patients tested with the MMPI was the only source of the descriptive statements studied in this research. The only material accepted from psychological reports was the IQ score and inferences from tests other than the MMPI concerning brain damage. All other numerical and narrative information found in the record was coded and analysed regardless of whether the note was made by the admitting office secretary, a first year medical student or the patient's 3-times-a-week psychotherapist, although the majority of the descriptive data were derived from the psychiatric evaluation, the social service report, and the nurses' notes.

The use of hospital records for this purpose can be criticized on several grounds. Although the clinical lore has it that hospital records are notoriously inadequate their ready availability, the wide range of content and contributors and the fact that they often do include longitudinal data, all argue for considering them as a potentially valuable source of information. In the course of the UMMC research program it has become obvious that the records maintained in a university medical center, a state hospital, and a state penitentiary all share a number of common defects. The major drawback to the use of such clinical records is the fact that in none of these three institutions is there a standard set of observations made and reported on every patient. In such a case the lack of a positive statement concerning any given attribute cannot be construed to denote the absence of that characteristic in the patient.

The fact that notes are often made in the charts by nonprofessional personnel seems on closer examination not to be a particularly unfortunate procedure. It will be recalled that the literature on judging others clearly indicates that professional training in psychology is not necessarily the only or the major factor that determines the accuracy with which one is able to describe persons.

One additional comment regarding the use of institutional records as the source of person descriptors is appropriate here. To the extent that the psychologist is concerned with predicting behavioral characteristics of patients that are most meaningful to the institutional personnel, the records that include notations of institutionally significant events and behaviors seem to be an eminently logical place to start. As Swenson and Pearson (1964) have pointed out, the psychological report may be much more valuable and palatable to many consumers if it is phrased in terms of those person-characteristics and behaviors that constitute the primary concerns of the consumer.

That the descriptive information in any one particular patient's record was not determined through a systematic and comprehensive survey of each patient relative to all potential characteristics presents a special problem for the investigator who would use the institutional chart as the source of criterion data. Several researchers have devised extensive listings of person-characteristics against which each patient is evaluated and in those instances the presence or absence of a large number of descriptive items is noted on every patient studied. There are, of course, many serious problems involved in such an approach too, not the least of which is the question of how one is to select initially the pool of criterion descriptors.

The unsettled issues involved in attempting to establish a standard format for recording patient data are the subject of a note by Berkley (1965) who recognized the importance of the composite medical record as a rich source of information concerning possibly quite subtle regularities that have not previously been noted. Two examples derived from the Missouri research may illustrate this point. One of our narrowly defined MMPI profile patterns among female patients is the 46 low 5 prototype.

We have observed that a high proportion of the women in this group have a history that include two, three, and sometimes even four of the following characteristics, but with no one of the descriptors occurring in the records of all 11 patients whose MMPI profiles fit this type: (1) difficulty in accepting the feminine role, (2) history of abrupt weight gain or loss, (3) menstrual irregularity, (4) dysmenorrhea, or (5) hirsutism. In one of our most frequently encountered MMPI profiles among men (the 4'3 type to be described below) severe personality disturbances have been noted to occur in a repetitive cycle that has a 1½ to 2½-year period.

The infrequency with which some of the descriptors occur in the medical records might not seem to justify their inclusion in a standard examination form for psychiatric patients. Or the possibility of a 1½- to 2½-year periodic cycle of nonaffective transitory personality disintegration has, *a priori*, such low probability that it too might not be included in the standardized admission check list. We maintain that by studying *all* of the contents of institutional records we may be alerted to unexpected patterns or events that occur in nature rather than being restricted to only those events or regularities that have, *in our a priori judgment*, high probability of occurrence.

This very heterogeneity of content and the inevitable individualized phraseology with which even the same event or characteristic may be described by different observers makes any composite record an extremely difficult document to deal with. In order to reduce the contents of the institutional records to analyzable form a procedure was developed that is in fact fairly efficient and does allow nearly all of the statements in a record to be categorized.

The total contents of all of the records available on 80 patients at UMMC or in a state hospital were used as our initial sample of patient data. Thirty-nine of the patients whose records were selected constituted our control group in that their MMPI profiles did not appear in any of the 11 computer-identified clusters. The remaining 41 records were on patients whose profiles fit one or another of our MMPI prototypes.

One of the investigators read each patient's entire record and dictated *all* patient-descriptive information onto tape. The stenographer's typed copy of these data was then edited only in order to designate the beginning and the end of each descriptor statement. At this point a descriptor was defined as a bit of information concerning the patient, his personality, his behavior, his responses to other persons, or responses of specified other persons to him. Examples will be given below. These edited statements were then retyped, each on a 3 × 5 card that carried the patient's hospital number in the upper right corner. There were approximately 40,000 cards, each carrying a descriptive statement and a number identifying the patient from whose record the statement was obtained.

These statements were then subjected to three different sortings by two psychologists working together. On the basis of the first sorting the statements were assigned to one of 10 broad categories that reflected the general content of the statement. Each of the categories was identified by a 2-digit number. These major categories and the 2-digit designation of each can be found in the first two columns of Table I.

The statements assigned to each of these major categories were then reviewed and sorted again, this time in order to specify in greater detail the subarea to which the content referred. As a result of this sorting a variable number of subareas were established under each major category. Each of the subareas was also designated by a 2-digit number that was to follow the 2-digit code for the major category. The subareas under each major category and the 2-digit subarea codes can be found in the second two columns of Table I.

TABLE I

AN OUTLINE OF THE MISSOURI SYSTEM FOR CODING THE INSTITUTIONAL NARRATIVE RECORD

Major area		Subarea		Specific statements	
Content	Numerical code	Content	Numerical code	Number	Numerical codes
Childhood	00	Adjustment	00	41	000-040
		Birth and early socialization	01	29	000-028
		Medical history	02	28	000-027
Children	01	None		45	000-044
Education	02	None		44	000-043
Health	03	Abdomen	01	12	000-011
		Admission and discharge	02	25	000-024
		Affect	03	64	000-063
		Allergies	05	8	000-007
		Appetite	06	31	000-030
		Back	07	19	000-018
		Bones and joints	08	26	000-025
		Breasts	09	8	000-007
		Cardio-vascular	10	32	000-031
		Catamentia	11	16	000-015
		Central nervous system	12	43	000-042

TABLE I (*Continued*)

Major area		Subarea		Specific statements	
Content	Numerical code	Content	Numerical code	Number	Numerical codes
		Chief Complaint	13	6	000-005
		Cognitive functioning	14	72	000-071
		Diagnosis	15	61	000-060
		Ears	16	9	000-008
		Extremities	17	24	000-023
		Eyes	18	38	000-037
		Gastro-intestinal	19	40	000-039
		Genito-urinary	20	68	000-067
		Hair	21	8	000-007
		Head	22	59	000-058
		Height and weight	23	56	000-055
		Interview Behavior	24	23	000-022
		Mental status	25	76	000-075
		Miscellaneous Health	26	89	000-088
		Mouth	27	15	000-014
		Nails	28	6	000-005
		Neck	29	12	000-011
		Neurological Pathology	30	55	000-054
		Nose	31	5	000-004
		Personality-phenotypic	32	109	000-108
		Personality-genotypic	33	73	000-072
		Posture	34	5	000-004
		Reaction to staff	35	8	000-007
		Rectal	36	5	000-004
		Respiration	37	38	000-037
		Response to treatment	38	52	000-051
		Sex behavior	39	75	000-074
		Skin	40	27	000-026
		Sleep	41	24	000-023
		Speech	42	27	000-026
		Suicide risk	43	10	000-009
		Throat	44	10	000-009
		Treatment received	45	42	000-041

TABLE I (*Continued*)

Major area		Subarea		Specific statements	
Content	Numerical code	Content	Numerical code	Number	Numerical codes
Miscellaneous	04	None		None classified to date	
Parents	05	Father	01	72	000-071
		Mother	02	86	000-085
		Parents	03	44	000-043
Siblings	06	Brother(s)	01	13	000-012
		Sibs in general or both brother and sister	02	27	000-026
		Sister(s)	03	10	000-009
Social	07	Age	01	11	000-010
		Family relationships	02	20	000-019
		Hobbies and interests	03	17	000-016
		Housekeeping	04	6	000-005
		Intelligence	05	4	000-003
		Marriage	06	26	000-025
		Physical appearance	07	23	000-022
		Relatives	08	7	000-006
		Religion	09	26	000-025
		Smoking	10	8	000-007
		Social-miscellaneous	11	9	000-008
		Peer Relationships	12	11	000-010
		Social relations and activities	13	24	000-023
		Social relations with females	14	23	000-022
		Social relations with males	15	11	000-010
		Use of alcohol	16	25	000-024
		Ward behavior	17	20	000-019
		Criminal record	18	13	000-012
		Service record	19	20	000-019
Spouse	08	None		135	000-134
Work	09	None		51	000-050

Two psychologists then re-sorted the statements that had been assigned to each of the subareas, this time to locate duplicate and synonymous statements. Exact duplicates presented no problem of course, but a great deal of individual judgment was required in assessing synonymous items. One example of the range of individual statements that were grouped together will be given below. On the basis of this third sorting a variable number of specific statements were assigned to each subarea. Each of these specific statements was designated by a 3-digit number. The numbers of specific statements to be found under each subarea are listed in the last two columns of Table I. Thus, each specific statement in this system is identified by a 7-digit number: the first 2 digits refer to the major category; the second 2 digits refer to the subarea; and the final 3 digits denote the specific statement itself.

An example of the range of statements found in patients' records that we considered to be synonymous are given in Table II. All of the

TABLE II
RANGE OF STATEMENTS CONSIDERED TO BE SYNONYMOUS WITH A CODED DESCRIPTOR

Descriptor Statement

0332035 Shows symptoms of anxiety and tension

Equivalent Statements:

anxiety
anxiety tension state
anxious expectation
became acutely upset shortly after her move to a new town
complained of feeling nervous
complained of marked nervousness
complained of nervous exhaustion
complains that she has continued to be nervous and upset
cries uncontrollably, cannot sit down, cannot walk, became so tense that she had
    to run out in the yard
denied emotional factor in symptoms of tenseness and nervousness
general nervousness, fears, and physical symptoms of anxiety for 15 years
nervous
nervous and upset
nervous exhaustion
nervousness
nervousness for a number of years
seen originally for nervousness
shows anxiety
symptoms of anxiety
talks about feeling nervous
tense
tense feelings
tension
unbearable tension prior to treatment

statements listed were considered to be synonymous with the statement "0332035—shows symptoms of anxiety and tension" and when any of these individual statements were found in a record an entry was made for statement 0332035, that is, the specific descriptor "Shows symptoms of anxiety and tension" was applied to that patient. The numerical code indicates that this statement may be found in the general category of Health (the first 2 digits, 03. . . . .) in the subarea of Personality-Phenotypic (the second 2 digits, . . 32 . . .) and as the thirty-fifth specific statement (the last 3 digits, ... 035).

Once each statement that was taken from a patient's institutional record had been given a 7-digit code designation, a set of 3 × 5 cards were prepared, each of which carried the patient's hospital number and a specific descriptor statement and its 7-digit code. We then had for each patient a deck of 3 × 5 cards that included all of the descriptors in this coding system that had been applied to that patient.

A set of IBM cards were then prepared for each patient. The numerical codes of all of the descriptors used were punched into cards, each card identified with the appropriate patient number. The coded data in these decks of patient cards can then be subjected to various analyses.

While this coding system may appear to be as formidable as the original institutional record it really is not. We have found that the time required to reduce an average institutional record (1 inch thick) to a deck of IBM cards that contains the numerical codes of all applicable descriptors is between 4 and 6 hours. No more than 2 of these hours are professional time and even that requirement can be further reduced by training clerical personnel to make all but the most highly judgmental sortings.

In its present form the UMMC coding system contains slightly fewer than 2500 specific statements. As these descriptor statements are further studied some may be combined and others added. As this system is organized, the elimination or addition of specific statements can be accomplished quite readily without disrupting the general format.

For example, current research using this system for coding the institutional record is proceeding not only in a university medical center and in a state hospital but in a prison as well. The coding system presently includes only 13 statements relating to "criminal record" (0718000 through 0718012). As we derive additional data from our prison records this section can quite easily be expanded to accommodate a much greater range of relevant descriptive information.

A detailed system such as this for coding the contents of the institutional record does not in itself insure criterion validity. There are, however, three aspects of this research program, two of them relating to the descriptive statements themselves and one procedural, that are reasonable arguments for use of institutional data as criteria. They are cited here as reasons for accepting this type of file data as sufficiently valid to justify at least more careful study than it has usually received in the past.

First, the overwhelming majority of the descriptor statements are closely tied to observable behavior. Whether the psychologist is interested in his patient's specific behavioral tendencies or in describing the more basic determinants of that behavior is not the question here. The point is, by using the institutional record as a source of criterion information one does thereby have access to descriptors that relate to a large number of his patient's specific behaviors, behaviors that are not only most often of primary concern to those responsible for the treatment and administrative supervision of the patient, but descriptors of the sort that have regularly been found to be most reliably judged. Secondly, judgments of these administratively important behavioral characteristics have most often been made by those persons who are in closest contact with the patient on the ward, for instance, or are based directly on reports obtained from members of the patient's family or his associates who were in the best position to observe and describe his extra-institutional behavior. That is, most of the criterion "judges" were persons who have a high probability of possessing several of the theoretically important attributes of "good judges."

A third way in which the validity of the criterion descriptors will be carefully scrutinized will be to cross-validate the findings concerning any profile type using relatively large groups of patients who fit into quite narrow test-defined classes. If, for instance, a criterion descriptor that may have an over-all low base rate is found to be applicable to a high proportion of persons who generate a narrowly specified test pattern whether those persons are found in a state hospital, a state penitentiary or a university hospital, the validity of that descriptor would appear to be fairly well demonstrated.

In summary the UMMC actuarial program consists of the following four specific steps:

1. the use of a test that not only relates reasonably well to the clinically relevant person-characteristics, but one that can also be administered and reliably scored without great expenditure of professional time,
2. the selection of a procedure for identifying classes of similar test profiles,
3. the development of procedures for identifying clinically relevant characteristics of the persons tested (the criterion attributes), and

4. determination of the contingencies between the several test patterns and criterion attributes.

d. The 4'3 Male Profile. Using the clustering procedure described above with a sample of 500 MMPI profiles obtained from male patients on admission to a state hospital, several major groups of similar profiles

TABLE III

INTERPROFILE MATRIX OF D2 VALUES FOR THE 4'3 MALE PROTOTYPE DEFINING PROFILES

	35237	34918	31544	34466	33463	32197	35625	34575	34564	34531	34444	34328	33399	33212
31599	696	756	457	483	402	469	312	390	471	366	593	470	525	323
33212	675	569	398	600	531	478	231	539	478	415	718	657	358	
33399	615	729	560	756	493	366	469	329	716	301	532	351		
34328	194	534	331	277	388	581	584	196	271	362	389			
34444	421	699	688	456	467	400	801	339	490	295				
34531	420	364	583	331	272	295	488	186	311					
34564	415	465	506	400	349	572	461	203						
34575	276	578	397	329	174	249	496							
35625	686	750	493	679	632	455								
32197	559	605	310	540	309									
33463	670	696	335	561										
34466	233	535	424											
31544	455	593												
34918	608													

were identified. One prototypic MMPI profile that has been most extensively studied (Davis & Sines, in preparation) will be described here. The matrix of inter-profile D^2 values for the prototype-defining MMPI profiles is presented in Table III. The mean of these 16 profiles is presented in Fig. 7.

When the prototypic profile was reinserted into the computer there

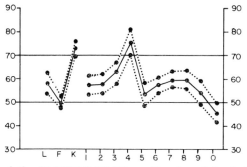

FIG. 7. Mean of the 16 UMMC MMPI profiles that defined the 4'3 MMPI prototype.

were 25 profiles that compared to it with a D^2 value of 484 or less. The contents of the hospital records of these 25 patients were coded in the system just described and the number of patients in this group to whom each descriptor had been applied was tallied. A control group of 20 patients whose MMPI profiles had not related to more than 2 other profiles with D^2 values of less than 625 was then selected from among the original sample of 500 patients. The mean of the profile generated by the control group patients has been presented elsewhere (Sines, 1964). The contents of the hospital records of each of the control patients were coded by the system described above. The number of records was counted in which each of the descriptors was used. The frequency with which each descriptor was used in these two groups was compared and those descriptors that were found to occur significantly more frequently among patients in the group defined by the 4'3 MMPI profile are listed in Table IV. Those descriptors that were used significantly less frequently to describe the patients in the 4'3 group are presented in Table V.

The incidence of this 4'3 profile type in a university hospital population was found to be less than 1%; in a state hospital it was 5%; and in the psychiatric ward in a state penitentiary it was 4.5%.

The records of the three patients who generated this 4'3 profile in a university hospital were reviewed and brief summaries are given below.

Patient A: This 46-year-old man came to the clinic at his wife's urging because of his inability to hold a job, his excessive drinking, and his tendency to abuse her when he drinks. He is reported to have always been shy and timid and even now expresses his feelings openly only when drinking. The patient's mother is said to have been the dominant parent and he is still notably dependent on her. The mother reports that he had no interest in girls until he was 25 or 26 years old and had his first date when he was 31 years of age. The father is said to have been partial to one of the patient's younger brothers and the patient still talks about this perceived paternal rejection. There is a history of psychiatric treatment while the patient was in the army and he was discharged with a diagnosis of schizophrenia, simple type. He married after leaving the army and began drinking heavily after the birth of his first child. He now feels that someone is keeping him from working but denies knowing who that might be. He occupies himself with housework and caring for the children while his wife works to support the family.

Patient B: This 32-year old man was referred to the clinic because of his acute nervousness of 1-month duration and a recent attempted suicide. He showed a fine tremor of both hands, more intense on the left, and there is a history of excessive drinking and recent impotence. The patient reported that both parents disliked him. The patient's mother died when he was 16 years of age, and his father remarried the next year. When the patient found himself unable to get along with his stepmother he left home and has not seen or communicated with his father for the last 15 years. The patient was married for the first time while he was in the Army and reports that before she was killed in an auto accident his first wife was unfaithful to him. His present wife, whom he also suspects of being unfaithful, reports that the patient usually keeps

TABLE IV

DESCRIPTORS STATISTICALLY MORE FREQUENT AMONG MEMBERS OF THE 4'3 MALE GROUP

Code	Statement	Code	Statement
0100032	close to own children	0337027	chest X-ray negative for TB
0200037	quit school before grade 12	0338045	escaped from hosptial one or more times
0303018	emotional instability		
0303054	worried	0501007	dependent on father
0312036	no history of seizures	0501019	father is physically ill
0314007	coherent	0501028	father was rejecting
0314017	general information good	0501035	relationship with father is not close
0314022	lack of judgment		
0314044	denies hallucinations	0502047	closer to mother than father
0315035	diagnosis: schizophrenic reaction, chronic undifferentiated type	0502071	mother is quite talkative
		0503009	dependent upon parents
		0503039	relates well to parents
0316008	some loss of auditory acuity	0602019	feels inferior to siblings
0322053	facial scars	0701002	age: 25-29
0323040	height: 6'	0703015	not interested in sports
0325025	little if any insight	0706019	planing or has planned to divorce spouse
0325049	seclusive		
0326028	history of several accidents	0707008	preoccupied with personal appearance
0332009	defensive		
0332010	demanding	0709021	did not attend church regularly
0332031	seeks attention	0711006	history of nomadic behavior
0332039	timid	0713004	socializes well
0332058	impulsive	0713009	financial irresponsibility
0332059	ingratiating manner	0713012	well liked by others
0332064	manipulative	0714005	attracted to young girls
0332081	history of hostile or aggressive behavior	0716007	denies excessive drinking
		0716017	turns to alcohol during periods of stress
0332089	said to be a follower		
0333023	immature	0718008	history of trouble with the law
0333027	lack of sense of responsibility	0719001	enlisted in armed forces
0333043	sensitive	0801036	spouse rejects patient
0333066	uses projection	0801071	antagonistic and hostile toward spouse
0342006	talkative		
0343000	attempted suicide	0900009	occupation is unskilled or semi-skilled
0343002	does not appear to be suicidal		
0343004	made suicidal threats	0900031	irregular work pattern while in the hospital
0345015	previous psychiatric treatment		
0345017	previously treated with EST		

his feelings to himself but has warned her not to have anything to do with certain men whom he thinks are plotting against him. His anxiety, nervousness, and withdrawal have become more apparent in the last month and he has been unable to work steadily. He was given a diagnosis of depressive reaction.

Patient C: This 32-year-old patient's father died when the patient was 9 years of age. The mother did not remarry and is said to have overprotected and pampered the patient who is an only child. The patient lived with and cared for his mother until

TABLE V

DESCRIPTORS STATISTICALLY LESS FREQUENTLY FOUND AMONG MEMBERS OF THE
4'3 MALE GROUP

Code	Statement	Code	Statement
0302000	admitted ambulatory	0335003	hostile toward staff
0303037	mild depression	0337034	history of pnuemonia
0303024	feelings of worthlessness	0338024	positive response to Rx
0303042	normal affect	0338042	responded well to EST
0306012	generally poor appetite	0341005	insomnia or sleeping difficulty
0310031	some degree of arteriosclerosis	0502022	mother is physically ill
0312019	EEG abnormal	0503005	feels rejected by parents
0314002	appeared confused	0601011	has been physically aggresive
0314021	indecisive		toward brothers
0314029	history of memory deficit	0702016	is a problem in the home
0314032	rational	0702018	threatened to injure or kill
0314050	indifferent		members of the family
0314069	distrustful of others	0707009	careless in personal habits
0315053	diagnosis: chronic brain syndrome	0707020	clean
		0712006	making new friends is difficult
0315056	diagnosis: psychoneurotic reaction, anxiety		for the patient
		0713022	upset when around groups of
0324022	indifferent during the interview		people
0325060	not spontaneous	0713023	worries about money matters
0325075	circumstantial	0716022	does not drink a great deal
0326012	denies illness is serious	0716024	low tolerance for alcohol
0326036	multiple somatic complaints	0717013	cooperative on the ward
0326041	no previous serious illnesses, operations or accidents	0717017	has been uncooperative on the ward
0326086	right handed	0717018	not talkative on the ward
0332035	shows symptoms of anxiety and tension	0719019	rejected from the armed services
0332010	generous	0801119	spouse afraid of patient
0332098	has a violent temper	0801120	spouse is a martyr type
0332099	felt to be dangerous	0900016	unemployed
0332102	mild mannered	0900094	occupation: farming
0332104	shy	0900045	does not relate well to co-workers
0332107	has not threatened or injured others	0900050	unable to work because of psychiatric illness
0330040	reflexes hyperactive		

her death 7 years ago and began dating for the first time 2 years after that. Three weeks after he married his present wife he made a suicide attempt and when he found out that his wife was pregnant he became very upset and attempted to castrate himself. Subsequently he reports that when driving his car he considers running it off the road to kill himself. He reports to his wife that someone is plotting against him. Since the wife's pregnancy the patient has become assaultive toward her. He openly neglects their only child and on one occasion was found burning the baby's clothes in the basement. In one of their arguments the patient held a knife to his wife's heart threatening to kill her and another time choked her into unconsciousness. Since the birth of the son the patient has lost interest in intercourse and does not respond to his wife's overtures. There is an EEG report of moderately severe diffuse cortical disturbance, more severe in left temporal leads. Although currently carrying a diagnosis of passive aggressive personality, aggressive type, the patient has previously been diagnosed schizophrenic reaction, paranoid type.

Although 24 examples of the 4'3 male prototype were located in our prison sample we have been able so far to review the records on only 18 of these men. Some of the descriptive data obtained are given in Table VI.

TABLE VI
SELECTED CHARACTERISTICS OF PRISONERS WHO GENERATE A 4'3 MMPI PROFILE

Offense	Number	Per cent	Offense	Number	Per cent
Murder	8	44	Total convicted		
Rape	6	33	of crimes of		
Armed robbery	3	17	violence	14	78
Burglary	3	17	Paternal absence		
Bad checks	1	5.5	or rejection	10	56

On the basis of the data that we now have concerning men who generate an MMPI profile that fits our 4'3 group we are reasonably confident that a fairly specific set of descriptors applies to such men. In general the 4'3 male MMPI profile as defined above implies, with a high probability, a fairly self-centered, nonsocial person who responds with intensely hostile-aggressive behavior to any of a variety of threats to his adequacy.

e. Summary of the Missouri Actuarial Program. The actuarial search for contingencies between MMPI profile patterns and administratively, clinically, and theoretically significant behavior and personality attributes now being developed at the University of Missouri involves several important methodological differences from previous research.

First, profile classes are being narrowly defined in terms of an arbitrary index of geometrical similarity without reference to an external criterion that includes any assumption regarding the psychological similarity of persons who generate various profiles. Since a large number of profiles is required for this type of approach we have systematically collected over 5000 profiles on persons to whose institutional records we have access.

Second, we have selected as descriptors those statements made about persons by the institutional staff members who have administrative and treatment responsibility and contact with the persons tested. A system has been devised by means of which the highly variably phrased statements found in the institutional records may be coded for more searching statistical analysis.

In spite of the unreliability of the MMPI, we are making the assumption that the predictive validity of membership in test-defined classes will be enhanced if the profile classes are defined quite narrowly. This is in contrast to the views expressed by Lykken and Rose (1963) and Meehl (1960) and results in clusters of profiles within which the variability is considerably less than that observed in the classes so far defined by Gilberstadt and Duker (1960) and by Marks and Seeman (1963).

An inevitable consequence of using narrowly defined profile types is that we find ourselves working with a large number of small classes. We do not consider this in any sense to be a liability of our approach in that accuracy of prediction is of much greater concern at this time than the total number of patients we are able to capture in any one group. It remains to be empirically determined whether the weighted utility value of the type and accuracy of our predictions will justify the expense of dealing with classes that include as few as 5% of our patients.

IV. Implications of Actuarial Prediction

Any serious attempt to study the utility of actuarial prediction of socially or clinically relevant person characteristics is seen to require detailed attention to a number of issues that often fail to concern the clinician. This seemingly tedious detail is indeed necessary if one is to achieve even the moderate degree of predictive accuracy that has been demonstrated so far by the use of actuarial methods. In addition to providing a moderate but practically important degree of predictive accuracy (accuracy that is consistently found, however, to equal or exceed that attainable even using expert clinical interpretation of tests) actuarial methods raise a number of heuristically important implications and questions concerning matters such as, among others, appropriate procedures for validation of our tests, the concern over reliability of tests, and the legitimacy of the diagnostic venture itself.

A. VALIDITY

Definitions of validity are quite variable and a dependable consensus is hard to come by. Regardless of, or possibly because of, the varied statements about validity that are to be found in the literature most validation studies have been designed to investigate the probability of a particular test score or pattern among persons who are members of some arbitrarily defined class and studies of this sort yield what was earlier referred to as partial validity data. The appropriately strong statement by Dawes (1962) that the only logical basis for test interpretation is knowledge of the probability of class membership given a test score or pattern applies equally to the determination of the validity of a test. The concurrent or predictive validity of a test is indicated by the magnitude of the probability that a test pattern implies class membership, not by the magnitude of $P(Rj/Ci)$.

Since many of the socially or clinically important classifications of persons (suicides, murderers, schizophrenics, or neurodermatitis patients) have each been shown to include a variable number of differentiable subclasses of persons we must entertain the highly likely possibility that all instances of membership in such classes may not be predictable from a single or even a few psychological test patterns. We are thus faced with the seemingly incongruous notion that accurate prediction of the criterion of interest may be more quickly and efficiently achieved if we concern ourselves initially not with instances of that criterion class but with classes of persons defined in terms of patterns of scores on currently available psychological tests.

B. Diagnosis

Even though there is the distinct risk of further reinforcing the antipathy that many clinicians have for actuarial methods, it should be pointed out that the strategy referred to above as "prediction from a taxonomic class" leads to a diagnostic nosology. Too often the utility of psychiatric diagnosis in principle is judged on the basis of the current gray-book nosology without consideration of the theory and logic underlying the development and purpose of taxonomic systems. The reader who is either interested in or highly critical of diagnosis per se should consult such writers as Crookshank (1926), Gleser (1961), Simpson (1961), and Zigler and Phillips (1961) for valuable discussions of this subject.

The most frequently voiced criticisms of diagnosis in general or of the existing psychiatric nosology are primarily focused on three topics. First, and most often noted is the fact that persons are not reliably assigned to one or another taxonomic class. The second type of objection is that the current diagnostic categories do not imply common etiological factors for all, or even a high proportion of class members. Finally, it is observed that membership in one of the existing diagnostic classes does not often imply the course of the patient's condition nor does it point to a specific treatment program.

Each of these criticisms is in some degree validly applicable to the existing psychiatric nosology. But the over-all rejection of diagnosis in general on such grounds may be seen on closer examination to be based on a number of unfortunate oversimplifications or the failure to make several basically important distinctions. These points may best be considered in relation to the three specific criticisms.

The lack of reliability that is reflected in the failure of an individual to be assigned to the same diagnostic class on different occasions may be due to at least two factors. One of these is the clinician's inaccuracy in assessing the class-defining patient characteristics that do not change over time. As has been noted above, the more inferential the class-defining characteristics are, the lower is the reliability of even expert judgments. This is in many respects analogous to the problems encountered in scoring a psychological test, where the maximum attainable reliability is achieved when the scoring procedures are reduced to a set of formal rules that can be specified in sufficient detail so that a clerk or a machine can execute them.

A second aspect of the reliability problem concerns valid change in the patient. This may be most clearly illustrated by referring to the 2-7-8 MMPI profile type described by Marks and Seeman (1963). Patients on initial evaluation who generate MMPI profiles that fit Marks and Seeman's 2-7-8 rules have been found to generate a markedly different profile on discharge (the discharge profile is an 0-2). We may thus conceive of two MMPI profile defined classes of patients in this case; the first made up of patients whose profile fit the 2-7-8 rules, and the second consisting of patients who generate profiles similar to the actual MMPI profile generated at the time of discharge by members of the original 2-7-8 group.

We have found 3 female MMPI profiles in the files at UMMC that fit Marks and Seeman's 2-7-8. Only one of these women took the MMPI just prior to discharge and that patient's discharge profile was very similar to the actual discharge profile generated by Marks and Seeman's 2-7-8 group (a D^2 of 511 was obtained when these two profiles were compared).

A search of the files yielded 3 additional profiles that were similar to the discharge profile generated by our member of the 2-7-8 group. Similarity was defined as a D^2 of 625 or less when compared to the discharge profile for the women who had originally generated a profile that fit the 2-7-8 type. A review of the hospital records of the 3 new patients indicated that there was a high degree of similarity in the sets of descriptors that were applied to patients in both groups—the Marks and Seeman 2-7-8 type as well as members of the 0'2 profile class.

The point here is that the marked changes in the degree to which persons manifest a set of class-defining characteristics (here MMPI scale scores) need not be interpreted as evidence of the uselessness of the taxonomic classes that are being used or studied. Any given set of class-defining characteristics may show dramatically low test-retest reliability resulting in the assignment of an individual to differently defined classes at different times yet the predictive validity of these unreliable classes may be quite high. While such a lack of test-retest reliability in a test based on content validity may be legitimately criticized, the lack of test-retest reliability in a test or in a set of class-defining characteristics derived on the basis of concurrent validity is not *in and of itself* a serious deficiency.

To the extent that the several different configurations of class-defining characteristics that are generated by a person over time each imply the same or similar constellation of nonclass-defining attributes of that person, the test or other set of class-defining characteristics may yield a usably valid taxonomy, even in the absence of high test-retest reliability. If we accept Simpson's statement that the purpose of a taxonomic system is to allow us to generalize beyond the set of class-defining attributes (Simpson, 1961), such a system may include several different classes from which identical or highly similar generalizations can be made.

It would appear therefore that while interjudge, inter-rater, or inter-scorer reliability must obtain, reliability in the degree to which a set of class-defining attributes is manifest in the same person at different times, test-retest reliability, is not essential for a useful taxonomic system. Viewed in these terms, the available literature on the current psychiatric diagnostic system does not include the type of studies that would be necessary to appropriately evaluate the validity of that taxonomy.

Relative to the second and third criticisms that have been leveled against the use of a diagnostic system, it should be clearly understood that most of the nonclass-defining characteristics that may ultimately be inferred from class membership must be determined empirically; actuarially, in fact. It is not feasible at this time, nor is it logically necessary, to make use of a large number of the etiologic or antecedent experiences and future behavioral characteristics (course, prognosis, and response to specific treatment) as class-defining characteristics. Those nonclass-defining characteristics that may be related to class membership are not usually or necessarily logically inherent in the definition of the taxonomic classes. In these terms it should be clearly emphasized that the predictive and postdictive value of a taxonomic system or the degree of generalization that a taxonomic system will allow must be determined empirically. The predictive and postdictive accuracy of any taxonomic system may be expected to be directly proportional to the relevance that the class-defining characteristics or dimensions have for the descriptive criteria of interest as well as to the narrowness with which the taxonomic classes are defined.

While any given diagnostic system may be criticized for demonstrated lack of utility, such criticisms must be based on empirical data and even then cannot be generalized in a wholesale fashion to the value of taxonomy in principle. It is obvious that the procedures and methods that are now being employed in research on actuarial prediction using the

MMPI lead quite logically to the development and critical examination of a precisely defined set of taxonomic classes of persons.

V. Concluding Comment

Although Meehl (1965) has recently expressed some disappointment that his analysis of prediction in the clinic has not materially affected psychological practice, the issues he raised are far from dead. A number of social, professional, and technological developments are making it inescapably clear that psychological clinicians *must* sharpen their predictive accuracy while increasing their efficiency. Facilities are becoming available so the interested clinician *can* do so.

If the clinician carefully attends to the numerous basic problems inherent in his usual routine psychodiagnostic activities he cannot fail to see the implication that a high degree of predictive accuracy can be achieved only if he restricts himself to a narrower range of events than has been his wont. He must be prepared to accept the fact that *some things are just not predictable* at this time. And it may well be that attempts to predict some of these currently quite unpredictable events have occupied a great deal of time for a large number of clinicians.

Those of us who attempt to explain and predict human behavior might profitably consider with great thoughtfulness the following comments made by Dr. E. P. Wigner in the lecture he delivered when he received the 1963 Nobel Prize in physics. "It is often said that the objective of physics is the explanation of nature, or at least of inanimate nature. . . . It is clear [however] that . . . physics does not endeavor to explain nature. In fact, the great success of physics is due to a restriction of its objectives: it only endeavors to explain the regularities in the behavior of objects. This renunciation of the broader aim, and the specification of the domain for which an explanation can be sought, now appears to us an obvious necessity. In fact, the specification of the explainable may have been the greatest discovery of physics so far" (Wigner, 1964).[1]

References

Allison, R. B., Jr., Korner, I. N., & Zwanziger, M. D. Clinical judgments and objective measures. *J. Psychol.*, 1964, **57**, 451-456.

Allport, G. W. Traits revisited. Address presented to the Amer. Psychol. Assoc. as a Recipient of the 1964 Distinguished Scientific Contribution Award, Chicago, 1965.

Ash, P. The reliability of psychiatric diagnosis. *J. abnorm. soc. Psychol.*, 1949, **44**, 272-276.

1 Copyright by the Nobel Foundation and quoted with permission of the Elsevier Publishing Company, Amsterdam.

Bendig, A. W., & Sprague, J. Rater experience and the reliability of case history ratings of adjustment. *J. consult. Psychol.*, 1954, **18**, 207-211.

Berg, I. A. The unimportance of test item content. In B. M. Bass and I. A. Berg (Eds.), *Objective approaches to personality assessment.* New York: Van Nostrand, 1959.

Berkley, C. Case histories—an untapped medical information resource. *Amer. J. Med. Electron.*, 1965, **4**, 4-5.

Birnbaum, A., & Maxwell, A. E. Classification procedures based on Bayes' formula. In L. J. Cronbach and G. C. Gleser (Eds.) *Psychological tests and personnel decisions.* Urbana: Univer. of Illinois Press, 1965.

Block, J., Levine, L., & McNemar, Q. Testing for the existence of psychometric patterns. *J. abnorm. soc. Psychol.*, 1951, **46**, 356-359.

Borke, H., & Fiske, D. W. Factors influencing the prediction of behavior from a diagnostic interview. *J. consult. Psychol.*, 1957, **21**, 78-80.

Briggs, P. F., & Wirt, R. D. Intra-Q deck relationships as influences and realities in personality assessment. *J. consult. Psychol.*, 1960, **24**, 61-66.

Canter, A. H. MMPI profiles in multiple sclerosis. *J. consult. Psychol.*, 1951, **15**, 253-256.

Cattell, R. B. R_p and other coefficients of pattern similarity. *Psychometrika*, 1949, **14**, 279-298.

Cattell, R. B., & Morony, J. H. The use of the 16PF in distinguishing homosexuals, normals, and general criminals. *J. consult. Psychol.*, 1962, **26**, 531-540.

Cattell, R. B., Saunders, D. R., & Stice, G. F. *Handbook to the Sixteen Personality Factor Questionnaire.* (3rd ed.) Champaign, Ill.: Institute of Personality and Ability Testing, 1957.

Cline, V. B., & Richards, J. M., Jr. Accuracy of interpersonal perception—a general trait? *J. abnorm. soc. Psychol.*, 1960, **60**, 1-7.

Cronbach, L. J. Processes affecting scores on "understanding of others" and "assumed similarity." *Psychol. Bull.*, 1955, **52**, 177-193.

Cronbach, L. J. *Essentials of psychological testing.* New York: Harper, 1960.

Cronbach, L. J., & Gleser, G. C. Assessing similarity between profiles. *Psychol. Bull.*, 1953, **50**, 456-473.

Cronbach, L. J., & Gleser, G. C. *Psychological tests and personnel decisions.* Urbana: Univ. of Illinois Press, 1965.

Crookshank, F. G. Theory of diagnosis. *Lancet*, 1926, **211**, 939-942 and 995-999.

Davis, K. R., & Sines, J. O. An antisocial behavior pattern predictable from a specific MMPI profile. (in preparation)

Dawes, R. M. A note on base rates and psychometric efficiency. *J. consult. Psychol.*, 1962, **26**, 422-424.

duMas, F. M. A quick method of analyzing the similarity of profiles. *J. clin. Psychol.*, 1946, **2**, 80-83.

duMas, F. M. The coefficient of profile similarity. *J. clin. Psychol.*, 1949, **5**, 123-131.

duMas, F. M. A note on the coefficient of profile similarity. *J. clin. Psychol.*, 1950, **3**, 300-301.

duMas, F. M. Quick methods for the analysis of the shape, elevation, and scatter of profiles. *J. clin. Psychol.*, 1953, **9**, 345-348.

Ebel, R. L. Must all tests be valid? *Amer. Psychol.*, 1961, **16**, 640-647.

Eber, H. W. Computer reporting of 16PF data. Paper presented to the Amer. Psychol. Assoc., Los Angeles, 1964.

Estes, S. G. Judging personality from expressive behavior. *J. abnorm. Psychol.*, 1938, **33**, 217-236.

Finney, J. C. Purposes and usefulness of the Kentucky program for the automatic interpretation of the MMPI. Paper presented to the Amer. Psychol. Assoc., Chicago, 1965.

Fisher, J. The twisted pear and the prediction of behavior. *J. consult. Psychol.*, 1959, **23**, 400-405.

Fowler, R. D. Computer processing and reporting of personality test data. Paper presented to the Amer. Psychol. Ass., Los Angeles, 1964.

Fowler, R. D. Purposes and usefulness of the Alabama program for the automatic interpretation of the MMPI. Paper presented to the Amer. Psychol. Assoc., Chicago, 1965.

Gage, N. L. Explorations in the understanding of others. *Educ. psychol. Measmt.*, 1953, **13**, 14–26.

Gage, N. L., & Cronbach, L. J. Conceptual and methodological problems in interpersonal perception. *Psychol. Rev.*, 1955, **62**, 411-422.

Gaier, E. L., & Lee, M. C. Pattern analysis: the configural approach to predictive measurement. *Psychol. Bull.*, 1953, **50**, 140-148.

Garfield, S. L., Heine, R. W., & Leventhal, M. An evaluation of psychological reports in a clinical setting. *J. consult. Psychol.*, 1954, **18**, 281-286.

Garland, L. H. The problem of observer error. *Bull. N. Y. Acad. Med.*, 1960, **36**, 569-584.

Gengerelli, J. A., & Butler, B. V. A method for comparing the profiles of several population samples. *J. Psychol.*, 1955, **40**, 247-268.

Ghiselli, E. E. Dimensional problems of criteria. *J. appl. Psychol.*, 1956, **40**, 1-4.

Ghiselli, E. E. The prediction of predictability. *Educ. psychol. Measmt.*, 1960, **20**, 3-8.

Giedt, F. H. Comparison of visual, content, and auditory cues in interviewing. *J. consult. Psychol.*, 1955, **19**, 407-416.

Gilberstadt, H. A modal MMPI profile type in neurodermatitis. *Psychosom. Med.*, 1962, **24**, 471-476.

Gilberstadt, H., & Duker, J. Case history correlates of three MMPI profile types. *J. consult. Psychol.*, 1960, **24**, 261-267.

Gilberstadt, H., & Duker, J. *A Handbook for Clinical and Actuarial MMPI Interpretation.* Philadelphia: Saunders, 1965.

Gilberstadt, H., & Farkas, E. Another look at MMPI profile types in multiple sclerosis. *J. consult. Psychol.*, 1961, **25**, 440-444.

Gleser, G. C. Logical constructs underlying various methods of grouping persons. Paper presented at the Sixth Ann. VA Res. Conf. on Cooperative Chemotherapy Stud. in Psychiat., 1961.

Gleser, G. C. Projective methodologies. *Ann. Rev. Psychol.*, 1963, **14**, 391-422.

Goldberg, L. R. Diagnosticians vs diagnostic signs: the diagnosis of psychosis vs neurosis from the MMPI. *Psychol. Monogr.*, 1965, **79**, No. 9 (Whole No. 602).

Gough, H. G. Clinical versus statistical prediction in psychology. In L. Postman (Ed.), *Psychology in the making.* New York: Knopf, 1962.

Gravitz, M. A., & Davis, N. High speed electronic computer scoring and analysis of the MMPI. Paper presented to the Amer. Psychol. Assoc., Chicago, 1965.

Grebstein, L. C. Relative accuracy of actuarial prediction, experienced clinicians and graduate students in a clinical judgment task. *J. consult. Psychol.*, 1963, **27**, 127-132.

Grigg, A. E. Experience of clinicians, and speech characteristics and statements of clients as variables in clinical judgment. *J. consult. Psychol.*, 1958, **22**, 315-319.

Grosz, H. J., & Grossmann, K. G. The sources of observer variation and bias in clinical judgments: I. the item of psychiatric history. *J. nerv. ment. Dis.*, 1964, **138**, 105-113.

Guertin, W. H. A computer package to identify clusters of similar profiles. Paper presented to the Southeast. Psychol. Assoc., 1963.

Haggard, E. A., Chapman, J. P., Isaacs, K. S., & Dickman, K. W. Intraclass correlation vs. factor analytic techniques for determining groups of profiles. *Psychol. Bull.,* 1959, **56**, 48-57.

Harris, C. W. Characteristics of two measures of profile similarity. *Psychometrika*, 1955, **20**, 289-297.

Hathaway, S. R. Clinical intuition and inferential accuracy. *J. Pers.,* 1956, **24**, 223-250.

Hathaway, S. R., & McKinley, J. C. *Manual for the Minnesota Multiphasic Personality Inventory.* New York: The Psychological Corporation, 1951.

Heerman, E. F. Comments on Overall's "Multivariate methods for profile analysis." *Psychol. Bull.,* 1965, **63**, 128.

Helmstadter, G. C. An empirical comparison of methods for estimating profile similarity. *Educ. psychol. Measmt.,* 1957, **17**, 71-82.

Henrichs, T. Objective configural rules for discriminating MMPI profiles in a psychiatric population. *J. clin. Psychol.,* 1964, **20**, 157-159.

Hoffman, P. J. The paramorphic representation of clinical judgment. *Psychol. Bull.,* 1960, **57**, 116-131.

Holt, R. W. Clinical *and* statistical prediction: a reformulation and some new data. *J. abnorm. soc. Psychol.,* 1958, **56**, 1-12.

Horst, P. Pattern analysis and configural scoring. *J. clin. Psychol.,* 1954, **10**, 1-11.

Irvine, D. G. Apparently non-indolic Ehrlich-positive substances related to mental illnesses. *J. Neuropsychiat.,* 1961, **2**, 292-305.

Jenkins, J. G. Validity for what? *J. consult. Psychol.,* 1946, **10**, 39-98.

Kleinmuntz, B. MMPI decision rules for the identification of college maladjustment: A digital computer approach. *Psychol. Monogr.,* 1963, **77**, No. 14 (Whole No. 577). (a)

Kleinmuntz, B. Personality test interpretation by digital computer. *Sci.,* 1963, **139**, 416-418. (b)

Kleinmuntz, B. Profile analysis revisited: a heuristic approach. *J. counsel. Psychol.,* 1963, **10**, 315-321. (c)

Kleinmuntz, B. Computer simulation of diagnostic judgments. Paper presented to the Midwest. Psychol. Assoc., St. Louis, 1964.

Kostlan, A. A method for the empirical study of psychodiagnosis. *J. consult. Psychol.,* 1954, **18**, 83-88.

Kubie, L. S. Multiple determinants of suicidal efforts. *J. nerv. ment. Dis.,* 1964, **138**, 3-8.

Ledley, R. S., & Lusted, L. B. Medical diagnosis and modern decision making. In *Mathematical Problems in the Biological Sciences, Proc. Sympos. Appl. Mathem.,* 1962, **14**, 117-158.

Levitt, H., & Fellner, C. MMPI profiles of three obesity sub-groups. *J. consult. Psychol.,* 1965, **29**, 91.

Lewinsohn, P. M., Nichols, R. C., Pulos, L., Lomont, J. F., Nickel, H. J., & Siskind, G. The reliability and validity of quantified judgments from psychological tests. *J. clin. Psychol.,* 1963, **19**, 64-73.

Lindzey, G. Seer versus sign. *J. exp. Res. Pers.,* 1965, **1**, 17-26.

Livson, N. H., & Nichols, T. F. Discrimination and reliability in Q-sort personality descriptions. *J. abnorm. soc. Psychol.,* 1956, **52**, 159-165.

Lodwick, G. S., Haun, C. L., Smith, W. E., Keller, R. F., & Robertson, E. D. Computer diagnosis of primary bone tumors. *Radiology,* 1963, **80**, 273-275.

Lubin, A., & Osburn, H. G. A theory of pattern analysis for the prediction of a quantitative criterion. *Psychometrika,* 1957, **22**, 63-73.

Lubin, A., & Osburn, H. G. The use of configural analysis for the prediction of a qualitative criterion. *Educ. psychol. Measmt.*, 1960, **20**, 275-282.

Lykken, D. T. A method of actuarial pattern analysis. *Psychol. Bull.*, 1956, **53**, 102-107.

Lykken, D. T., & Rose, R. Psychological prediction from actuarial tables. *J. clin. Psychol.*, 1963, **19**, 139-151.

McHugh, R. B., & Apostolakos, P. Methodology for the comparison of clinical with actuarial predictions. *Psychol. Bull.*, 1959, **56**, 301-308.

McQuitty, L. L. Rank order typal analysis. *Educ. psychol. Measmt.*, 1963, **23**, 55-62.

McQuitty, L. L. Capabilities and improvements of linkage analysis as a clustering method. *Educ. psychol. Measmt.*, 1964, **24**, 441-456.

Marks, P. A. An assessment of the diagnostic process in a child guidance setting. *Psychol. Monogr.*, 1961, **75**, No. 3 (Whole No. 507).

Marks, P. A., & Seeman, W. *The actuarial description of abnormal personality.* Baltimore: Williams and Wilkins, 1963.

Meehl, P. E. Configural scoring. *J. consult. Psychol.*, 1950, **14**, 165-171.

Meehl, P. E. *Clinical versus statistical prediction.* Minneapolis: Univer. of Minnesota Press, 1954.

Meehl, P. E. Wanted—a good cookbook. *Amer. Psychol.*, 1956, **11**, 263-272.

Meehl, P. E. A comparison of clinicians with five statistical methods of identifying psychotic MMPI profiles. *J. counsel. Psychol.*, 1959, **6**, 102-109.

Meehl, P. E. The cognitive activity of the clinician. *Amer. Psychol.*, 1960, **15**, 19-27.

Meehl, P. E. Seer over sign: the first good example. *J. exp. Res. Pers.*, 1965, **1**, 27-32.

Meehl, P. E., & Dahlstrom, W. G. Objective configural rules for discriminating psychotic from neurotic MMPI profiles. *J. consult. Psychol.*, 1960, **24**, 375-387

Meehl, P. E., & Rosen, A. Antecedent probability and the efficiency of psychometric signs, patterns, or cutting scores. *Psychol. Bull.*, 1955, **52**, 194-216.

Mehlman, B. The reliability of psychiatric diagnoses. *J. abnorm. soc. Psychol.*, 1952, **47**, 577-578.

Meier, M. J., & French, L. A. Some personality correlates of unilateral and bilateral EEG abnormalities in psychomotor epileptics. *J. clin. Psychol.*, 1965, **21**, 3-9.

Melda, R. J., & Linden J. D. The homogeneous classification of neuropsychiatric patient profiles: a multivariate approach. Paper presented to the Amer Psychol. Assoc., Chicago, 1965.

Miller, G. A. The magical number seven, plus or minus two: some limits on our capacity for processing information. *Psychol. Rev.*, 1956, **63**, 81-97.

Miller, H., & Bieri, J. An informational analysis of clinical judgment. *J. abnorm. soc. Psychol.*, 1963, **67**, 317-325.

Moos, R. H., & Solomon, G. F. Minnesota Multiphasic Personality Inventory response patterns in patients with rheumatoid arthritis. *J. Psychosom. Res.*, 1964, **8**, 17-28.

Mosel, J. N., & Roberts, J. B. The comparability of measures of profile similarity: an empirical study. *J. consult. Psychol.*, 1954, **18**, 61-66.

Nunnally, J. The analysis of profile data. *Psychol. Bull.*, 1962, **59**, 311-319.

Osgood, C. E., & Suci, G. A measure of relation determined by both mean difference and profile information. *Psychol. Bull.*, 1952, **49**, 251-262.

Oskamp, S. The relationship of clinical experience and training methods to several criteria of clinical prediction. *Psychol. Monogr.*, 1962, **76**, No. 28 (Whole No. 547).

Overall, J. E. Note on multivariate methods for profile analysis. *Psychol. Bull.*, 1964, **61**, 195-198.

Overall, J. E., & Hollister, L. E. Computer procedures for psychiatric classification. *J.A.M.A.*, 1964, **187**, 115-120.

Pearson, J. S., Swenson, W. M., Rome, H. P., Mataya, P., & Brannick, T. L. Further experience with the automated Minnesota Multiphasic Personality Inventory. *Proc. Mayo Clin.*, 1964, **39**, 823-829.

Piotrowski, Z. A. Digital-computer interpretation of inkblot test data. *Psychiat. Quart.*, 1964, **38**, 1-26.

Rimm, D. Cost efficiency and test prediction. *J. consult. Psychol.*, 1963, **27**, 89-91.

Robins, L. N., & Braroe, N. W. The lay interviewer in psychiatric research. *J. nerv. ment. Dis.*, 1964, **138**, 70-78.

Rome, H. P., Swenson, W. M., Mataya, P., McCarthy, C. E., Pearson, J. S., & Keating, R. F. Symposium on automation techniques in personality assessment. *Proc. Mayo Clin.*, 1962, **37**, 61-82.

Rorschach, H. *Psychodiagnostics*. Berne: Verlag Hans Huber, 1942.

Rosen, W., Hales, W. M., & Simon, W. Classification of "suicidal" patients. *J. consult. Psychol.*, 1954, **18**, 359-362.

Sarbin, T. R. A contribution to the study of actuarial and individual methods of prediction. *Amer. J. Sociology*, 1943, **48**, 593-602.

Sawrey, W. L., Keller, L., & Conger, J. J. An objective method of grouping profiles by distance functions and its relation to factor analysis. *Educ. psychol. Measmt.*, 1960, **20**, 651-673.

Seeman, W. Some persistent misconceptions about actuarial (statistical) description of personality. Paper presented to the Midwest. Psychol. Assoc., St. Louis, 1964.

Simpson, G. G. *Principles of animal taxonomy*. New York: Columbia Univer. Press, 1961.

Sines, J. O. The variety and frequency of usage of descriptive terms in psychological reports. Unpublished data, 1960.

Sines, J. O. Actuarial methods as appropriate strategy for the validation of diagnostic tests. *Psychol. Rev.*, 1964, **71**, 517-523.

Sokal, R. R. Numerical taxonomy and disease classification. In J. A. Jacquez (Ed.), *The diagnostic process*. Ann Arbor: Malloy Lithogr. Inc., 1964.

Sullivan, P. L., & Welsh, G. S. A technique for objective configural analysis of MMPI profiles. *J. consult. Psychol.*, 1952, **16**, 383-388.

Swenson, W. M. Purposes and usefulness of the Mayo Clinic program for the automatic interpretation of the MMPI. Paper presented to the Amer. Psychol. Assoc., Chicago, 1965.

Swenson, W. M., & Pearson, J. S. Automated techniques for personality assessment. Paper presented to the Midwest. Psychol. Assoc., St. Louis, 1964.

Taft, R. The ability to judge people. *Psychol. Bull.*, 1955, **52**, 1-23.

Taft, R. Multiple methods of personality assessment. *Psychol. Bull.*, 1959, **56**, 333-352.

Tellegen, A. The Minnesota Multiphasic Personality Inventory. In L. E. Abt and B. F. Reiss (Eds.), *Progress in clinical psychology*. New York: Grune & Stratton, 1964.

Turner, M. W. On the mathematical basis of medical diagnosis. *Med. Coll. Virginia Quart.*, 1965, **1**, 22-27.

Ward, J. H., Jr. Hierarchical grouping to optimize an objective function. *J. Amer. statistical Ass.*, 1963, **58**, 236-244.

Ward, J. H., Jr., & Hook, M. E. Application of an hierarchical grouping procedure to a problem of grouping profiles. *Educ. psychol. Measmt.*, 1963, **23**, 69-81.

Webster, H. A note on profile similarity. *Psychol. Bull.*, 1952, **49**, 438-439.

Wedell, C., & Smith, K. V. Consistency of interview methods in appraisal of attitudes. *J. appl. Psychol.,* 1951, **35,** 392-396.

Weiss, Janice H. Effect of professional training and amount and accuracy of information on behavioral prediction. *J. consult. Psychol.,* 1963, **27,** 257-262.

Wheeler, L., Burke, C. J., & Reitan, R. M. An application of discriminant functions to the problem of predicting brain damage using behavioral variables. *Percept. mot. Skills,* 1963, **16,** 417-440.

Wigner, E. P. Events, laws of nature, and invariance principles. *Sci.,* 1964, **145,** 995-999.

Williams, R. J., Reed, J. G., Berry, H. K., Cain, L., & Rogers, L. L. Individual metabolic patterns and human disease: an exploratory study utilizing predominantly paper chromatographic methods. The Univer. of Texas Publ., 1956, No. 5109.

Zigler, E., & Phillips, L. Psychiatric diagnosis: a critique. *J. abnorm. soc. Psychol.,* 1961, **63,** 607-618.

PERSONALITY AND THE RESOLUTION OF INTERPERSONAL DISAGREEMENTS[1]

Ivan D. Steiner

DEPARTMENT OF PSYCHOLOGY,
UNIVERSITY OF ILLINOIS,
URBANA, ILLINOIS

I. Introduction

In his classic studies of conforming behavior Asch (1952) noted that many of his subjects did not yield to the social pressures created by a unanimous majority. However, all of them showed signs of being dis-

---

[1] Several of the studies by Steiner that are reported in this review were supported by a grant from the United States Public Health Service, National Institutes of Health, No. M-4460.

turbed or disoriented when they discovered that their own judgments were not shared by their colleagues.

Interpersonal disagreements are not always troublesome. If the issue is of little importance, or the antagonist is believed to be an undependable source of information, contrary opinions may be tolerated with little difficulty. But many disagreements are not readily resolved or easily tolerated. Beliefs are usually embedded in larger attitude structures (Rosenberg, 1960) and thus assume an importance that extends beyond their own immediate significance. Moreover, even seemingly unimportant opinions, like those concerned with the lengths of lines, may become critical when they are challenged in a way that suggests one lacks some basic ability. Were it not so, the "forces toward uniformity" that Festinger (1950) says impinge on interacting individuals should make conformists of us all.

This paper is concerned with disagreements that are not likely to be tolerated with equanimity, that pose at least some threat to the self-percepts or attitude structures of the parties concerned, and that make at least some minimal form of reprisal likely. Such disagreements, we shall assume, represent a state of imbalance analogous to that described by Newcomb (1953) in his discussion of the A-B-X-model, and by Osgood (1960) in his treatment of the congruity principle. Though we do not postulate a universal "drive" to achieve balance, it is believed that the conditions specified above are generally sufficient to prompt individuals to seek balance-restoring resolutions of their interpersonal conflicts. Several such resolutions are possible, and on the following pages we shall examine some of the variables that favor the use of one rather than another response to interpersonal disagreements. Both personality and situational variables will be considered, for there is reason to believe that these two types of determinants sometimes interact strongly with one another.

II. Responses to Interpersonal Disagreements

A. Types of Responses

In their simplest forms, the conflicts under examination here involve the elements pictured in Fig. 1. The individual whose responses are to be understood and predicted has an attitude toward an issue. He receives a message from one or more associates (a source) with whom he has a positive relationship. The message expresses an attitude toward the issue that is at variance with that held by the individual. According to the formulations of Heider (1958), Newcomb (1953), and Osgood (1960), these conditions represent an imbalanced state, and the individual will attempt to restructure the relationships in a way that reduces or eliminates the imbalance.

What *can* he do? According to balance theory a triangle of the kind under consideration here is balanced if the relationships represented by all three sides are positive, or if the relationship represented by *only one* side is positive. Consequently, the individual may achieve balance by "altering" any one of the relationships depicted by the triangle. He may change his own attitude so that it is brought into accord with the position expressed by the message (conform), or he may change his evaluation of the source so that it is no longer positive (reject the source). He may also alter the message by misconstruing its meaning or by autistically

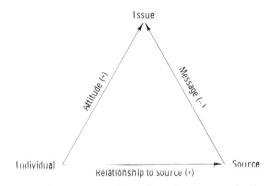

Fig. 1. Schematic representation of an interpersonal disagreement.

forgetting its disagreeable features (assimilation or underrecall of disagreements). In addition, he may be able to convince the source that the message should be revoked (proselytism).

Under certain circumstances still other reactions may be feasible. If the message has not come directly from the source, the individual may conclude that it has been garbled in transmission, or that the attributed source did not, in fact, originate the message at all (disbelief). Or he may decide that the message, though authentic enough, does not represent the true beliefs of the source who must have been jesting, looking at the issue from an extremely atypical point of view, or talking about a completely different issue (rationalization).

Finally, the individual may employ a response that is not directly derivable from an examination of Fig. 1. He may, as Rosenberg (1960) has suggested, isolate the issue from the larger ideological framework of which it is normally a part, and convince himself that disagreements concerning this inconsequential issue do not threaten other beliefs or imply that he or the source is inadequate or culpable (devaluation of the issue). This reaction permits all three sides of the triangle to remain unchanged.

B. EMERGING AGREEMENT CONCERNING THE NATURE OF RESPONSES

The responses enumerated above closely parallel the dissonance-reducing reactions that Festinger and Aronson (1960) believe to be available to the person whose judgments have been contradicted by an associate.

> In general, he may attempt to convince himself that the content area in which the disagreement exists is relatively unimportant; he may attempt to derogate the person or group that disagrees with him; he may attempt to eliminate the disagreement either by changing his own opinion or by attempting to influence the disagreeing persons to change theirs; or he may seek additional social support for the opinion he holds, thus, in essence, adding new cognitions which are consonant with his own opinions (p. 222).

Other writers (Brehm & Cohen, 1962; Newcomb, 1953; Osgood, 1960; Secord & Backman, 1961) who have approached the problem from the point of view of balance theory have proposed lists of responses that partially duplicate those cited above. Working within the framework of learning theory, Hovland (1959) suggested that influence attempts may produce a number of responses, which include attitude change (conformity), assimilation of the message, and rejection of the source. An early study by Schachter (1951) reflected the Lewinian tradition and led to the conclusion that proselytism and rejection are alternative responses to disagreements; this study also emphasized the "relevance" of the topic, thus anticipating the present concern about devaluation of the issue. In a theoretical treatise on conceptual systems and personality organization, Harvey, Hunt, and Schroder (1961) have examined a wide range of reactions to disconfirming communications. Although their discussion is phrased in language that differs markedly from that of the present paper, most of the responses that they describe appear to duplicate or resemble those mentioned above. Writers who have considered the problem of interpersonal disagreements from more eclectic points of view (Kelman & Eagly, 1965; Manis, 1961) have also emphasized some of the same responses.

This review is focused upon studies dealing with conformity, rejection, underrecall, and devaluation. Each of the first three of these responses has received considerable attention in theory and research; the last is included because it is of special interest to the writer. Other responses to interpersonal disagreements, such as proselytism, disbelief, and rationalization, are examined much less thoroughly. Because they have not often been linked to one another in empirical studies, they are less amenable to systematic treatment in a review that is concerned with the identification of personality characteristics that favor the use of one rather than another response.

Evidence that disagreements actually do prompt people to produce balance-restoring reactions is not lacking, although some types of response have received far less study than others. An extensive review of the pertinent literature would take us well beyond the intended scope of this paper, but a few illustrative studies may be mentioned. The studies by Asch and Schachter cited previously document the use of conformity, rejection, and proselytism. Hovland (1959) and Manis (1961) have shown that people sometimes assimilate discrepant arguments, and Lewis (1941) has reported evidence that they also "explain away" disagreements by concluding that the source has been facetious or concerned with a different issue. The research of Osgood and Tannenbaum (1955) not only reveals the use of conformity and rejection, but also indicates a tendency toward disbelief when the position advocated by the source is highly discrepant from the individual's own view. Evidence concerning devaluation of the issue is less direct. Subjects' conceptions of the significance of topics or tasks have often been manipulated, but researchers have rarely asked whether people change their appraisals of the importance of issues when disagreements occur. Results of several studies (e.g., Deutsch & Gerard, 1955; Schachter, 1951; Zimbardo, 1960) involving the manipulation of issue-importance suggest that imbalance is much more readily tolerated when the issue seems trivial or irrelevant to the individual's self-percept than when it is made to appear critical. These studies do not, of course, demonstrate that subjects spontaneously conclude that controversial issues are unimportant in order that they may more readily tolerate the controversy, but such investigations do at least suggest that devaluation, if it occurs, should make disagreements less frustrating. It may also be recalled that some of Rosenberg's (1960) subjects, who were hypnotically induced to alter their opinions on an important issue, dissociated the topic from other beliefs with which it had formerly been linked. Presumably this step made the issue seem less consequential, and thus made the individual's new and (in his social environment) unpopular stand more tolerable.

C. Situational and Personality Determinants

Although the studies mentioned above constitute only a very small fraction of the relevant research, they are sufficient to indicate that a variety of different responses to interpersonal disagreements *do* occur. Furthermore, detailed inspection of these studies suggests that an individual's choice of response is strongly influenced by the nature of the experimental situation to which he is exposed. But situational variables do not account for all of the variance. Marked individual differences are sometimes noted between the reactions of persons who are exposed to very similar situations. Thus some of Asch's (1952) subjects showed strong evidence of conformity, whereas others showed none at all. Such diversity of reactions suggests that the individual who receives a message that contradicts his own belief has some margin of freedom to choose from among several balance-restoring strategies. It is this margin of freedom that is examined in the present paper.

It is true, of course, that situational variables often impose serious restraints on the individual's freedom of action, and make some responses more probable than others. Extremely prestigeful sources are not readily rejected; previous public expressions of one's views inhibits conformity; and messages that are received in face-to-face encounters cannot easily be attributed to the wrong sources. Ingenious experimenters have shown great ability to devise situations in which many potential responses rarely occur, and in which subjects rely primarily upon the balance-restoring techniques that are the major interest of the investigator.

There is often good reason for restricting the freedom of experimental subjects. If a manipulation may evoke any of several different responses, and if the occurrence of one response precludes or limits the occurrence of others, the average effect of the manipulation on any one response is likely to be very slight. Consequently, if an investigator is interested in testing a predicted relationship between a manipulated variable (e.g., degree of imbalance) and a specific balance-restoring response, it may be advantageous to suppress the occurrence of alternative responses. Otherwise the expected effect of the manipulated variable may be seriously diluted.

Since most experimental studies of balance theory have been concerned with the effects of manipulated variables on one (or, at most, very few) responses, it is not surprising that relatively little has been learned about the implications of personality variables, or about the interrelationships of balance-restoring responses in comparatively free situations. Because subjects' freedom of choice has usually been rather severely restricted, we may agree with Kelman and Eagly (1965, p. 64) who have maintained that the major unresolved issues in balance theory and its derivatives is "the question of what determines the particular mechanism that a person chooses, out of a range of possibilities available to him in a given situation, in order to restore balance or reduce dissonance." Answers to this question must be sought in situations that allow a wider "range of possibilities" than has generally been permitted in experimental studies.

The individual's "free" responses to interpersonal disagreements may be expected to reflect important personality characteristics. If personality "is the dynamic organization within the individual of those psychophysical systems that determine his unique adjustment to his environment" (Allport, 1937, p. 48), then stable individual differences in response to interpersonal disagreements must, by definition, be indicative of personality differences. Horney (1945) has seen interpersonal conflicts as a primary cause for the development of personality, and has described three persistent strategies for coping with such conflicts (moving against people, moving toward people, and moving away from people). According to this view, man's social life makes interpersonal disagreements inevitable and creates the arena in which certain preferred responses are learned. Depending upon the details of his life history, the individual may have been encouraged to adopt one or another strategy for avoiding or minimizing the threat that is implicit in interpersonal disagreements. In a somewhat less striking manner Fromm (1941) has also argued that many of life's most pressing problems concern our dealings with other persons, and that we come to rely upon favored techniques for managing such relationships. Even Freudian theory, which tends to be *intra*personal in its orientation, contends that people employ favored adjustive processes in maintaining relationships with their associates. Some of the mechanisms that Freud described have more than a faint resemblance to the balance-restoring responses mentioned above. (Thus assimilation and underrecall of disagreements may be special cases of "repression," conformity may be seen as a form of "introjection," and rejection may be the antithesis of "identification.")

The fact that different experimental subjects sometimes employ different balance-restoring techniques, even when the situation appears to favor a single response, suggests that reactions are guided by fairly strong preferences. Probably the individual's choice of response is governed by a "habit family hierarchy" that has been learned through earlier experience with interpersonal disagreements. Undoubtedly, such hierarchies of responses vary not only among people but also for a single individual as he encounters drastically different types of interpersonal conflicts. But it would be uneconomical for the individual to attempt to discriminate between every pair of situations he encounters or to employ balance-restoring responses in a purely random manner. Consequently, it seems reasonable to postulate that individuals learn response hierarchies that are applicable to broad classes of situations. Probably the cognitive boundaries that separate one class of situations from another are subject to social influences, as are the response hierarchies that are associated with each situational domain. Both are presumed to be shaped by the norms of the groups in which the individual has experienced interpersonal conflicts, the socialization procedures that have been employed by parents and associates, and the "accidents of life" that have made some responses seem peculiarly effective.

III. An Approach to the Study of Response Preferences

Research designed to reveal preferred modes of response to interpersonal disagreements should not only permit a variety of responses to occur, but should also include measurement of each mode. The purpose of this section is to describe techniques used by the present author to achieve these ends. Findings obtained through the use of these techniques will be reported in subsequent sections along with data from other sources.

Fifty multiple choice questions were devised. Items dealt with the characteristics of animals, the areas and shapes of geometrical designs, important features of well-known personages and events, and number, letter, and figure series modeled after items contained in I.Q. tests. Some questions were extremely easy, whereas others called for very difficult discriminations or for information that very few persons are likely to possess. Sample items are as follows.

> Which of the following is a silhouette of Monticello, Thomas Jefferson's home? (The three alternative answers included silhouettes of two skyscrapers and the correct silhouette.)
> Which letter comes next in this series? abvcdvefvghv—(Alternative answers were k, n, and i.)
> Which of the following did the ancient Greeks regard as the most pleasing proportions for a building? (In addition to a rectangle depicting the correct proportions, two rectangles of displeasing proportions were offered as alternative answers.)
> Which of the following is a silhouette of Radio City in New York? (Answers included silhouettes of three very similar skyscrapers.)
> Which of the following is a footprint of a wolf? (Alternatives included footprints of a dog, coyote, and wolf.)
> Which number comes next in this series? 40-10-2-40-20-8-40-30—(18, 24, 64)
> Which is Adlai Stevenson's I.Q. score? (120, 153, 174)

Most and least popular answers to each question were determined by administering all items to a large number of college students who were allowed 30 seconds in which to read each question and to write their answers on a piece of paper. Eighteen items were subsequently eliminated from the battery because their content was very similar to that of other questions, or because no single answer proved to be most or least popular. Each of the thirty-two questions retained in the battery was printed, along with the three alternative answers, on a card approximately 10 by 12 inches in size.

These stimulus cards have been used in a series of studies disguised as inquiries into the "dynamics of impression formation." Although the details of the studies have varied, the general procedures have involved putting a college student (the naive subject) into a laboratory situation with one or two experimental accomplices of the same sex. After being informed that they are participating in a study of impression formation, subjects (Ss) and accomplices are asked to reveal their home town, year in college, major, and academic average. When only one accomplice has been employed, he has reported that his home is in Chicago, that he is a junior majoring in physics, and that his academic average is higher than "B." When two accomplices have been used, the second accomplice has claimed the same credentials as the first, except that he has asserted that he is a pre-medical major. After all participants have revealed this limited amount of background information about themselves they are asked to indicate their impressions of one another on a series of six-step graphic rating scales. The ends of some of these scales are identified by polar adjectives indicative of general personality variables, such as confident–unsure, energetic–tired, and immature–mature. The other scales call for judgments about associates' abilities to answer questions of the kinds included on the thirty-two stimulus cards described above. Thus the participants are asked to guess how competent their associates are likely to be on tasks involving the solution of mathematical puzzles, judgments of geometrical designs, identification of animals, and familiarity with historical, political, and economic events.

After rating their associates, participants are told that the experimenter (E) will administer a test that is to be answered orally, and that they should pay attention to one another's answers so that they may improve the accuracy of their interpersonal impressions. On the pretext that "it is much easier to record answers if they are always given in the same order," E requests the accomplice(s) to give their answers first, and instructs S to announce his replies as soon thereafter as he is ready. However, participants are told that they will have no more than 30 seconds for each question. The thirty-two stimulus cards are then exposed in a predetermined order.

The answers announced by the accomplice(s) have been systematically varied from one study to the next, and across treatments within a single study. However, within a single experimental treatment each accomplice always gives a standard set of responses. Typically about twenty of these answers are those that have been found to be most popular among control subjects.

After all thirty-two cards have been exposed, participants are asked to rate one another again on the same graphic rating scales employed earlier. They are also requested to record a written estimate of the number of times they have disagreed with their associate(s) and to indicate their judgments of the extent to which the thirty-two questions measure important personal qualities. The latter data are obtained through the use of a series of graphic rating scales calling for judgments of the extent to which correct answers are indicative of intelligence, general knowledge, good social adjustment, personality traits, etc.

Data obtained in the manner outlined above permit the computation of four different response scores for each S. A conformity score is obtained by counting the number of times the S agreed with the accomplice when the latter gave least popular answers, or by counting the total number of times (out of 32) that the S agreed with the accomplice. Scores obtained in these two ways have correlated .80 or higher, and the latter procedure has been used in most studies because it has been found to distinguish a little more sharply between experimental Ss and control Ss who have not heard anyone else's answers to the thirty-two stimulus cards.

Rejection of the source is indexed by the difference between the numerical values of the ratings given the accomplice before and after hearing his responses to the thirty-two questions.

A score for underrecall of disagreements with the source is obtained by subtracting the S's estimated number of disagreements from the true number of disagreements.

A devaluation score is computed by summing the numerical values of the S's ratings of the significance that should be ascribed to people's answers to the thirty-two stimulus cards. (High numerical values indicate little significance.) Because significance ratings are obtained *after* S has experienced disagreements, but not before, this score constitutes only a crude estimate of devaluation. However, it does indicate S's final evaluation of the importance of the topics, and thus provides an index of the extent to which S may be expected to regard the experimentally induced disagreements as inconsequential.

Information concerning the stability of scores was obtained in a study (Steiner & Vannoy, 1965) in which 61 Ss returned 5 to 15 days after the experimental session and responded privately to the rating scales and the thirty-two stimulus cards. The product moment correlations of scores obtained in the two sessions were as follows: underrecall of disagreements, .51; devaluation, .52; rejection of the source, .74; and conformity, .16. It should be noted that the accomplice was not present during the second session and that subjects were instructed to change their responses if they felt inclined to do so. Thus the very low correlation for the two sets of conformity scores should not be construed to indicate that conforming responses were almost totally unreliable. If the second session had duplicated the first, and if Ss had not been invited to change their answers, the correlation might have been much higher. Indeed, in several studies the split-half reliabilities of conformity scores have varied from .68 to .82. Split-half reliabilities for the other three responses have been of the same magnitude.

The research procedures described above are designed to permit the S to employ his preferred response to disagreements. Although some of the deviant answers announced by the accomplices are obviously incorrect, most of them are not so clearly wrong that conformity is made difficult. The accomplices' academic averages and major areas of study establish them as credible sources (they are evaluated highly *before* the thirty-two cards are exposed) but they are not so unimpeachable that rejection cannot occur when they subsequently express improbable judgments. Many of the questions on the thirty-two stimulus cards can reasonably be interpreted as measures of intelligence, or of other personal qualities, but the content and difficulty of the items are so varied that the entire battery may also be viewed as measuring nothing at all of importance. Consequently, devaluation is a possible response. Finally, because thirty-two pairs of answers are far too many to be remembered accurately, under-recall of disagreements is easily accomplished.

IV. Relationships among Responses to Disagreements

A. Theoretical Considerations

If a situation permits several different responses to occur, an individual might conceivably use one response to the virtual exclusion of others, or he might use two or more simultaneously. Strong use of any one response (e.g., conformity, rejection) should restore balance and make additional responses unnecessary. But moderate use of several responses may also provide a comfortable solution to the problem created by interpersonal disagreements. Whether the individual will employ *one* or *several* techniques for restoring balance is a question that has received comparatively little attention.

Among balance theories, Osgood's (1960) congruency principles come closest to dealing systematically with this problem. In his analysis of responses to persuasive messages, Ogood emphasizes the importance of two critical factors: the individual's initial attitude toward the issue with which the message deals, and the individual's initial attitude toward the source. Both of these attitudes are conceived to fall somewhere on an evaluative dimension that ranges from extremely favorable to extremely unfavorable. Consequently, both attitudes may be said to represent positions that are separated by some distance (including zero distance) from the neutral point on the evaluative dimension. The more polarized the attitude (i.e., the greater its distance from the neutral point), the more resistant it is to change. Thus if a neutral source expresses an opinion that contradicts a subject's highly favorable (highly polarized) view on an issue, little or no conformity will occur; the subject will, instead, reject the source. Rejection will be manifested by a change in the subject's attitude toward the source; this change being such that it tends to equalize the polarization of attitudes toward the issue and the source. If a highly favorable source expresses a very positive view of an issue toward which the subject's initial attitude is slightly unfavorable, both conformity and rejection will tend to occur. However, conformity will be more pronounced than rejection because the subject's initial attitude toward the issue was less polarized than was his appraisal of the source. It should be noted that Osgood does not assume that complete congruency (equal polarization) will always be achieved; other responses, including disbelief that the source actually originated the message, may make total congruency unnecessary. Osgood has also suggested other reasons why the law of polarization may not always predict reactions to interpersonal disagreements. Opinions concerning an issue are often embedded in attitude structures that render them comparatively inflexible, and sources may be somewhat immune from rejection if they are seen as representing large categories of respected and credible persons. Moreover, messages generally focus attention upon the issue rather than upon the source. Thus the impact of a message upon an individual's attitude toward the issue is likely to be greater than the law of polarization would predict, and the effect on attitude toward the source is likely to be smaller.

In spite of these limitations, the law of polarization permits predictions concerning responses to interpersonal disagreements. When both the attitude toward the source and the attitude toward the issue are moderately positive, a disconfirming message should simultaneously produce conformity *and* rejection; unless, of course, some other response such as disbelief renders these changes unnecessary. Other conditions being equal, the greater the incongruity produced by a message, the greater will be the subject's use of both responses. If a message produces different amounts of incongruity for different persons in a sample, the correlation between conformity and rejection will be positive for that sample. If one sample receives a message that uniformly creates great incongruity, and another sample receives a message that creates little incongruity, the correlation between conformity and rejection should be negligible within either sample, but should be highly positive for the two samples combined.

Osgood's theory does not deal explicitly with the subject's involvement in the attitudinal issue about which he has received a disconfirming message, nor is it concerned with the degree to which the message deviates from the subject's initial attitude.

Festinger takes these factors into account when he states that the amount of dissonance created by the expression of a contrary opinion is a positive function of (a) the credibility and attractiveness of the communicator, (b) the extent of the discrepancy in opinion, and (c) the importance of, or the involvement in, the cognitive elements of the situation (Festinger, 1957, p. 178). Presumably Festinger would agree that the magnitude of dissonance experienced by an individual can be *reduced* by decreasing the attractiveness of the source (rejection), by minimizing the discrepancy in opinion (conformity to, or underrecall of, the discrepant content in the message), or by lowering one's evaluation of the importance of the issue (devaluation). Festinger does not attempt to specify the use that individuals will make of these several responses in situations that permit maximum freedom of choice. Either complete reliance upon a single response, or partial reliance on each of several, should be adequate to minimize dissonance.

Although both Osgood and Festinger point to conditions that may be expected to favor the use of certain balance-restoring responses, they do not tell us what occurs when the decision is left to the individual. In short, they do not concern themselves with personality characteristics that may influence the individual's choice of response.

If personality variables do, in fact, establish preferences for certain types of balance-restoring responses, individuals should show a tendency to make unequal use of the alternatives that are open to them. In situations that impose few restraints some persons should emphasize one response and some another. People who find it easy to conform should rely strongly on conformity, and should have little need to employ other responses, whereas people who "prefer" rejection should make little use of conformity, devaluation, or underrecall. If the situation creates approximately equal levels of imbalance for the subjects in a sample, the correlations between scores on any pair of the four responses should be negative.

B. CORRELATIONAL EVIDENCE

Few attempts have been made to perform the kind of research that is needed to determine whether people in relatively free situations tend to employ only one or several balance-restoring techniques. Festinger and Maccoby (1964) found conformity and rejection to be negatively correlated in three replications of an experiment involving oral messages concerning the disadvantages of fraternity life. However, the correlations were significant only when the arguments were accompanied by irrelevant visual material. When the visual material was relevant to the arguments of the speaker, the correlations, though negative, were very low. Kelman and Eagly (1965) obtained a slight negative relationship between conformity and underrecall (positive displacement of message content) when the source of a disconfirming message was positive, but the relationship was reversed when the source was negative.

In a more deliberate attempt to examine relationships between responses, Johnson (1964) created an experimental situation in which Ss received adverse evaluations from a moderately credible source (a college senior majoring in psychology who had examined Ss' responses to several personality scales). The discrepancy between Ss' own self-evaluations and the evaluations rendered by the source were systematically varied across eight different levels, and a variety of response measures were taken. Correlations between conformity and other responses tended to be negative, as did correlations between rejection and underrecall. But rejection was positively associated with measures of devaluation and rationalization, possibly because the latter variables were measured by items that elicited Ss' appraisals of the information available to the source, and of the care with which the source had examined that information. Thus both devaluation and rationalization, *as measured in this study,* implied that the source was undependable. It seems reasonable to conclude that Johnson's measures of rejection, devaluation, and rationalization reflected the same general response.

A study by Steiner and Rogers (1963) employed the procedures outlined earlier in this paper (Section III). Table I reports the intercorrelations of response scores. Although the correlations are low, only one is positive, and it should be noted that the correlations in a matrix cannot possibly be uniformly high *and* negative. If the correlation between variables A and B is —1.00, and the correlation between variables A and C is also —1.00, the correlation between B and C must necessarily be +1.00. If all of the correlations in a matrix of n variables are equal and negative, the correlations cannot be larger than $1/(n-1)$. Thus with four variables the largest obtainable negative correlation (assuming all correlations are equal and negative) is —.33.

In addition to the ceiling effect that is present when dealing with a matrix of predominately negative correlations, there is another reason for anticipating that obtained negative correlations will not be high. If some Ss prefer one response and some another, and if the use of one response is generally sufficient to restore balance, Ss should typically receive one high score (on their favored response) and three fairly low scores. Correlations between any two responses will tend to be low because the many Ss for whom neither response is a favored reaction will have rather low scores on both (zero correlation), and only those Ss who favor one of the two responses will contribute to the negative relationship.

To test the hypothesis that Ss tend to use one, *and only one*, response to a high degree, Ss' positions in the four distributions of response scores were examined. Each distribution was dichotomized as closely to the seventy-fifth percentile as possible, and Ss scoring above that point were regarded as having used the response to a high degree. Fifty-three Ss were found to have scored above the cutting point on only one response. By chance, a total of 41.98 Ss should have been above the cutting point on only one response. The difference is significant at the .01 level by chi square test. When males and females were considered separately the same trends appeared, but the obtained frequencies were not significantly greater than might be expected to occur by chance.

TABLE I

INTERCORRELATIONS OF RESPONSE VARIABLES[a, b]

	Sex	Underrecall	Devaluation	Rejection
Conformity	M	—.15	.00	—.22
	F	—.41[c]	—.26	—.19
Underrecall	M		—.06	—.08
	F		—.03	.16
Devaluation	M			—.13
	F			—.22

[a] From Steiner and Rogers (1963).
[b] The Ns for both sexes were 50.
[c] $p < .01$.

An additional test of Ss' propensity to employ one response to a high degree involved ranking all 100 Ss on each of the four responses. Ss' ranks on three of the responses were summed and the resulting sum-of-ranks scores obtained for Ss who fell in the top quarter (or top half) of the distribution for the fourth response were compared with the sum-of-ranks scores of Ss who fell below the cutting point on the fourth response. No matter which of the four responses provided the basis for the dichotomy, the differences were always in the expected direction. Ss who were in the top quarter (or top half) of any distribution had lower average ranks on the other three responses than did Ss who were not high on the dichotomized distribution. Differences were not uniformly significant, but the consistency of the results lent support to the conclusion that Ss who employed any single response to a high degree had little need to produce other balance-restoring responses.

The previous analyses have dealt only with immediate reactions to interpersonal disagreements. But if responses serve as functional alternatives, this fact should also be evidenced by delayed reactions. If, over a period of time, a *S* becomes less rejecting of the source, he should simultaneously make more use of some other balance-restoring response. A decrease in the use of one response should be accompanied by an increase in reliance on another response. Thus the correlations between *changes* in scores for any two responses should tend to be negative. This derivation has been tested in an unpublished study by Steiner and Vannoy (1964).

The procedures outlined earlier were employed to create interpersonal disagreements for 61 male college students. In addition to the usual four response scores, a measure of rationalization was also employed. After all thirty-two stimulus cards had been exposed, Ss responded to graphic rating scales that called for appraisals of the accomplice's effort to give correct answers. Since the accomplice's behaviors were highly stan-

TABLE II
CORRELATIONS BETWEEN CHANGES IN RESPONSE SCORES

	Underrecall	Devaluation	Rejection	Rationalization
Conformity	—.24	—.05	—.15	—.09
Underrecall		—.12	—.17	—.20
Devaluation			—.07	—.02
Rejection				—.14

dardized in a fashion designed to create the impression of utter seriousness and determination, it was assumed that low ratings of his efforts to be accurate were indicative of rationalization.

Several days after the experimental session, each *S* returned for a second testing period. The accomplice was not present at this time. Ss were told that *E* wanted them to respond once more to the rating scales they had encountered before because "people sometimes change their minds about things after they have thought about them for a while." Ss were instructed that it did not matter whether or not they gave the same replies as before so long as they tried to be completely accurate. After Ss had reacted to the rating scales, they also responded to the thirty-two stimulus cards, being allowed 30 seconds for each answer.

With the data obtained in the second session it was possible to compute a new set of response scores for each *S*. Thus the number of times a *S*'s answers to the thirty-two stimulus cards agreed with the answers the accomplice had given during Session 1 was treated as his new conformity score, and the numerical values of his ratings of the accomplice were subtracted from the values of the first ratings he had given the accomplice during Session 1 to obtain a new rejection score. The differences between the *S*'s scores in Sessions 1 and 2 were then determined and treated as change scores. Table II reports the intercorrelations of these measures. All ten of the relationships are negative, as they should be if a decrease in the use of one response is accompanied by an increase in the use of other responses. The correlations are low, but the maximum correlation that can be obtained (if all correlations are equal) is only —.25 for a matrix of this size. The findings are consistent with the contention that responses are functional alternatives.

C. THE SIMULTANEOUS USE OF TWO RESPONSES

The evidence reviewed above suggests that people who are free to employ any of several balance-restoring techniques tend to emphasize one response and to make relatively little use of others. But such evidence does not indicate that the simultaneous use of two or more responses is necessarily inefficient or troublesome. Indeed, Osgood's (1960) congruency theory holds that under many circumstances people should be expected to reject and conform at the same time. Dissonance theory is somewhat less clear on this point. Dissonance theorists (Brehm & Cohen, 1962; Zimbardo, 1960) have argued that forced compliance with a rejected person is dissonance arousing. Consequently, a person who is free to choose his own responses should presumably avoid the simultaneous use of rejection and conformity. But dissonance theory also contends that forced compliance with a rejected source leads to genuine attitude change. The conclusion that seems justified by an examination of the literature on dissonance theory is that people who reject a source will not ordinarily conform unless they are forced to do so. But if conformity is forced, genuine attitude change and increased *acceptance* of the source will follow. If this interpretation is correct, the free situation may lead either to conformity *or* to rejection, but not to both. The forced compliance situation produces conformity *and acceptance*. In either case, conformity and rejection should not occur together.

As the foregoing discussion indicates, balance theorists are not in complete agreement concerning the consequences of multiple responses. Osgood clearly contends that effects are additive, at least when the responses are conformity and rejection. Dissonance theorists have suggested that the simultaneous use of these two responses arouses "new dissonance," although it is not clear whether the new dissonance should be expected to outweigh the consonance-producing effects that such theorists ordinarily attribute to conformity and rejection when they occur separately.

In an effort to determine whether the effects of these two responses are additive, Steiner and Johnson (1964) experimentally induced some of their Ss to conform, some to reject, and some to reject and conform simultaneously. Still other Ss were inhibited from employing either of these responses. Conformity was manipulated by telling Ss that they were serving as experimental assistants and that their job was to agree with their partner's answers whenever E held a stimulus card in his right hand but to give the most accurate answer whenever a card was held in E's left hand. Conformity was inhibited by telling other Ss they should always disagree with their partner when a card was held in E's right hand, but should give accurate answers to all cards held in E's left hand. The same eight cards were always held in E's right hand, and the accomplice always gave the least popular answer to each of these cards.

Rejection was induced by telling Ss that their partner had recently participated in an experiment where he answered questions similar to those on the stimulus cards, and that he had done very poorly. When the accomplice arrived he reported that he was majoring in physical education, was a sophomore, and had an academic average lower than "B." Other Ss were inhibited from rejecting the accomplice by being told that the accomplice had recently answered questions similar to those on the stimulus cards and had done very well. To reinforce this treatment the accomplice reported that he was a physics major, a junior, and had an academic average of "B" or higher.

If the balance-restoring effects of conformity and rejection are additive, Ss who have been induced to produce both of these responses should make less use of other available responses than should subjects who have been induced to make only one of these responses. Ss who have been inhibited from employing either response should make the greatest use of other balance-restoring techniques. The findings support these expectations. Scores representing Ss' total use of underrecall, devaluation, and conformity (on the twenty-four unmanipulated stimulus cards) were highest for Ss who had been inhibited from using the two manipulated responses, and were lowest for Ss who had been induced to produce these responses. Thus the category of Ss who, according to dissonance theory, might have been expected to experience "new dissonance" (those who had been induced to conform and reject simultaneously) showed the least inclination to employ other available responses. Although it could be argued that the "new dissonance" was more than canceled by the independent effects of the two induced responses, or that it was resolved in a manner that was not measured in the present study, we are inclined to view these outcomes as contradictions of dissonance theory. On the other hand, these results seem consistent with Osgood's congruency principle. The data are not detailed enough to demonstrate strict additivity, but at least they suggest that the moderate use of two balance-restoring responses has a greater effect than the moderate use of one.

D. Experimental Manipulation of Responses

Many researchers have manipulated Ss' freedom to employ certain responses, and have observed the consequences of such manipulations on Ss' use of alternative responses. Although such studies have little to say about Ss' *preferred* reactions to interpersonal disagreements, they do test the contention that people who are prohibited from employing one response make greater than average use of the alternatives that are available to them.

1. Rejection

Ss should find it somewhat difficult to reject associates who have been made to seem highly attractive, and thus should show a general tendency to make strong use of nonrejecting techniques for restoring balance. Several studies have indicated that conformity is more pronounced when the Ss' associates are attractive than when they are not (Back, 1951; Bovard, 1951; Gerard, 1954; Lambert & Lowy, 1957; Lott & Lott, 1961). But negative findings have been reported by Downing (1958), Harper (1961), and Wilson (1960). Negative findings are not altogether surprising because the manipulations by which associates are made to seem attractive have rarely involved an explicit attempt to establish them as credible sources of information about the issues that are discussed during experimental sessions. Consequently, the manipulation of attractiveness cannot always be assumed to have inhibited the use of rejection of the limited kind that is needed to restore balance.

More directly pertinent are those investigations in which the source has been established as highly credible. Hovland, Janis, and Kelley (1953) have reviewed a number of attitude change studies that indicate a general tendency for conformity to be greatest when the source of discrepant information is unimpeachable. More recent research by Aronson, Turner, and Carlsmith (1963) and by Steiner and Johnson (1965) supports the same conclusion.

Underrecall of disagreements has also been found to be most pronounced when the source of discrepant messages cannot readily be rejected. Kelman and Eagly (1965) manipulated the credibility and general attractiveness of attributed sources and found a marked tendency for Ss to perceive messages received from positive sources as being more highly supportive of their own views than they actually were. Messages from negative sources were displaced away from the Ss' own positions on the attitude continuum. Manis (1961) has also reported a tendency for Ss to minimize the extent to which the expressed views of high prestige communicators have deviated from their own opinions. Kelley and Woodruff

(1956) noted a significant tendency for Ss to displace the content of a tape-recorded message in the direction of their own views when it was accompanied by applause coming from a positive reference group. Sampson (1954) and Berkowitz and Goranson (1964) have obtained supportive findings in somewhat different situations.

2. Conformity

Researchers have not often examined the effects of induced conformity on Ss' use of other responses. Gerard (1961a,b) employed an electronic device to convince some of his Ss that their "first impulse" was to agree with the discrepant opinions of their associates, and to convince others that their first impulse was to disagree. The former rated their associates more highly (were less rejecting) at the conclusion of the experiment. Dissonance theorists (cf. Brehm & Cohen, 1962) have employed a variety of means to persuade people to express views that contradict their own personal beliefs. "Forced compliance" has been reported to encourage more favorable attitudes toward the stand the individual has been induced to defend, and toward other people who take that stand.

3. Devaluation

Evidence concerning the effects of manipulations of the importance of issues (devaluation) is sparse and contradictory. Zimbardo's (1960) Ss conformed more highly when they were led to believe that task performance would reveal important information about their personalities and social values. Deutsch and Gerard (1955) obtained far more conformity when Ss were told that their answers would determine whether or not their group received a desired reward. Schachter (1951) noted more rejection of deviants when the issue under discussion was pertinent to the avowed purposes of the group than when it was not. These findings suggest that Ss who cannot readily devaluate the importance of a topic are especially prone to use other techniques for restoring balance. But DiVesta (1959) obtained contrary results when he told some of his Ss that good performance was indicative of high I.Q.; and studies in which Ss have been selected on the basis of their interest in topics have yielded negative correlations between "involvement" and conformity (Snyder, Mischel, & Lott, 1960; Vaughan & Mangan, 1963). Some of the deviant opinions expressed in DiVesta's study were blatantly incorrect, and it is possible that Ss may have been unable to reconcile conformity with high I.Q. In the case of the studies involving selection of Ss, rather than manipulation of the importance of the issue, involvement is undoubtedly confounded with other determinants of conformity, such as knowledge and previous commitment. If these interpretations of the negative findings

are correct, the available evidence would seem to suggest that manipulations that inhibit devaluation tend to encourage strong use of other
responses.

4. Underrecall

The writer is not aware of research in which underrecall of disagreements has been directly manipulated. Several investigators have systematically varied the magnitude of the discrepancy created by bogus
messages, a procedure which is known to affect Ss' propensities to underrecall. Research of this variety has been reviewed by Johnson (1964).

E. CONCLUSIONS

Both the correlational evidence and the results of studies involving
the experimental suppression of responses suggests that the several techniques for restoring balance are functional alternatives. In free situations
people who use one response to a high degree tend to make relatively
little use of other responses; and when one or more reactions are experimentally blocked, Ss employ the available options to a greater than usual
degree.

However, the studies reviewed above do not justify the conclusion
that responses to interpersonal disagreements are functional *equivalents*.
Ss' general tendency to make unequal use of available responses suggest
that, for most persons, complete equivalence does not exist. Later in
this paper we will examine evidence linking personality variables to
response preferences.

V. Disagreements and the Assumptions of Consistency Theory

Although many empirical studies have provided general support for
consistency theories, there are reasons to suspect that the assumptions such
theories make about human processes are not equally valid for all individuals. The purpose of this section is to examine some of these assumptions and to note their implications for the study of interpersonal
disagreements.

A. THE ROLE OF EXPECTATIONS

All varieties of consistency theory contend that people expect certain
events to co-occur, and expect certain other events not to co-occur. These
assumptions seem unassailable. Sooner or later any human with the
ability to learn is likely to develop the expectation that heavy, dark clouds
mean a storm is imminent, and that bright sunlight and a cloudless sky
indicate that rain is unlikely. But it is also true that different persons

learn to link quite different pairs of events, some believing that "absence makes the heart grow fonder," and others maintaining with equal vigor that "out of sight means out of mind." Moreover, it is probable that no individual ever comes close to developing expectations concerning the co-occurrence of *all* possible pairs of events. As Francis Bacon observed, the subtleties of nature are greater many times over than the subtleties of human comprehension. Most of us undoubtedly plot our courses from very fragmentary probability charts. Consequently, for some people in some situations, consistency theory may be inapplicable because nothing is expected. In other situations the expectations of one person may be quite different from those of another person; and consistency theory, though it is applicable, must predict individual differences in responses. Unfortunately, researchers (including the present writer) have rarely taken the trouble to determine what the relevant expectations of their *S*s really are, or whether they have any relevant expectations at all. Experimenters commonly assume that their *S*s expect prestigeful sources to express accurate judgments, count upon their respected associates to share their own appraisals of geometric designs or political issues, and believe that hard work dependably leads to valuable rewards. But outside the laboratory the behaviors of individuals sometimes indicate that they do not hold such expectations, and it is reasonable to suspect that a certain percentage of our laboratory *S*s also do not. If this is the case, individual differences in responses to experimental situations may sometimes reflect differences in *S*s' expectations, rather than differences in response preference.

B. The Motivating Effects of Disconfirmed Expectations

When a person's expectations are violated he is said by the consistency theorist to experience dissonance, incongruity, asymmetry, or imbalance. Although the physiological characteristics of these states are not specified, they are assumed to involve motivational arousal that is reduced through the performance of one or more responses of the kind discussed earlier in this review. Thus violated expectations are believed to instigate aversive states that, in turn, prompt corrective readjustments.

Festinger (1957, p. 3) contends that dissonance is "psychologically uncomfortable," but he does not attempt to describe the precise nature of the discomfort. Newcomb (1961, p. 13) speaks of a "strain" that motivates the individual to restore balance. Osgood (1960, p. 345) suggests that incongruity is responsible for "a kind of motivation, analogous to other drive states like hunger, sex, and anxiety, but purely cognitive in origin." Cognitive inconsistency is said to set up "pressures" that prompt the individual to produce the responses by which he maintains "a kind of mental homeostasis." Harvey, Hunt, and Schroder (1961, p. 7) assert that "refutation results generally in the experience of negative affect with accompanying avoidant tendencies toward the perceived agent of refutation."

The aversive character of "inconsistency" has more often been assumed than tested. Experimenters have typically created situations in which *they believed the expectations of their Ss would be violated,* and have noted that their Ss produced responses that were consistent with that belief. While these procedures establish the presumption that an aversive motivation has been aroused, they do not provide a clear demonstration that such has been the case, or even that the Ss' expectations have been violated. Retrospective reports by Ss are sometimes offered as evidence that a stressful disconfirmation has occurred, but in the majority of studies even this form of documentation is lacking. Failure to obtain evidence concerning Ss' affective responses to experimental situations has permitted critics (e.g., Chapanis & Chapanis, 1964) to reinterpret many research reports in a manner which avoids the major assumptions of consistency theory. Although these deficiencies have been most notable in studies prompted by dissonance formulations, they have also occurred in other types of consistency research.

However, a few investigators have reported evidence that unbalanced situations are unpleasant. Jordan (1953) asked Ss to rate the pleasantness of sixty-four hypothetical triadic situations, and found that balanced triads were regarded as more pleasant than unbalanced ones. That Ss *expect* such triads to be balanced is suggested by an unpublished study of the present writer who confronted college students with a series of triangles like the one shown in Fig. 1 of this report. Only two sides of each triangle were labeled, and Ss were asked to supply a plus or minus label for the third side. With few exceptions Ss supplied more balance-producing than imbalance-producing labels. When shown triangles with all three sides labeled, most Ss rated the balanced triads as more pleasant than those that were not balanced, thus supporting Jordan's findings.

Measures of physiological arousal have also been employed to detect reactions to inconsistency. The major advantage of such techniques is that they yield an index of the success of an experimental manipulation (e.g., the induction of "inconsistency") at the time the manipulation is applied. Consequently, it is not necessary to rely solely upon self-report data obtained after the experiment has been completed. Because post-session self-reports are always subject to distortion; and, in any case, are likely to be influenced by events subsequent to the manipulations they are intended to evaluate; physiological indexes have a special utility in studies of interpersonal disagreements.

On the other hand, present knowledge of autonomic functioning does not provide a very secure basis for identifying a S's arousal state as fear, anger, disappointment, or joy. Even the act of attending to a stimulus is known to affect many common measures of arousal, suggesting that such indexes are measures of "activation" rather than tools for identifying precisely definable emotional states. However, they at least provide evidence that experimental manipulations are commanding the attention of the S, and are evoking autonomic changes in him. In some cases the nature of the stimulus situation, and of other response data, permits the experimenter to apply a tentative psychological label to the state or process that is manifested by the observed physiological arousal.

Changes in skin resistance have been the most frequently employed measure of autonomic response to interpersonal disagreements. For a discussion of other physiological indexes that have been used in studies of social behavior, the reader is referred to Leiderman and Shapiro (1964).

As early as 1936, C. E. Smith employed a psychogalvanometer to measure changes in the skin resistance of Ss who were informed that a fictitious majority did or did not share their opinions. Ss showed greater reactivity when the majority was said to disagree with them than when it was said to agree. They were also more strongly aroused if they held their own view with strong rather than weak conviction. However, Ss who held their opinions with extreme conviction reversed this trend, leading Smith to suggest that people who are very firmly convinced of the rightness of their own views are not challenged by the contrary opinions of others. A much more recent study by Gerard (1961a, 1961b) obtained parallel results and, in addition, produced evidence that repeated disagreements involving large discrepancies tend to stimulate greater arousal than do repeated disagreements involving smaller discrepancies. Burdick and Burnes (1958) measured skin resistance changes while male college students discussed "life after death" and "the draft" with a faculty member. In a balanced design, E agreed with S on one topic and disagreed with him on the other. Results indicated that autonomic arousal was greater when E disagreed with the S. Finally, in a study that will be reviewed in some detail on pages that follow, Steiner (1964) noted that the skin resistance of male Ss remained high when an accomplice gave popular answers to a series of thirty-two questions, but showed significant decreases when eleven of the accomplice's thirty-two answers were unpopular ones.

Considered collectively these studies provide moderate support for the contention that disagreements stimulate more intense autonomic activity than do agreements. And, in view of the conditions under which the disagreements occurred and the fact that painful stimuli are known to instigate such reactions, it seems reasonable to believe that the increased autonomic activity noted in these studies was indicative of stress. However, these findings have little to say about the reasons for individual differences in arousal. It is possible that some Ss showed little reaction to disagreements *because they did not expect agreements to occur*, and that others manifested little arousal because they were highly tolerant of disconfirmed expectations. Thus, although the findings provide support for the belief that most Ss (*a*) expect attractive associates to agree with them, and (*b*) experience stress when this expectation is violated; the findings do not indicate which (if either) of these two assumptions of consistency theory is invalid for those Ss who do not react in a manner that is indicative of stress.

C. Responses to Disconfirmed Expectations

Consistency theories contend that people expect certain events to co-occur (or not to co-occur), that violations of these expectations instigate aversive motivational states, and that people's responses to violated expectations (e.g., conformity, autistic underrecall, devaluation, etc.) have the effect of reducing the aversive motivation. The previous discussion has examined the first two contentions, but has not offered evidence concerning the third.

Hoffman (1957) conducted a study in which Ss found that a (fictitious) majority of their associates disagreed with the judgments they had previously expressed concerning a variety of issues. Ss who conformed (changed their judgments to agree with those of the fictitious majority) showed smaller decreases in skin resistance than did Ss who reasserted their original views. However, there were substantial individual differences, and the findings were significant only for those Ss who had scored highly on the California F scale and on a similar paper-and-pencil instrument devised by Hoffman. Supportive evidence has been reported by Gerard (1964) who told Ss that he was able to detect their "first reactions" to Asch-type stimuli through the use of an electrical recording device. Ss who were repeatedly informed that their first impulse was to disagree with the bogus majority (i.e., to give the correct answers to the questions) showed greater arousal than did Ss who were told that their first impulse was to agree with the bogus majority. Thus Ss who were led to believe that they were privately conforming to the group consensus showed less evidence of situationally induced stress.

Speisman, Lazarus, Mordkoff, and Davison (1964) measured the skin conductance of Ss as they watched a potentially threatening movie. Ss who heard an oral commentary that encouraged intellectualization or denial of the picture's threatening qualities showed less skin conductance (less stress) than did Ss who did not hear such a commentary. Moreover, the data of this study suggested that the oral manipulations were most effective in minimizing stress when the intellectualization or denial advocated by the commentary was consistent with the S's "usual" strategy for coping with threatening situations. Although the stress engendered in this study was not a consequence of interpersonal disagreements, the findings are reported here because they indicate that certain noncon- forming responses to threatening situations also have the effect of pre- venting or reducing autonomic arousal. In addition, the study offers indirect support for the contention that people have preferred strategies for coping with conflict situations.

In a study designed to explore the effects of nonconforming re- sponses on autonomic arousal, Steiner (1964) employed the experimental task described earlier (Section III). A single naive S answered thirty-two questions after hearing the responses of a prestigeful accomplice. Under control conditions the accomplice always gave popular answers, but under experimental conditions eleven of his last twenty-two replies were those least often given by persons who had responded privately to the items in a preliminary investigation. The accomplice gave the same series of answers in all experimental sessions. Continuous records of Ss' basal skin resistance were obtained, and each S's average base rate was computed for five intervals during the session.

Figure 2 reports both initial base rates and average base rates over blocks of five trials. It is to be noted that the base rates of fourteen con- trol Ss decreased much more slowly than did those of sixty experimental Ss, and that the major discrepancy between the two categories occurred when they encountered trials 11 to 15. It was at this point that the accomplice began giving unpopular answers in the experimental sessions, three of his five answers in this block of trials being of the unpopular variety. The differences between the mean *decreases* in base rate from trials 6–10 to 11–15 are highly significant ($t = 8.62$, $p < .001$) for these two categories of Ss, indicating that interpersonal disagreements (unpopu- lar answers) led to greater autonomic arousal than did agreements (popu- lar answers).

A score on conformity, rejection, underrecall, and devaluation was obtained for each S in the manner described in Section III of this paper. Experimental Ss who ranked in the top quarter of one distribution of scores, but not in the top quarter of any of the other three distributions, were assigned the label of the response on which they had ranked high. Thus, for example, the eight Ss who ranked in the top quarter on con- formity, but not in the top quarter on any other response, were called conformers. (The criteria were relaxed slightly when identifying rejectors because too few Ss met the prescribed standards.) Figure 2 reports the average base rates for each of the four categories of responders. With the very small *n*s involved in these groups no significant differences between categories were obtained. However, when the thirty experimental Ss who ranked high on one response but not on any others were combined into a

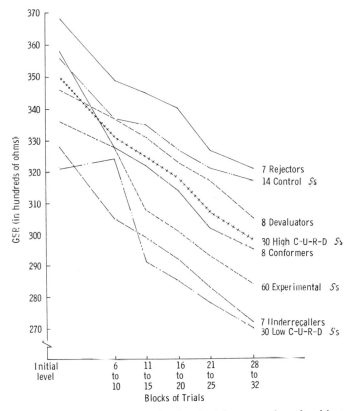

FIG. 2. Mean skin resistance levels of eight categories of subjects.

single category (called High C-U-R-D in Fig. 2), interesting findings were obtained. These thirty Ss showed markedly less autonomic arousal than did the thirty Ss who did not emphasize a single response (called Low C-U-R-D in Fig. 2). Twenty-three of the latter Ss did not rank in the top quarter on *any* of the four responses, and seven ranked in the top quarter on more than one. Because the average decrease in basal skin resistance from trials 6–10 to 11–15 is significantly larger for Low C-U-R-D than the High C-U-R-D Ss ($t = 14.04$, $p < .001$), it may be concluded that Ss who made great use of *one* response showed less autonomic arousal than did Ss who did not.

Because the Low C-U-R-D category included both Ss who ranked low on all four responses and Ss who ranked high on more than one, an additional analysis was conducted. Each experimental S was given a score representing the discrepancy between his rank on the response he had emphasized most and his average rank on the three other responses. A high score on this measure indicates that the S ranked much higher on one response than on the others. The thirty experimental Ss with the highest scores on this measure showed significantly less ($t = 4.11$, $p <$ .001) decrease in base rate from trials 6–10 to 11–15 than did the thirty Ss with the lowest scores. This finding suggests that it is strong use of a *single* response, rather than strong total use of several responses that provides the most effective "relief" from interpersonal disagreements.

Although none of the differences between the initial base rates shown in Fig. 2 are significant, the existence of moderate discrepancies between categories even before disagreements were created suggests the possibility that a S's "normal" level of anxiety or stress may tend to influence his choice of response to disagreements. Particularly suggestive is the fact that the thirty High C-U-R-D Ss showed substantially, though not significantly, less initial arousal than did the thirty Low C-U-R-D Ss. Perhaps larger samples would reveal that people who are characteristically "unexcited" in social situations rely heavily on a single strategy when disagreements arise, whereas their more worrisome counterparts make indiscriminate use of several responses. Such a finding would suggest either that the individual's level of chronic stress influences his responses to disagreements, *or* his responses to disagreements tend to determine the level of arousal he typically experiences in social situations. Goldin (1964) has suggested that defensive strategies that have worked in the past provide the individual with assurance that he can handle future conflicts that may arise, and that *successful* reliance on a defensive technique may be associated with *low* anxiety. Similarly, Hoffman (1957) has argued that a pattern of persistent conformity may be a device for avoiding anxiety, rather than a response to anxiety. Hoffman's contention would seem to be equally valid for nonconforming reactions to disagreements.

A final comment about Fig. 2 is concerned with the comparatively high levels of arousal manifested by the seven underrecallers. While the *n* is too small to yield statistical significance, the precipitous drop in skin resistance that occurred when these Ss encountered disagreements suggests that these persons were not immediately successful in coping with the conflict. Even during the last block of trials, their skin resistance scores are lower than those of people who emphasized conformity, rejection, or devaluation. It may be surmised that underrecall was accomplished *after* the completion of the experimental series, whereas the other responses may have occurred almost as soon as disagreements were encountered. Had measurements of skin resistance been continued during the 5-minute interval that separated the test series from the administration of the post-session questionnaires, evidence concerning this possibility might have been obtained.

D. SUMMARY AND DISCUSSION

Throughout this review interpersonal disagreements have been treated as special cases of inconsistency. It has been assumed that people expect attractive associates to share their views on a variety of issues, and that violation of this expectation establishes an aversive state within the individual. Although empirical support for the first of these assumptions is rather sparse, it is clear that experimental Ss have tended to react negatively to disagreements created in laboratory settings. Moreover, responses that are commonly assumed to restore consistency have appeared to yield a measure of control over the autonomic arousal that usually accompanies disagreements.

The findings reviewed above can be interpreted as supporting the view that disagreements constitute inconsistency, but the precise nature of the inconsistency remains to be determined. Even when a source of information is highly esteemed, disagreements may not be unexpected. Students expect that favorite teachers will occasionally correct their uninformed or illogical beliefs, senators are reported to be quite aware that respected colleagues will oppose their legislative proposals, and people who write reviews of psychological literature anticipate receiving criticisms from interested readers. The fact that such reactions are expected does not always make them pleasant, and we may surmise that it is not merely the "shock of contradiction" that gives disagreements their aversive stimulus value. Even when they are anticipated, interpersonal controversies may presage impending disaster, predict future hardships, or confirm the existence of personal faults. Undoubtedly it is the symbolic meaning of a disagreement, rather than its inherent qualities, that is inconsistent with valued goals.

A major implication of this view of disagreements is that any particular controversy may have very different meanings for different persons. Consequently, a complete theory of responses to interpersonal disagreements must be a theory of cognitive processes as well. To some degree the development and use of valid measures of physiological arousal may lessen the necessity for studying the interpretative schemes of individuals, but it is apparent that some means must be found for determining that the individual whose reactions are being studied has, in fact, experienced a conflict.

Needless to say, most of the research cited in this review has failed to provide a guarantee of this sort. Therefore, it is entirely possible that some of the individual differences in response tendencies that have been noted in the literature may ultimately be explainable as consequences of variation in conflict level. This warning has a special relevance to the discussion of personality variables that follows.

VI. Relationships between Personality Variables and Responses to Interpersonal Disagreements

Although many studies have linked personality variables with one or another response to interpersonal disagreements, the total success of such research has been rather meager. Most studies have measured only one response, and thus have provided only indirect evidence concerning *preferred* balance-restoring techniques. In many cases experimental procedures appear to have imposed "situational demands" that strongly favored a single response. Moreover, the reaction elicited and measured has almost always been conformity. In spite of the fact that other responses seem equally relevant to many theories of personality, experiments relating them to personality measures have been exceedingly rare.

Unfortunately, the literature is not only focused upon a single response; it is also replete with weak and even inconsistent findings. In a review of research relating personality variables to conformity behaviors, Mann (1959) examined studies that included measures of conservatism, dominance, extroversion, and general adjustment. In no case was the *median* of several correlations between a personality variable and conformity found to be higher than .25. To some degree the weak and inconsistent character of the findings probably can be attributed to the use of invalid measurement techniques. Mann noted that self-ratings of extroversion and adjustment tended to correlate positively with conformity, whereas scores on these variables obtained by other techniques usually correlated negatively with conformity. This pattern of findings is strongly suggestive of a social desirability factor that operates when people are confronted by social norms *and* when they are asked to provide descriptions of themselves. Several other possible explanations of the generally weak and inconsistent character of research findings may also be cited. Maybe the really critical personality variables have not yet been investigated, or perhaps situational and personality variables interact to a degree that makes trans-situational uniformity of findings an unlikely occurrence. The techniques by which responses to interpersonal disagree-ments are measured have varied from study to study, and may involve low reliabilities. Finally, it should be noted that there is reason to believe that correlations between personality variables and responses to inter-personal disagreements *should be low* when people are free to employ any of several responses. If, as is suggested elsewhere in this review, some people make moderate use of several responses, the correlations between personality variables and any particular response measure are likely to be modest. To the extent that two responses are functional equivalents, they may be combined in innumerable ways to satisfy a particular per-sonality "need." And the fact that a few subjects in some of the studies described earlier have, in fact, employed two or more responses simul-taneously suggests that functional equivalence is not an extremely rare phenomenon.

Research linking personality variables to conformity behavior has been reviewed in a number of places (Blake & Mouton, 1961; Hovland & Janis, 1959; Krech, Crutchfield, & Ballachey, 1962; Mann, 1959). The present discussion will emphasize recent findings and research evidence (old or new) that seem to bear most directly on the problem of alternative response modes.

A. AUTHORITARIANISM

Although the California F scale has typically been found to be positively correlated with conformity scores, contrary findings have also been reported. Hoffman (1957) found that high F scorers were no more prone to conform to a false group consensus than were low scorers, and were even less likely than the latter to repeat their conforming responses 2 weeks later in a "private" situation. Hardy (1957) and Johnson (1964) also failed to note greater conformity on the part of high scorers, and other investigators have reported *negative* correlations between authori-tarianism and conformity (Harvey, 1958, 1959; Wagman, 1955). After examining the pertinent literature, Wright and Harvey (1965) have suggested that authoritarian Ss tend to conform when the source has high prestige and involvement in the issue is not too high, or when involvement is high and the authority of the source is also very high and unimpeachable. According to these authors, authoritarians are likely to be nonconformists when the source is a person of low status or the issue is one of very high involvement. Support for this interpretation is re-ported by Vidulich and Kaiman (1961) who found that Ss who had scored high on dogmatism showed greater conformity to a high prestige source than they did to a low prestige source, whereas Ss who had scored low on dogmatism were unaffected by the prestige of the source. Even more pointed evidence has been obtained by Harvey and Beverly (1961) whose Ss were exposed to a message that contradicted the Ss own attitude but which was believed to be endorsed by a very high status source. High F scorers not only showed a greater tendency than low F scorers to conform to the view expressed in the message, but also showed less evidence of having understood the arguments of the speaker. Since the arguments were not very complex, it seems reasonable to conclude that the high scorers paid less attention to the details of the message, and that they reacted primarily to the authoritative status of the source rather than to the evidence he advanced in support of his recommendations.

There is a dearth of findings concerning relationships between authoritarianism and other responses to interpersonal disagreements. But Harvey's (1962) authoritarian Ss who received negative information about themselves were less inclined to reject the source and more inclined to underrecall the adverse contents of the message than were his nonauthoritarian Ss. In other investigations, Harvey (1959) found that authoritarianism was associated with a tendency to minimize the discrepancy between one's own and the source's judgments of autokinetic movement, to minimize the negativity of a speech arguing against one's own view of prohibition, and to underestimate the heaviness of an extreme anchor weight. These findings suggest that the authoritarian is prone to underrecall disagreements, although it is not clear whether this tendency, like the authoritarian's propensity to conform, is contingent upon the prestige of the source. Newcomb (1961) has also reported that authoritarians are especially prone to minimize attitudinal differences between themselves and positive sources, although this tendency became evident only after Ss and sources had lived in the same rooming house for a period of several weeks.

Steiner and Johnson (1963) examined the effects of authoritarianism in a study that varied the unanimity of sources. Procedures were essentially those described earlier (Section III). In one experimental treatment, two moderately prestigeful accomplices almost invariably gave the same answers to 32 questions, eleven of these being replies least often given by control Ss. In another treatment one accomplice gave the same 11 unpopular answers as in Treatment One, while the second accomplice gave only popular answers. In a third treatment, each accomplice gave 11 unpopular answers, but the questions to which one accomplice gave deviant replies were always different from those to which the other accomplice gave unpopular answers. Thus in the three experimental treatments the accomplices disagreed among themselves twice, 11 times, and 22 times, respectively.

For Ss who received Treatment One, California F scores were positively correlated with conformity (number of agreements with one accomplice plus number of agreements with the other accomplice). In this group, authoritarianism was also negatively correlated with anxiety as measured by a perspiration measure taken at the conclusion of the experimental session. Thus when the two accomplices supported one another, authoritarian Ss were inclined to conform more than other Ss and to show less evidence of stress after they had experienced the conflict situation. In Treatment Two, authoritarianism was unrelated to total conformity, but authoritarian Ss showed a greater tendency than did nonauthoritarian Ss to agree as often with the accomplice who gave 11 unpopular answers as with the accomplice who gave only popular answers. Authoritarian Ss also avoided rejection of the accomplice who gave unpopular answers. The correlation between authoritarianism and anxiety was negative, but too low to reach an acceptable level of statistical significance. For Treatment Three, there was again no relationship between authoritarianism and total conformity; but high F scorers were significantly more prone than low scorers to agree more frequently with one accomplice than the other, and significantly less inclined to under-recall the number of disagreements among the accomplices. They also were more rejecting of one accomplice than the other, but this difference did not reach significance. No relationship between authoritarianism and anxiety was noted.

This pattern of findings suggests that when two moderately prestigeful persons agree with one another, thus constituting a highly credible source, authoritarians conform and obtain substantial relief from stress by doing so. But when the views of one such person are contradicted a moderate number of times by another such person, the authoritarian maintains relative impartiality in his responses to the two sources, even though one of them has advocated views that are difficult to defend. Under these circumstances, maintenance of amicable relationships with the two sources is apparently more important to the authoritarian than is the correctness of the opinions that they express. In both Treatment One and Treatment Two the reactions of authoritarians are consistent with the contention that they are "source-oriented" rather than "message-oriented" (Kelman & Eagly, 1965; McDavid, 1959). When two moderately prestigeful persons disagree very frequently with one another (Treatment Three), it should be difficult to maintain the belief that both are highly credible and accurate sources of information. Under these circumstances the authoritarian is prone to ally himself with one or the other of his disagreeing partners and to exaggerate the differences between them. In this way he maintains a highly supportive relationship with one of his associates, whereas if he divided his allegiance he would be deprived of a self-satisfying alliance presumed to be highly desired by source-oriented individuals.

As the previous discussion indicates, relationships between authoritarianism and nonconforming responses to interpersonal disagreements have not been widely studied; and the available findings do not fit neatly into a single interpretative schema. But the evidence suggests that authoritarianism predisposes one to be concerned with the maintenance of amicable and supportive relationships with prestigeful sources, rather than with the correctness of one's own or the source's opinions. If this is the case, authoritarian Ss should conform to high status sources, but not to those with low status. They should be reluctant to reject a prestigeful source, and should tend to underrecall their disagreements with authoritative persons. In general, the available evidence seems to support these expectations, though as Wright and Harvey (1965) have noted, very high involvement in the issue may prevent the authoritarian from employing his characteristic responses to disagreements. Perhaps high involvement compels even the authoritarian to become message-oriented.

B. Self-Esteem

The more competent an individual believes himself to be, the easier he should find it to (a) resist conformity pressures, and (b) derogate the source of contrary opinions. There is considerable empirical evidence in support of the first of these propositions, but the relationship between self-esteem and rejection has received little attention. Several investigators (DiVesta, 1959; Hochbaum, 1954; Kelman, 1950; Samelson, 1957) have manipulated Ss' perceived competence, and have noted that high levels of assumed ability are associated with low levels of conformity. However, Croner and Willis (1961) have demonstrated that experimental manipulations of perceived competence may have little effect on conformity in situations not involving the specific resources that Ss have been led to believe they do (or do not) possess. These authors' findings suggest that it is perceived ability with respect to the issue in question, rather than global self-esteem, that affects responses to interpersonal disagreements. Inverse relations between general self-esteem and conformity have been reported with fair regularity (Janis, 1954, 1955; Janis & Field, 1959; Janis & Rife, 1959; Lesser & Abelson, 1959).

Cohen (1959) has maintained that high self-esteem is associated with preference for certain defense mechanisms. Thus persons with high self-esteem are assumed to favor avoidance defenses (reaction formation, repression, and denial) that deny the existence of threat to one's self-system, whereas persons with low self-esteem are said to employ expressive defenses such as projection and regression. Silverman (1964) has interpreted Cohen's arguments to mean that a threat to self-esteem will have the effect of reducing conformity on the part of high self-esteem Ss, but will increase conformity among persons with low self-esteem. In an empirical test, Silverman obtained evidence supporting this derivation, but he also found that when Ss had not been exposed to prior conditions designed to heighten self-defensiveness, high and low self-esteem Ss conformed equally and to a greater degree than did Ss with moderate self-esteem. This curvilinear relationship is interpreted by Silverman as suggesting the operation of a "social desirability" factor when people respond to self-rating scales. High scores on such instruments may reflect either high self-esteem or a propensity to give socially desirable answers. The latter tendency is assumed to favor conformity and thus to suppress the inverse correlation between self-ratings and conformity scores.

Evidence concerning self-esteem and specific nonconforming responses to interpersonal disagreements is lacking. Cohen's formulation implies that high self-esteem should encourage the use of underrecall and devaluation as alternatives to conformity, but these contentions have not been adequately tested. Work in the present author's laboratory has produced very low and inconsistent correlations between self-ratings and responses to interpersonal disagreements, including conformity. Perhaps the social desirability factor so thoroughly confounds responses to self-rating scales that no very stable relationships can be obtained. If this is the case, satisfactory tests of the effects of unmanipulated self-esteem may require the use of techniques that partial out this influence.

Silverman (1964) has suggested that low self-esteem Ss should be expected to identify more readily with high prestige sources than should high self-esteem Ss. Findings of Stotland and Hillmer (1962) are consistent with this contention, and thus lend some credence to the assumption that low self-esteem encourages source-orientation. Such an assumption harmonizes well with the notion that people who think poorly of themselves do not ordinarily trust their meager abilities to evaluate messages and must, therefore, rely upon the presumed authenticity of positive sources.

C. Cognitive Styles

Harvey, Hunt, and Schroder (1961) have described four "conceptual systems" said to be characteristic of children at various ages, and postulated to guide the responses of adults as well. Persons operating in System 1 are responsive to cues concerning social status and propriety, and are prone to react submissively to authoritative sources. Sensitivity to cues that suggest restricted autonomy is typical of System 2. Rebellion, denial, and rejection are common reactions to this type of threatening situation. System 3 emphasizes acceptance by others, and involves a sensitivity to cues indicating other persons' reactions to one's behaviors. People operating in this manner are said to be "outer-directed," whereas System 1 encourages individuals to be "tradition-directed." The outer-directed person is expected to respond to refutation by relying on others, by manifesting overgeneralized submission, and by producing behaviors that invite interpersonal support. System 4 is characterized by "openness" of one's own standards, by an ability and propensity to relate the content of incoming messages to previously learned materials, and by a tendency to evaluate messages from a variety of standpoints. In this respect, System 4 is more flexible, tolerant, and message-oriented than are the other three.

It is difficult to translate Harvey, Hunt, and Schroder's theoretical statements into precise predictions concerning responses to interpersonal disagreements. The authors themselves indicate that similar responses may serve different purposes for persons relying upon different systems. However, Janicki (1964) has employed the four systems as a basis for explaining some of the "errors" in predictions made by Osgood and Tannenbaum's (1955) congruency formula.

Rokeach's (1954) concept of dogmatism, like the authoritarianism that is measured by the California F Scale, implies cognitive inflexibility. (Harvey, Hunt, & Schroder assert that high F Ss emphasize System 1.) The dogmatic person is presumed to have a "closed mind" that prevents him from reacting to a message on its own merits. Powell (1962) has provided support for this contention in a study showing that separate evaluations of a political candidate and a statement attributed to him were further apart in semantic space for nondogmatic than for dogmatic Ss.

Authoritarianism and dogmatism suggest a general intolerance of ambiguity which might be expected to affect reactions to interpersonal disagreements. Thus Feather (1964) found that Ss who scored highly on Budner's measure of intolerance of ambiguity were more inclined than low scorers to evaluate syllogisms in terms of their own personal beliefs about the issues involved rather than on the basis of syllogistic logic. But Vannoy's (1964) factor analytic appraisal of many measures of cognitive complexity-simplicity suggests that intolerance of ambiguity is far from being a unitary personality characteristic. Although Vannoy noted certain parallels between his findings and the hypothetical systems of Harvey, Hunt, and Schroder, the obtained factor structure only partially supports those authors' views.

In order for a measure of "intolerance of ambiguity" or "need for consistency" to predict responses to disagreements, the measure should identify the cognitive elements between which the individual desires to maintain consistency. It is possible that some people can tolerate inconsistency between a source and his message rather easily, but find inconsistency between the message and their own views very troublesome. Perhaps for other people it is the disagreements between various sources, or the contradictions within a single message, that are most threatening. Until this possibility has been explored, and appropriate measures developed, scores on intolerance of ambiguity are unlikely to be very accurate predictors of individuals' responses to interpersonal disagreements.

A measure that seems relevant to the notion of cognitive consistency is Pettigrew's (1958) Category Width Scale. Wide categorizers should presumably be regarded as comparatively tolerant of inconsistency since they are willing to include fairly diverse events within a single category. Steiner and Johnson (1965) found that wide categorizers conformed less markedly than did narrow categorizers, and tended to underrecall disagreements with their associates. They also showed a propensity to underrecall disagreements among two positive sources from whom they had received very contradictory messages. These findings suggest that wide categorizers may see little real difference between their own views and those advocated in messages. Thus they may have little reason to conform, and may find it easy to minimize disagreements. But it is also possible that wide categorizers are insensitive to inconsistencies between sources and messages, or between various sources. Category width affects responses to interpersonal disagreements, but it is not entirely clear at what point in the cognitive process this effect is accomplished. Like other measures of tolerance of ambiguity, category width fails to specify the kinds of elements between which inconsistency is tolerated.

D. Manifest Anxiety

Earlier in this paper (Section V,3) it has been suggested that an individual's responses to interpersonal disagreements may depend in part upon his level of chronic anxiety or nervousness. The Taylor Manifest Anxiety Scale has been widely used to identify people who are characteristically tense or worrisome, and though it is subject to the "social desirability" bias that characterizes most self-rating instruments, it represents a convenient tool for evaluating this variable.

In an early study, Goldberg, Hunt, Cohen, and Meadow (1954) found MAS to be positively correlated with conformity among females and negatively correlated with conformity among males. These findings have been supported by Mangan, Quartermain, and Vaughan (1960) who obtained a negative correlation for males, and by Vaughan (1964) who reported a nonsignificant positive correlation for females. The findings of Steiner and Rogers (1963) were also consistent with those of Goldberg *et al.*, although the correlation for male *S*s did not reach an acceptable level of significance. On the other hand, Tuddenham (1959) obtained nonsignificant negative correlations for both sexes.

There have been few attempts to relate MAS to nonconforming responses, but Steiner and Rogers (1963) noted that MAS was negatively correlated with underrecall on the part of male (but not female) *S*s, and that it was negatively correlated with rejection among females. (For male *S*s the correlation between MAS and rejection was approximately zero.) Thus, a pattern of sex differences was found for nonconforming as well as conforming responses.

The interaction of manifest anxiety and sex that is indicated by the above findings may reflect the effects of male and female roles. It is probable that conformity is more socially appropriate for women than for men in our society. And if it can be assumed that worrisome *S*s are especially prone to do what is regarded as socially appropriate, the tendency of high MAS females to conform is not surprising. Anxious males, for whom independence is probably a social virtue, should, according to this view, show reduced conformity and a moderate willingness to reject those who challenge their judgments.

It is possible, too, that females are generally more "source-oriented" (Kelman & Eagly, 1965) than are males. Anastasi (1958, pp. 479–481) has cited evidence that females are more inclined than are males to be concerned about interpersonal relationships, whereas the latter are more strongly oriented toward actions and objects. If this is the case, females should probably be expected to show greater conformity and less rejection than do males when the source of contrary information is an attractive or prestigeful person. However, it should be noted that the issues about which disagreements have been created in the typical conformity study appear to have been ones that are more familiar and ego-involving to males. Consequently, it is possible that many of the sex differences noted in the literature reflect differences in knowledge and commitment, rather than differences in personality variables or normative values.

E. PERSONALITY VARIABLES ASSOCIATED WITH CONFORMITY

Research linking personality variables with conformity behavior has proceeded much more rapidly than have investigations of nonconforming responses. The literature dealing with the "compliant personality" is too extensive to be reviewed here, but a few studies that indicate the general nature of the findings will be cited.

Tuddenham (1959) employed a large battery of tests in an effort to describe Ss who yield to a bogus majority in laboratory situations of the type devised by Crutchfield (1955). Conformers were said to be characterized by conventionality, conscientiousness, cooperativeness, patience, sincerity, and docile socialization. The self-ratings of such persons emphasized nurturance, affiliativeness, abasement, and denial of psychiatric symptoms. These interpretations are in close accord with the findings of DiVesta and Cox (1960) who concluded that the conforming individual is restrained, cautious, submissive, and oriented toward consideration of others. Vaughan (1964) found conformers to rank *low* on intelligence, assertiveness, neural reserves, extroversion, realism, and theoretical value. They ranked high on anxiety, authoritarianism, and religious value. Izard (1959) has reported evidence indicating that compliant Ss score low on measures of autonomy and dominance and high on deference and abasement.

These studies suggest that there is indeed a personality syndrome that predisposes individuals to conform. People who are submissive in laboratory situations respond to paper-and-pencil instruments in a manner that implies a general (and perhaps excessive) concern for the approval and respect of their associates. They appear to be especially sensitive to social conventions and to have strong affiliative needs. The latter interpretation is buttressed by Byrne's (1961) observation that Ss low in affiliative need tend to respond to disagreeing strangers with indifference, whereas those high in affiliative need do not. Hardy (1957) has also noted the important role of affiliative motivation in determining whether or not Ss conform.

The findings and interpretations discussed above suggest that some people are so strongly disposed to maintain amicable relationships with positive sources that they readily bring their own views into accord with those of their immediate associates. This pattern of adjustment has been called normative conformity (Kelman & Eagly, 1965), and is thought to be typical of persons who are source-oriented. Presumably this type of conformity is short-lived, being rapidly superseded by compliance to the preferences of other positive sources with whom the individual comes into contact. Thus it may be argued (Hoffman, 1957; Steiner & Vannoy, 1965) that the conformity that is manifested in many laboratory situations does not involve any very genuine or pervasive attitude change, and that normative compliance is primarily a strategy for avoiding, rather than for resolving, interpersonal disagreements. On the other hand, the message-oriented individual is probably much less likely to indulge in facile conformity, and more inclined to produce nonconforming responses. However, when the message-oriented person does conform, his behaviors should reflect more lasting changes of the kinds Kelman and Eagly have called identification and internalization.

Because researchers have rarely studied the permanence of conforming responses, investigations of personality correlates are subject to varied interpretations. Even the trans-situational generality of conforming responses remains in doubt, though Vaughan (1964) has recently reported modest relationships across a range of situations. So long as personality scores are based primarily on self-ratings there will be room for skepticism concerning the meaning of any particular outcome (Mann, 1959).

It may be suggested that one of the biggest deficiencies in this area of investigation is the general failure to examine alternatives to conformity. Confidence in findings that link personality variables to conformity behaviors could be increased markedly if such connections were shown to be part of a larger network of meaningful relationships.

VII. Concluding Comments

Consistency theory provides guidelines for the examination of interpersonal disagreements. It identifies some of the conditions that make disagreements uncomfortable, and specifies a number of responses that individuals may employ to minimize the impact of disconfirming communications. Evidence from studies that have investigated physiological reactions has tended to support the most relevant propositions of consistency theory. When people find that their opinions on salient issues are not shared by respected associates, they are likely to manifest autonomic arousal. When they make the balance-restoring responses enumerated by consistency theorists, arousal is inhibited or reduced. But consistency theory has little to say about the factors that determine which of several balance-restoring responses an individual will employ. Choice of response is known to be influenced by certain situational variables, but there is evidence indicating that many people have fairly strong response preferences that operate when situational constraints are not very compelling. Although the stability of such preferences over time and across situations remains to be determined, it is clear that different persons favor different responses. The individual's preferred mode of response to interpersonal disagreements would appear to reflect important aspects of his personality.

Few attempts have been made to identify the personality characteristics that are associated with response preferences. Investigators have usually emphasized situational variables, and have rarely explored Ss' predispositions in relatively "free" situations. But the limited evidence that has been accumulated to date strongly suggests that a substantial portion of the error variance of studies that have neglected personality variables may be due to individual differences in response preferences. It is probable, too, that the interaction effects of personality and situational variables will account for some of the inconsistent findings reported in the literature dealing with situational effects.

It is unfortunate that research on interpersonal disagreements has generally dealt with only a few facets of an exceedingly complex network of relationships. Most studies have manipulated one or a few qualities of the stimulus situation, and have measured only one or two of many possible responses. Moreover, the same limited number of stimulus and response parameters have received attention in the vast majority of investigations, while other variables have remained largely unexplored. Although a single study can examine only a limited number of variables, it may be hoped that future research will involve a broader sample of situational and response variables than has so far been the case. And the glaring underrepresentation of personality variables should certainly be remedied.

Even more critical is the need for theory that will order the many pertinent stimulus and response parameters into meaningful patterns. Consistency theories provide a broad frame of reference, but at their present level of development, are too general and unspecific to deal with some of the complexities of interpersonal disagreements. Whether such theories can be refined to predict the wide range of outcomes reported in this review is a question for future consideration.

References

Allport, G. W. *Personality: A psychological interpretation*. New York: Holt, 1937.

Anastasi, Anne. *Differential psychology*. New York: Macmillan, 1958.

Aronson, E., Turner, Judith, & Carlsmith, J. M. Communicator credibility and communication discrepancy as determinants of opinion change. *J. abnorm. soc. Psychol.*, 1963, **67**, 31-36.

Asch, S. E. *Social psychology*. New York: Prentice-Hall, 1952.

Back, K. The exertion of influence through social communication. *J. abnorm. soc. Psychol.*, 1951, **46**, 9-24.

Berkowitz, L., & Goranson, R. Motivational and judgmental determinants of social perception. *J. abnorm. soc. Psychol.*, 1964, **69**, 296-302.

Blake, R. F., & Mouton, Jane S. Conformity, resistance, and conversion. In I. A. Berg and B. M. Bass (Eds.), *Conformity and deviation*, New York: Harper, 1961.

Bovard, E. W., Jr. Group structure and perception. *J. abnorm. soc. Psychol.*, 1951, **46**, 398-405.

Brehm, J. W., & Cohen, A. R. *Explorations in cognitive dissonance*. New York: Wiley, 1962.

Burdick, H. A., & Burnes, A. J. A test of "strain toward symmetry" theories. *J. abnorm. soc. Psychol.*, 1958, **57**, 367-370.

Byrne, D. Interpersonal attraction as a function of affiliation need and attitude similarity. *Human Relat.*, 1961, **14**, 283-289.

Chapanis, Natalia P., & Chapanis, A. Cognitive dissonance: Five years later. *Psychol. Bull.*, 1964, **61**, 1-22.

Cohen, A. R. Some implications of self-esteem for social influence. In C. I. Hovland and I. L. Janis (Eds.), *Personality and persuasibility*, New Haven: Yale Univer. Press, 1959.

Croner, M. D., & Willis, R. H. Perceived differences in task competence and asymmetry of dyadic influence. *J. abnorm. soc. Psychol.*, 1961, **62**, 705-708.

Crutchfield, R. S. Conformity and character. *Amer. Psychologist*, 1955, **10**, 191-198.

Deutsch, M., & Gerard, H. B. A study of normative and informational social influences on individual judgment. *J. abnorm. soc. Psychol.*, 1955, **51**, 629-636.

DiVesta, F. J. Effects of confidence and motivation on susceptibility to informational social influence. *J. abnorm. soc. Psychol.*, 1959, **59**, 204-209.

DiVesta, F. J., & Cox, L. Some dispositional correlates of conformity behavior. *J. soc. Psychol.*, 1960, **52**, 259-268.

Downing, J. Cohesiveness, perception and values. *Human Relat.*, 1958, **11**, 157-166.

Feather, N. T. Acceptance and rejection of arguments in relation to attitude strength, critical ability, and intolerance of inconsistency. *J. abnorm. soc. Psychol.*, 1964, **69**, 127-136.

Festinger, L. Informal social communication. *Psychol. Rev.*, 1950, **57**, 271-282.

Festinger, L. *A theory of cognitive dissonance.* Evanston, Ill.: Row, Peterson, 1957.

Festinger, L., & Aronson, E. The arousal and reduction of dissonance in social contexts. In D. Cartwright and A. Zander (Eds.), *Group dynamics: Research and theory.* Evanston, Ill.: Row, Peterson, 1960, 214-231.

Festinger, L., & Maccoby, N. On resistance to persuasive communications. *J. abnorm. soc. Psychol.*, 1964, **68**, 359-366.

Fromm, E. *Escape from freedom.* New York: Farrar and Rinehart, 1941.

Gerard, H. B. The anchorage of opinions in face-to-face groups. *Human Relat.*, 1954, **7**, 313-326.

Gerard, H. B. Disagreement with others, their credibility, and experienced stress. *J. abnorm. soc. Psychol.*, 1961, **62**, 554-564. (a)

Gerard, H. B. Inconsistency of beliefs and their implications. Paper read at Amer. Psychol. Ass., New York, September, 1961. (b)

Gerard, H. B. Physiological measurement in social psychological research. In P. H. Leiderman, and D. Shapiro (Eds.), *Psychobiological approaches to social behavior.* Stanford: Stanford Univer. Press, 1964.

Goldberg, S. C., Hunt, R. G., Cohen, W., & Meadow, A. Some personality correlates of perceptual distortion in the direction of group conformity. *Amer. Psychologist*, 1954, **9**, 378. (Abstract)

Goldin, P. C. Experimental investigation of selective memory and the concept of repression and defense: A theoretical synthesis. *J. abnorm. soc. Psychol.*, 1964, **69**, 365-380.

Hardy, K. R. Determinants of conformity and attitude change. *J. abnorm. soc. Psychol.*, 1957, **54**, 289-294.

Harper, F. B. W. The sociometric composition of the group as a determinant of yielding to a distorted norm. Unpublished Ph.D. Thesis, Univer. of California, Berkeley, 1961.

Harvey, O. J. Reactions to unfavorable evaluations of self by others. Tech. Rep. No. 8, 1958, Vanderbilt Univer., Contract NONR 2149(02), Office of Naval Research.

Harvey, O. J. Personality correlates of concept functioning and change across situations.

Tech. Rep. No. 3, 1959, Univer. of Colorado, Contract NONR 1147(07), Office of Naval Research.

Harvey, O. J. Personality factors in resolution of conceptual incongruities. *Sociometry,* 1962, **25**, 336-352.

Harvey, O. J., & Beverly, G. D. Some personality correlates of concept change through role playing. *J. abnorm. soc. Psychol.,* 1961, **63**, 125-130.

Harvey, O. J., Hunt, D. E., & Schroder, H. M. *Conceptual systems and personality organization.* New York: Wiley, 1961.

Heider, F. *The psychology of interpersonal relations.* New York: Wiley, 1958.

Hochbaum, G. M. The relation between group member's self-confidence and their reactions to group pressure toward uniformity. *Amer. Sociological Rev.,* 1954, **19**, 678-687.

Hoffman, M. D. Conformity as a defense mechanism and a form of resistance to genuine group influence. *J. Pers.,* 1957, **25**, 412-424.

Horney, Karen. *Our inner conflicts.* New York: Norton, 1945.

Hovland, C. I. Reconciling conflicting results derived from experimental and survey studies of attitude change. *Amer. Psychologist,* 1959, **14**, 8-17.

Hovland, C. I., & Janis, I. L. (Eds.). *Personality and persuasibility.* New Haven: Yale Univer. Press, 1959.

Hovland, C. I., Janis, I. L., and Kelley, H. H. *Communication and persuasion.* New Haven: Yale Univer. Press, 1953.

Izard, C. E. Personality characteristics associated with resistance to change. Tech. Rep. No. 2, 1959, Univer. of Colorado, Contract NONR 1147(07), Office of Naval Research.

Janicki, W. P. Effect of disposition on resolution of incongruity. *J. abnorm. soc. Psychol.,* 1964, **69**, 579-584.

Janis, I. L. Personality correlates of susceptibility to persuasion. *J. Pers.,* 1954, **22**, 505-518.

Janis I. L. Anxiety indices related to susceptibility to persuasion. *J. abnorm. soc. Psychol.,* 1955, **51**, 663-667.

Janis, I. L., & Field, P. B. Sex differences and personality factors related to persuasibility. In C. I. Hovland and I. L. Janis (Eds.), *Personality and persuasibility.* New Haven: Yale Univer. Press, 1959.

Janis, I. L., & Rife, D. Persuasibility and emotional disorder. In C. I. Hovland and I. L. Janis (Eds.), *Personality and persuasibility.* New Haven: Yale Univer. Press, 1959.

Johnson, H. H. Some effects of discrepancy level on responses to adverse information about one's self. Unpublished Ph.D. Thesis, University of Illinois, 1964.

Johnson, H. H., & Steiner, I. D. Responses to adverse information about the self, 1965. (In preparation)

Jordan, N. Behavioral forces that are a function of attitudes and of cognitive organization. *Human Relat.,* 1953, **6**, 273-287.

Kelley, H. H., & Woodruff, C. L. Members' reactions to apparent group approval of a counternorm communication. *J. abnorm. soc. Psychol.,* 1956, **52**, 67-74.

Kelman, H. C. Effects of success and failure on "suggestibility" in the autokinetic situation. *J. abnorm. soc. Psychol.,* 1950, **45**, 267-285.

Kelman, H. C., & Eagly, Alice H. Attitude toward the communicator, perception of communication content, and attitude change. *J. Pers. soc. Psychol.,* 1965, **1**, 63-78.

Krech, D., Crutchfield, R. S., & Ballachey, E. L. *Individual in society.* New York: McGraw-Hill, 1962.

Lambert, W. E., & Lowy, F. H. Effects of the presence and discussion of others on expressed attitudes. *Canad. J. Psychol.,* 1957, **11**, 151-156.

Leiderman, P. H., & Shapiro, D. *Psychobiological approaches to social behavior.* Stanford: Stanford Univer. Press, 1964.

Lesser, G. S., & Abelson, R. P. Personality correlates of persuasibility in children. In C. I. Hovland and I. L. Janis (Eds.), *Personality and persuasibility.* New Haven: Yale Univer. Press, 1959.

Lewis, Helen B. Studies in the principles of judgments and attitudes: IV. The operation of "prestige suggestion." *J. soc. Psychol.,* 1941, **14**, 229-256.

Lott, A. J., & Lott, B. E. Group cohesiveness, communication level, and conformity. *J. abnormal. soc. Psychol.,* 1961, **62**, 408-412.

Mangan, G. L., Quartermain, D., & Vaughan, G. M. Taylor MAS and group conformity pressure. *J. abnorm. soc. Psychol.,* 1960, **61**, 146-147.

Manis, M. The interpretation of opinion statements as a function of recipient attitude and source prestige. *J. abnorm. soc. Psychol.,* 1961, **63**, 82-86.

Mann, R. D. A review of the relationships between personality and performance in small groups. *Psychol. Bull.,* 1959, **56**, 241-270.

McDavid, J., Jr. Personality and situational determinants of conformity. *J. abnorm. soc. Psychol.,* 1959, **58**, 241-246.

Newcomb, T. M. An approach to the study of communicative acts. *Psychol. Rev.,* 1953, **60**, 393-404.

Newcomb, T. M. *The acquaintance process.* New York: Holt, Rinehart & Winston, 1961.

Osgood, C. E. Cognitive dynamics in the conduct of human affairs. *Publ. Opin. Quart.,* 1960, **24**, 341-365.

Osgood, C. E., & Tannenbaum, P. H. The principle of congruity in the prediction of attitude change. *Psychol. Rev.,* 1955, **62**, 42-55.

Pettigrew, T. F. The measurement and correlates of category width as a cognitive variable. *J. Pers.,* 1958, **26**, 532-544.

Powell, F. A. Open- and closed-mindedness and the ability to differentiate source and message. *J. abnorm. soc. Psychol.,* 1962, **65**, 61-64.

Rokeach, M. The nature and meaning of dogmatism. *Psychol. Rev.,* 1954, **61**, 194-204.

Rosenberg, M. J. A structural theory of attitude dynamics. *Publ. Opin. Quart.,* 1960, **24**, 319-340.

Samelson, F. Conforming behavior under two conditions of conflict in the cognitive field. *J. abnorm. soc. Psychol.,* 1957, **55**, 181-187.

Sampson, H. The influence of "attraction" on perceived symmetry of attitude. *Amer. Psychologist,* 1954, **9**, 464.

Schachter, S. Deviation, rejection and communication. *J. abnorm. soc. Psychol.,* 1951, **46**, 190-207.

Secord, P. F., & Backman, C. W. Personality theory and the problem of stability and change in individual behavior: an interpersonal approach. *Psychol. Rev.,* 1961, **68**, 21-33.

Silverman, I. Differential effects of ego threat upon persuasibility for high and low self-esteem subjects. *J. abnorm. soc. Psychol.,* 1964, **69**, 567-572.

Smith, C. E. The autonomic excitation resulting from the interaction of individual opinion and group opinion. *J. abnorm. soc. Psychol.,* 1936, **30**, 138-164.

Snyder, A., Mischel, W., & Lott, B. E. Value, information and conformity behavior. *J. Pers.,* 1960, **28**, 333-341.

Speisman, J. C., Lazarus, R. S., Mordkoff, A., & Davison, L. Experimental reduction of stress based on ego-defense theory. *J. abnorm. soc. Psychol.,* 1964, **68**, 367-380.

Steiner, I. D. Galvanic skin resistance and responses to interpersonal disagreements. Tech. Rep., NIH Grant M-4460. Univer. of Illinois, August, 1964.

Steiner, I. D., & Johnson, H. H. Authoritarianism and conformity. *Sociometry*, 1963, **26**, 21-34.

Steiner, I. D., & Johnson, H. H. Relationships among dissonance reducing responses. *J. abnorm. soc. Psychol.*, 1964, **68**, 38-44.

Steiner, I. D., & Johnson, H. H. Category width and response to interpersonal disagreements. *J. Pers. soc. Psychol.*, 1965, **2**, 290-292.

Steiner, I. D., & Rogers, E. D. Alternative responses to dissonance. *J. abnorm. soc. Psychol.*, 1963, **66**, 128-136.

Steiner, I. D., & Vannoy, J. S. The stability of responses to interpersonal disagreements, 1964. (Unpublished study)

Steiner, I. D., & Vannoy, J. S. Personality correlates of two types of conformity behavior, 1965. *J. Person. and Social Psychology* (In press)

Stotland, E., & Hillmer, M. V. Identification, authoritarian defensiveness, and self-esteem. *J. abnorm. soc. Psychol.*, 1962, **64**, 334-342.

Tuddenham, R. D. Correlates of yielding to a distorted norm. *J. Pers.*, 1959, **27**, 272-284.

Vannoy, J. S. A study of the generality of cognitive complexity as a personality construct. Unpublished Ph.D. Thesis, Univer. of Illinois, 1964.

Vaughan, G. M. The trans-situational aspect of conforming behavior. *J. Pers.*, 1964, **32**, 335-354.

Vaughan, G. M., & Mangan, G. L. Conformity to group pressure in relation to the value of the task material. *J. abnorm. soc. Psychol.*, 1963, **66**, 179-182.

Vidulich, R N., & Kaiman, I. P. The effects of information source status and dogmatism upon conformity behavior. *J. abnorm. soc. Psychol.*, 1961, **63**, 639-642.

Wagman, M. Attitude change and authoritarian personality. *J. Psychol.*, 1955, **40**, 3-24.

Wilson, R. S. Personality patterns, source attractiveness, and conformity. *J. Pers.*, 1960, **28**, 186-199.

Wright, J. M., & Harvey, O. J. Attitude change as a function of authoritarianism and punitiveness. *J. Pers. soc. Psychol.*, 1965, **1**, 177-181.

Zimbardo, P. G. Involvement and communication discrepancy as determinants of opinion conformity. *J. abnorm. soc. Psychol.*, 1960, **60**, 86-94.

INFORMATION DEPRIVATION IN HUMANS[1]

Austin Jones

DEPARTMENT OF PSYCHOLOGY, UNIVERSITY OF PITTSBURGH,
PITTSBURGH, PENNSYLVANIA

I. Introduction

Beginning in the early 1950's, two research areas rapidly emerged which brought very different strategies to bear on the proposition that organisms are motivated by the absence or reduction of certain kinds of stimulus variability. The two areas are commonly designated as explora-

1 This study was supported by research grants M2479 and MH 07632 from the National Institute of Mental Health, United States Public Health Service.

tory-curiosity behavior and sensory deprivation. The exploratory-curiosity research emerged earlier by a brief period, the studies of "manipulatory drives" by Harlow and his associates (Harlow, 1950; Harlow, Harlow, & Meyer, 1950) being the first of the contemporary studies in the area, although exploratory behavior and closely related topics were the objects of occasional studies in the 1920's and 1930's (e.g., Dashiell, 1925, and Nissen, 1930). The first sensory deprivation studies appeared four years later, in 1954 (Bexton, Heron, & Scott), without any readily discernible prior experimental history, and were the outcome of the Canadian government's support of research which, it was hoped, would shed light on the psychological mechanisms underlying the techniques recently employed by the Russians for the elicitation of spurious confessions by military prisoners.

In the exploratory and curiosity experiments, the Ss, usually animals, are allowed to make instrumental responses for access to manipulatory or perceptual incentives, such as mechanical puzzles, complex visual stimuli, checkerboard mazes, and stimulus onset, or are required by the forced-choice procedure to choose between stimuli varying in degree of novelty or complexity. Some studies have been concerned simply with demonstrating that Ss will learn and maintain for substantial periods of time responses which bring them into contact with exploratory or curiosity incentives, incentives which do not derive in any obvious way from physiological drives such as hunger and sex. Other studies, which bear more closely on the research to be discussed in this chapter, have shown further that the strength of the exploratory response is directly related to the length of time during which the S was deprived of the incentive, and to the magnitude of the complexity or novelty associated with the incentive. Butler's (1957) study of visual exploration in monkeys who had been subjected to varying periods of visual deprivation, and Berlyne's (1957a) study of human perceptual curiosity as a function of the relative entropy of visual stimuli, are, respectively, among the first to provide supporting evidence on these two points. Fowler (1965) has recently provided a comprehensive review of the exploratory-curiosity literature.

The basic theoretical proposition of the sensory deprivation studies, that organisms are characterized by a need for certain kinds of variable exteroceptive stimulation, is the same as that underlying the exploratory-curiosity research, but the experimental strategy has been quite different, being directed mainly to the possible psychopathological consequences in humans of prolonged deprivation of such stimulation (e.g., Bexton, Heron, & Scott, 1954; Heron, Doane, & Scott, 1956). The principal hypotheses have been concerned with various impairments and distortions in the processes of perceiving, thinking, and remembering, rather than with testing directly the assumption that organisms require variable exteroceptive stimulation.

In 1958, a series of studies was begun in the Psychology Laboratory of the University of Pittsburgh which was designed to explicate, at the human level, the motivational assumptions underlying the exploratory-curiosity and sensory deprivation experiments. These studies have been concerned particularly with the assessment of possible drive states associated with sensorily restricted environments and with the nature of the stimulus incentives associated with such drives. Put somewhat colloquially, with what do humans feed their stimulus hunger, if in fact they have one at all? Or, more properly, what are the dimensions of variable exteroceptive stimuli which are relevant to the reduction of the drive or drives presumed to be associated with maintenance in sensorily restricted environments?

To the question "What is meant by variable stimuli?," the answers provided thus far in published studies have been themselves highly variable, and this perplexity led to the provisional selection of information theory concepts as the basic approach to measurement of the stimulus incentives in the studies reported here. The information measures, which were introduced to psychologists by Miller and Frick (1949), have the advantage of being completely general in the sense that they may be applied in principle to any stimulus situation, and thus hold out the possibility of reconciling the highly heterogeneous operational definitions of stimulus variability (or complexity or novelty, etc.) which have been employed in prior studies. In addition to the metrical advantages, there are, as Berlyne (1957b) has noted, "unmistakable affinities" between information theory and S-R reinforcement theory, and a secondary goal of the present studies has been the delineation of the relationships between these two theories—or to be more precise, between information concepts and S-R reinforcement theory, since information theory is really not a theory at all in the sense that psychologists use that term, but rather a set of definitions and measures.

In the initial study of the series (Jones, Wilkinson, & Braden, 1961) an attempt was made to demonstrate that information deprivation generates a drive variable, and that information-deprived Ss will execute, with increasing frequency, instrumental responses which serve to introduce increasing amounts of information into the environment. Information is defined as the reduction of uncertainty in a receiver (Shannon, 1948); thus a condition of information deprivation is one in which uncertainty reduction does not occur. This is most easily established by providing an environment in which all stimulation is of maximal certainty, i.e., maximal predictability by the S. In the limiting case, if all stimulation is perfectly predictable, then uncertainty reduction, or information, is necessarily at zero, since no uncertainty exists to be reduced. Any sensorily homogeneous and constant environment might be employed as an information deprivation condition, regardless of the absolute intensity of sensation, since information refers to the probabilistic aspects of stimuli rather than to their intensity. Because of technical convenience, maximal certainty of environmental stimulation was, in the present study, approximated by isolating S in a lightproof chamber with audition greatly restricted. Although the procedure also caused restrictions in the variability of auditory, tactile, and kinesthetic stimuli, the experimental condition was regarded as producing effective information deprivation in the visual modality only, and the tests of experimental effects were limited to measures of instrumental response for visual incentives. The incentives consisted of faint light flashes arranged in series of varying information value. The principal hypotheses were as follows: (a) Human Ss deprived of visual information will learn and maintain an instrumental response associated with the occurrence of light stimulation. (b) Instrumental response rate will be an increasing monotonic function of hours of deprivation. (c) The frequency of instrumental response will be an increasing monotonic function of the amount of information associated with the patterning of the stimuli.

Two experiments comprised the initial study, the second of which served as the model for most of the subsequent studies in the series. The method of this prototypal experiment (Jones et al. 1961: Exp. II) will be described in some detail in the following paragraphs. Except when noted to the contrary, the method of the subsequent studies was the same.

II. The Prototypal Experiment

A. SUBJECTS

Students in the University's introductory psychology course are requested as part of their course participation to serve as Ss in several hours of psychological experimentation, the particular experiments selected being entirely optional. For the present study, male Ss between the ages of 17 and 22 were accepted who were either currently enrolled in the course or who had taken it previously, provided they had completed no more than three courses in psychology. The latter requirement was adopted to minimize the probability of Ss having had some academic contact with literature related to the study, while the requirement of present or past enrollment in the introductory psychology course was based upon the observation that these students are typically more acceptant, less critical, and less suspicious of experimental participation than are those who have not had that experience.

Potentially serious sampling problems were apparent from the beginning. The dramatic cognitive and perceptual effects reported in the early investigations of sensory deprivation were the object of some discussion among the undergraduate psychology students, and preliminary experimentation indicated that some Ss tended to interpret the present study as one designed to induce such effects or to be stressful in some other way. Because the number of Ss to be utilized in each of the experiments constituted but a small percentage of the formally defined pool, there was concern that those volunteering might represent a highly atypical sample with regard to certain personality dimensions. In order to minimize such sampling bias, the solicitation of Ss was conducted in such a way as to dissociate the experiments from studies of stress or sensory deprivation, and a relatively attractive cash stipend was provided. Subjects were solicited from class groups by written announcements posted on a bulletin board, sometimes preceded by oral announcements in the class meeting. Prospective Ss were told that participants were needed for a single, 10-hour session, for which they would receive $12.00, and during which meals would be provided; that the experiment was sponsored by the United States Public Health Service; and that the procedure involved nothing that was in any way dangerous, painful, or embarrassing. Although a formal study of the characteristics of the volunteer samples has not yet been undertaken, preexperimental interview and postexperimental questionnaire and interview data do not suggest any appreciable personality bias. Volunteers were plentiful, and financial motivation seemed to weigh considerably more heavily than "thrill-seeking." Only very rarely did volunteers display apprehension in advance concerning the experimental procedure, and these typically withdrew before their scheduled appearance at the laboratory.

B. Experimental Design

Twenty-six Ss were maintained in the visual deprivation environment for one 10-hour period. The Ss were divided into two groups of 13 each. Group I was not allowed to perform the instrumental response for light incentives until they had received a signal 1 hour after the beginning of the session; Group II was similarly restricted for a period of 5 hours. In all other respects the groups were treated identically.

Each S was provided a small control panel with a five-position switch and one button, which permitted a "cafeteria" selection from among light series with relative information values of .00, .33, .67, and 1.00, plus a control series, $.00_A$, which will be described below. The order in which the various light series were assigned to the dial positions was systematically varied.

Because response functions plotted over the 10-hour experimental session would be difficult to interpret if S's fluctuations between wakefulness and sleep were not known, the decision was made to try to keep all Ss awake throughout by the administration of a 15 mgm. dexedrine spansule. This dosage was sufficiently low that no side effects of any sort were observed by Es or reported by Ss.

C. The Information Variable

Each instrumental response, consisting of a button press, activated electronic programming apparatus which caused a series of 24 light flashes to appear at 1-second intervals on a panel in the ceiling of the experimental room. There were two classes of light flashes, red and green, each produced by a very weak current to a small neon bulb behind a glass lens. The two lenses were 4 inches apart. The flashes were sufficiently faint that no part of the room was illuminated to the dark-adapted eye. The apparatus was so constructed that a light series in progress would not be affected by additional presses of the button.

The relative information values of the series depended upon the proportion of the 24 flashes which were random (or "uncertain" from S's standpoint) with respect to the determination of color. Series of .00 relative information value are associated with zero randomness, i.e., 24 lights of the same color. Series of 1.00 relative information value were associated with a random determination of color for each of the 24 flashes. The intervening values of .33 and .67 were associated, respectively, with series in which the color of one-third and two-thirds of the 24 flashes was determined randomly. The latter two series may be summarized as follows, where F refers to a flash of fixed (i.e., redundant) color, and R to a flash of randomly determined color:

$$I_{rel} = .33 \text{ FFRFFR etc.}$$
$$I_{rel} = .67 \text{ FRRFRR etc.}$$

The color of F, the fixed flash, was systematically varied over Ss but was constant within each S's experimental session.

A fifth light series was included as a control for the possible incentive properties of simple stimulus change, or alternation of the stimuli. Should it be demonstrated that Ss respond more frequently for series of higher information value, it might be argued that the critical dimension of the light series is its alternation rather than its uncertainty, or randomness, per se. For this reason, a control series was included which had .00 relative information value, because the color of the flash was entirely pre-dictable, but which had maximal alternation of stimulus classes—i.e., a fixed, single alternation of red and green flashes. If degree of alternation or stimulus change is the critical dimension of light incentives, then Ss' response rates for this control series, designated .00A (zero information, alternation) should be as high or higher than those for 1.00 information series, which contain maximal information and also a high degree of stimulus change (random alternation). Conversely, if information is the critical dimension of the incentive, then response for the .00A series should not differ significantly from response for the .00 series, both being less frequent than response for series of higher information values.

D. The Deprivation Environment

In the studies following the prototypal experiment, certain specific technical im-provements in the deprivation environment were made which did not affect in any way the experimental design and which were associated with only minute changes in procedure. Therefore, for descriptive convenience, the following paragraph applies generally to the entire series of experiments.

Subjects were placed in individual experimental rooms, each of which were about 7 feet $\times$ 10 feet. Aside from the apparatus, the only furnishings were a comfortable bed, mounted on heavy felt pads, and a portable, chemically treated toilet. The rooms were entirely lightproof and were acoustically insulated. Thermostatically regulated air conditioners maintained temperature at about 75°F. In one wall, two, separated, double-doored compartments were located, one door of each opening from inside the experimental room, the other from the corridor outside. One compartment was used for the delivery and retrieval of food trays, the other for containers used with the portable toilet; both were equipped with microswitches which signaled to the E their use by the S. On the wall near the head of the bed there was a buzzer which was used to signal the arrival of food and for certain other purposes noted below. Fastened to one side of the bed was a signal switch by which S could acknowledge his reception of a signal from E or summon him in case of an emergency.

The S's control panel, containing the dial and button by which he could initiate series of light flashes, was attached to a long, flexible cable which permitted it to be located either on the bed or on the floor at the side of the bed in accordance with particular stages in the experimental procedure. The red and green lights were mounted about 8 feet, 7 inches above the floor in a small panel fastened to the ceiling over the foot of the bed. For comfort in viewing, the light panel was oriented perpendicularly to the S's line of regard while lying on his back with his head on the pillow. The electronic programming apparatus which regulated the light series, and the Esterline-Angus equipment, by means of which records of instrumental response were kept, were located in a separate control room that was not adjacent to the experimental chambers.

E. PROCEDURE

Subjects were scheduled by telephone calls by the E, during which certain preliminary instructions were given. In the interest of minimizing individual differences in response due to variations in fatigue, diet, and associated physiological factors, Ss were requested not to drink alcoholic beverages and to go to bed by 11:00 p.m. on the evening prior to their experimental session, and not to eat or drink anything in the morning prior to the experiment, as they would be given breakfast upon their arrival.

Subjects arrived at the laboratory at 8:20 a.m. in groups of three, the number of Ss run concomitantly, and received breakfast and group instructions prior to beginning the deprivation condition at 9:00 a.m. At that time the purpose of the dexedrine spansule was explained and the S's permission formally requested. Permission was granted in each case (in all the subsequent experiments, involving several hundred Ss, only two declined, and two others reported being physically unable to swallow the capsule). An effort was made to verify S's compliance with the requests concerning sleep and diet.

The experiment was introduced as a "study of boredom." The Ss were informed that they were to lie quietly on a bed in a darkened room throughout the 10-hour session and that no activity of any kind would be permitted other than eating and using the toilet. Still in a group, the Ss were then administered the following instructions orally:

"It has been found in previous research that such boredom may be alleviated somewhat by the presentation of series of brief light flashes in the room. The purpose of this experiment is to find out what kinds of series work best—that is, what kinds of patterns of lights are most helpful in relieving boredom. As you lie on the bed in the darkened room, there is one thing you will be allowed to do. Whenever you wish, you may push a button at the side of the bed which will result in a series of brief light flashes in the ceiling. There will be a dial which may be set in any one of five positions, which will determine the kind of series, or pattern, which will occur. Exactly what the different series will look like you will see later. The main thing to remember is that you may push the button as often as you wish, for whichever pattern you wish.

"This is a purely exploratory study. We have no expectations of which dial position should be used or how often the button should be pushed. And your responses tell us nothing whatever about your personality or ability or anything like that. Instead, you are telling us something about what kinds of light flashes are most helpful in the alleviation of boredom. There are no tricks or hidden meanings in the experiment. In the past, some subjects have become somewhat distracted by trying to figure out what we were really after—thinking that the procedure was a cover for the study of some other psychological topic. This is a needless complication and one which you should avoid. When you are in the room, just lie back and relax, and push the button for the lights whenever the impulse moves you. It's as simple as that.

"When the session is over, we will have a few questions to ask you about your experience. These will require easy, matter-of-fact answers, and again have nothing to do with your personality or ability. Subjects occasionally wonder, or even worry, about what we will ask them, and are later surprised by the ordinariness of the questions.

"A distinction needs to be made between this study and some researches that have been conducted elsewhere under the title 'sensory deprivation.' It was found that subjects spending very long periods, 3 or 4 days, in darkened isolation chambers sometimes experienced false visual or auditory sensations—hallucinations, in other words. Our procedure is only very superficially related and is not expected to result in such experiences. The period of 10 hours would ordinarily be far too short. If such hallucinatory phenomena should by chance occur, there is no cause for alarm since everybody is susceptible to them to a degree and they do not persist after you leave the experimental room.

"Are there any questions?"

Further instructions were given concerning such mechanical aspects of the experimental environment as the method of feeding, use of the toilet, etc., following which each S was taken to his individual experimental room to await breakfast. Subjects were asked to practice going from the bed to the toilet and back, and to the food compartment and back, so that they could later do so in the dark without danger of falling.

After S had eaten breakfast, E entered to give final instructions. Complete and detailed information was given concerning operation of the apparatus and the nature of the light series associated with each of the dial positions. In explaining the nature of each of the light series, E pointed out the serial position of the fixed and random flashes, and ascertained that S understood the concept of randomness and that flashes designated as random would be "re-randomized" in subsequent selections of that series. It was emphasized that the rules relating the different light series to particular dial positions would not change in any way during the course of the experiment. The S was then given the following further instructions:

"The light apparatus is not to be used all the time you are in here. It may be used only for a portion of the 10-hour period. When that will be even I don't know yet, since the time will be determined randomly. There will be a signal so that you will know when the apparatus may be used." (The signal, described next, was a rapping on the leg of the bed, which was replaced in all subsequent experiments but one, with a series of five short buzzes from an electric buzzer mounted on the wall near the head of the bed. Subjects in these experiments were instructed to distinguish this signal from the signal for food, which was two buzzes, and were asked to acknowledge receipt of the signal by throwing the signal switch provided for them on the side of the bed.) "The apparatus, once the signal is given, may be used until the end of the session. Until the signal is given, leave the dial on the floor at the side of the bed. When the signal is given, bring the dial onto the bed within easy reach and leave it there, whether you use it or not."

The S was then given a card which presented in summary fashion the kind of series associated with each dial position and was asked to study it so that he would be able to remember it during the experimental session. This was thought to be important as a precaution against the possibility of instrumental responding as a "check" on memory rather than for the light incentives per se. After allowing the S about 5 minutes alone to study the card, E returned, answered any questions, and instructed S, upon the beginning of the experimental session (marked by the closing of the door, with the room light out), to execute two practice trials for each of the five light series in order to verify his understanding of the operation of the apparatus. The S then fitted beeswax and cotton plugs in his ears and put on acoustical "ear-muffs" (a product of Mine Safety Co. called "Noise-Foe") while waiting for the above-mentioned signal. Following the practice trials, the S was again permitted to ask questions, although usually none occurred at this point. The 10-hour experimental period was timed from the termination of the practice trials or, when questions occurred, from the termination of the usually brief discussion required to resolve them.

At the conclusion of the experimental period, Ss individually answered a questionnaire concerning their reactions to the experiment, including their physical comfort, and were interviewed briefly. These data were principally for the future guidance of the E's and were not intended as experimental variables.

III. Stimulus Information as an Incentive

A. INITIAL DEMONSTRATION IN THE PROTOTYPAL EXPERIMENT

An incentive is defined for this discussion as an object or event which may serve as a reinforcer of instrumental activity, with the proof of an incentive dimension resting upon the demonstration that instrumental response, assuming an appropriate drive level, is an increasing function of the degree or magnitude of the hypothesized incentive. This usage of the term incentive dimension is consistent with the incentive-motivational formulations of Spence (1956) and Hull (1952). In the present study, the incentive-motivational hypothesis was that the frequency of instrumental response by information-deprived Ss will be an increasing monotonic function of the amount of information associated with the patterning of the stimuli.

In Fig. 1, the mean proportion of responses for each of the five light series is shown. The proportion for $.00_A$ is plotted with the abscissa broken to acknowledge that a different stimulus dimension (variability or alternation, rather than information) is involved. For each S, the proportion of his total responses made for each of the five series was computed separately (thus, five proportions summing to 1.0), and the proportions for each series then averaged to yield the data of Fig. 1. This was done in order to provide equal weighting of each S in the data despite differences in absolute number of responses, since the hypothesis was concerned not with how many responses Ss made, but rather with the shape of their distribution over the scale of information values. An analysis of variance of trends of these data was computed for the 1-hour and 5-hour deprivation groups combined, excluding the data for $.00_A$, however, since, as noted previously, a different stimulus dimension is involved. The analysis showed proportional response rate to be a highly significant ($p < .0001$) increasing linear function of the information values associated with the light incentives. In a separate test, no significant difference was found between the proportions of response to .00 and to $.00_A$.

These results were interpreted as providing strong support for the view that the relative information value of stimuli constitutes an incentive variable. The stimulus "hunger" which the Ss appeared to have experienced was not a hunger simply for sensation, since the frequency,

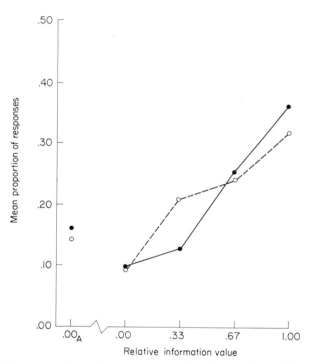

FIG. 1. Mean proportion of responses as a function of the relative information value of visual stimulus series (broken line) and auditory stimulus series (solid line). (From, respectively, Jones, Wilkinson, & Braden, 1961, and Jones & McGill, in press).

intensity, and quality of sensation were the same for each information value; thus response would have been approximately constant rather than increasing over information values if only a "hunger" for sensation were involved. Similarly, it was shown that when Ss respond maximally for series of 1.00 information value, they are not responding simply or primarily for the alternation of stimulus categories, since response rate for $.00_A$, a series containing maximal alternation (more than in the 1.00 series) but zero information was relatively low and not significantly different from the response rate for .00 series. This does not prove that differences in degree of alternation may not be associated with differences in incentive value in situations in which information value is a constant, but from the present results it may be inferred at least that information is by far the more potent dimension of incentive. [Because of apparently discrepant findings, a recent study by Munsinger and Kessen (1964) of preference for random visual forms should be noted. Their subjects showed preference for visual forms to be a curvilinear and nonmonotic, rather than a linear, function of degree of randomness, with maximal preference being associated with forms of intermediate randomness. Although there are further differences between their procedure and that of the experiment reported here, it appears probable that differences in drive level account for much of the difference in the preference functions of the two experiments. In the Munsinger and Kessen study, subjects indicated their preferences under conditions of presumably very low information drive, relative to that of the subjects in the study discussed above, inasmuch as their performance was not preceded by any period of perceptual deprivation. Being under conditions of low information drive, it would seem reasonable that their preference for informational incentives would be shifted "downward" to incentives of lesser magnitude relative to those selected under conditions of higher information drive.]

Are there incentive properties associated with informational stimuli in other modalities? The theoretical preference of the author and his collaborators has been to view information motivational phenomena as entirely general with respect to sensory modalities. It seems reasonable to assume that information transmission, or discrimination, is a central, rather than peripheral process, in which case informational incentive variables should be demonstrable in any modality. But since the history of science is characterized by the many instances in which hypotheses of obvious validity were unnecessarily tested only to be disconfirmed, it is acknowledged that the question requires an empirical answer. Although executed at a later date that the foregoing experiment of visual information deprivation, partial evidence on this point was provided by an experiment of identical design utilizing auditory information deprivation and auditory informational incentives (Jones & McGill, in press; Expt. I).

Twelve Ss, in two groups of six each, served in 10-hour auditory deprivation sessions. Each S lay on a bed in a sound-insulated, darkened room, wearing earphones which effectively masked the few background noises which penetrated the walls of the room. The first group was permitted access to the apparatus controlling the stimulus series after 1 hour, and the second group after 5 hours of deprivation. Each press of the button caused a series of 24 tones to be delivered to the S via the earphones at 1-second intervals. The stimulus categories, analogous to the red and green lights, were 300 cps and 1000 cps tones at a comfortable and clearly audible sound level. The relative information values of the tone series were identical to those of the prior experiment. The analysis of variance again showed proportional response rate to be a significant linear function of information values (see Fig. 1). The slope of the auditory incentive function appears slightly greater than that of the visual incentive function; the difference in slopes does not, however, attain statistical significance.

Although replication with still other modalities is perhaps warranted, the results of the auditory deprivation experiment nevertheless suggest strongly that the incentive properties of informational stimuli are general with respect to modalities.

Supporting evidence for the incentive properties of auditory information has been provided by the studies of Zuckerman and Haber (1965), whose Ss responded for random series of both auditory and visual signals, and Smith and Myers (1966), whose Ss were permitted to listen to segments of a stock market report, which may be regarded as containing a relatively high degree of sequential randomness.

B. POTENCY OF INFORMATIONAL INCENTIVES OVER LONGER PERIODS OF DEPRIVATION

The over-all significance of information motivation is not readily inferred from the preceding demonstrations that stimulus information constitutes an incentive dimension. The magnitude of the motivational process was not under investigation, either in the sense of the present intensity or of the persistence over time of the motivation. Should it be discovered, for example, that the effects demonstrated in 10-hour deprivation conditions dissipate rapidly over longer periods and are negligible after, say, 48 or 96 hours, then the information motivational phenomena would be revealed as relatively transient processes playing only a very subordinate role in the "motivology" of humans. If, on the other hand, the experimental effects should be shown to persist, or to be heightened, after such extended periods of deprivation, then information motivation would be evaluated as of correspondingly greater significance.

There is also a particular theoretical issue which may possibly be clarified by experimentation with extended periods of deprivation—the question of the ultimately innate or acquired status of information motivation. If the motivation for stimulus information is innate, then instrumental activity should be maintained or increased over longer periods of information deprivation, and the S's discrimination of differing values of stimulus information, as reflected in his more frequent selection of series of successively higher information value, should similarly be maintained or increased. If, on the other hand, instrumental activity should decline substantially, or the S increasingly fail to discriminate information values in his selection of stimulus series, then it would appear that extinction was in process, i.e., that the decrement in response rate and in discrimination was occurring because of the repeated execution of the response in the absence of whatever primary rewards reinforced it initially, perhaps very early in the S's development.

The persistence of the S's discrimination of informational incentive values was evaluated by Gardner (1961) in a study of information motivation during experimental sessions of 48 hours. (The experiment also provided evidence concerning the maintenance of over-all instrumental response rate, discussion of which will be deferred to Section IV, B.) Twelve Ss, divided in two groups of six each, served in continuous 48-hour sessions. The first group was allowed access to visual information incentives after 5 hours, and the second group after 24 hours; the present discussion, however, is concerned principally with the combined data. The procedure was otherwise parallel to that of the prototypal experiment, except for the omission of the dexedrine spansule for the control of sleeping, and for the fact that the experimenter was female. An analysis of variance of the responses made during the first 10 hours of access to the light incentives for each group again showed proportional response rate to be an increasing linear function of the information value of the incentives, but when the total period of access to the incentives was considered (hours 5–48 and 24–48 for Groups I and II, respectively), no significant relationship between response rate and information values could be demonstrated, either for the data as combined or as treated separately for each group. It appeared that the incentive properties of visual information had declined over time as measured by the lack of discrimination of information values, and that the interpretation of informational incentives as reflecting transient learned reward phenomena was supported. It was difficult, however, to feel that the question had been unequivocally resolved since, despite considerable variation among Ss, response was most frequent for the 1.00 information series, and the relatively small n caused the likelihood of a Type II error to appear great.

The question was next taken up in an unpublished study by the author (Jones, 1963a) in which 18 Ss, divided into three groups of six each, were maintained in deprivation environments for 96 hours. Groups I, II, and III were allowed access to the light incentives after 0, 24, and 48 hours of deprivation, respectively. The procedure was otherwise similar to that of Gardner's, except that the laboratory was in a new location which provided somewhat better control of background auditory stimulation and that the experimenters were both male. (It would not seem likely that the sex of the E would be a major determinant of instrumental performance in these experiments, but the possibility cannot be dismissed that interaction with an attractive and obviously female E, in the context of a procedure requiring 2 days' confinement in a laboratory

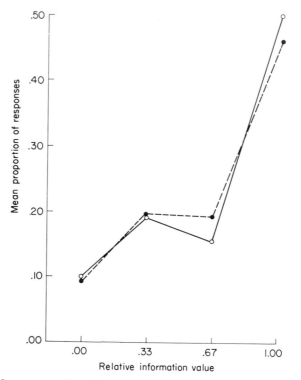

Fig. 2.   Mean proportion of response as a function of the relative information value of the stimulus series during the first 6 (broken line) and first 48 hours (solid line) in the deprivation environment. (From Jones, 1963a)

"bedroom," would elicit various sorts of irrelevant drives in the male undergraduates which might in some way affect performance. This possibility had been anticipated in Gardner's study, and the E took care to dress austerely, with a lab coat, to speak in a friendly but impersonal manner to the Ss, and to dissociate herself, in the Ss' perception, as much as possible with the management of feeding and toilet arrangements throughout the experimental session. In addition to the differences already noted, the procedure of the 96-hour experiment included a somewhat greater automation of the feeding, toilet, and other arrangements, with a corresponding deemphasis of the E's activity during the session as viewed by the Ss.)

As may be seen in Fig. 2, the performance of Ss in the 96-hour experiment indicates a very strong discrimination of information values, with the 1.00 information series being responded for about five times as often as series of .00 information. The data were combined for the three groups of Ss, and plotted in Fig. 2 both for the first 6 hours of access to the light incentives and for the total period of access (96, 72, and 48 hours for Groups I, II and III, respectively). The analysis of variance of trends showed the linear component of both functions to be highly significant ($p < .001$). The results provide strong evidence for the persistence of informational incentive phenomena over the course of many hours (96, in the case of Group I) of access to the light incentives, which is consistent with, although not proof of, the view that information motivation is innate rather than acquired. Although the linear components of both functions were significant, it is apparent from inspection of Fig. 2 that the group data are in each case better fitted by an exponential than a linear function, or, to be more precise, by a function with an exponent greater than 1.0. The fact that the function is "steeper" for responses over the total session than for responses during the first 6 hours of access to the incentives, suggests that Ss' discrimination of information values, and preference for maximal information, are sharpened rather than diminished or held constant over extended periods of time. Should this effect be found stable upon replication, it would add further indirect support to the innate basis of information motivation, since the "sharpening" of discrimination with the passage of time would be an effect opposite to that ordinarily expected were extinction in progress. Such evidence can only be indirect, however, as the argument may easily be raised that evidence of extinction, and decrement in preference for higher information values, might be readily demonstrated if the length of the experimental session were sufficiently extended.

C. INFORMATION COMPARED WITH OTHER DIMENSIONS OF STIMULUS INCENTIVES

The principal conclusion of the studies discussed thus far has been that, for information-deprived Ss, series of stimuli have incentive values which are directly related to the degree of information associated with them. Series of stimuli have, of course, statistical properties other than information, and the significance of information motivational phenomena rests partly upon the outcome of research seeking to establish the motivational phenomena, if any, which are associated with other statistical properties. In a series of experiments designed to provide evidence on this point (Jones, 1964), two such additional properties or dimensions were defined, stimulus *complexity* and stimulus *fluctuation*, and the motivational phenomena associated with these dimensions were evaluated both individually and in "competition" with each other and with the information dimension, in order that the hierarchical organization, or relative motivational dominance, of the three dimensions might be established. Brevity and clarity may frequently be positively correlated, but in the present case clarity of exposition would seem to require that the definitions of these dimensions, and the description of the values assigned them in the experiments, be taken up in some detail. The following paragraph is a modified version of definitional statements expressed elsewhere (Jones, 1964, p. 423).

Stimulus information refers to the degree of uncertainty or unpredictability of a sequence of stimuli as experienced by the *S*. Stimulus *complexity* is defined as the degree of "physical" randomness in a sequence of stimuli, i.e., it is measured directly without reference to the predictive response of an *S*. A stimulus series may have a high degree of complexity but zero information, as when a particular randomly ordered sequence repeatedly presented to the *S* becomes predictable by him. Stimulus *fluctuation* refers to the degree to which stimulus categories alternate, or fail to succeed themselves in a series. A stimulus series may have a high degree of fluctuation but zero complexity as, for example, the single alternation A, B, A, B. . . . There is, then, a logical hierarchical organization of the dimensions in the order information, complexity, fluctuation. Non-zero values of each dimension are always accompanied by non-zero values of dimension(s) subordinate to it, while superordinate dimensions may have zero values. A zero value of a dimension requires zero values for superordinate dimensions, while subordinate dimensions may be non-zero. Thus, a sequence cannot contain information without containing also some degree of complexity and fluctuation, and a series cannot contain complexity without also some degree of fluctuation.

In the present experiments, each concerned with incentives in the visual modality, a maximum information series (relative information value of 1.0) is one in which the color of successive flashes is determined randomly upon each selection of that series so that the *S* is always maximally "uncertain" as to the sequence. A .5 information series is defined as one in which the odd-numbered flashes (or even numbered) are fixed, always of the same color, with the remaining flashes randomized; further selection of that series by the *S* results in the odd-numbered (or even-numbered) flashes being fixed as before, but with the remaining flashes "re-randomized" on each occasion. A maximum (1.0) complexity series with zero information consists of a particular randomly ordered series of red and green flashes, which is repeated exactly each time it is selected by the S. A .5 complexity series (again with zero information) is one in which odd-numbered flashes are of the same color, with the intervening flashes randomized, and which is repeated exactly each time it is selected by the S. In parallel fashion, a maximum fluctuation series (with information and complexity at zero) consists of a sequence of flashes each of which constitutes an alternation of color with respect to the preceding flash (which will be recognized as the series designated $.00_A$

TABLE I

SAMPLE VALUES OF THE INFORMATION, COMPLEXITY, AND FLUCTUATION VARIABLES[a]

Relative Value	Information Serial order of flash: 1 2 3 4	Complexity (information at .00) Serial order of flash: 1 2 3 4	Fluctuation (information and complexity at .00) Serial order of flash: 1 2 3 4 . . . .
1.0	R R R R . . .	r r r r . . .	a b a b . . .
.5	a R a R . . . or b R b R . . .	a r a r . . . or b r b r . . .	a a b b a a b b . . . or b b a a b b a a . . .
.0	a a a a . . . . or b b b b	a a a a . . . . or b b b b	a a a a . . . . or b b b b . . . .

[a] R is a flash whose color is randomly determined anew on each selection of the series by S; r is a flash whose color is initially randomly determined but is thereafter fixed upon further selections of the series; a and b represent red and green flashes whose sequential position is either repetitive or symmetrically alternating and is invariant over repeated selections of the series.

in prior experiments); and a .5 fluctuation series (information and complexity again at zero) consists of a series of flashes, half of which are alternations of color with respect to the preceding flash, and half of which are the same color, with the requirement that the sequence be "symmetrical" or non-random. The zero value for all three dimensions—information, complexity, and fluctuation—consists of successive flashes of a single color. Table I provides a summary of these conditions.

Experiment I: Information vs. Complexity. In each of the prior experiments instrumental response rate was found to be an increasing linear function of the information value of the light (or tone) series. It was not entirely clear, however, that the crucial dimension of the incentives was information, for the reason that increasing values of information of the series were paralleled by and confounded with increasing values of the statistically subordinate dimension, complexity. The purpose of the first experiment was to compare the relative strengths of the incentive properties associated with these two dimensions. The comparison was simultaneous and "competitional."

Subjects deprived of both stimulus information and stimulus complexity were permitted to make responses causing the appearance of either information or complexity series. In this discussion, complexity series will refer to series having some value of complexity ranging from .00 to 1.00, but always with zero information value. As noted earlier, information series of greater than zero value necessarily contain above-zero complexity values as well, since a series cannot be uncertain or unpredictable without also containing some degree of physical randomness. Thus, in the present experiment should response be found to have the same increasing linear function over complexity values as over information values, then the crucial dimension of the light incentives would be established as complexity since the complexity series contain zero information.

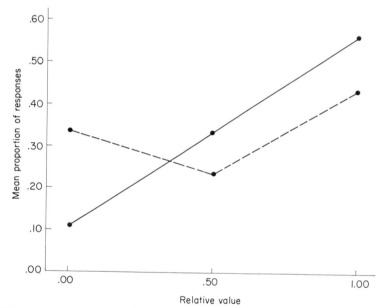

Fig. 3. Mean proportion of responses as a function of the relative value of the information (solid line) and complexity (broken line) series. From Jones, 1964; Expt. I)

The simultaneous visual conditions of information and complexity deprivation were provided by maintaining Ss in light-proof chambers for 8 hours. Thirteen Ss were each provided a five-position dial and button permitting selection of three comparable values of information and complexity—.00, .50, and 1.00. As zero complexity and information are represented by identical series, repeated flashes of a single color, only five series (and dial positions) were required to provide the three values of both dimensions. The procedure was similar to that of the prototypal experiment above, execpt that Ss were allowed access to the incentives from the beginning, that each button press initiated a series of six light flashes at 1-second intervals, and that a tactile code identifying the principle of each of the five series was attached to the base of the dial box. The tactile code was employed simply as a further effort to insure that the Ss would remember the nature of the series as described in their instructions.

The data consisted of the proportions of total responses for complexity series which were made for each of the three complexity values, and, computed separately, the proportions of total responses for information series which were made for the three information values. In Fig. 3, these two functions are presented graphically. The analysis of variance again shows response to be a significant ($p < .001$) increasing linear function over information values. The corresponding complexity function was neither linear nor monotonic although the quadratic component was significant ($p < .001$).

The results indicate that when information and complexity incentives are simultaneously and equally available, it is only the informational attribute of series of stimuli which qualifies as an incentive dimension. The shape of the complexity function, however, was interesting and puzzling. The Ss' preference for 1.00 complexity was not much stronger than for .00 complexity and the preference for .50 complexity

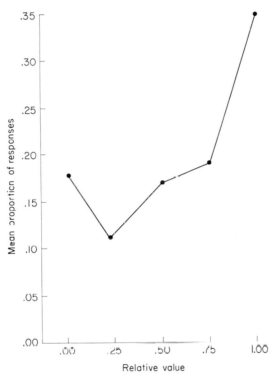

FIG. 4. Mean proportion of response as a function of the relative complexity value of the stimulus series. (From Jones, 1964; Expt. II)

was significantly less than either. It seemed possible that the motivational phenomena associated with stimulus information might obscure or suppress the motivational phenomena associated with stimulus complexity when both variables are operating, but that the latter might become manifest under conditions in which information is held at zero. The second experiment was designed to test this possibility.

Experiment II: Complexity Incentive Relationships When Information Is Zero. Twelve Ss served in an experiment similar to the preceding one except for the light series; the five complexity values .00, .25, .50, .75, and 1.00 were employed (with zero information in each case). The results are shown in Fig. 4. In contrast to the preceding findings, both the linear and quadratic components of the function were significant ($p < .05$). A comparison of Fig. 3 and 4 shows that the shape of the function did in fact change greatly in the direction of increased linearity when "competing" information incentives were not available. The function remains nonmonotonic, however, due to the relatively high frequency of response for .00 complexity; the function is monotonic from .25 complexity upward. Thus, the two experiments taken together suggest that the strength of the incentive-motivational properties of the complexity dimension varies inversely with the presence of simultaneously available information incentives.

Experiment III: Complexity versus Fluctuation. The purpose of Expt. III was to compare the incentive properties of stimulus complexity and stimulus fluctuation when both classes of incentives are equally available. In view of the results of the preceding experiment, it was expected that proportional response rate would again be an increasing linear (and probably also quadratic) function of complexity values. Since complexity series of greater than zero value are statistically superordinate to fluctuation series in the sense that they contain values of fluctuation within them, whereas fluctuation series have zero complexity, it was hypothesized that response for complexity series in a "competitive" condition with fluctuation series would "suppress the evidence" for incentive-motivational properties of fluctuation, just as response for information series had suppressed evidence of the incentive properties of complexity series. Thus, it was expected that response would be neither an increasing, linear, nor monotonic function of fluctuation values.

Eleven Ss served in a procedure similar to that of the preceding experiments except for the light series. Complexity and fluctuation series were each represented by the values .00, .50, and 1.00. As zero values of complexity and fluctuation (as well as information) are represented by the same stimulus series, only five series were required to provide the three values of each dimension.

The results are shown in Fig. 5. Contrary to expectations, *both* functions are significantly linear ($p < .02$), and the difference between their slopes is not significant. This appears to indicate that stimulus complexity does not constitute an independent incentive dimension, that the incentive properties associated with physically random stimulus series are reducible solely to the fluctuation of stimulus categories rather than to the attribute of randomness. Had complexity series possessed incentive properties unique to the physical randomness which characterize them, the function over complexity values should have been significantly "steeper" than the function over fluctuation values, where physical randomness is zero.

Experiment IV: Fluctuation Incentive Relationships When Complexity Is Zero. Further evidence that the incentive value of physically random stimulus series is solely or principally a function of the fluctuation or alternation of stimulus classes was provided by a final experiment in which Ss had access to series of varying fluctuation value, with complexity (and information) held at zero. If the incentive value of complexity series is associated only with the fluctuation of stimulus categories, then the response function over fluctuation values when only fluctuation incentives are available should be similar to the response function over complexity values when only complexity incentives are available, just as the two functions were found to be similar in a competitional situation.

The method was identical to that of Expt. II, except that the values of the fluctuation series were .00, .33, .50, .67, and 1.00 whereas the values of the complexity series had been .00, .25, .50, .75, and 1.00. The change in values was dictated by the need to provide stimulus series of similar over-all length, each of which terminated with the completion of a fluctuation "cycle." The Ss' proportional response rates are plotted over the fluctuation values in Fig. 6. Despite the slight differences in the units of the abscissa, it is apparent that this function is highly similar to that shown in Fig. 4, which is based on response for complexity series only. The analysis of variance shows the fluctuation function to be significantly quadratic ($p < .05$) as was true of the complexity function. The linear component, however, in contrast to that of the complexity function was not significant.

Inasmuch as the presence of competing information series appeared to suppress the incentive value of complexity series, and as the incentive

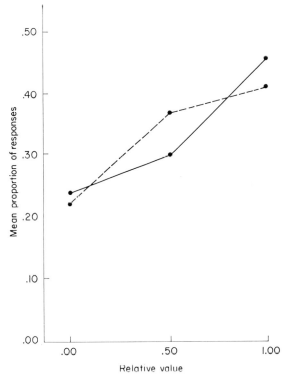

FIG. 5. Mean proportion of response as a function of the relative value of the complexity (solid line) and fluctuation (broken line) series. (From Jones, 1964; Expt. III)

properties of complexity appear to be reducible entirely or nearly entirely to the fluctuation contained within complexity series, it seemed logically to be required that competing information series would also suppress the incentive value of fluctuation series. This transitivity in the relationships among the three dimensions was not tested in the present experiments, but some evidence is provided by the results of the prototypal experiment described earlier, in which the series designated $.00_A$ corresponds to the fluctuation value 1.00. In that experiment the proportional response rate for the 1.00 fluctuaton series was about .14, which was only slightly and nonsignificantly higher than that for .00 information, whereas in Expts. III and IV of the present series, where there were again five response options but with information constant at .00, the response rate for 1.00 fluctuation rose sharply to .42 and .37, respectively. Thus the expected transitivity of the incentive functions associated with the three dimensions appears to be verified.

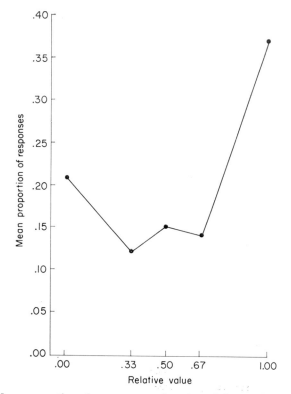

Fig. 6. Mean proportion of response as a function of the relative fluctuation value of the stimulus series. (From Jones, 1964; Expt. IV)

In summary, the results of the four experiments considered jointly, and in comparison with the results of the prototypal experiment, support the following generalizations: (1) Of the three statistical properties evaluated, it is only stimulus information which meets the criterion of an incentive dimension, i.e., that response be an increasing monotonic function of the value of the hypothesized incentive. (Increasing monotonic functions were shown for complexity and fluctuation only in Expt. III, where each function was plotted over but three points; in Expts. II and IV, where the functions were plotted over five points, neither was monotonic.) (2) When information incentives are not available, Ss tend in general to respond for higher rather than lower values of complexity and fluctuation. (3) When information incentives are simultaneously available, however, the incentive properties of complexity and fluctuation are substantially suppressed, i.e., preference for high vaules of complexity and fluctuation is sharply attenuated. (4) Complexity, or physical randomness, appears to be associated only very slightly or not at all with the incentive properties of stimulus series; preferences for high values of complexity series are related principally or entirely to the correlated values of the statistically subordinate fluctuation dimension.

IV. Information Deprivation as a Drive Variable

A. Initial Demonstration in the Prototypal Experiment

The results reviewed thus far appear to indicate clearly that the condition of information deprivation strongly motivated the Ss to respond for informational incentives, but they do not indicate whether the motivational process constitutes a drive variable. The term drive is used here, as in the S-R reinforcement theory of Hull (1952) and Spence (1956), as a motivational construct correlated with the degree or temporal extent of deprivation of incentive, and which serves as a multiplier of habit strength in the determination of performance.

An experiment preliminary to the prototypal experiment (Jones et al., 1961: Expt. I) provided some indirect evidence relevant to the hypothesis that information deprivation generates a drive. The procedure was similar to that of the prototypal experiment except that each S served in four, separate, 12-hour sessions, with access to but one value of information per session and with the values .00, .33, .67, and 1.00 being varied over sessions. In addition, the Ss were allowed to use the apparatus from the beginning of each session. As in each of the experiments which followed, the stimulus series were designed with the expectation that their incentive value would be exceedingly small relative to that of the series of stimuli to which the S is typically exposed in his daily life; that is, the total absolute information value of a series would be infinitesimal compared to the absolute information value of the stimuli ordinarily transmitted to S. Specifically, it was believed that the series of brief light flashes contained such low absolute values of information that even continuous responding would not produce but a very small fraction of the information which would typically be received in a comparable period outside the deprivation environment. Therefore, if the rate of information to which Ss expose themselves is regulated by a drive, no amount of responding for light series should be sufficient to offset the cumulative effects of successive hours of deprivation. Allowed access to the light series from the beginning of the session, response rate should increase hour by hour as drive increases, at least for a period of time until sleep or exhaustion intervene and response rate is necessarily suppressed. (If response for information can never "keep up" with ever-increasing drive, the question may be raised as to why responding should not rise immediately to its maximal rate, i.e., continuous responding, and remain constant. According to a part of the theory initially held by the investigators, about which empirical evidence will be presented later, information drive is of central rather than peripheral origin, and may be reduced by informational incentives in any modality. Therefore, in the initial hours of the deprivation condition, information drive may be substantially or, intermittently, completely offset by information transmission in the relatively uncontrolled, nonvisual modalities. With the passage of time, however, and continued experience in the deprivation environment, the stimuli of nonvisual modalities gradually become more predictable to the S, i.e., decline in information value, and progressively lose their capacity for reducing information drive. Concomitantly, the informational incentives in the visual modality, as their unpredictability remains constant over time, increase in motivational relevance, and instrumental response rate rises accordingly.)

The results of the preliminary experiment, based upon the pooled data of four 12-hour sessions for eight Ss, are shown in Fig. 7. The analysis of variance showed both the linear and quadratic components of the response function over hours to be highly significant ($p < .001$). The response rate rose sharply over the first 9 hours, falling off somewhat in the final 3 hours. These results appeared to support the hypothesis that information deprivation generates a drive. The 9-hour period over which response rate steadily increased is about as extended a temporal interval for the demonstration of drive effects as one might expect under the particular experimental conditions. During the final 3 hours, about 11 to 14 hours after the Ss had arisen to come to the laboratory, many Ss appeared to have become drowsy, the residual effect of the dexedrine spansule presumably having become slight. Similar findings of increasing response rate over the initial hours of deprivation have been reported also for the briefer period of 3 hours by Zuckerman and Haber (1965), whose Ss were permitted to respond for exposure to random arrays of colored strips.

Although clearly consistent with a drive interpretation of information deprivation, these results were not conclusive because of a confounding of drive and habit strength variables. In the present experimental procedure, all Ss were free to respond for the information incentives from the beginning of each session; thus, with the premise that performance is a multiplicative function of drive and habit strength, the increasing response function over the first 9 hours could be mainly or entirely a result of increased habit strength associated

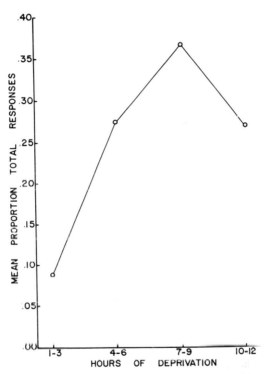

FIG. 7.   Mean proportion of total responses as a function of hours in the deprivation environment. (From Jones, Wilkinson, & Braden, 1961; Expt. I)

with the cumulatively increasing numbers of reinforced trials—without any contribution of an information drive variable.

The prototypal experiment (Jones *et al.*, 1961: Expt. II) was designed to remedy this deficiency. As was noted earlier, Ss were divided into two groups of 13 each. The first group was not allowed to use the apparatus until given a signal 1 hour after the beginning of the session, and the second group not until given a signal after 5 hours; following the signal, all Ss were free to use the apparatus as they wished until the end of the session. Thus, any differences obtained in response functions between the two groups over comparable periods of time following the signal could be attributed only to the drive construct, as habit strength prior to the signal was a constant due to absence of response. Figure 8 compares the data of the two groups in their first 5 hours of access to the light series. Data are the mean absolute numbers of responses during each hour. Subject attrition reduced the n to eleven and eight for the 1-hour and 5-hour

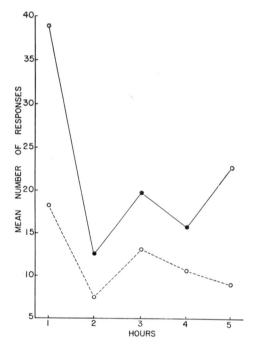

FIG. 8.   Mean absolute number of responses during the first 5 hours of access to the incentives, following one hour of prior deprivation (Group I; broken line) and 5 hours of prior deprivation (Group V; solid line). (From Jones, Wilkinson, & Braden, 1961; Expt. II)

signal groups respectively. (Other than mechanical malfunction of apparatus, the most important source of attrition was an S's "jumping the gun" and using the apparatus before the signal was given. That this was possible at all was due to an unforeseen deficiency in the apparatus which was corrected in all following experiments. With reference to the drive hypothesis, however, it is perhaps worth noting that of the four Ss who made such anticipatory errors, three were in the group deprived for 5 hours before the signal was given.) The two functions were compared by analysis of variance of trends, equal ns

being achieved by utilizing the first eight Ss run under the 1-hour signal condition and the total of eight Ss (after attrition) in the 5-hour signal condition. The finding of principle interest regarding the drive hypothesis was the significant ($p < .02$) difference in the shapes of the two functions over time. Subjects delayed in access to the light incentives for 5 hours began by responding at a much higher rate than Ss delayed for 1 hour, but in successive hours responded at a lesser rate, more nearly approximating that of the latter Ss, finally increasing their rate differential again in the fifth hour. The initially higher rate of the Ss delayed 5 hours is interpreted as due to their greater initial drive, as habit strength was presumably the same for both groups. With successive hours of access to the incentive, the differences in response rate became reduced, which would be expected as the effects of the differential drive manipulation are dissipated over time. The only discrepant aspect of the data is the increased difference in response rate during the fifth hour of the Ss delayed for 5 hours, the interpretation of which does not seem immediately clear. It may be noted, however, that the significant difference betwen the shapes of the two functions is determined principally by the disparity in relative response rates between the first and second hours.

The question may be raised as to why the response rates, once the Ss were allowed to use the apparatus, did not rise over the first 9 hours or so as they had in the preliminary experiment in which there was no delay in access to the light series. Although this finding was not anticipated, the following *post hoc* explanation appears plausible. In the preliminary experiment, Ss began responding infrequently in the first hour without delays imposed by the E, under conditions of low drive. Habit strength, because of the relative infrequency of response, remained fairly low for the first 1 or more hours. As drive increased slowly with the passage of time, response rate and habit strength increased, so that the response rates continued to increase for a substantial period of time, about 9 hours. In the experiment which followed, however, in which Ss were initially deprived of access to the incentives for 1 or 5 hours, the drive accompanying the initial response was considerably higher and motivated a greater number of responses. Factors of reactive inhibition and some diminution of drive then led relatively quickly to a decrease in response rate. But as reactive inhibition and the diminution of drive are factors which dissipate over periods of time during which instrumental response rate is reduced, response rate should again increase until reactive inhibition and diminution of drive again supervene, i.e., some sort of cyclical function of response over time should be observable. Subjects with no initial delay in response, as in the preliminary experiment, would not be exempt from this expectation, but, as drive and response rate are initially lower, it would take a longer period of time before reactive inhibition and appreciable diminution of drive would check response, thus the cycles into which response falls, at least the first ones, would be expected to be of longer duration.

Some support for this interpretation is provided by the data shown in Fig. 9 in which the response rates of the 1-hour and 5-hour delay groups are plotted over their total period of responding, 9 hours and

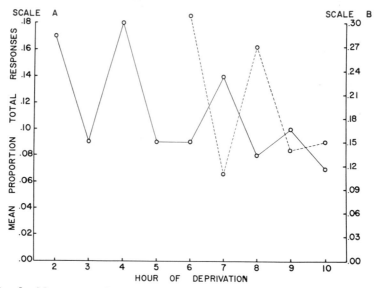

Fig. 9. Mean proportion of total response as a function of hours in the deprivation environment following signal indicating availability of information series. (One-hour signal Ss, solid line; five-hour signal Ss, broken line. For ease of comparison, the 1-hour group is plotted on Scale A and the 5-hour group on Scale B.) (From Jones, Wilkinson, & Braden, 1961; Expt. II)

5 hours, respectively. The response rates are plotted in proportional form in order to clarify the manner in which the Ss distributed their responses over time. A cyclical character to the functions is apparent, and if the two are superimposed it may be seen that their correspondence is quite close. The cycles in each case have an average duration of about 2½ hours. These cycles are reflected in the septic and quadratic components of the functions for the 1-hour and 5-hour delay groups, respectively, and a compound test of the two cycles shows them to be significant at $p < .03$. In order for the pooled cycles of the two groups to have been significant, not only must a majority of the Ss have responded in approximately 2½-hour cycles, but the crests and troughs of the Ss'

cycles must have shown close correspondence temporally throughout the 9- and 5-hour periods. This interesting periodicity is evidently tied to the time of first availability of the light series, which is consistent with the interpretation offered here, rather than to the elapsed time in the deprivation environment, as may be seen by comparing the succession of high and low points in the response functions of the two groups over their first five hours of responding.

B. Persistence of Information Drive Over 48-Hour and 96-Hour Periods

The support reviewed thus far for the hypothesis that information deprivation generates a drive is limited by the relatively brief total periods of maintenance in the deprivation environment (10 or 12 hours) and by the relatively brief total periods of deprivation (one and five hours) preceding the crucial comparisons of response rate. As noted previously (Section III, B), evidence concerning the persistence of information motivational phenomena over extended periods of time may permit some inferences concerning the innate versus acquired status of information motivation. In the case of Ss permitted access to the incentives from the beginning of greatly extended periods of deprivation, a declining response rate over the total period would suggest that the underlying motivation is secondary, or acquired, and that extinction is occurring. The inference would be less clear if response rate should be maintained or increased throughout the total period. Such a finding would be consistent with, although not proof of, the view that information drive is innate—the argument always being tenable, no matter how long the period of deprivation, that a response decrement might be demonstrable were the period to be extended still further. Similarly, in comparisons of response rates of groups differing in extent of prior deprivation in which such periods of deprivation are longer than those previously employed, a failure to replicate the support for the drive hypothesis would suggest that an acquired drive underlies response and that differences in extent of deprivation are not generally motivationally relevant; should support for the drive hypothesis again be found, the inference would continue to be tenable that the information drive has an innate basis.

In Gardner's (1961) study of information motivational phenomena over 48 hours, the Ss of Group I were deprived for 5 hours, and the Ss of Group II for 24 hours, before being allowed access to the light incentives. The initial response rates (i.e., beginning with the fifth hour for Group I and the twenty-fourth hour for Group II) were compared separately for the first one-half hour, the first hour, first 10 hours, and the first 24 hours of access to the incentives. In each comparison, the absolute number of responses made by Group II was significantly greater ($p < .01$). As there were no initial differences in habit strength between the groups, the greater response rate of the Ss deprived 24 hours provides important additional support for the drive interpretation. [It is interesting to note that the 24-hour deprivation was sufficiently more motivating

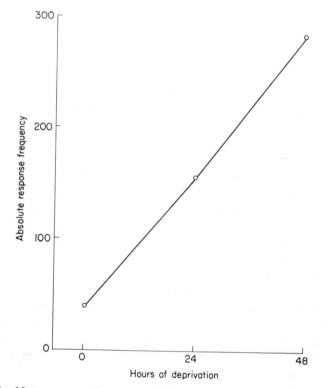

FIG. 10. Mean response frequency during the first six hours as a function of numbers of hours of prior deprivation. (From Jones, 1963a)

than the 5-hour deprivation that the former Ss' total response rate over the remainder of the session was significantly ($p < .05$) the greater, even though they had but 24 hours in which to respond, while the other group had 43 hours; the means were 160 and 130, respectively.]

In the 96-hour deprivation experiment which followed (Jones, 1963a), Ss were divided into three groups associated with delays of 0, 24, and 48 hours, respectively, before being allowed access to the light incentives. The mean absolute response rates of each group during their first 5 hours of access to the incentives are shown in Fig. 10. Analysis of variance shows response rate to be a highly significant ($p < .001$) linear function of the number of hours of prior deprivation, thereby providing what would seem to be relatively conclusive evidence of the drive-generating character of information deprivation. The magnitude or intensity of the drive experienced by the Ss appears to have been highly variable, as inferred from differences in response rates. For example, in the 48 hours during which the six Ss of Group III were allowed to respond (after 48 hours initial delay), their total response rates were 134, 247, 551, 1290, 1702, and 2588. The performance of the last S listed assumes heroic proportions when one considers that he responded, on the average, once every 67 seconds over the course of 2 days.

With regard to possible inferences concerning the innate or acquired nature of information drive, the data of Group I, allowed to respond from the beginning of the 96-hour session, are the most relevant. The proportion of each S's total responses made during each of the successive 24-hour periods was computed. The mean proportions rose slightly, but nonsignificantly, over the 4 days, from about .24 to about .30, thus failing to provide evidence of extinction or support for an acquired drive interpretation. The hypothesis of an innate basis for information drive thus remains tenable but unproven.

Analysis of the potential cyclic aspects of response becomes, in the present experiment, much more complicated than in that reported earlier, due to probable superimposition of cycles associated with irrelevant biological factors and cycles associated with information motivation, and have not yet been executed in any detail. An analysis is available, however, of the manner in which responses were distributed over the first 24 hours of access to the incentives. Fig. 11 shows the proportions of the total responses over the 24 hours that were made during each block of 6 hours. The differences in "shape" among the three functions are significant ($p < .05$) and are consistent with the expectation that differences in initial drive level will affect the initial cyclic character of response. As drive is lowest in the 0-delay group, response rate is initially relatively low, but rises substantially during the second block of 6 hours, falls sharply in the third block, and begins to rise again in the fourth. The group delayed for 24 hours, and thus under much higher drive, has a much higher initial response rate, which in the second block rises only slightly and which falls off sharply in the third and fourth blocks, without recovery. The group delayed 48 hours, and thus under the highest drive level, has still a slightly higher initial response rate, which, instead of rising in the second block, is followed by a steady decrement in response throughout the remainder of the 24 hours. The 0-, 24-, and 48-hour delay groups thus show two, one, and zero

inflections, respectively, in their response functions over 24 hours, suggesting that successive increments in initial drive level set into motion cycles
of successively longer duration. The 0-delay group, for example, appears
in the fourth block to be beginning a second cycle within the 24-hour
period, while the 48-hour delay group shows no evidence of a cycle at
all within 24 hours, its first cycle presumably requiring a much longer

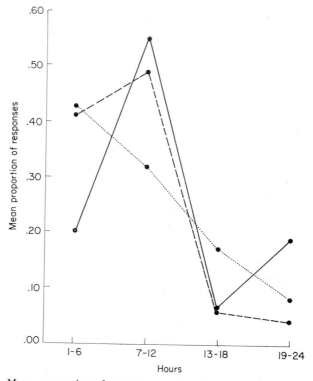

Fig. 11.   Mean proportion of response as a function of the first 24 hours following
access to the incentives. (0-hour delay, solid line; 24-hour delay, dashed line; 48-hour
delay, dotted line.) (From Jones, 1963a)

period for completion, and the 24-hour delay group has an intermediate
status. Although not shown in Fig. 11, the data for the 48-hour delay
group in their second 24-hours of access to the incentives confirm a
cycle of longer duration, response rising again to a rate almost as high
as during the first 6 hours of the first day, then falling to a point slightly
lower than at the end of the first day. The duration of the first cycle of
response for the 48-hour delay group is approximately 30 hours, as compared with a duration of about 15 hours for the first cycle of the 0-delay
group. The interpretation appears plausible that the Ss deprived 48

hours began responding under very high drive and therefore "consumed" information at a high rate, attaining substantial satiation (perhaps even hypersatiation for some Ss) in the first 6 hours, following which a prolonged successive decrement in response occurred as Ss went into a "recovery" phase, which was in turn followed by a rise in response as information drive gradually increased. The Ss of the 0-delay group, in contrast, began responding under low drive and thus tended less to "overconsume" the information incentives with the result that the recovery phases are briefer and the cycles of lesser total duration. Taking into consideration the much briefer 2½ hour cycles discussed in the preceding section which occurred to Ss deprived initially for 1 or 5 hours, it would appear that duration of cycles is not a linear but a curvilinear function of hours of initial deprivation, with maxima at zero and at some indefinitely large number of hours. Should future study confirm the existence of such cycles over longer periods of time and support this type of interpretation, the tenability of the hypothesis that information drive has an innate basis might be regarded as having been somewhat strengthened. Although cyclic aspects of response are conditionable, the appearance of highly regular cycles over long temporal periods would perhaps be more suggestive of a homeostatic principle at the physiological level.

The recording of physiological measures of arousal during experimental sessions was beyond the scope of the present studies, but it should be noted that important data of this sort have been provided by several recent experiments. Zubek and his associates have reported a series of studies of EEG changes as a function of 14 days of perceptual deprivation which indicated that mean occipital frequencies showed a progressive decrease over that period [Zubek, Welch, & Saunders (1963)] and that disturbances of EEG were evident as long as 10 days following termination of the experiment (Zubek, 1964). Several studies of galvanic skin responses, however, have shown an increase in conductance over the period of deprivation (e.g., Vernon McGill, Gulick, & Candland, 1961; Zuckerman, Levine, & Biase, 1964).

The Zuckerman and Haber (1965) experiment cited earlier is of particular relevance to the present discussion of information drive, and suggests the probable convergence of the drive and arousal concepts. Subjects in the prior experiment of Zuckerman, Levine, and Biase had been maintained for 3 hours in visually deprived, auditorily deprived, or visually and auditorily deprived environments. The nonspecific GSR measures were significantly higher for the visually and auditorily deprived Ss, indicating that the degree of perceptual restriction (two modalities rather than one) is related to the degree of autonomic arousal. This is a finding of great interest in itself, but of special significance in the present discussion is the fact that Zuckerman and Haber then took the further step of relating the magnitude of the GSR measure to the rate of instrumental response for informational incentives. From the Ss of the prior experiment, 12 high GSR reactors (i.e., Ss who showed either low increase or decrease in conductance) were selected. Both groups were maintained in a condition of visual and auditory deprivation for 3 hours, during which they were free to respond for random visual or auditory stimulation. The high GSR reactors made significantly more responses than did the low GSR reactors. The effect was both highly reliable ($p < .001$) and of great magnitude; response frequency for the high GSR group was almost four times that for the low GSR group. These results support the interpretation that the two groups differed in the drive level with which they entered the experiment. The two groups, however, had been selected previously as representing different levels of autonomic arousal; thus the results may be regarded essentially as a validation of autonomic arousal as a predictor or inferential measure of the drive associated with information deprivation.

C. Summation of Information Drive and Irrelevant Drives

Common to the theories of both Freud and Hull is the principle that the physiological bases of the various drives or categories of emotional arousal are highly interactive and that instrumental activity motivated by one drive may be enhanced by the simultaneous arousal of another, seemingly unrelated drive. As part of the over-all assessment of the drive properties of information deprivation, an experiment was designed to determine whether the irrelevant drives of hunger and anxiety would summate with information drive in the motivation of responses for informational incentives (Jones, 1961). Control, hunger, and anxiety groups of 12 Ss each were maintained in the information deprivation environment for 8 hours and were allowed access to the light series from the beginning. The hunger group entered the experiment at 9:00 a.m., as did the others, but without having eaten since 6:00 p.m. the preceding day, and was deprived of food throughout the 8-hour session. Thus, at the beginning of the session their irrelevant hunger drive was equivalent to that of a delay of an hour or two in the normal time of breakfast. The anxiety group, which would be more correctly referred to as the "pain-plus-anxiety" group, was given ten brief electric shocks at irregular intervals throughout the session. In keeping with the results of a prior experiment (see Fig. 7) in which Ss were allowed to respond from the beginning of a 12-hour session (Jones et al., 1961; Expt. I), it was hypothesized that control Ss' proportional response rate would increase over hours, falling off slightly toward the end of the session, but that responses in the anxiety group would be facilitated in the initial hours of the session, then show a decrement over the remaining hours as a result of accomodation to the repeated presentation of the shock. [Evidence for such accomodation has been shown in a conditioned avoidance procedure reported by MacDonald (1946)]. It was hypothesized that Ss of the hunger group would have higher proportions of responses in the initial hours than would control Ss, and that proportional response rate would be an increasing monotonic function of hours, rather than declining in the final hours as was predicted for control Ss. The hypothesis of an increasing monotonic function is required by the assumption that the drive stimuli associated with food deprivation increase over hours of deprivation, at least over the moderate range of hours employed in this experiment.

In order to avoid the potentially serious sampling bias which might occur if Ss scheduled to serve in the anxiety group volunteered with the expectation of being shocked, while hunger Ss volunteered with the expectation of not being fed, and control Ss volunteered with neither expectation, it was decided to recruit all Ss on the basis of the same expectation, that of receiving shock. In the solicitation of Ss, students were told simply that they would receive a small number of brief electric shocks, the maximum intensity of which they would themselves determine in advance, and that they would receive a $10.00 stipend for their participation. Hunger and control Ss were not told of their true status until arriving at the laboratory for the scheduled session. Because of the risk that the Ss would react negatively to the deception or fail to trust the E's subsequent statements about experimental procedure, a particular effort was made to justify the deception of the Ss. For the hunger group, the following explanation was made:

"In research with human subjects we have followed the policy, as have most psychologists, of never deceiving subjects about the conditions under which they serve. Occasionally, however, an experiment cannot be carried out successfully without a measure of deception. That is true of this experiment. The deception has already occurred. I will tell you about it now, so that you may have an entirely accurate picture of the procedure before we actually begin.

"This experiment requires the services of subjects who are willing to undergo the discomfort of a series of electric shocks. Now that you have been selected on this basis, however, I am able to tell you that there will be no electric shocks during any part of the experiment. Instead, you are asked to accept another kind of discomfort—during your eight-hour session you will receive no food, nor will any breakfast be served. Water, however, will be available in very small quantities.

"We regret that the requirements of the experiment did not permit us to discuss this with you in advance—and although I hope that you will agree to stay, we acknowledge completely your right to drop out at this point. If you decide not to continue, you will receive the full stipend of $10.00, since you acted in good faith according to your original understanding.

"How about it—will you stay?"

None of the volunteers declined to participate.

Subjects of both the anxiety and control groups were told, "You are already aware that electric shock is involved in this experiment. Not all subjects will receive shock, however. Who receives shock and who does not will be determined randomly. I will now determine your case by consulting a table of random numbers." The *E* then paused to enact the random determination. Subjects in the control group were then told; "You have just been selected to serve in the non-shock group. This means that at no time will you receive any sort of shock whatsoever. Everything else will be just as you have been told. There are no tricks involved." Subjects assigned to the anxiety group were informed that they had been selected to receive shock and were then ad-

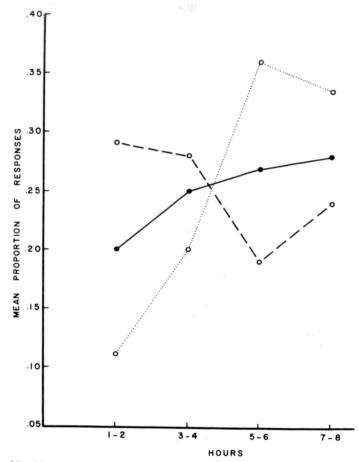

Fig. 12. Mean proportion of response as a function of hours in the deprivation environment, plotted separately for the shock (dashed line), hunger (solid line), and control (dotted line) groups. (From Jones, 1961)

ministered a preliminary scaling series of shocks in order to determine their tolerance. They were requested to set a distinctly aversive upper limit of shock intensity which they would agree to receive during the experiment. The shocks were administered during the session through electrodes attached to the forearm. Shock duration was 1.5 seconds and intensity was constant for each *S* at his upper limit. Other than the shock and hunger manipulations, the procedure was similar to that employed in the proto-typal experiment.

The results are shown in Fig. 12 in which the proportional response functions over hours are plotted separately for the three groups. It should be recalled that the hypotheses were concerned with the proportional distribution of responses over the 8 hours, rather than with absolute response rates, thus the mean of the four data points for each function is .25. The trends of the hunger and the shock groups over hours each differed significantly ($p < .01$ and $p < .05$, respectively) from that of the control group. The nature of the three functions was almost exactly as hypothesized. As compared with the control group, the responses of the shock group were strongly facilitated in the initial hours, during which anxiety may be presumed to have been most acute. In the second half of the session, response rate declined as accomodation to the shock occurred. The hunger group showed a lesser degree of initial facilitation, which would be in keeping with the expectation that mild hunger is less aversive than shocks of an intensity set by Ss as their upper limit. As predicted, the fact that hunger presumably increased throughout the 8-hour session resulted in offsetting the tendency, under control conditions, for response to decline in the final hours.

The results are interpreted as further evidence that information drive has the same properties, including that of summation with irrelevant drives, as do such "classical" drives as hunger, thirst, and pain. Although not the primary purpose of the experiment, the results provide an unusually clear illustration of the drive summation principle itself. A chronic difficulty in many past studies has been that of establishing an irrelevant drive that is really irrelevant, i.e., the drive stimuli of which are independent of and dissimilar to the relevant drive stimuli. It is difficult, for example to feel confident that such independence exists between the stimuli of hunger and pain, hunger and thirst, or pain and thirst. The present experiment, however, appears to provide a situation of maximal independence of drive stimuli. However the drive stimuli associated with information deprivation be conceptualized, they are apparently quite unrelated to the drive stimuli either of hunger or of the pain and anxiety associated with electric shocks. Thus the present experiment appears to have provided an unusually stringent test of the drive summation hypothesis with positive outcome.

D. Are There Drives Associated with the Deprivation of Complexity and Fluctuation Incentives?

In an earlier section (III, C) evidence concerning possible incentive properties of statistical attributes of stimuli other than information was discussed. It was concluded that while Ss showed some tendency to respond for higher rather than lower values of stimulus complexity and fluctuation, neither response function was monotonic over relative complexity and fluctuation values (Jones, 1964). Only response for information showed a clearly monotonic function over relative values of the incentives, and, for that reason, only information met the criterion of an incentive dimension as defined for the purpose of the studies reported here. The other side of the motivational process may now be considered. Is the drive for information paralleled by other drives for the statistically subordinate variables of complexity and fluctuation? If such drives may be demonstrated, will they be found to decline when deprived Ss are allowed to respond for "competing" information incentives, just as the preference for high complexity values was suppressed when information incentives were simultaneously available?

It will be recalled that in Expt. I of that study (Jones, 1964) visually deprived Ss were allowed to respond from the beginning of the session for three values of information series and three values of complexity series. As in a prior experiment (Jones et al., 1961; Expt. I), response for information series was an increasing function ($p < .01$) of hours in the deprivation environment. This was interpreted, in the prior experiment, as consistent with a drive hypothesis of information deprivation, but not conclusive because of the confounding of habit strength and drive, thus requiring the further step of showing that Ss deprived for varying initial periods (1 and 5 hours) before being allowed access to the light series respond initially at a rate directly related to the hours of prior deprivation. Had Ss responding for information from the beginning of the session not shown an increasing response rate over most or all of the session, the results would be interpreted as evidence against the drive hypothesis. As the complexity series were shown to have weaker incentive properties than the information series, with the implication that satiation would occur even more slowly than with the information incentives, a drive for complexity should manifest itself in an even more prolonged upward trend of response over hours when Ss are allowed to respond from the beginning, and, as in the case of information motivation, absence of such an upward trend would be interpreted as evidence against a drive associated with the deprivation of complexity incentives.

The evidence discussed in this section comes exclusively from the set of experiments in the Jones (1964) study previously cited. In Expt. I. of that series, which assessed the drive and incentive relationships associated with information and complexity under "competitional" conditions, response for information incentives rose sharply over hours, as was noted above. The response rate of the same Ss for complexity series, however, not only failed to increase over hours, but declined slightly (and non-significantly) over successive hours, thus providing evidence against a drive for complexity incentives. In order to test the possibility that a complexity drive does exist but that its effects are supressed when information incentives are available, an analysis was made, in Expt. II, of the trend of the responses over hours when only complexity series were available with information held at zero. Again there was no significant trend over hours. In Expt. III, in which Ss responded for both complexity and fluctuation incentives, both response functions rose slightly in the third to fourth hours, but declined substantially through the remainder of the session. The analysis of variance showed the complexity function to be a significantly ($p < .05$) *decreasing* linear function of hours. The similar-appearing trend of response for fluctuation series did not attain significance, nor did it in the final experiment in which S's responded for fluctuation incentives only. Thus, of the three assessments of motivation for stimulus complexity and the two for fluctuation, none showed a significant increasing trend, and one showed a significant decreasing trend of response rate over hours. Two interpretations appear possible. The first, which appears more plausible to the writer, is that there is no drive variable associated with complexity or fluctuation deprivation, that only information deprivation functions as a drive. It is at least theoretically possible, however, that there are drive variables associated with deprivation of complexity and fluctuation incentives, but that they are extremely weak relative to that associated with information deprivation, so that such minute incentives as were comprised by the complexity and fluctuation light series were sufficient to produce satiation.

The results of Expt. III showed a significant decreasing trend over hours of response for complexity incentives, thus suggesting that extinction was taking place. It appears likely that experimentation over somewhat longer periods of time, which might provide a better opportunity for extinction to be demonstrated, if it occurred, would help to resolve whatever doubt remains as to the existence of weak drives for complexity and fluctuation incentives. Should clear additional evidence of extinction emerge, it would seem to indicate that the motivation underlying the prior responses for complexity and fluctuation incentives is either acquired or represents the generalization of information-producing responses to partially similar stimulus series, such generalization declining as the S attains additional experience with the incentives over successive hours.

E. The Homeostatic Character of Information Drive

The general strategy of both the exploratory-curiosity studies and the sensory deprivation studies has been to show that Ss maintained in perceptually restricted environments become motivated for contact with novel or variable stimuli, i.e., they have been concerned with the drive effects of only deprivation of such stimuli. The information deprivation studies reported thus far have involved a similar strategy in that they dealt exclusively with the motivating effects of deprivation of information. The experiment to be discussed in this section, however, was addressed to the "obverse" motivational problem, to the hypothesis that satiation with information generates a drive state under which Ss will demonstrate a preference for lower rather than higher information values, or for absence of information (Jones & McGill, in press; Expt. II).

Because of greater convenience of instrumentation, the auditory rather than the visual modality was utilized for this experiment. Subjects were exposed for 1 or 5 hours to continuous auditory signals of 1.00, or maximal, information value, following which they were allowed to determine the information value of the signals but not to escape from them. The first part of the procedure will be referred to provisionally as "satiation," it being acknowledged that although true satiation was intended, its actual occurrence is a matter of empirical demonstration; the second part of the procedure will be referred to as the forced-choice condition.

It will be recalled that evidence was presented (Section III, A) that the response rate of auditorily *deprived* Ss was an increasing linear function of the information value of auditory stimulus series, just as was the response rate of visually deprived Ss for visual information series (Fig. 1). In the present experiment, the effects of *satiation* were measured as alterations in the slope of that incentive function. It was hypothesized that the preference for higher information values would be less during the forced-choice condition following auditory information satiation than that observed previously following auditory information deprivation, and that the magnitude of such alteration of preferences would be greater for Ss satiated for 5 hours than for those satiated for 1 hour. As the effects of the satiation procedure presumably would dissipate over time following its conclusion, it was hypothesized further that the alteration of preferences would diminish over time in the forced-choice condition, the incentive function more nearly approximating that found previously under information deprivation.

Eighteen Ss, divided into two groups of nine each, served in a continuous 10-hour session. One group received 1 hour of information satiation and the other group 5 hours. The satiation condition consisted of the broadcasting of a continuous series of tones at the rate of 1 per second through a speaker in the ceiling over the S's bed. Throughout the satiation period, the relative information value associated with the sequential patterning of the two tone categories (300 and 1000 cps) was

1.00. The sound level was high enough to be relatively distinctive and attention-compelling, but not aversive of itself. Following the termination of the satiation period, Ss were allowed to manipulate the apparatus controls which varied the information value of the stimuli. The information values available were .00, .33, .67, and 1.00, plus $.00_A$ which was retained simply in the interest of maintaining comparability of procedure with prior studies.

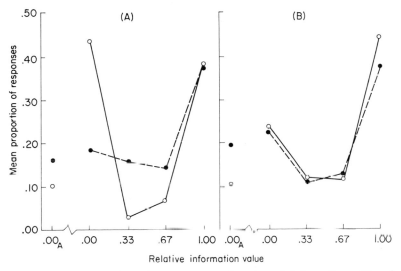

FIG. 13. Mean proportion of response as a function of information value of the auditory series during (A) the first hour of access to apparatus controls (1-hour satiation group, broken line; 5-hour satiation group, solid line), and (B) the first 5 hours of access to apparatus controls (1-hour group, broken line; 5-hour group, solid line). (From Jones & McGill, in press)

The results of principal interest are plotted in Fig. 13. In Fig. 13A, proportional response rate during the first hour of the forced-choice condition is plotted as a function of information value separately for the 1-hour and 5-hour satiation groups. The mean proportion of responses, as the ordinate is designated, refers to the proportion of time in the forced-choice condition during which S selected the various information values, rather than to the number of discrete dial-manipulation responses, since a single turn of the dial to a different position may be followed by an indefinite exposure to the corresponding information series. Analysis of variance showed the pooled response of the 1-hour and 5-hour groups to be a significant quadratic function of information value ($p < .001$); a similar analysis for the pooled response made during the first 5 hours in the forced-choice condition (see Fig. 13B) showed the function to remain quadratic ($p < .01$). In each case, but particularly in the first hour following satiation (Fig. 13A), it may be seen that the response rate for .00 information was far greater than that observed following auditory deprivation (Fig. 1); the slopes of the incentive functions under those two conditions differ significantly at the .05 level (two-tailed test). These results are generally consistent with the first hypothesis, that the preference for higher information values would be less following satiation then following deprivation. In the first hour following satiation, Ss in the 5-hour delay group preferred .00 information over all other values, and those in the 1-hour delay group preferred .00 information over all other values except 1.00, whereas Ss' response rate following deprivation was consistently lowest for .00, increasing monotonically to 1.00 information. In each of the present satiation groups, however, the next highest preference was for 1.00 information. Thus the satiation condition clearly produced a rather gross alteration of preferences for information values, but apparently by enhancing strongly the incentive value of .00 information rather than simply modifying the incentive values of the whole range of information values which were previously established following deprivation. The simplest expectation would have been that, following satiation, .00 information would be most preferred, .33 information next most preferred, etc., with 1.00 information being least preferred, i.e., that the incentive function obtained during deprivation would have been simply rotated downward, with linearity retained. That this did not occur appears somewhat puzzling upon first consideration. The authors tentatively suggested as perhaps the most plausible explanation, ". . . that the high-information tone series had positive reward value during the first portion of the satiation procedure and that considerable habit strength was established for the responses involved in attending to the stimuli. By the end of the satiation procedure, however, the high-information input had become distinctly aversive, and the Ss, then permitted control over the series, tended strongly to select the .00 information series as it differed most discriminably from the satiation series. After some period of exposure to the .00 series, the effects of the satiation procedure would be presumed to have dissipated. The choice of series then shifted to that value for which the greatest habit strength had previously been associated—1.00. Further exposure to 1.00 series resulted in a second satiation process and in turn to the renewed selection of .00, with which substantial positive reward value had recently been associated. The period of time over which such extreme fluctuations in performance might persist would presumably be a function of the degree of aversiveness associated with the initial satiation" (Jones & McGill, in press).

Evidence supporting the second hypothesis, that the preferences of the group satiated 5 hours would be more greatly displaced toward lower information values than those of the group satiated 1 hour, is provided by a comparison of the two functions in Fig. 13A, where it may be seen that during the first hour of the forced-choice condition the proportional rate for .00 information in the 5-hour satiation group was more than twice the rate in the 1-hour group; analysis of variance showed the over-all functions for the two groups to differ significantly at $p < .02$. When a similar comparison is made, however, of the two incentive functions during the first 5 hours of forced-choice responding (Fig. 13B), they are found no longer to differ significantly ($F < 1.0$), and visual inspection confirms that the two functions have, in fact, converged so closely that three of the four data points are almost identical. This convergence is interpreted as support for the third hypothesis, that the effects of satiation dissipate over time, thereby causing initial differences due to different periods of satiation to be gradually eliminated.

The hypothesized dissipation of satiation effects should also be manifested in changes in the mean information value per response (mean I/R, hereafter). Immediately following satiation, mean I/R should be lowest, as Ss prefer .00 information, but should rise gradually over successive hours in the forced-choice condition as satiation effects dissipate. A significant ($p < .05$) increasing trend of this type was found for the 5-hour satiation Ss. For the 1-hour group, the trend was also upward, but slight and nonsignificant, presumably reflecting the substantially weaker effect of satiation of but one hour's duration.

It was noted earlier that the extent to which the procedure produced a condition of true satiation (in the same sense that an animal forcibly fed an amount of food considerably greater than its characteristic consumption would be expected to become temporarily avoidant of consummatory response for food) was a matter to be determined empirically. Such "true" satiation would be demonstrated by the slopes of the incentive function following satiation. Under information deprivation, as under other drive conditions, response rate would ordinarily be expected to be an increasing monotonic function of incentive magnitude, in the present discussion, of relative information value. Under information satiation, as, presumably, under other satiation conditions, the response rate of Ss forcibly required to respond would ordinarily be expected to be a decreasing monotonic function of incentive magnitude. As the extent of the satiation induced is increased, the trend of responses over incentive magnitudes should decrease more "steeply," i.e., show a greater negative slope. If, however, the satiation procedure is only partially effective, i.e., if information deprivation is reduced, but not to the point of true satiation, the increasing trend of response over information values associated with information deprivation should persist but with reduced positive slope. In the present experiment, the mean I/R expresses the slope of the linear component of the incentive functions. The mean I/R may take values from .00 (response only for .00 information) to 1.00 (response only for 1.00 information), with .5 corresponding to zero slope (equal preference for all information values) and the lower and upper limits corresponding to negatively and positively infinite slopes, respectively. The mean I/R obtained in the prior experiment of auditory deprivation (pooling the values for the 1-hour and 5-hour deprivation groups as they were very similar and did not differ significantly) was .58, which is related to the positive slope of the incentive function shown in Fig. 1. In Table II, this is compared with the mean I/R for the two satiation groups during the first and fifth hour of the forced-choice procedure. Considering only

TABLE II

ABSOLUTE MEAN I/R VALUES FOR THE 1-HOUR AND 5-HOUR SATIATION GROUPS DURING THE FIRST AND THE FIFTH HOUR OF THE FORCED-CHOICE PROCEDURE IN COMPARISON WITH THE ABSOLUTE MEAN I/R OBTAINED FOLLOWING DEPRIVATION

Forced-choice procedure	Satiation		Deprivation
	1-hour group	5-hour group	
First hour	.51 ($N = 10$)	.37 ($N = 12$)	.58 ($N = 12$)
Fifth hour	.53 ($N = 9$)	.67 ($N = 9$)	

the first hour of the forced-choice condition, it may be seen that the mean I/R of the 1-hour satiation group, relative to the value for the prior deprivation group, represents a reduction of slope of the incentive function to about zero, while the mean I/R for the 5-hour satiation group represents a reduction of slope to a substantially negative value. Thus, true satiation appears to have been approached closely after 1 hour of the continuous broadcating of 1.00 information auditory series, and to have been clearly attained after 5 hours. It was noted above that the dissipation of the satiation effects should be manifested in a rise of mean I/R values over time following termination of satiation, and that this expectation was verified for the 5-hour satiation group but not for the 1-hour group. Considering, in Table II, the data during the fifth hour of the forced-choice condition (i.e., the fifth hour after satiation) the mean I/R for the Ss satiated 5 hours has risen, not only significantly, but well beyond the value for Ss of the auditory deprivation experiment, while the mean I/R for Ss satiated only 1 hour has risen only from .51 to .53. This would appear puzzling in light of the intuitively reasonable theory that the effects of satiation should be most rapidly dissipated in those Ss most briefly satiated; in the present experiment, however, the 1-hour satiation Ss show almost no recovery while the 5-hour satiation Ss not only recover quickly but by the fifth hour have increased their mean I/R to a value considerably greater than that of Ss who had been deprived of auditory information. The authors suggest the following explanation: "It appears probable that the satiation condition at the end of five hours was sufficiently aversive as to lead the Ss to selection of .00 series for a period exceeding that which is consistent with their characteristic rate of information transmission. Such an 'overshooting' phenomenon would bring the S into a phase of information deprivation which would motivate the relatively rapid shift of response toward higher information values. The adequacy of this explanation appears to rest upon future experiments in which satiation conditions of more widely varied duration are compared. If the degree of 'overshooting' (depression of mean I/R below .50) and the speed of dissipation of the satiation effect (rise in mean I/R above that value associated with information deprivation) are both directly related to length of satiation, the present explanation would be supported" (Jones & McGill, in press).

Although at least as many questions are raised as answered by this initial experiment in information satiation, the results are interpreted as providing considerable support for the view that information satiation generates a drive, under which the incentive value of stimulus series is negatively related to their information value. Together with the demonstration, in previous studies, of similar but "opposite" drive-incentive relationships associated with information deprivation, the present findings support a homeostatic theory of information drive. Drive states appear to be induced in human Ss whenever their rate of information transmission varies in either direction from some characteristic value, the parameters of which remain to be established.

F. Some Further Questions Concerning Information Drive

In this section we shall consider briefly two questions which are basic to an understanding of information drive but for which only partial and tentative answers are as yet available.

1. Afferent versus Central Interpretations of Information Drive

Is the drive associated with information deprivation a drive for certain kinds of afferent activity, or may it be "satisfied" by stimuli of central origin as well? This question is raised by the observation that not all Ss appear to experience the deprivation procedure as aversive, and that those who do not are sometimes quite explicit as to the prominence of their ideation and fantasy throughout the experiment. Do these stimuli of central origin substitute for the afferent activity that other Ss appear to crave? A firm proof of this point would appear difficult, but experimentation appears feasible which might clarify the issue. One approach would be to select extreme groups of Ss on the basis of their ideational and fantasy performance; possibly measures derived from the TAT (Thematic Apperception Test) could serve this purpose. Groups representing the two extremes (and equated on such variables as intelligence and emotional stability) would then be subjected to an "endurance" type of deprivation situation, without any access to sensory incentives, in which Ss may earn financial reward for each hour or day completed, with no limit set on the duration of the experiment. If the high fantasy Ss remain in the experiment significantly longer than the low fantasy Ss, it would seem reasonable to conclude that stimuli of central origin offset the development of information drive in the same sense that exteroceptive stimuli are presumed to do.

On the assumption that fantasy and creativity are correlated variables, the first evidence on this point appears to have been provided by Levin and Brody (1966) in a recent study of the relationship between creativity and information drive. The creativity of potential Ss was the object of a preliminary evaluation by means of the Remote Associates Test (RAT) devised by Mednick (1962), on the basis of which extreme groups of high-creative and low-creative Ss were formed, with mean RAT scores of 20.5 and 11.0, respectively. Subjects were maintained in an information deprivation environment for a total of 8 hours. Half the Ss of each group were allowed access to visual information incentives after 1 hour, and half after 5 hours. The method was similar to that of the prototypal experiment discussed above except that Ss could choose between only two values of information, $.00_A$ (zero information, repetitive single alternation) and 1.00, and that the intersignal interval, as well as the sequence of red and green lights, was randomly varied in the 1.00 series. In this methodological variation, employed initially by Thornton and Jones (1965), the intersignal interval of the 1.00 information series is randomly varied between .5 and 8.5 seconds, while the intersignal interval of the $.00_A$ information series is constant at 4.5 seconds. The absolute information value of the 1.00 series is thus considerably increased as two dimensions are randomly varied rather than one.

The data most relevant to the present discussion are the trends of responses for the 1.00 information series tabulated over the hours during which Ss were allowed access to the incentives. In a comparison of the high- and low-creative groups deprived for 1 hour before being allowed to respond, it was found that the high-creative group responded about

ten times as often in the first hour as did the low-creative group. Their
response rate was maintained or increased slightly over the first 4 hours,
thereafter falling off to about two-thirds of the initial rate during the
final (seventh) hour. The relatively low initial response rate of the low-
creative Ss rose slightly over the first 4 hours then sharply over the remaining 3 hours, surpassing slightly (nonsignificantly) the response rate of
the high-creative group. The differences in the two functions are significant at the .05 level.

These results suggest that the information drive of low-creative Ss
is at a very low level during the initial hours of information deprivation,
requiring, in the present experiment, about 5 hours of deprivation before
it becomes sharply mobilized, while the high-creative Ss appear to be
characterized by an information drive that is readily mobilized during
a single hour of deprivation. If it may be assumed that the high-creative
Ss were also the more apt to engage in fantasy during the deprivation
condition, the results suggest that the information drive is not "satisfied"
by such stimuli of central origin, but requires instead the afferent activity
associated with exteroceptive stimuli. The assumption involved is, of
course, considerable, but the implications of Levin and Brody's experiment, which was not addressed principally to the afferent versus central
issue, are sufficient to encourage further efforts to clarify the issue.

2. Is Information Drive Specific to Sensory Modalities?

If we accept provisionally the view that the drive associated with
information deprivation is dependent upon alterations in the informational characteristics of afferent activity and cannot be accounted for in
terms of central processes only, a further question may be raised concerning the extent to which the drive is specific to sensory modalities. Does
the stimulus information received through the visual, auditory, tactile
and other systems all converge in the reduction (or, in the case of satiation, production) of a generalized drive? Or does each modality have a
"hunger" all its own?

Two experiments have been conducted which provide some evidence
on this point. In the first (Thornton & Jones, 1965), the experimental
strategy involved information deprivation in the visual modality for both
experimental and control groups, with simultaneous information satiation in the auditory modality for the experimental group. Upon termination of the deprivation and deprivation-plus-satiation conditions, both
groups were then allowed to respond freely for visual information incentives. If information drive is generated separately in each modality as a
function of alterations of the information value of the stimuli appropriate to that modality, then both groups should respond equally for

visual information incentives since both were equally deprived of visual information. But if information input in one modality acts to reduce a general information drive which may be generated by deprivation in another modality, than the experimental Ss should show a lesser preference for visual information incentives than the control Ss since they were previously exposed to auditory information while the control Ss were not.

Twenty-two Ss, randomly assigned to experimental and control groups, were each maintained in the information deprivation environment for 8 hours. During the first 6 hours, the experimental Ss were subjected to auditory information satiation by means of brief, randomly ordered 300- and 1000-cps tones of 1.00 information value with respect both to the sequence of tone categories and to the intersignal intervals. Control Ss were exposed to series of $.00_A$ information value, which consisted of the single alternation of 300- and 1000-cps tones at constant intersignal intervals. The Ss were instructed to lie quietly on their beds in the darkened experimental rooms while the continuous series of auditory signals were broadcast from speakers in the ceiling. They understood that at some time during the 8-hour session (actually the end of the sixth hour) the tones would stop permanently, and from that point they would have unrestricted use of the apparatus controlling the light series. As in the Levin and Brody (1966) experiment, Ss were limited to two selections of series, those of 1.00 information value on both the temporal and sequence-of-category dimensions and those of $.00_A$ information, a single alternation of red and green flashes at a constant rate. Each button press initiated a series of six flashes, extending over an average period of 25 seconds.

Response rate was tabulated for each of the 30-minute periods in the 2 hours during which the Ss were allowed access to the apparatus producing the light series. During the first half hour, 43% of the experimental Ss' responses were made for visual incentives of 1.00 information value as compared with 67% of the control Ss' responses. This difference is significant at the .01 level. In the following half-hour periods, however, the preferences of the two groups converged closely (t's < 1.0) presumably due to the dissipation of the satiation effects.

The results support the view that information drive is not specific to sensory modalities but is instead at least partially a generalized drive to which alterations of information input in any modality contribute. The results do not rule out the possibility that sensory modalities may be associated with some degree of information drive specific to them. The generalization of the results is also limited by the "directionality" of the satiation procedure employed—satiation in the auditory modality with subsequent testing of the effects of satiation in the visual modality. Had the auditory and visual conditions been reversed, or had still other modalities been employed, it is possible that the results might have been significantly different.

Some evidence concerning the "directionality" of satiation is provided by a study by Thornton (1966) in which all Ss were subjected to a satiation procedure for 5 hours before being allowed to control the apparatus generating the stimulus series for a final 3 hours. During the last 3 hours, all Ss were allowed to choose between auditory series of .00$_A$ and 1.00 information value, but not to escape them; thus this period constituted a forced-choice condition. The Ss were divided into three groups (the complete study, however, involved additional groups not relevant to the present discussion) according to the nature of the satiation procedure. One group received auditory information deprivation by means of a continuous series of .00$_A$ information value; a second group received auditory information satiation by means of a continuous series of 1.00 information value; and the third group received visual information satiation by means of a continuous series of visual stimuli of 1.00 information value. These three groups will be referred to hereafter as the auditory deprivation, auditory satiation, and visual satiation groups, respectively.

The visual satiation procedure, newly developed for this experiment, involved the use of a mask-like device fitted over the S's eyes, which contained light sources behind a frosted plastic panel. The two categories of stimuli were a relatively bright and a relatively dim flash of light. In order to prevent the S from escaping the stimuli by closing his eyelids, the absolute brightness of the flashes was set high enough to require the S to receive them through his closed lids, and preliminary investigation was conducted to verify that the discrimination of light categories was not impaired by this manner of "viewing."

The data consisted of the proportion of time in the forced-choice condition during which each S selected the 1.00 auditory information series. For the auditory deprivation group, the mean of such proportions was .72, indicating that the Ss deprived of auditory information for 5 hours subsequently showed a strong preference for auditory information incentives (the 1.00 series) rather than for stimuli lacking in information (the .00$_A$ series). For the auditory satiation group, the mean proportion of responses for the 1.00 information series dropped to .58, indicating that the 5 hours of satiation with 1.00 series substantially reduced (in comparison with the group who had been deprived of information for 5 hours) the subsequent drive for informational incentives in the same modality.

With these two values established, the mean proportion of responses for the 1.00 auditory series in the *visual* satiation group may be taken as an indication of the extent to which information input in one modality offsets the development of information drive in another. If the visual satiation Ss were to show a mean proportion of .72 for the 1.00 auditory information series as did the auditory deprivation group, it would indicate that the 5 hours of visual information input in no way offset the development of information drive in the auditory modality, i.e., that the drive generated by the auditory deprivation was entirely specific to that modality. If the visual deprivation group were to show a mean proportion of .58 for the 1.00 auditory series, it would indicate that the 5 hours of visual information input had reduced the subsequent level of auditory information drive just as effectively as the same number of hours of information satiation in the *same modality*, i.e., that the drive associated with auditory information deprivation is a generalized drive containing no component specific to the auditory system. Mean proportions of response values falling between .72 and .58 would be interpreted as evidence that the visual satiation procedure offset partially the subsequent level of auditory information drive but that some component of that drive is, in fact, specific to the auditory system.

With these alternative implications in mind, the results obtained for the visual satiation group in the first half-hour of the forced-choice procedure are quite striking. The mean proportion of responses for the 1.00 auditory series was .52, which indicated a decrement in preference for 1.00 series *greater* than that occurring in the group satiated with information in the same modality. As the difference between the two proportions (.58 and .52) was not reliable ($t < 1.0$), they will be considered here as but two estimates of the same population value. Therefore, the results appear to indicate that the drive for auditory information following 5 hours of auditory deprivation may be offset to the same degree by information satiation in either the visual or auditory modality. The drive generated by auditory information deprivation is thus regarded as a generalized drive, no component of which is specific to the auditory system. The differences among the preferences of the three groups declined after the first half-hour, indicating, as in the prior experiment, the progressive dissipation of the satiation effects.

The combined results of the two experiments indicate that the drives associated with visual and with auditory information deprivation are to an important extent generalized rather than modality-specific drives. In the case of auditory deprivation, the drive appears to be entirely nonspecific, while the drive associated with visual deprivation was shown to be at least partially nonspecific to the visual modality, the exact degree remaining to be established in future experimentation which provides the comparison of a visual satiation group subsequently responding for visual incentives, which was not included in the first experiment.

G. Clinical Observations of Ss' Emotional Reactions

In each of the studies reported above, Ss were asked to fill out a comprehensive questionnaire concerning the emotional, cognitive, perceptual, and other aspects of their experience. As noted earlier, the questionnaire responses were not regarded as dependent variables but were obtained for the informal guidance of the *E*s as they "monitored" the clinical aspects of the *S*s' performance. Consequently, brief, and for the most part nonquantitative discussion of these data will be offered here. Zuckerman (1964) has provided a recent review of the affective phenomena reported as a function of sensory deprivation.

How unpleasant, in general, did our *S*s find their experience in the deprivation environment? In the questionnaire for each experiment, one multiple-choice item was: "I found the experimental situation to be— (a) extremely unpleasant, (b) moderately unpleasant, (c) neither pleasant nor unpleasant, (d) slightly enjoyable, (e) very enjoyable." For all experiments pooled, excluding the one extending 96 hours, the modal response was "neither pleasant nor unpleasant," and "slightly enjoyable" was checked more often than "moderately unpleasant." Even in the anxiety group receiving shock in the study of drive summation (Jones, 1961; Section IV, C above), only three *S*s checked alternative (b), and none reported the experiment to be extremely unpleasant. Only in the 96-hour experiment did the modal response shift to alternative (b), and only three *S*s checked (a). Even in this experiment, however, affective reactions were highly variable, and several *S*s reported the experiment to be "slightly enjoyable." For the *S*s who found the experiment to be either moderately or extremely unpleasant, the more frequent sources of discomfort included disturbing and unusually vivid nightmares, spatial disorientation within the experimental chamber, and some difficulty (although apparently not extreme) in maintaining organized series of thoughts. Subjects in all experiments described their feelings during the experiment by checking one or more of the following adjectives in a checklist included in the questionnaire: bored, fatigued, listless, depressed, restless, tense, apprehensive, frightened, excited, and relaxed. Considering all experiments combined, including the 96-hour experiment, the adjectives most frequently checked were bored, restless, and relaxed; in the 96-hour experiment, there was a moderate increase in the "tense" responses, but the adjectives apprehensive, frightened, and excited remained infrequently checked. These findings appear generally consistent with those reported by Myers (1964), who employed the Subjective Stress Scale of Kerle and Bialek (1958) in the evaluation of the stress presumably associated with sensory deprivation. Although the Scale, bounded by "in agony" at one end and "wonderful" at the other, reliably differentiated control *S*s from *S*s maintained in perceptual isolation 4 days, the average rating shifted only from "comfortable" to "indifferent," suggesting that most of their *S*s, also, did not experience the deprivation procedure as distinctly aversive.

The attrition rates of the various experiments provide further, indirect evidence concerning the degree to which the deprivation procedures were experienced as stressful. The rate of attrition due to voluntary withdrawal of Ss was quite high between the time the S agreed to participate and the time, usually several days later, when the preliminary instructions had been completed in the reception room of the laboratory, ranging from about 25% in the 8- and 10-hour deprivation experiments to about 50% in the 96-hour experiment. It is especially revealing to note, however, that out of the several hundred Ss who actually began the deprivation procedure, less than ten voluntarily terminated the experiment before its scheduled termination. One became physically ill in a manner apparently unrelated to the experiment. The others terminated prematurely as reactions to varying degrees of boredom, physical discomfort, or emotional tension. The emotional reactions were in each case judged to be of but slight intensity, and post-experimental interviews with the Ss convinced the Es that the emotional reactions were principally a function of personality processes of long duration rather than of the deprivation procedure per se. The differences in attrition rates between the period leading up to the deprivation procedure, and the period of that procedure itself, suggest that the stress associated with the deprivation experiments was almost entirely of an anticipatory nature, and that, once actually "embarked" upon their experimental adventures, the Ss found them overwhelmingly boring and minimally frightening.

Post-hoc efforts to explain the surprisingly low incidence of clearly discernible stress reactions have led to the tentative conclusion that the instructional set of the Ss was probably the most critical factor. That Ss may be highly suggestible with regard to both emotional and cognitive impairments appears to be clearly established (Jackson & Kelly, 1962; Orne & Scheibe, 1964). In each of the present experiments it was emphasized to Ss that the procedure was not designed to study personality or stress variables, and that while it was possible (though not expected) that some unusual sensory experiences might occur, they were not to be regarded as "serious" in any way. In addition to this effort to manipulate the Ss' set regarding the purpose and intended effects of the experiments, the Es attempted to reduce irrelevant anxiety drive by instructing Ss thoroughly as to the details of the experimental environment, the use of apparatus, etc. From their instructions, these Ss had a very clear and complete knowledge of the procedure in which they were to serve. Care was taken to answer all questions as thoroughly as possible, and to elicit them when E perceived any doubt or insecurity on the part of the S. With very few, and very minor exceptions, the Ss had in advance precisely the same foreknowledge of the experimental procedure as did the Es. Although a variable obviously difficult to quantify, it appears that the Ss had a very high degree of "trust" in the Es. In the writer's opinion, it was this attitude of trust, and its role in mediating the reduction of irrelevant anxiety associated with the deprivation procedure, which was most responsible for the low incidence of adverse emotional reactions.

Some informal support for the "trust hypothesis" is provided by the reports of several Ss following conclusion of the 96-hour deprivation procedure. In that experiment, the round-the-clock maintenance of Ss was rotated among a rather large number of research assistants, who monitored the apparatus and gave the Ss their meals, among other duties. Each meal was arranged in a square metal tray before being placed in the double-doored compartment of the S's experimental chamber. The food items and their arrangement on the tray were standardized. Subjects had previously been informed of the food they would receive and given certain choices, e.g., carrot or celery sticks, and plastic cartons of milk or orange drink. The assistants were instructed to open each plastic carton for the S, so that he would not have the minor difficulty of opening it in the dark. On the top of each tray was to be placed a moistened paper towel with which the S might clean his hands before eating.

It became apparent, in the postexperimental interviews, that these details were of the greatest importance to the Ss if they were executed inaccurately. In each of the following examples, a small error was apparently made in the standardized feeding procedure, with very distinctive emotional reactions on the part of the S. The first of these incidents involved, on one meal out of the total of twenty served over the 96 hours, the mistaken inclusion of celery sticks instead of the carrot sticks the S had initially selected. The S reported that he was very puzzled about the unexpected change, thought about it at length, and finally concluded that the E was trying to communicate to him that he had been selecting the stimulus series incorrectly. For a second S, the carrot sticks at one feeding were inadvertently omitted, and this annoyed and upset him so that he declined to eat the entire meal. Another S discovered, again on one meal only, that his milk carton had not been opened in advance; after some deliberation, he concluded that the E had chosen this manner of communicating to him that his response rate was deficiently low. Finally, a fourth S reported that, at one feeding, the moistened paper towel was missing from his tray. Although this occurred well before the end of the experiment, he recalled his angry reaction vividly and still appeared distinctly irritated with the E. These several observations led the Es to redouble their efforts at securing completely standardized feeding procedures, and further incidents of this sort were avoided.

Rather than being merely somewhat embarassing demonstrations of insufficient experimental precision, however, these incidents suggest an important generalization concerning the emotional condition of Ss in deprivation environments. It appears likely that information deprivation procedures are minimally stressful or anxiety-producing of themselves as long as nothing occurs to impair the S's attitude of trust toward the E and the experimental environment into which he has placed the S. Against the relatively homogeneous or redundant stimulus background of the deprivation condition, however, any stimuli, however weak, which are perceived as inconsistent with statements made by the E, tend to elicit doubt and apprehension. Having been once "betrayed," the S may well feel that he cannot safely trust anything E has told him. Because the S is in a peculiarly dependent relationship to the E, being fed, observed, and eventually released by him, while he, the S, is in an impotent and at times slightly disoriented condition, it would seem reasonable that any evidence of untrustworthiness of the E would elicit strong anxiety and, frequently, anger. Thus, it appears that the source of anxiety and other forms of aversive emotional arousal in perceptually restricted environments may be more importantly related to interpersonal than to perceptual variables.

There is also an informational analysis to be made of the incidents noted above. The various stimuli to which the Ss reacted so negatively were very much unexpected by them; that is, they had high information or "surprise" value. The further generalization is suggested that, for Ss in conditions of information deprivation, any stimuli, however neutral in other contexts, which are of high information value tend to elicit generalized alarm and apprehension. Should these suppositions prove correct, they may find peculiarly apt demonstration in the highly homogeneous environments in which future space travelers may be maintained. A traveler on a long voyage may be in a condition of much higher information drive, and far more vulnerable and dependent on others, than our terrestrial 96-hour Ss, and his reactions of fear and paranoid-like ideation may, correspondingly, be very much more acute should a sudden and utterly unpredicted stimulus be presented. His reactions would perhaps be exceeded only by those of the hero of that old one-sentence suspense story written by an unknown information theorist: "The last man in the world was sitting in his room when he heard a knock upon the door."

V. Cognitive and Perceptual Effects

Several of the relatively early sensory deprivation studies, e.g., Bexton, Heron, and Scott (1954) and Scott, Bexton, Heron, and Doane (1959), reported evidence suggesting that Ss experienced a progressive impairment of various intellectual abilities as measured by psychometric instruments, with subjective reports of difficulty in concentration and in organization of thought. More recent reports, however, e.g., Zubek, Sansom, and Phrsiazniuk (1960) and Zubek *et al.* (1962), suggest that whatever impairing effects occur are slight and do not ordinarily persist after the experiment.

In the various information deprivation studies discussed above, no tests of cognitive functioning were made either during or following deprivation so that only tentative conclusions based on questionnaire and interview data may be drawn. Subjects were asked, in the questionnaire, to describe what they did or thought about during the experiment. Most *S*s replied by listing the various topics with which their thoughts had been concerned. Considering all experiments except that extending 96 hours, the incidence of *S*s reporting confusion or disorganization of thought at any time was almost nil. In the 96-hour experiment (Jones, 1963a), several *S*s reported some difficulty in pursuing organized trains of thought but apparently not to a severe degree, and with no evidence of such difficulty in the interview immediately following termination of the deprivation condition. As nearly all *S*s were currently enrolled in undergraduate psychology courses, there was considerable opportunity for the *E*s to become aware of any persistent adverse effects which might emerge. Despite the acknowledged informality of the observations, it seems significant that not a single instance of even briefly persistent adverse cognitive or perceptual effects came to the attention of the *E*s, who were strongly motivated to detect them should they occur, out of the several hundred *S*s who served in deprivation sessions of 8, 10, 12, 48, or 96 hours. This does not, of course, constitute proof that impairing cognitive or perceptual effects may not occur, but it does suggest that such impairments as may occur are not severe.

The recent trend in the sensory deprivation literature to de-emphasize the adverse cognitive effects of deprivation has been paralleled by a perhaps stronger reconsideration (e.g., Zubek, 1964; Rossi, Fuhrman, & Solomon, 1964; Vernon, Marton, & Peterson, 1961; Suedfeld and Vernon, 1964; Schultz, 1965) of the hallucinatory phenomena which were reported with great frequency by the *S*s of the early experiments. Rossi *et al.*, for example, have pointed out that the incidence of hallucinatory experiences reported by *S*s increases with decreasing levels of arousal as measured by the EEG, suggesting that hallucinations may be facilitated by levels of arousal similar to those accompanying sleep, and that subjects' reports may fail to discriminate clearly between waking and sleeping "hallucinatory" phenomena. Zuckerman and Cohen (1964) in their comprehensive review of the literature on hallucinatory effects associated with perceptual isolation suggest that "reported visual sensations" be grouped into two categories—Type A, including such meaningless sensations as patches and spots of light, undifferentiated noise, etc., and Type B, including meaningful sensations of objects, people, complex scenes, etc. The criteria for determining when a "reported visual sensation," or auditory sensation, is truly an hallucination, are a subject of considerable ambiguity. Vernon, Marton and Peterson (1961) and Suedfeld and Vernon (1964) have suggested the desirability of applying the following rather stringent set of criteria: (a) uncontrollability of onset, content, and termination; (b) "out-thereness"; (c) scannability; and (d) apparent reality. Applying these criteria to the reports made by the Ss of all the information deprivation studies combined, not more than 1 or 2 per cent of the Ss would be regarded as having experienced a single "true" hallucination. Approximately 25% of the Ss reported some form of visual sensations during the deprivation procedure; for all but three of these Ss, their reports would fall in Zuckerman and Cohen's category A, usually with a failure to meet any of the criteria above except (a), uncontrollability of onset, content, and termination. As in the evaluation of cognitive effects, it is acknowledged that the observation of hallucinatory phenomena was informal and incomplete in these experiments; it is quite possible that some Ss experienced visual and other sensations which they did not report. It seems reasonable, however, to conclude at least that hallucinatory phenomena, as defined by Vernon and his associates, were not a salient feature of the information deprivation conditions.

Although perceptual phenomena were not a major focus of the information deprivation experiments, discussion with some Ss of their perception of time during the deprivation procedure led to an experimental "digression" in an effort to determine what effect, if any, the statistical character of stimuli may have on perceived duration. The most thought-provoking comment on this topic was made by an S in the 96-hour experiment, who explained that while he felt some impulse to respond for the light series, he found that viewing them seemed to cause time to pass more slowly (i.e., a standard interval to be overestimated) than when he simply rested in the dark. His explanation implied that it was the frequency of the sensory events rather than their statistical character which was at issue, and the first experiment (Jones & MacLean, 1965) was directed to that hypothesis. Subjects were asked to make magnitude estimations of intervals ranging from 8 to 250 seconds while lying on a bed in a darkened room. From a speaker in the ceiling, auditory clicks were broadcast at a constant rate during each trial. The click frequencies varied from .25 per second to 10 per second. It was expected that the magnitude estimations would be an increasing monotonic function of click frequency, but the results showed instead that the estimations rose from the comparatively slow rate of .25 per second to the rate of 1.5 per second, thereafter falling off slightly to 10 per second. This "frequency effect" on perceived duration was highly reliable over the briefer durations, but was greatly reduced in the region of 175 seconds to 250 seconds.

The second experiment (Jones, 1965) was directed to the hypothesis that perceived duration is an increasing function of the information value of stimuli. In an otherwise similar procedure, Ss made magnitude estimations during trials filled with auditory tone series of varied information value. The relative information values were .00, .50, and 1.00. Zero information was represented by a series of repeated 300-cps tones (or, for half the Ss, 1000-cps tones); .50 information was represented by a series in which the odd-numbered tones were of a fixed category, with the rest randomly varied; and 1.00 information series was composed of an entirely random sequence of 300-cps and 1000-cps tones. The results supported the hypothesis; the mean magnitude estimations were an increasing function of the relative information value of the tone series.

It is acknowledged that the generalization of these findings to periods of information deprivation of many hours is limited because of the relatively very brief durations employed. Should, however, replications over much longer periods be successful, i.e., should perceived duration continue to be distorted "upward" by increments in the information value of stimuli, it would suggest that Ss in information deprivation environments may experience a seemingly paradoxical dilemma as follows: The deprivation procedure generates a drive for information which motivates response for series of stimuli of informational character. The occurrence of the stimulus series, however, has the effect of lengthening the perceived duration of the experimental procedure. As information drive magnitude is defined as a function of length of deprivation, is it not possible that the perceived increment in duration dependent upon viewing the stimuli may function as does an objective increment in duration, in raising information drive level? Thus the S would be in the position of making a response which momentarily reduces the drive which motivated it, but the net effect of which is to increase that drive. Such paradoxes are not new, of course, in psychology (e.g., the "neurotic paradox" of Freud). Stated colloquially, information deprivation may produce boredom and restlessness, and be mildly aversive, but will pass quickly if simply endured. If series of stimuli are introduced, boredom may be alleviated and the environment made more interesting, but time will pass more slowly.

No other studies of the relationship between statistical characteristics of stimuli and time perception in perceptually deprived conditions have been reported, but the motivational relevance of perceived duration for deprived Ss has been established in a study by Murphy, Hampton, and Myers (1962). These investigators compared the time-estimation ability of Ss who completed a 96-hour deprivation procedure with those who requested early release and for whom the procedure was presumably substantially more aversive. The time estimations were obtained after 4 hours; Ss were asked simply to estimate the day and time of day. The early-release Ss overestimated the passage of time significantly more often than did those who completed the experiment. Thus, although the causal direction of the effect is not specified, the possibility is raised that the overestimation of elapsed time resulted in the greater aversiveness of the deprivation environment for those Ss.

VI. Extension of the Information Drive Model: The Reduction of Uncertainty concerning Future Pain

That information deprivation generates a drive, and that information constitutes an incentive dimension of stimuli, appears well established by the experiments discussed earlier in this chapter. The information, or reduction of uncertainty, occurring through the presentation of series of light flashes or tones of varying degrees of unpredictability appears to constitute a reinforcement principle that is independent of any observable, direct association with either a primary or previously established secondary reinforcement, which suggests that the reduction of uncertainty may be a dimension of reinforcement of considerable generality, serving to modify a wide range of human behavior.

In this section we shall consider an attempt to apply the information motivational principles gained from such studies of abstract, or "content-free" information incentives to a condition in which the S, in a state of uncertainty, may respond for information about certain contingencies of independent motivational relevance. The condition selected for this effort to extend the application of the information drive model is that of uncertainty regarding the characteristics of future painful stimuli. Knowing only that the experimental procedure required them to receive an unspecified number of shocks to the forearm at unknown intervals, Ss were permitted to respond for information concerning the temporal schedule and other aspects of the shocks, with the understanding that their response or lack of it would in no way affect the predetermined sequence of shocks. Where Ss in the prior information deprivation experiments were responding for informational stimuli which reduced uncertainty only about those stimuli, the present Ss were responding for information about particular future events.

From the prior experiments, the hypotheses were drawn that (1) information about future pain would for most Ss serve as a reinforcer of instrumental response, and (2) that response rate would be an increasing monotonic function of the degree of uncertainty associated with future painful stimuli. The first hypothesis reflects the evidence that uncertainty reduction constitutes a general class of reinforcers, and, as a sub-classification of such stimuli, uncertainty reduction regarding future pain should also function as a reinforcer. In addition to the incentive value of information per se, it was expected that such information might have additional, secondary reward value associated with its role in alleviating either anxiety or pain, or both. For example, the S who has just learned that the next shock is not due for 3 minutes and 15 seconds may be thereby enabled to feel less anxious during the period which he knows to be "safe," and may also be able to minimize the painful effect of the shock by "clenching" or otherwise providing competing kinesthetic feedback just before and during shock. It should be noted, however, that the most direct application of the principle of secondary reinforcement would generate an opposite prediction; as stimuli regularly associated with pain would be expected to acquire negative reward value, informational stimuli associated with the occurrence of shock should be the objects of avoidance, rather than approach, and Ss would be expected in general to refrain from responding.

In the first experiment addressed to this problem (Jones, Bentler, & Petry, 1966; Expt. 1), college Ss each served in counterbalanced order in three different 12-minute conditions, associated with low, medium, and high degrees of uncertainty regarding the temporal schedule of shocks. Twelve shocks were administered in each condition. The Ss understood that the shocks would occur only at the quadrants of the clock dial, as the second hand crossed 3, 6, 9, or 12. Under low temporal uncertainty, the shocks were scheduled randomly throughout the 12 minutes, with the constraint of a minimum intershock interval of 45 seconds. Under medium temporal uncertainty, the shocks were randomly scheduled with a minimum intershock interval of 30 seconds, and under high uncertainty they were randomly scheduled with a constraint of but 15 seconds. Shock intensity was randomly varied over five levels established in preliminary scaling conducted separately for each S. At least the upper three levels were distinctly aversive, the highest level corresponding to the upper limit of intensity which the S could be induced to accept.

All Ss were treated as just described, but were assigned to two groups differing in the amount of information contained in the messages given S contingent upon his instrumental responses. In Group I, information about only the temporal schedule was given; in Group II, information about both the temporal and intensity dimensions of shock were given. It was expected that the Ss receiving information about two dimensions of shock would show a higher response rate than those receiving information about only one dimension. The groups were otherwise treated identically.

Following the preliminary shock-scaling and the administration of instructions, the first of the three conditions was begun by placing S in a room by himself, wearing earphones and sitting before a well-illuminated clock dial. The S understood that whenever, if ever, he wished, he could press a button which would result in the communication of information over the earphones. In Group I, the message would be of the form "one minute, forty-five seconds"; in Group II, it would be of the form "one minute, forty-five seconds—level five," the intensities designated by the numbered levels having been previously explained to S. With regard to the temporal information, S understood that he was to note the position of the clock dial when he pressed his button for information, and that the exact occurrence of the next shock was to be measured from the quadrant of the clock dial immediately preceding the position of the second hand when he responded. For example, if the S responded when the second hand was at some point between 6 and 9, and the message was "forty-five seconds," he would begin counting from the preceding quadrant, 6, and thus would know that the next shock would occur when the second hand next passed 3. Prior to beginning each condition, the S was given a thorough explanation of the appropriate constraint governing the temporal schedule of shocks.

The results indicate that information concerning future pain functioned as a positive reinforcer for a majority of the Ss. Only 8 of the 32 Ss failed to respond; the mean number of trials on which the remaining Ss responded was 16.75. The response rate of Group II was higher, but not significantly so, than that of Group I. In Fig. 14, proportional response rate is shown as a function of degree of temporal uncertainty for the two groups. The hypothesis that response rate would be an increasing function of temporal uncertainty was supported by an analysis of variance of trends for Group I and for Groups I and II pooled ($p < .01$). For Group II considered alone, the overall differences in response rate over levels of uncertainty were significant, but neither the linear nor quadratic components. As the observed downward inflection of Group II response rate at high uncertainty is not reliable, it would appear that the pooled function, which is significantly linear, may be regarded as the best estimate of the true relationship between response rate and degree of temporal uncertainty. Thus, the principle that stimuli have incentive value that is directly related to their information value appears to be supported in this context of "meaningful" messages correlated with future events of motivational significance, as well as in the context of prior studies in which the informational stimuli were meaningless and not correlated with future events. In the present experiment, with attributes of painful stimuli being the content of the informational messages, it is acknowledged that motivational processes other than information drive may have

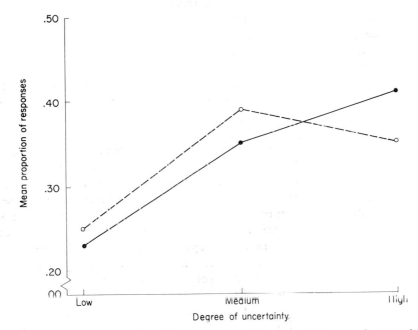

Fig. 14. Mean proportion of response as a function of degree of uncertainty concerning the temporal occurrence of shock (Group I, solid line; Group II, broken line.) (From Jones, Bentler, & Perry, 1963; Expt. I)

contributed to the increasing function of responses over uncertainty values. The results are, for example, consistent with the theory that higher degrees of uncertainty are associated with parallel increments in anxiety, and that it is such increments in anxiety which motivate the increasing rates of uncertainty-reducing responses. Evidence on this interpretation is not as yet available. A further interpretive question, and one anticipated sufficiently early that some evidence has already been obtained, concerns the possibility that the actual level of pain experienced by the Ss may have increased over the conditions as a function of increasing uncertainty. If that were true, the increments in response rate over uncertainty conditions may reflect simply the increments in generalized drive associated with greater magnitudes of pain, rather than the degree-of-uncertainty variable per se. In order to evaluate this possibility, Stineman (1963) conducted a study of magnitude estimation of the pain intensity associated with a standard series of shocks as a function of the uncertainty in the temporal sequence of the shocks. Her results indicate that the Ss' perceived pain intensity associated with shock is remarkably invariant over variations in temporal uncertainty. Thus, while their responses may reflect increments in anxiety due to increments in temporal uncertainty, they do not appear to have been determined by differential pain reactions to the uncertainty conditions.

That the Ss of Group II, who received information about intensity as well as temporal occurrence did not respond significantly more often than those of Group I, who received temporal information only, suggests that uncertainty reduction concerning temporal occurrence may be of much greater motivational relevance than uncertainty-reduction concerning pain intensity, possibly because of its greater role in reducing anxiety. In order to compare directly the motivational relevance of the two dimensions of information, a second experiment was carried out, employing a generally similar method (Jones, Bentler, & Petry, 1966; Expt. II). A further purpose was to determine whether the rate of response, and percentage of Ss responding, could be increased by increasing the absolute uncertainty of the experimental conditions. Three levels of uncertainty, low, medium, and high, again constituted the independent variable, but the absolute uncertainties associated with these conditions were higher than in the previous experiment. Each S received 14 shocks in each of three 14-minute conditions. Subjects were allowed to press one button for information about temporal occurrence and another for information about shock intensity. One or both buttons could be pressed, in either order. As in the previous experiment, Ss could respond for information only about the next shock; response for information about a subsequent shock could not be made until the presently pending shock had occurred. Details of the procedure are available in the report cited above and in that by Petry (1963).

The results of this second experiment, in which the absolute values of the uncertainties induced were somewhat higher than before, provide strong additional support for the view that the reduction of uncertainty concerning future pain functions as a positive reinforcement for the majority of the Ss. Because of the requirements of certain statistical analyses, discussion of which is beyond the scope of this chapter, the criterion of a minimum of ten responses was set for inclusion of Ss' data in the study. Only three of a total of 27 Ss failed to meet that criterion. Of the 24 who did, the number of trials on which one or both buttons was pressed ranged from 10 to 42 with a mean of 34.75. As in the preceding experiment, response rate was an increasing linear function of degree of uncertainty. The hypothesis that "temporal" information is more motivationally relevant than is "intensity" information was tested by a comparison of the mean response frequencies for the two classes of response. The frequency of response for temporal information was significantly greater ($p < .05$), by more than 100%, than the frequency of response for intensity information. Subjects were strongly motivated to find out when the shock was coming, but the additional knowledge of the shock intensity to be expected was apparently of little motivational relevance. The particular mechanism or mechanisms involved in the information reinforcement were again not considered directly in this experiment, but questionnaire data and informal interviews with Ss suggested that uncertainty concerning future pain elicits anxiety and that the uncertainty-reducing responses mediate the reduction of anxiety, chiefly through ideational responses by which the S reassures himself that a certain temporal period is "safe."

In the final experiment of this series (Jones, 1963b) the informational aspect of the painful stimuli was their probability of occurrence, rather than uncertainty of schedule or intensity. Subjects sat before a visual display in which the offset of a white light signaled the beginning of a two-minute trial, and a succession of amber lights marked the termination of 30-second segments of the trial. The S understood that the trials were continuous, and that at the end of each trial, signaled by the onset of the white light, he would or would not receive a shock on a chance basis. The probability that a shock would occur was correctly communicated to the S at the beginning of each trial by the lighting of one of three probability indicators on the visual display. Three probabilities of shock —.1, .5, and .9—were randomly varied over thirty trials. Subjects were allowed to respond at any time within the trial, and understood that their responses would not affect in any way the shocks which they would receive. Following each response (button press) one of two lights would flash on at the top of the visual display, red if the trial was to be terminated by shock and green if not, and remain on until the end of the trial. The intensity of the shocks was held constant at the upper limit of shock intensity which the S could be induced to accept in pre-experimental pain scaling of shock. All Ss appeared to have set shock limits which were in fact highly aversive.

The method of this experiment provides a particularly clear comparison of the positive and negative reward factors associated with information about future pain. If, from the previous experiments, we assume that information about pain is positively reinforcing and that response rate will be an increasing function of the degree of uncertainty associated with the trials, then the response rate should be highest for the .5 probability trials, as they are the trials on which the S is most uncertain; and, if only the positive reinforcement aspect of information is operating, response rate on the .1 and .9 trials should be equally low. As noted above, the most direct application of the principle of secondary reward

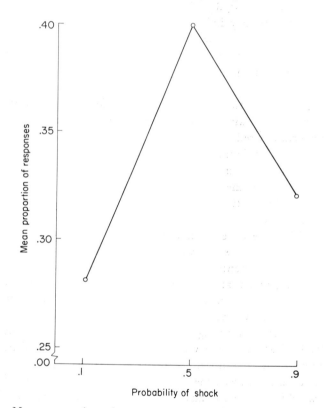

Fig. 15. Mean proportion of response as a function of probability that a trial will be terminated by shock. (From Jones, 1963b)

would lead to the hypothesis that informational signals associated with shock will function as negative reinforcers and will be avoided, and that response for such information will be nil. Conversely, informational signals associated with omission of shock would be expected to function as positive reinforcers. In the present experiment, response rate should then be highest, not on the .5 probability trials in which uncertainty is greatest, but on the .1 probability trials in which response will most often be followed by a "positive" (green light) signal; intermediate on .5

probability trials; and lowest for .9 probability trials in which responses will usually be followed by a "negative" (red light) signal.

The results are shown in Fig. 15 in which proportional response rate is plotted as a function of the probability of shock. The shape of the function conforms closely to that which would be expected if the information-incentive aspects of the signals are dominant over the more direct secondary reward aspects of the signals; the response rate was highest on .5 probability trials, falling off sharply and significantly ($p < .01$) on both the .1 and .9 probability trials. Thus, in situations of uncertainty concerning the occurrence of future pain, it appears that uncertainty-reducing responses are increasingly likely to occur as the uncertainty experienced by the S is increased, regardless of whether "good news" or "bad news" is imminent. These results are generally consistent with the recently reported findings of Lanzetta and Driscoll (1966) whose Ss strongly preferred information (rather than absence of information) about both unavoidable shock and unavoidable monetary reward, with no significant difference between the two conditions.

The combined results of the series of experiments discussed in this section add support to the view that the reduction of uncertainty constitutes a strong positive reinforcer in a broad range of motivational conditions, and suggest the desirability of extending the information drive model into the study of additional behavioral topics.

References

Berlyne, D. E. Conflict and information theory variables as determinants of human perceptual curiosity. *J. exp. Psychol.*, 1957, **53**, 399 401. (a)

Berlyne, D. E. Uncertainty and conflict: A point of contact between information-theory and behavior-theory concepts. *Psychol. Rev.*, 1957, **64**, 329-339. (b)

Bexton, W. H., Heron, W., & Scott, T. H. Effects of decreased variation in the sensory environment. *Canad. J. Psychol.*, 1954, **8**, 70-76.

Butler, R. A. The effect of deprivation of visual incentives on visual exploration motivation in monkeys. *J. comp. physiol. Psychol.*, 1957, **50**, 177-179.

Dashiell, J. F. A quantitative demonstration of animal drive. *J. comp. Psychol.*, 1925, **5**, 205-208.

Fowler, H. *Curiosity and exploratory behavior.* New York: Macmillan, 1965.

Gardner, Jo-Ann. Information drive produced by extended periods of information deprivation. Unpublished master's thesis, Univer. of Pittsburgh, 1961.

Harlow, H. F. Learning and satiation of response in intrinsically motivated complex puzzle performance by monkeys. *J. comp. physiol. Psychol.*, 1950, **43**, 289-294.

Harlow, H. F., Harlow, Margaret K., & Meyer, D. R. Learning motivated by a manipulatory drive. *J. exp. Psychol.*, 1950, **43**, 289-294.

Heron, W., Doane, B. K., & Scott, T. H. Visual disturbances after prolonged perceptual isolation. *Canad. J. Psychol.*, 1956, **10**, 13-18.

Hull, C. L. *A behavior system.* New Haven: Yale Univer. Press, 1952.

Jackson, C. W., & Kelly, E. L. Influence of suggestion and subjects' prior knowledge on research in sensory deprivation. *Sci.*, 1962, **132**, 211-212.

Jones, A. Supplementary report: Information deprivation and irrelevant drive as determiners of an instrumental response. *J. exp. Psychol.*, 1961, **62**, 310-311.

Jones, A. Information drive and incentive phenomena following ninety-six hours of visual deprivation. Unpublished research report, Univer. of Pittsburgh, 1963. (a)

Jones, A., Response for information about shock as a function of shock probability. Unpublished research report, Univer. of Pittsburgh, 1963. (b)

Jones, A. Drive and incentive variables associated with the statistical properties of sequences of stimuli. *J. exp. Psychol.*, 1964, **67**, 423-431.

Jones, A. Distortions of time perception associated with the information value of auditory stimuli. Unpublished research report, Univer. of Pittsburgh, 1965.

Jones, A., & MacLean, Marilyn. Perceived duration as a function of auditory stimulus frequency. *J. exp. Psychol.*, 1966, **71**, 358-364.

Jones, A., & McGill, D. W. The homeostatic character of information drive in humans. *J. Exp. res. Pers.* in press.

Jones, A., Wilkinson, H. J., & Braden, I. Information deprivation as a motivational variable. *J. exp. Psychol.*, 1961, **62**, 126-137.

Jones, A., Bentler, P., & Petry, Georgia. The reduction of uncertainty concerning future pain. *J. abnorm. Psychol.*, 1966, **71**, 87-94.

Kerle, R. H., & Bialek, H. The construction, validation and application of a subjective stress scale. Presidio of Monterey, Calif.: U. S. Army Leadership Human Research Unit, 1958.

Lanzetta, J. T., & Driscoll, J. M. Preference for information about an uncertain but unavoidable outcome. *J. pers. soc. Psychol.*, 1966, **3**, 96-102.

Levin, J., & Brody, N. Information deprivation and creativity. Paper presented to the East. Psychol. Ass., New York, 1966.

MacDonald, Annette. The effect of adaptation to the unconditioned stimulus upon the formation of conditioned avoidance response. *J. exp. Psychol.*, 1946, **36**, 1-112.

Mednick, S. The associative basis of the creative process. *Psychol. Rev.* 1962, **69**, 220-232.

Miller, G. A., & Frick, F. C. Statistical behavioristics and sequences of responses. *Psychol. Rev.*, 1949, **56**, 311-324.

Munsinger, H., & Kessen, W. Uncertainty, structure, and preference. *Psychol. Monogr.* 1964, **72**, No. 9.

Murphy, D. B., Hampton, G. L., & Myers, T. I. Time estimation error as a predictor of endurance in sustained sensory deprivation. Paper presented to the Amer. Psychol. Ass., 1962.

Myers, T. I. Some further data from the Subjective Stress Scale (SSS). Paper presented to the Eastern Psychol. Ass., 1964.

Nissen, H. W. A study of exploratory behavior in the white rat by means of the obstruction method. *J. genet. Psychol.*, 1930, **37**, 361-376.

Orne, M. T., & Scheibe, K. E. The contribution of nondeprivation factors in the production of sensory deprivation effects: the psychology of the "panic button." *J. abnorm. soc. Psychol.*, 1964, **68**, 3-12.

Petry, Georgia. Responses which reduce uncertainty concerning pain. Unpublished master's thesis, Univer. of Pittsburgh, 1963.

Rossi, A. M., Fuhrman, A., & Solomon, P. Sensory deprivation: arousal and rapid eye movement correlates of some effects. *Percept. mot. Skills*, 1964, **19**, 447-451.

Schultz, D. P. *Sensory restriction*. New York: Academic Press, 1965.

Scott, T., Bexton, W. H., Heron, W., & Doane, B. K. Cognitive effects of perceptual isolation. *Canad. J. Psychol.*, 1959, 13, 200-209.

Shannon, C. E. A mathematical theory of communication. *Bell System tech. J.*, 1948, 27, 379-423, 623-656.

Smith, S., & Myers, T. I. Stimulation seeking during sensory deprivation. Mimeographed research report, Naval Medical Research Institute, Bethesda, 1966.

Spence, K. W. *Behavior theory and conditioning.* New Haven: Yale Univer. Press., 1956.

Stineman, Carolyn A. Magnitude estimation of shock as a function of temporal uncertainty. Unpublished master's thesis. Univer. of Pittsburgh, 1963.

Suedfeld, P., & Vernon, J. Visual hallucinations during sensory deprivation: A problem of criteria. *Sci.*, 1964, 145, 412.

Thornton, D. The function of visual information in cross-modality satiation of auditory information drive. Unpublished doctoral dissertation, Univer. of Pittsburgh, 1966.

Thornton, D., & Jones, A. The nonspecific character of information drive with respect to sensory modalities. Paper presented to the Midwest. Psychol. Ass., 1965.

Vernon, J., Marton, T., & Peterson, E. Sensory deprivation and hallucinations. *Sci.*, 1961, 133, 1808-1812.

Vernon, J., McGill, T., Gulick, W., & Candland, D. Effect of sensory deprivation on some perceptual and motor skills. In P. Solomon *et al.* (Eds.), *Sensory deprivation.* Cambridge, Mass.: Harvard Univer. Press, 1961.

Zubek, J. P. Effects of prolonged sensory and perceptual deprivation. *British Medical Bull.*, 1964, 20, 38-42.

Zubek, J. P., Sansom, W., & Phrsiazniuk, A. Intellectual changes during prolonged sensory isolation (darkness and silence). *Canad. J. Psychol.*, 1960, 14, 83-100.

Zubek, J. P., Aftanas, M., Hasek, J., Sansom, W., Schludermann, E., Wilgosh, L., & Winocur, G. Intellectual and perceptual changes during prolonged perceptual deprivation: low illumination and noise level. *Percept. mot. Skills,* 1962, 15, 171-198.

Zubek, J. P., Welch, G., & Saunders, M. EEG changes during and after 14 days of perceptual deprivation. *Sci.*, 1963, 139, 209-210.

Zuckerman, M. Perceptual isolation as a stress situation. *Arch. gen. Psychiat.*, 1964, 11, 255-276.

Zuckerman, M., & Cohen, N. Sources of reports of visual and auditory sensations in perceptual isolation experiments. *Psychol. Bull.,* 1964, 62, 1-120.

Zuckerman, M., & Haber, Merry M. The need for stimulation as a source of stress response to perceptual isolation. *J. abnorm. soc. Psychol.*, 1965, 70, 371-377.

Zuckerman, M., Levine, S., & Biase, V. Stress response in total and partial perceptual isolation. *Psychosom. Med.*, 1964, 26, 250-260.

AUTHOR INDEX

Numbers in italics indicate the pages on which the complete references are listed.

SUBJECT INDEX

A

Achievement motivation, 86

Actuarial assessment, *see* Assessment of personality

Actuarial predictions, M.M.P.I., 159-183

Affiliative motivation, 233

Anxiety
  during disagreement, 222-223, 227, 231-232, 233
  information deprivation and, 274-277

Assessment of personality
  actuarial, 133-193
  actuarial method defined, 134-136
  actuarial prediction, 146-187
  automated assessment, nonactuarial, 155-156
  Bayes's theorem, 153-155
  clinical judgment compared, 139
  college grades, 140
  configural models, 150-151
  cost factor, 140-141
  criteria
    content, 143-145
    "free," 141-147
    psychiatric, 141
    selection, 141-146
  diagnosis, validity of, 184-186
  fixed criteria, 147-150
  "free" criteria, 141, 147
  Goldberg's Index, 150
  homosexuality, 152-153
  hospital records
    coding, 172-175
    validity, 169-170
  implications, actuarial prediction, 183-187
  judges, attributes of, 145-146
  linear models, 150-151
  medical diagnosis, 153-155
  Minnesota Multiphasic Inventory (M.M.P.I.), 134, 135, 137, 138, 146, 148, 151, 155, 159-185, *see also* Minnesota Multiphasic Inventory
  Missouri Medical Center program, 166-183
  predictor data, availability, 151

Q-sort, reliabilities, 144

rules, Meehl-Dahlstrom, 150-151

16-PF Scales, 138

suicide risk, 148, 149, 184

taxonomic class predictions, 156-183

taxonomies, logic of, 158-159

Thematic Apperception Test (T.A.T.), 138, 139, 140, 152

validities
  diagnosis, 184-186
  hospital records, 169-170
  of tests, 136-138

Authoritarianism, 225-230, 233

Autonomic responses
  during disagreement, 218-219, 220-223, 227
  during information deprivation, 273-274

Aversive behavior, modeling and, 116-127

B

Balance, in interpersonal disagreement, 197

Bayes's theorem, 153-155

Boredom, 291

"Brain-washing," 242

C

Cases, clinical data, 27-29, 60-61, 63, 179-182

Cheating, delay of reward and, 86

Childhood schizophrenia, 39-42

Clinical judgment, actuarial assessment and, 139

Cognition, changes during deprivation, 294-298

College grades, actuarial prediction, 140

Complexity, stimulus, as need, 256-263, 277-278

Concordance, twin studies, *see also* Schizophrenia
  corrections for age, 10, 67
  methods, 9, 17, 45, 52, 70-71
  rates for schizophrenia, 11, 21, 27-29, 45-46, 50-52, 67-69

Configural models, actuarial assessment, 150-151